Perspectives on Gender in Post-1945 German Literature

Studies in German Literature, Linguistics, and Culture

Perspectives on Gender in Post-1945 German Literature

Georgina Paul

 CAMDEN HOUSE
Rochester, New York

First published 2009
by Camden House

Camden House is an imprint of Boydell & Brewer Inc.
668 Mt. Hope Avenue, Rochester, NY 14620, USA
www.camden-house.com
and of Boydell & Brewer Limited
PO Box 9, Woodbridge, Suffolk IP12 3DF, UK
www.boydellandbrewer.com

ISBN-13: 978-1-57113-423-3
ISBN-10: 1-57113-423-9

Library of Congress Cataloging-in-Publication Data

Paul, Georgina.
 Perspectives on gender in post-1945 German literature / Georgina Paul.
  p. cm. — (Studies in German literature, linguistics, and culture)
 Includes bibliographical references and index.
 ISBN-13: 978-1–57113-423-3 (acid-free paper)
 ISBN-10: 1-57113-423-9 (acid-free paper)
 1. German literature—20th century—History and criticism. 2. Sex
(Psychology) in literature. 3. Identity (Psychology) in literature. I. Title.

 PT405.P3455 2009
 840.9'353—dc22

                                                    2009020101

A catalogue record for this title is available from the British Library.

This publication is printed on acid-free paper.
Printed in the United States of America.

Contents

Acknowledgments

I SHOULD LIKE TO EXPRESS MY SINCERE THANKS to the Arts and Humanities Research Council of Great Britain, to the University of Warwick, and to the Governing Body of St. Hilda's College, Oxford, all of whom granted me periods of funded research leave that greatly assisted the completion of this book.

Barbara Köhler's poem cycle "Elektra. Spiegelungen," from her first collection *Deutsches Roulette* (1991), is quoted in chapter 8 by kind permission of the Suhrkamp Verlag, Frankfurt am Main.

The cover image, one of a series of six woodcuts that, together with Köhler's seven poems, constituted the first, freestanding, limited-edition publication of *Elektra. Spiegelungen* (1985), is used by kind permission of the artist, Gudrun Höritzsch. My thanks to her, and to Barbara Köhler and Werner J. Hannappel for their help in scanning the image.

Chapters 7 and 8 draw in part on material that first appeared in an article entitled "Multiple Refractions, or Winning Movement Out of Myth: Barbara Köhler's poem cycle 'Elektra. Spiegelungen,'" published in *German Life and Letters* in 2004 (57, no. 1: 21–32).

The seed for this book was sown in a series of guest lectures I gave in the Taylor Institution at the University of Oxford in 1998. I am immensely grateful to Karen Leeder, of New College, Oxford, who extended the invitation, thus creating the conditions for one of the most intellectually stimulating experiences of my career. I also owe a debt of thanks to the students in the Department of German Studies at the University of Warwick who took part in my subsequent seminar on gender in post-1945 German literature, especially to the *Jahrgang* 2000 (Eleanor Astell, Rachel Cook, Karen Hudson, Jane Kelly, Helen Mullins, Jonathan Orange, and Malvina Wilson) and to Visiting Student Fabian Lettow, lively debates with whom helped me to clarify the interpretations of the texts presented here.

This book has had a long maturation, and many colleagues and friends have been generous in their support in the course of the writing process. Special thanks are due to Karen Leeder and Ursula Hudson-Wiedenmann, who read along with me as I wrote and offered invaluable comments and suggestions. Birgit Dahlke invited me to read an early version of chapter 6 to her seminar at the Humboldt-Universität Berlin in 1998, which proved a useful test of my approach. The following read and responded to individual chapters: Richard Dyer (whom I also thank for helpful secondary references), Louise Hide, Elizabeth Boa, Erica Carter, Angelica Goodden, Tony Phelan, Frank Zipfel. I thank them all for their comments and corrections. Any errors that remain are my own responsibility.

I feel very fortunate in my publisher. Jim Walker, editorial director at Camden House, has been both thoroughly supportive and stimulatingly critical, and the end product owes a great deal to his input, as well as to the work of the editorial team, and to the two anonymous readers who read and reported so constructively on the manuscript.

Finally, for their personal support and encouragement throughout the project, I should like to thank, in addition to those already mentioned, Carol Nelson, James Legg, and Simon Heighes. My mother, Ellen Paul, gave me house-room for one long, productive writing summer, though sadly she did not live to see the publication. Reading would not have been the same without the help of Tabitha. In a league quite of her own, though, in this as in so many other respects, is my partner Judith Unwin, whose generous-heartedness, good humor, and unfaltering belief in me have borne me along through every stage of the writing. It is to her that I dedicate this work.

St Hilda's College, Oxford
May, 2009

Note on the Translations

IT HAS BECOME INCREASINGLY IMPORTANT to me during my work on this study that it should be accessible to readers who do not read German, notwithstanding the importance of textual detail, including linguistic texture, to the way literature works. For this reason, all quotations from primary texts are given in both German and English, the latter from published translations where these are available. For reasons of length, all works of theory, philosophy, and critical commentary are, where the language of the original is not English, given in English translation only. So, too, are most (though not all) statements made by the authors in interviews and other non-literary forms. English sources of non-English texts are indicated throughout; where only the German source is given, the translations are my own.

Introduction

THROUGHOUT HUMAN HISTORY and in all forms of human society, the existence of two sexes and the social organization of their relationship to each other have generated a diversity of concepts and meanings, ideal characteristics and qualities, that come together in abbreviated form in the gender terms "masculine" and "feminine." What masculinity and femininity mean in any given society is, among other things, mediated through culturally symbolic forms such as art, dance, music, and literature. This book is an investigation of gender as a culturally symbolic category in a sequence of major literary works by key German-language writers in the period since 1945. Conceived as a comparative study of works by male and female authors, the book focuses on the way gender has played into the conceptualization and representation of human subjectivity within European modernity since the Enlightenment — and how notions of the masculine and the feminine interact in literary works from the post-1945 period that critique the culturally predominant masculine-connoted conceptualization of subjectivity and historical agency. I argue that the critique of masculinity, as the condensed expression of the cultural values of Enlightenment modernity, and the projection of the feminine, as the symbolic site of resistance to those values, underlie gender's function as a symbolic category in the literature of the postwar era and also shape writers' conceptualization of their own gendered positions as authors.

The study comprises two parts. Part I presents a summarizing historical account of the way gender functioned as a cultural-critical category in late nineteenth- and twentieth-century German thought in order to provide a frame of reference for the textual readings that follow in part II. The relevance of gender to the cultural critique of modernity in German-language culture has been investigated in a number of important recent studies, above all in relation to the turn of the nineteenth to the twentieth century, and for this reason chapter 1 begins at that historical juncture. By investigating the use of the gender metaphor in the critique of modern culture in the early modernist period and in the reaction to that critique, notably in the form of the fascist reformulation of gender roles during the Nazi period, the book opens up a perspective on the theoretical continuities between the fin de siècle and the gendering of cultural critique in the post-Holocaust era, the period that is the focus of chapter 2. There were not only continuities, however. A significant difference was that, in the postwar period and especially after the watershed of 1968, women writers and theorists began taking control of the meanings ascribed to gender for their own cultural-critical purposes, a move that changed the parameters within which male writers deployed gender symbolism in their works.

Part II presents a sequence of readings of thematically linked pairings of texts, one by a male writer, the other by a female writer. The themes on which I have chosen to focus reflect the dominant concerns of gender-inflected cultural critique in the post-1945 period. Chapters 3 and 4 consider the construction of subjectivity, including the way identity is determined by conventions of self-narrative, through a comparative reading of Ingeborg Bachmann's 1971 novel, *Malina*, and Max Frisch's *Mein Name sei Gantenbein* of 1964. In chapter 5, Frisch's *Homo faber* (1957) and Christa Wolf's *Störfall* (1987) exemplify the literary critique of instrumental rationality as the defining characteristic of the de facto male Enlightenment subject. Pathology, as a form of subjective rebellion against a too-restrictive social status quo, is examined with reference to Elfriede Jelinek's *Die Klavierspielerin* and Rainald Goetz's *Irre* (both 1983) in chapter 6, and chapter 7 looks at the "end visions" of Heiner Müller's *Die Hamletmaschine* (1977) and Christa Wolf's *Kassandra* (1983), two works imbued with pessimism at the prospects for a radical renewal of the Western philosophical and cultural tradition in which they are self-consciously located. Considering writings by male and female authors alongside each other illuminates the extent to which they share common cultural concerns, though the authors' respective sex places them quite differently in terms of their perspectives on issues of identity, cultural-historical agency, and what they wish of the opposite sex. Chapter 8, the last chapter, presents not a textual pairing, but the response of Barbara Köhler, the youngest writer to be considered in the book, to the problems involving the representation of gendered subjectivity that haunt the texts explored earlier. Köhler's early poem-cycle "Elektra. Spiegelungen" (1984–85), I shall argue, initiates a concern in her work with exploring ways out of the impasse of gender conflict and gender difference. While there is some movement back and forth in time between the chapters, taken all together, the readings offer a broadly chronological review of the period from the 1950s to the late 1980s.

My methodology of detailed textual analysis in comparative pairings in part II means that I argue my central theses concerning the relation between gender symbolism, the gender of authorship, and the cultural critique of modernity on the basis of a relatively small range of works from the period under study. The works I have selected are (with the exception of the lesser-known Köhler and possibly also Goetz's novel) generally regarded as key articulations of underlying cultural concerns in post-1945 German-language literature and as such are intended to be exemplary of wider trends. I chose to focus on few texts rather than many because the real work of cultural critique in literature takes place at the detailed level of structure and form, character interaction, and linguistic texture, aspects that cannot be treated adequately in a broad literary-historical overview. It is my hope that this book identifies underlying patterns in the functioning of gender symbolism in the literature of the period that can be tested, refined, complemented, and if necessary corrected through the examination of other works not treated here.

Part I: Gender, Subjectivity, and the Cultural Critique of Modernity: Twentieth-Century Perspectives

1: Gender, Subjectivity, and Cultural Critique from the Fin de Siècle to Fascism

In 1911, THE BERLIN SOCIOLOGIST and cultural commentator Georg Simmel published an essay entitled "Weibliche Kultur" (Female Culture). Written against the background of the increasing public impact of the women's movement and widespread debate on the so-called "Woman Question," Simmel's essay set out to consider the specific contribution that women might be expected to make to the shaping of human culture in the future. The objective manifestations of culture had — on this point he was unequivocal — hitherto been exclusively the creation of men: "It is men who have created art and industry, science and commerce, the state and religion."[1] The belief, he wrote, that there was a purely "human" culture for which the difference between men and women was irrelevant had its origins in the same premise from which it followed that such a culture did not exist — "the naïve identification of the 'human' with 'man'" (67). What was needed, he argued, was the acknowledgement of the completely different basis of female existence: "The naïve conflation of male values with values as such can give way only if the female existence as such is acknowledged as having a basis fundamentally different from the male and a stream of life flowing in a fundamentally different direction: two existential totalities, each structured according to a completely autonomous rule" (72).

There can be no doubt that Simmel was politically progressive in his intentions; indeed, his views were used by some contemporary campaigners for women's political and civil rights to support their arguments.[2] Yet when he comes to defining the constitutive values (*Wesenswerte*) of the two sexes in this essay, as the logic of his argument requires he must, Simmel slips as if inevitably into the repetition of familiar cultural preconceptions. On the one hand, he represents gender as a set of cultural norms or obligations (his word is *Sollen*) to behave in accordance with historically determined ideal social roles, in apparent acknowledgement of the extent to which gender might be regarded as a cultural construction. Reduced to an abstract expression, he argues, the norms are that man is required to be "significant" (*bedeutend*) while woman should be "beautiful" (*schön*) — though "naturally," he adds, such beauty is not restricted to the possession of a pretty face (88). On the other hand, however, within a few sentences his abstract "man" is represented no longer in the

hypothetical, but in the actual fulfillment of the cultural expectations leveled at him, all dynamism, activity, and achievement (in terms, moreover,
which reek of sex), while the "constitutive idea of woman" is projected in
static and organic form:

> While man externalizes himself, discharges his energy into his achieve-
> ments, and thus "signifies" something that is in some sense external
> to himself, dynamically or ideally, creating or representing — the
> constitutive idea of woman is that unbroken character of the periph-
> ery, the organic containment in the harmony of the constituent parts
> in relation to each other and in the symmetry of their relationship to
> their center — precisely the formula of the beautiful.[3]

From here, it is just a short step to the metaphysical — "For she is, in the
symbolism of metaphysical concepts, the one who is [*die Seiende*] and
man the one who becomes [*der Werdende*]" — and from the metaphysical
back, in a perfect circular movement, to the ideal social roles of the sexes,
whereby man now notably "must" as opposed to "should," while woman
remains obligated to the principle that defines her: "It is for this reason
that he must attain his significance in relation to a thing or an idea, a historical or a cognitive world, while woman should be beautiful in the sense
of this 'bliss in and of itself'" (88–89, translation modified).

Simmel's essay of 1911 is not the most obvious starting point for a
study concerned with the culturally symbolic significance of gender in the
German-language literature of the much-later post-1945 period. Yet his
contemplations of gender are illuminating for the arguments of this book
for a number of reasons. In the first place, the passage cited demonstrates a
characteristic of discourse on gender so commonplace that it may not even
seem surprising, yet it is a characteristic that this study is intent on subject-
ing to scrutiny. This is the constant slippage in the referentiality of gender,
its historically derived and tendentiously dualistic metaphoricity. Gender,
while rooted in the perception of sexual difference — that is, the perception of the existence of two sexes, male and female, whose relations with
one another must be socially regulated — has throughout the history of
human culture been persistently placed at the head of sequences of dual-
isms that underpin the conception not only of sexual and social interaction,
but also of psychological and cultural dynamics, of cosmic and metaphysical systems, of the principles of life itself in all its forms. As Simmel himself
argues in the rather earlier *Philosophie der Geschlechter* (Philosophy of the
Sexes) of 1906, wherever human beings think in dualistic oppositions —
and the pervasive tendency to do so may have its self-perpetuating basis in
the gender dualism — the gender metaphor will be at hand:

> Whether we think to grasp the true reality of phenomena in the qui-
> escent state of being or in the Heraclitan flow of becoming; whether

things in their metaphysical significance come together into an absolute and indivisible unity or are dissolved into independent elements with differentiated properties; whether the individual places the accent of his existence on its receptivity or its productivity; whether the life of a society rests more on the legacies of the past, on tradition, the principle of conservatism and of loyalty, or on variability, adaptability, and ruthlessly progressive development — on one respective side of such antitheses a more feminine essence will be perceived to resonate, on the other a more masculine one.[4]

The implications are far-reaching. Gender has a long history of carrying a great many cultural meanings besides sexual difference, many of them mutually or even self-contradictory, for gender is a far-from-stable symbolic category. Yet at the same time, the significations of gender remain attached, however tenuously, to representations of persons of the male and female sex or to ideal social "types," coloring (self-) perceptions of male and female behavior and social positioning and, more overtly and constrictingly in some historical periods than others, projecting a pervasive sense of social obligation to fulfill certain cultural roles. Infringements of such prescribed roles tend to be judged socially as behavior that contravenes gendered nature, a crossing-over from one sex to the other or a strange, even uncanny, intermingling. Moreover, the way in which gender *means* at any given place and moment in history, precisely because it oscillates between its broader culturally symbolic significations and its function as a framework for personal behavior, acts quite specifically upon the individual. The socialization of individual subjects is always also a socialization into a symbolic system of gender difference. Historical shifts in the social roles of the sexes, meanwhile, involve an often-complex process of adaptation and contestation of the significations already operating in the socially symbolic sphere of cultural representation. The exploration of this latter aspect will be a central concern in this study.

In this respect, Simmel's views are illuminating in that they provide an entry point into the prehistory of the gender symbolism operative in the post-1945 period. As will be discussed later in this chapter, the way in which Simmel reads gender is premised upon the construction of gender roles characteristic of the European bourgeois social order of the late eighteenth and nineteenth centuries, the first phase of the period that will be referred to as Enlightenment modernity.[5] It was an era active in the propagation of strictly defined and divided gender roles, spreading the message through a historically unprecedented degree of literary and other forms of legible representation that reached out to possess the minds of an unprecedentedly large readership. By the time Simmel was writing, the social positioning of women was shifting very considerably, so that he was beginning to think about the cultural changes that this shift might bring. Yet from our point of view, the fact that he could not imagine the "feminine" or the "masculine" other than in bourgeois nineteenth-century terms draws attention to the difficulty of breaking free from cultural conceptualizations so entrenched that they have come to seem "natural." The chapters of textual readings in this book will show how the notions of masculinity and femininity that structure the relative positionings of the characters within the fictions draw on symbolic attributes inherited from much earlier in the modern period while simultaneously trying to accommodate the fact that these fixed preconceptions no longer match subjectively experienced reality.

The fact that gender became so ineluctably attached to certain symbolic attributes in the course of the bourgeois Enlightenment's ideological construction of itself and of the relations between the two sexes forms the basis for the centrality of gender in the cultural critique of modernity, which is a primary concern of all the fictions to feature in this study. In this context, too, it is instructive to begin by looking back to the earlier part of the twentieth century, for this illuminates aspects of continuity in the operation of gender symbolism even after 1945, as well as crucial differences. The prevalence of gender as a cultural-critical metaphor — in particular, in German-language modernist culture and thought — has been far more thoroughly examined in scholarship to date in relation to the period of cultural crisis at the turn of the nineteenth to the twentieth century than it has with regard to the postwar era. Yet all of the texts from the post-1945 period that form the object of close study in this book draw on the conceptual inheritance of modernism, and the way in which they deploy gender symbolism can only really be properly understood if the historical roots of their cultural critique are taken into account. It is for this reason that the study begins with a cultural-historical review of the interplay between cultural critique and notions of gender in the twentieth century in order to establish a frame of reference for the readings of texts that follow. The aim is to illuminate the highly complex web of relations between economic and political modernization, the changing social roles of the sexes, and the generation of symbolic meanings attaching to gender that operate in the sphere of culture, literature, and the arts. At all points in what follows, the crucial issue is what it is that gender is *meaning* in the respective historical contexts.

Gender and the Critique of Modernity at the Fin de Siècle

Simmel was just one among a great many writers of both sexes who were writing about gender at the turn of the nineteenth to the twentieth century in Western Europe. That it was a subject matter that excited tempers so greatly was above all due to the very marked transformation in the social roles of the sexes as a result of economic modernization. Most obviously, the campaigners for women's suffrage and civil rights were, by the early years of the new century, making significant political headway, so that ideological battle was joined between the cultural conservatives, afraid of the overthrow of all social order through this "unnatural" incursion of women into public affairs, and the cultural progressives, armed with arguments concerning the salutary effect upon society to be expected from women's greater public participation. This advancement of the cause of women's civil rights was itself premised upon the shifts that had already taken place in particular in bourgeois women's social positioning in the last decades of the nineteenth century: their increased access to education, even (despite considerable obstacles) to higher education, and consequently their more prominent activity in bourgeois social institutions such as politics, medicine, and science, and in the cultural sphere as writers, artists, and publicists. Furthermore, the expansion of the urban-based industrial and commercial economy gave rise to new patterns of employment for women. Stereotypical bourgeois notions of ideal femininity as passive, subordinate, morally pure, and primarily maternal were by the 1880s and 1890s being challenged by the increasingly overt presence in the public sphere of active, independent-minded, and sexually liberated "new women," insisting on their right to earn their own means to live and intent on rebelling against the imprisonment of their sex within the strictures of bourgeois norms.[6] They did so, however, in the face of a still very strong cultural sense of what was denoted by appropriate feminine behavior. To some extent, the campaigners for women's rights worked with (and no doubt also believed in) the predominant conceptualizations of "femininity." If the domesticated woman of nineteenth-century ideology was cast as "invariably gentle, pious, moral and self-sacrificing," and the mother as the guardian of her offspring's moral upbringing (Abrams, 61, 102–4), then women's participation in the public arena of politics could be strategically justified in terms of the superior moral sense considered "natural" to women. It was this, the suffragists argued, that would ensure the general moral improvement of society, once women were granted the vote.[7] At the same time, however, given the prevailing rigidity of gender norms, the woman staking a claim to being regarded on equal terms with men, and in particular the woman actively engaged in the political or intellectual spheres, could only be understood as "masculinizing," since to be active in the public sphere was de facto to behave in a masculine manner. In the campaigns against the women's franchise, the specter was raised of a degenerate, culture-threatening, double-gendered monster: the "Man-Woman."[8]

This unsettling of female social roles was complemented by what have been widely discussed in studies of masculinity as the diverse symptoms of a crisis in masculine identity. The causes of this crisis appear complex and various. On the one hand, the processes of modernization that assisted the emancipation of women undermined established concepts of masculinity to a certain degree. If modernization was interpreted in a certain light — for example, in order to stress the increasing anonymity of the individual in the urban crowd, the functionalization of the worker in the public-institutional or commercial environment, or his reduction to the status of passive consumer as opposed to active producer within the modern mass economy — then it inevitably heralded a crisis in bourgeois notions of masculine subjectivity as active, creative, singular, "significant." The rise of new medical and scientific discourses at the turn of the century, most notably those of psychoanalysis and sexology, posed further challenges to notions inherited from the Enlightenment tradition of the bounded, rational self with a distinct and stable psychosexual identity. Studies of the unconscious presented for consideration the extent to which mas-culine identity was achieved only at the cost of a veritably superhuman work of psychic repression, while in a range of scientific and pseudosci-entific treatises, all manner of deviants from conceptual social and gender norms were discussed, dissected, and pathologized.[9] Meanwhile, art and literature from the Pre-Raphaelites and Jugendstil to the Symbolists and beyond was exhibiting an intense, and often morbid, interest in figures of an idealized archaic "feminine," an engagement with an "imaginary femi-ninity" that Andreas Huyssen has diagnosed as a symptom of "the increas-ingly marginal position of literature and the arts in a society in which masculinity is identified with action, enterprise, and progress — with the realms of business, industry, science, and the law."[10] On the other hand, the interests of modern political, economic, and military enterprise in a period marked by the contest of the European imperial states were vested in an aggressive and virile male subjectivity. Contemplations of cultural decline and "feminization" would therefore habitually present as their solution the reassertion of virile character traits and the expulsion from the male personality of vestiges of "feminine" weakness and softness.[11] In all manner of ways, then, discussions of gender became a touchstone of social and cultural development. As Rita Felski observes in her study of *The Gender of Modernity,* the "saturation of cultural texts with metaphors of masculinity and femininity is nowhere more obvious than in the case of the modern."[12]

While gender was prevalent in the metaphorical discussion of social decline or social transformation in many European cultures at the fin de siècle, it was, as Felski also observes, "particularly pronounced in Ger-many, where a long-standing tradition of Romantic organicism combined with a relatively late and rapid experience of industrialization to encour-age a profound ambivalence vis-à-vis the supposed benefits and values of the modern" (50). That this was not limited to Germany, but extended to other German-speaking parts of the former Holy Roman Empire, is demonstrated by Jacques Le Rider's study of *Modernity and Crises of Identity*, which explores the evidence for a "crisis of masculinity" and the projection of a variously interpreted culturally redemptive or destructive femininity within Viennese modernism.[13] Felski's chapter "On Nostalgia: The Prehistoric Woman" and the section of Le Rider's book specifically concerned with "Crises of Masculine Identity" engage with a broadly similar range of cultural phenomena and set of meanings being ascribed to gender at the turn of the century in German-speaking cultures. In Le Rider's reading, the crisis of masculinity "relates closely to a crisis of modernization, interpreted and experienced as a too-exclusive affirmation of values connected with the masculine element," such as scientific and technical rationality, self-mastery, and mastery of the object (89–90), that were seen as having alienated the individual subject from the relationship to organic nature and to the transcendent realm of spiritual truth and harmony. Felski, meanwhile, observes among writers, artists, and intellectuals a "sense of estrangement from a positivistic world view and an ever more urban and technologized society," which expresses itself "through an orientation to the past and an explicit cult of the mythic and the nonrational" (50). In this context, artists and intellectuals turned to a conceptualization of the "feminine" as the repository of values counter to the fragmentation and alienation of the modern male subject. Woman here becomes equated, as she is in Simmel, with un-self-conscious wholeness and organicism, closeness to and harmony with nature and thus the sources of life itself, though she is also associated with darker and more dangerous mythic and archaic forces. In Felski's summary: "From the paintings of Gustav Klimt to the writings of Lou Andreas-Salomé, the figure of woman emerged as an erotic-mythic creature, an enigmatic incarnation of elemental and libidinal forces that exceeded the bounds of reason and social order. In the modern yearning for a preindustrial world, she embodied everything that modernity was not, the living antithesis of the ironic self-estrangement of urban man" (50).

The quest of three modernist artists — Frank Wedekind, Thomas Mann, and Wassily Kandinsky — to overcome this masculine self-estrangement in their art is the subject matter of Gerald N. Izenberg's *Modernism and Masculinity*. Izenberg, keen to distinguish his own position from Le Rider's and Felski's, offers a useful corrective to their arguments with his insistence that the "crisis of masculinity" signified in early modernist art and literature in Germany reveals itself not so much as a flight from masculinity toward the feminine as an active, conscious, form-imposing, and thus properly "masculine" attempt to remodel male subjectivity through the appropriation of the ideal "feminine" within the artwork: "Early Modernists were concerned both with recovering a true self that was threatened or lost by uncovering its true instinctual and spiritual foundations, and reuniting that self with the world and with truth."

Izenberg's aim is to show "that at least for a number of canonical Modernists, the self that was to be recovered or reconstructed was the truly masculine self, and that this was to be accomplished, most paradoxically, by the masculine appropriation of ideal femininity."[14] Nevertheless, Izenberg is both broadly in agreement with Le Rider's and Felski's readings of the social causation and psychological symptoms of the crisis of masculinity — "Beneath the ideological optimism of modern capitalist materialism lay hidden a self ravaged by suppressed longings both instinctual and transcendental, longings contemporary society could neither account for nor satisfy" (3) — and consistent with them in the interpretation of the feminine as signifying an idealized harmonious completeness, spirituality, and connectedness with the totality of being to which the male artist aspired.

This projection of the feminine was highly ambivalent in its symbolic potential, though, and variations upon it were as likely to appear in analyses of cultural decadence and decline that needed to be opposed by the reassertion of virile self-mastery and masculine spiritual superiority. Both Le Rider and Felski point to the importance of the influence of the work of nineteenth-century thinkers such as J. J. Bachofen (1815–87) and Friedrich Nietzsche (1844–1900) upon turn-of-the-century male intellectuals' conceptualizations of the masculine and the feminine. Bachofen's *Mutterrecht* (Mother Right, 1861) is of interest to the critique of modernity in that his hypotheses concerning the matriarchal organization of pre-Hellenic ancient societies (later discredited, but nevertheless of very considerable significance for the subsequent development of the study of this period) form part of a progressive philosophy of history according to which human culture passes through differently gendered phases. Already in Bachofen, the "feminine" is associated above all with the mystic and mythical premodern past. However, the ascendancy of the patriarchal organization of society is taken as a sign of humankind's overcoming of the "maternal" bondage to the body and to materiality: "The triumph of paternity brings with it the liberation of the spirit from the manifestations of nature, a sublimation of human existence over the laws of material life. [. . .] Spiritual life rises over corporeal existence, and the relation with the lower spheres of existence is restricted to the physical aspect. Maternity pertains to the physical side of man, the only thing he shares with the animals: the paternal-spiritual principle belongs to him alone."[15] In Bachofen's reading, patriarchy represents progress; it marks the triumph of humanity over the material conditions and limitations of life: nature, the body, mortality. This progress he sees as being under threat in his own time, however. In this context, the "feminine" signifies potential cultural regression, equated as it is in Bachofen's view with sensuality, decadence, and the unwarranted political influence of "the indistinguishable masses."[16]

Nietzsche is rather more difficult to position because his often-associative and contextual — and thus not necessarily consistent — views do not fit neatly into the categories with which the gender metaphor is operating in other works of the period. On the one hand, his condemnation of the too-exclusive emphasis on rationality and of the "weak" Christian moral ethos, which he saw as characteristic of the bourgeois order of his day, and his cultivation in their stead of the "Dionysian" element, understood by him as instinctive energy and flux, but also as a destructive, even evil force, points to the aspects of his cultural critique that he shared with (and to an extent influenced in) the artists examined by Izenberg and Le Rider. (In Bachofen, as Le Rider points out, Dionysos is the god of sensuality and luxuriant nature, and associated therefore with the feminine.[17]) The Nietzschean conceptualization of the opposition and tension between the Apollonian principle of Hellenic rationality and form on the one hand and archaic Dionysian sexual energy and self-dissolution on the other was, for example, of considerable importance for the work of Thomas Mann, as Izenberg discusses in the chapter of his study devoted to Mann.[18] Yet Nietzsche was also among those who expressed disgust for the modern age in gendered terms, finding it "effeminate," while his central notion of the *Übermensch* or "superman" as the one who enforces his will upon the vicissitudes of life and rises above the inchoate mass brings together a wealth of specifically "manly" virtues. Le Rider summarizes:

> Nietzsche poured scorn on the decadence of his times, of which the confusion and atrophying of sexual characteristics were, he thought, a symptom. Women were turning into viragos; men were going soft and evincing moral cowardice. The feminization of men and the virilization of women were making humanity culturally sterile, incapable of producing superior personalities. More than one passage in Nietzsche calls for a new opposition of sexual attitudes, a fertile polarity which would renew the libidinal tension between "true" men and "real" women. (106)[19]

The negative assessment of the modern age as intrinsically "feminine" in its dedication to sensual and sexual license, only redeemable through the reassertion of the masculine principles of self-mastery and self-contained individuation, came to a head in the compendious, and at the time highly successful, 1903 study of *Geschlecht und Charakter* (Sex and Character) by the twenty-three-year-old Otto Weininger, based on his doctoral thesis submitted to the Philosophical Faculty of the University of Vienna the year before. The opening section of Weininger's study considers in some detail the natural bisexuality of all human beings (i.e., the combination of masculine and feminine aspects or characteristics in every individual), a theory in keeping with the contemporary standpoint in the biological science of the sexes and one that would become, as it were, canonized for twentieth-century psychology by Freudian psychoanalysis. The much longer second section of the book, however, revolves around the extrapolation of two polarized "ideal types" of the "masculine" and the "feminine" that define Weininger's construction of those terms. In his reading, the pervasive cultural association of the feminine with bodily materiality, organic nature, and libidinal forces reappears, but in negative guise: the feminine is now characterized by its complete absorption in the sexual function, as projected into two contrasting female figures, the Mother and the Prostitute. Weininger's account of masculinity, meanwhile, focuses on the absolute ideal type of the Genius: the thinker, the artist, the great mind, who, through the strength of his own supreme individuality, is able to unite within his singular self the entire gamut of human types and experiences. The model of the ultramasculine personality type is Goethe. According to John Toews's useful summary: "'Masculinity' denoted the pole of conscious subjective agency, rational control, ethical individuality, freedom and spiritual transcendence (all epitomized as 'being') and 'femininity' designated the pole of unconscious objective passivity, sexual determinism, amorality, and material de-individualized immanence (summarized as nonbeing or 'nothing')."[20]

As Chandak Sengoopta has discussed, Weininger's project in this book was to counter the perceived threat to the conceptualization of the male subject posed by developments in contemporary psychology and philosophy. Of particular note is the influence of Ernst Mach, professor of philosophy in Vienna from 1895, whose study of the psychology of sensations led him to the conclusion that "there was no such thing as a coherent unified self or 'ego.' What people thought of as their unique, distinct self was simply a complex of sensations that was differently configured in different individuals. There was no clear gulf 'between bodies and sensations . . . between what is without and what is within, between the material world and the spiritual world.'"[21] In short, according to Mach's most famous dictum: "The self is beyond salvage" (*Das Ich ist unrettbar*).[22] In the face of this challenge, Weininger sets out to rescue a distinctly German idealist conceptualization of the self (*Ich*): a Kantian "intelligible self," bounded and rational, the foundation and guarantor of logic and ethics.[23] This is achieved in Weininger's system by the expulsion from the masculine self of all that is connoted "feminine." Bodily instincts, sensations, and impulses are to be rigorously brought under the control of the masculine-connoted will and intellect.

Taken as symptomatic of a particular historical moment, what is striking about Weininger's text is the way in which it distils an underlying cultural anxiety — signs of which are broadly evident in the contemporary cultural environs — about the threatened loss of singular and distinctive selfhood, that coherent, bounded, and "significant" individuality bestowed upon the male subject by the great philosophers of the Enlightenment. Weininger's interest in the great-artist-as-genius can be seen as a reactive grasping after the apogee of that conceptualization of the individual: the author-genius as individual ne plus ultra (a concern he in essence shares with Nietzsche and most of the artists so far touched upon). The "feminine," meanwhile, functions as a figure: it marks the cultural site at which is gathered everything that is opposed to and threatens the Enlightenment self, both from within and without. Sexuality, with which femininity is primarily associated in Weininger's text, stands for a merging or mingling of selves that smudges the boundaries between self and other. A being dedicated to the pursuit of the sexual and the sensual is, in Weininger's estimation, the figuration of nonentity. Moreover, it is the too-exclusive pursuit of material interests and sensual urges that, in Weininger's most startling connection, marks the similarity between women and Jews, discrediting the latter as viable subjects also. For Weininger, femininity/Jewishness embodies a form of behavior — sexual and sensual concupiscence — that threatens at an individual level the boundaries of the rational and self-contained male subject of Enlightenment provenance. Importantly, though, he also perceives the threat in broader cultural terms. Weininger condemns his age as degenerate and degraded: it is "not only the most Jewish, but also the most feminine of ages"[24] — an age, in the terms of his argument, dedicated to material and sensual interests that erode the foundations of individuated and autonomous selfhood. What he seems to have been seeing around him was the developmental trend within the new phase of urban-based and commercial modernity toward the mass society, a form of social organization that has the tendency to deprive human beings of their distinctive, singular selves and to cast them in generic terms. The "femininity" or "Jewishness" of the age is really simply a shorthand, generated out of contemporary prejudices and themes and out of the contrast with a masculinity traditionally conceived as the epitome of individuation, for the feared reduction of selves to an unreflective, undifferentiated, and consumerist mass.

It would be possible to extend considerably further this account of conceptualizations and representations of the masculine and the feminine in German-speaking culture in the early part of the twentieth century. However, the intention here is not to provide an exhaustive overview. Rather, the aim of the discussion so far has been to establish some points of reference for the ways in which gender is taken up as a metaphor in the representation and discussion of cultural crisis, since a number of thematic strands already present in the critique of modernity at the turn of the century will reappear in the post-1945 period, albeit now significantly transformed by the post-fascist and post-Holocaust perspective. In between lies the assertion of an extreme form of masculinity under National Socialism, readable as a cultural reaction to the challenges posed by rapid modernization and the democratization of the political system. However, before moving on to consider this and the post-1945 reactions,

it is worthwhile pausing to reflect a little further on the cultural preconditions that permitted the masculine and the feminine to be projected in
the terms encountered in the discussion so far.

Gender in the Bourgeois Era:
The Ideology of "Separate Spheres"

In the account above, two countervailing trends have been identified that,
in discussions of cultural decadence and decline in the period around 1900,
are seen to signify the threatening collapse of social order: the virilization of women and the feminization of men. The "virilization" of women
refers primarily to the appearance of women in a domain marked within
Enlightenment modernity's ideology of strictly gender-segregated "separate spheres" as the preserve of masculinity: this is the public domain of
politics, the state, and the institutional infrastructure that upholds these.[25]
The "feminization" of men, by contrast, signals above all a failure in the
achievement of masculine identity, a falling short of the normative model
of the male subject, defined as physically and mentally disciplined, bounded
and self-contained, rational, logical, and in control of the passions.[26] The
"feminine," as the oceanic element of non-differentiation (also conceived
as the mythic and the prerational) that threatens to engulf the male individual and deprive him of his singular identity, is thus different from the
"femininity" promoted as a code of behavior for women in the bourgeois
era. That it is denoted "feminine" at all has at least in part to do with the
fact that, from the culturally predominant heterosexual male perspective, it
is in men's encounters and relationships with women as love-objects that
the challenge to the bounded, rational self is most likely to be experienced.
Otto Weininger's identification of this aspect of the "feminine" with the
two archetypal figures of the Mother and the Prostitute has, after all, a certain cultural logic. The one bears, from the male standpoint, the association
with a symbiotic merging, a maternal envelopment out of which the autonomous individual must go forth under the sign of the law of the father,
repeating, as it were, in each individual's life the passage from matriarchy
to patriarchy that characterized the nineteenth century's conceptualization
of human history. The other is the emblem of pure sexuality, set aside from
the sphere of respectability, duty, self-control, and the bourgeois male's
public status as husband and father.

For what is notable about the model of the male subject characteristic
of Enlightenment modernity is that it is constituted above all in terms of
publicly required and approved behavior: it is an essentially *public* self,
which supports the pursuit of collective social aims. George L. Mosse,
interested in the *visual* construction of ideal masculinity in the modern period — the well-proportioned, muscular torso, the trained physique — stresses the significance of this body as a fighting body, the body

of the warrior-hero who defends not only his personal honor, but also the nation.[27] Yet the rational, self-disciplined male subject is also the linch-pin of the bourgeois Enlightenment's public political arena, and, importantly, the driver behind the nation's increasing knowledge and wealth. As scientist, the ideal Enlightenment male subject works to comprehend the principles of nature, the body, the mind, and society in order at all times to contribute to the improvement of man's ability to control his environment. As businessman, he pursues enterprise, expands markets, manages his finances, controls his workforce, invests for the future. As military or naval commander or as colonialist, he pushes out the boundaries of his nation's international influence and conquers the territories that will ensure its trading networks. No room here for rash emotions, hasty judgements, dissipation, or self-indulgence.[28] Risk and venture are important, but they must be calculated and clever, the mental equivalents of the physical daring and self-confidence exhibited by the disciplined masculine body. The sum of desirable qualities means that for the ideal type of the bourgeois male subject, self-realization is coterminous with impact on historical processes, changing the world, "making a name" — hence Georg Simmel's still inherently bourgeois notion of "significance" as the male's primary goal. Moreover, to the extent that this essentially public construction of the self is open to the public sphere even at home, the home life, too, must project achievement in the interests of the social collective. The bourgeois male increases his public status by marrying advantageously, fathering children (this, too, an investment in the future), and matching his ability to rule in public with the ability to rule over his household as paterfamilias (Frevert 113). In short, the publicly accepted and acceptable male subject of the bourgeois era is the emblem of Enlightenment values. As Mosse states: "The construction of masculinity had fashioned a stereotype that [. . .] reflected the view society liked to have of itself" (56).

Where the ideal-typical bourgeois male subject is essentially the creature of the public sphere, the "ideology of separate spheres" casts his female counterpart, or more precisely, complement, as the guardian of the private sphere. As Lynn Abrams elaborates in her study of *The Making of Modern Woman*, the containment of women within the domestic sphere in the modern age took as its basis the historically long-established notion of female bodily functions as binding women far more than men to their physical nature. She quotes Jean-Jacques Rousseau's famous maxim: "The consequences of sex are wholly unlike for man and woman. The male is only a male now and again, the female is always a female . . . everything reminds her of her sex."[29] Specifically, of course, this refers to the identification of the female with the reproductive function necessary to the continuation of the species. This primary social role dictates the conceptual link between what it means to be female and a passive subordination to the body's natural cycles and functions that, unlike the trained male physique, cannot be significantly altered by acts of will (though they can, of course, be influenced by masculine medical intervention). Anatomical difference, not just in terms of the reproductive organs but also differences in the nervous system and brain size, became in turn a plank in the argument for the social segregation of the sexes, "the belief that woman was fitted for the private or domestic sphere and the male for the public or civic and political arena" (Abrams 23).

As Abrams points out, the notion of separate spheres of labor for men and women predates the bourgeois era, but the differences between the roles for men and women were exacerbated under the conditions of "nascent industrial power" in the late eighteenth and nineteenth centuries. Woman became defined as possessing "natural" characteristics that "fitted the conception of home as a moral haven and refuge from the disruption of industrial society" (45, 129). Within the home, the ideal-typical bourgeois wife may have been mistress, but her own interests were nevertheless strictly subordinated to those of her husband. Her role was to ensure his private well-being through the ordering and administration of his domestic and family life, while also lending his public activities her personal support. Interestingly, this private sphere was itself divided, however, into the part that touched upon the public role of the family and was on display, and the part, in which the actual physical functioning of the home took place, that was kept concealed. "Bourgeois interiors were segregated so that the home would not be contaminated by the appearance of industry. The domestic area was physically separated from spaces used for preparing and cooking food, cleaning, washing and sleeping" (132). This is important to bear in mind because it indicates a pervasive tendency within the public culture of bourgeois modernity to repress or deny all that touches upon human beings' physical and mortal existence (and, by extension, their psychological and emotional vulnerabilities). It was part of a woman's job to keep these aspects concealed, even though she had knowledge of them, just as it was her role to bear children while appearing sexually chaste.

Georg Simmel found that the constitutive idea of womanhood could be summed up in the requirement that a woman be beautiful, quickly adding that this demand "naturally rejects any restriction of beauty to a pretty face" (88). The construction of woman as a creature not only of physical, but also of moral beauty — of refined sensibilities, a gentle and charitable nature, and a deep natural piety that radiated through her physical appearance — was one of the signatures of the nineteenth-century bourgeois era. Izenberg sees this as "a bourgeois reworking of an older aristocratic ideal." If the aristocratic code of chivalry had required of the true man that he both idealize and protect women, then its bourgeois modern variant raised woman onto the imaginary pedestal of her own moral purity in order that she provide inspiration for the man embroiled in public affairs: "Women embodied the higher spirituality that men must also aspire to but could not always achieve because of the worldly, often violent nature of their other duties" (Izenberg 5). Furthermore, with bourgeois modernity's conflation of the religious and the aesthetic spheres, the cultivation of aesthetic culture, too, passed to an observable degree into the guardianship of women:

> Aesthetic culture was, like religion, the realm of a "higher sphere of spiritual life" that "ennobled" the "lower sphere" of gainful activity. A wife's cultural involvement and attainments were necessary contributions to her husband's social standing and thus his masculinity, yet at the same time culture was a quintessentially feminine pursuit. In part because they were confined to the domestic sphere, women could pursue the spiritual inwardness that made them the humanistic and Romantic "whole beings" that men aspired to be but that their worldly striving made all but impossible to achieve.[30]

This summary account of the ideology of separate spheres characteristic of the bourgeois era of the late eighteenth to the nineteenth centuries provides a somewhat altered basis on which to revisit the cultural motifs of the virilization of women and feminization of men. For it was the nineteenth century's very polarized definitions of what constituted the differential nature of men and women that formed the background to the fin-de-siècle questioning of those norms. By the turn of the century, groups among both sexes were mobilizing against the respective extremes in the ideological projection of masculine and feminine social roles, and moving conceptually toward a center ground marked by the acknowledgement of the degree to which the two sexes shared psychological characteristics and requirements, were in fact in large degree *alike* — a finding borne out by the contemporary theories of universal bisexuality that Otto Weininger, for example, cites in the first section of *Sex and Character*. As already discussed, the turn toward the "feminine" in the work of German and Austrian writers and artists at the turn of the century has been primarily read in terms of a revolt against the "too-exclusive affirmation of values connected with the masculine element" (Le Rider 90) in a society that was modernizing rapidly, and as an expression of a "sense of estrangement from a positivistic world view and an ever more urban and technologized society" (Felski 50). But what is also evident when one looks at their works is that this was a generation of writers and artists who were asking questions about what is repressed within the psyche in the course of the construction of the publicly accepted and acceptable male self, spurred on by the fact that their specifically *aesthetic* sensibilities often made them feel their inadequacy in the face of the demand that they become a certain kind of man — at least until they had made their name as significant authors or painters.[31] The emergent sciences such as psychoanalysis and sexology, meanwhile, provided the conceptual tools with which to begin to grasp what was going on in the recesses of the mind behind the constructed façade of the public male subject — or simply in his private life. Here the conceptual ground was being laid for the later insight that what was denoted "feminine" within the culture's framework of gender oppositions — physical nature, bodily instincts, material reality on the one hand; aesthetic and spiritual experience, the memory of humankind's mythical past on the other — was in effect a psychological projection away from the individuated, autonomous, rational entity, that product of culture called "modern man."

At issue for the women engaged in the struggle for women's civil rights, by contrast, was the rebellion against the confinement in the corset of the "feminine" behavioral code that imposed a considerable range of social and moral duties and responsibilities, but did not acknowledge women as civil or moral subjects. In order to gain the crucial recognition as subjects within the public polity, arguments needed to be made about equivalences between women and men. The German Social Democrat August Bebel, in his classic text *Die Frau und der Sozialismus* (Women and Socialism) of 1879, argued that, since an increasing number of women were now participants in the labor market and many were obliged by their social circumstances to make their own living, their inclusion in the processes of law-making had become imperative (Frevert 104–5). He also drew explicit parallels between working-class men's fight for the franchise and the campaign for the vote for women. Moreover, both he and fellow Social Democrat Wilhelm Liebknecht supported the appeal of feminists such as Hedwig Dohm to the principle of *human* rights as the basis for civil enfranchisement: political rights were human rights, not men's rights, and so should be extended to the female constituents of humanity (Frevert 104). For the antifeminists, however, precisely this claim was inadmissible. Max Scheler, for example, writing on the women's movement in 1915, cited Simmel's observation of the "error" of referring to human culture when in fact culture was specifically masculine and concluded "that the woman who claims to be generally human becomes *eo ipso* more masculine in the process [*daß die Frau, die allgemein menschlich sein will,* eo ipso *hierdurch männlicher wird*]."[32]

Scheler's aperçu, at first glance more an indication of the lengths to which the antifeminists would go in their argumentation than an observation to be taken seriously, nevertheless draws attention to the way in which masculinity continues to occupy the definition of human subjectivity at this period, a subjectivity from which women qua sex remained excluded, not only legally, but also philosophically. This means that what was described above as the movement of both sexes toward a conceptual center ground where the intermediacy of both sexes is acknowledged does not produce structural sameness in the resulting male and female cultural positionings. If the "virilization" of women refers, as I have argued, to the increasing active participation of women as individual subjects in the public domain, that is, to their public appearance in social roles that the ideology of separate spheres decreed to be viable only for men, it also indicates that women entering the public life of the state had to develop characteristics — rationality, autonomy, agency, combativeness, and so on — that were defined a priori as "masculine." In actuality these characteristics were dictated by the structures and norms of the public sphere rather than by any qualities essential to masculinity. ("Masculinity" is as much of an imposition on male subjects as it is on female would-be subjects, as the psychoanalysis of identity formation demonstrates.) The adoption of characteristics not attributed to women by the dominant culture meant that women remained self-conscious about "masculinity" as a role, and this gap of self-consciousness ensured that the move by women into the public domain was always only a partial masculinization. Moreover, the suffragists may have argued for women's claim to equal civil rights with men, but they were also, as we have seen, insistent that there were positive effects to be gained for society at large from the influence of "feminine" characteristics on the public sphere — that morality, piety, and self-sacrifice, for example, which nineteenth-century ideologues had proclaimed to be the natural features of the feminine temperament.[33] When women did achieve positions in civil life, whether in politics, the academy, or in other social institutions, they were arguably most often successful when they understood how to mobilize specifically feminine-connoted virtues in the interests of the public good: defending the family, working for public health, promoting social justice, and so on. In thus working with the *difference* in their relationship to the wielding of public power generated by the conventional meanings attached to "femininity," the women who came to occupy positions of prominence in civil life conceptually straddled the conventional norms of both genders. Put differently, as a public personage still visibly female, a woman could retain the legacy of the qualities projected as "feminine" within the ideology of separate spheres, while simultaneously and in addition taking on aspects of the conventionally masculine subject. This "double-gendering," and the problems it poses, is a prominent feature in the fictions to be examined in the chapters of textual readings in this book, and is a theme to which I will return at the end of chapter 2.

The typical male scenario is structured differently. If what was at stake in the fin-de-siècle turn to the idealized "feminine" in art and literature was the attempt to reconstitute masculinity in opposition to what was perceived as a too-narrow and restrictive conception of publicly endorsed male subjectivity, masculinity nevertheless remained a priori wedded to a conceptualization of selfhood as "conscious subjective agency, rational control, ethical individuality, freedom and spiritual transcendence."[34]

Woman, as the male-authored abstract figure of the nonsubject within
Enlightenment thought, may have radiated self-contained aesthetic harmony (Simmel's "beautiful") or literally em-bodied the corporeal, the
sensual, and the erotic, but she always did so in the express absence of any
dimension of conscious agency or will. In incorporating the "feminine"
into the artwork, thereby imposing aesthetic form and the artist's individual signature on its representation, the male artist *consciously* appropriated
it for the project of his reconstituted masculine subjectivity.[35] As Felski
concludes in the chapter in which she considers the "imaginary identification with the feminine" among male artists and aesthetes at the turn
of the century: "The aesthete's performance of femininity is depicted as
authentically modern precisely because of its *self-conscious* transcendence
of the constraints of corporeality and natural sexual identity within which
woman remains imprisoned. Thus while challenging the ideal of a phallic,
unified, repressed masculinity, the cult of aestheticism contains a mysogy-
nistic [*sic*] dimension that is closely linked to, rather than dissolved by,
its antirepresentationalism and antinaturalism"; further: "To demateral-
ize the 'natural' by insisting upon the totalizing power of the textual may
thus to be to echo rather than challenge a long-standing aesthetic tradition which has sought transcendence through a denial and erasure of
the female body."[36] In this respect, the works that turn most obviously
toward the representation of the corporeal and the sensual can in the end
be seen as sharing the goal of the spiritual transcendence of the corporeal encountered in the work of those most concerned to repudiate the
abstracted feminine, such as Bachofen and Weininger.

"An age . . . of pure, of self-assertive virility": Fascism and Gender

In her 1929 landmark essay *A Room of One's Own*, Virginia Woolf
reflects on the adverse cultural effects of what she terms the "state of sex-
consciousness" that she sees as having, since the fin de siècle, disturbed
and distorted a formerly more harmonious and balanced — by implication
because less self-conscious — relationship between the sexes. The emancipation of women had, Woolf argues, challenged the cultural superiority
of men. Now she anticipates with some foreboding the reaction, envisaged as "an age to come of pure, of self-assertive virility" that, she notes,
is already being realized in contemporary fascist Italy.[37] Woolf's causal
connection is undoubtedly oversimplified, but given the diffuse equation
that had been created in the German-language critique of modernity, in
particular, between "femininity," sensuality, materialism, decadence, and
cultural malaise, it is in many respects unsurprising that the reassertion on
a collective scale of overtly masculine-connoted characteristics was eventually

found by many to offer a way out of the difficulties presented by social and economic modernization.

In George L. Mosse's account, the "crisis of masculinity" that characterized the turn of the century was resolved in the first instance by the onset of the First World War: "The crisis of masculinity at the fin de siècle had not changed but stiffened the ideal of normative manhood. Whatever challenge remained, it was temporarily drowned out by the August days of 1914 as European youth rushed to the colors. The Great War was a masculine event, in spite of the role it may have played in encouraging the greater independence of women" (107). Although not an explicit theme in Mosse's narrative of this period, what nevertheless emerges from his discussion of the norm of masculinity asserted during the First World War and after, in particular in Germany, is the extent to which the war assisted the transition from a bourgeois conceptualization of masculinity, which rested, as I have been arguing, on a notion of autonomy, individuation, and singular personality, to a model of masculinity compatible with the postbourgeois, mass organization of society. As becomes clear in retrospect, bourgeois masculinity's ideological investment in singularity and autonomy was in fact only sustainable on the basis of the opposition between an elite bourgeois class that controlled the levers of social power and the mass of the ruled who were excluded, as women were, from conceptual subjectivity. As long as this structure held, an ideological opposition could be maintained between the undifferentiated physicality and raw bodily force of the working and peasant classes and the individuated bourgeois intellect required to direct and control them — another of Enlightenment modernity's oppositions of body and mind, structurally not dissimilar to that between the feminine and the masculine, with the undisciplined body once again featuring as the locus of cultural threat.[38] The enfranchisement of the working classes in the early years of the twentieth century created a new form of civil society structured by the opposition within a parliamentary democracy of mass political parties, representing conflicting social interests, while the emergent modern mass economy continued as the driver of major demographic change. For a society such as Germany's, which was modernizing very quickly, the threat of social instability as well as ideological incoherence was considerable. The war, though, provided at least a temporary solution. In creating the need for national unity, it gave the conflicting social forces directional focus and also aided the remodeling of ideal-typical masculinity. Aspects of the bourgeois ideal of masculinity were retained, notably the dedication of the individual to the aims of the social collective and the trained and disciplined physique, together with willpower, perseverance, and mental control.[39] But the bourgeois drive toward individuation and singularity was now substituted by the patriotic sacrifice of self to the specifically *national* cause and the disappearance of individuality in the coordinated marching mass. "Significance" was now to be found in a mass form of heroism or in the formal recognition accorded to physical bravery, especially where dangerous action was undertaken without regard for personal safety. Curiously, this unleashing of physical aspects of the self presented a potential answer both to the dissatisfaction with the narrowly rationalistic constraints of bourgeois masculinity and to the longings for self-transcendence surfacing in German-language art and literature in the prewar years. In the war memories of Ernst Jünger, for example, which enjoyed considerable popularity when they were published in the 1920s, one notes the ecstatic depiction of the release of primordial energies from the constraints imposed by Enlightenment rationality and the laws of civil society, and the hint at the fulfillment of spiritual or transcendent longings in the experience of violence. Counter to the threat posed by self-dissolution in the engulfing embrace of the archaic feminine, however, this release of the senses is presented in terms entirely compatible with conventional notions of virility:

> As sons of an age intoxicated by matter, progress seemed to us perfection, the machine the key to godliness, telescopes and microscopes organs of enlightenment. Yet underneath the ever more polished exterior, beneath all the clothes in which we bedecked ourselves, we remained naked and raw like men of the forest and the steppes.

> That showed itself when the War ripped asunder the community of Europe, when we confronted each other in a primordial contest behind flags and symbols which many sceptics had long mocked. Then it was that, in an orgy of frenzy, the true human being made up for everything he had missed. At this point his drives, too long pent up by society and its laws, became once more the ultimate form of reality, holiness, and reason.[40]

There was, as Mosse and many others have argued, a direct line between the restoration of the virile self-image of the male subject in the First World War period — and, by extension, of the nation he defended — and the more extreme version promoted by the National Socialist movement in Germany in the years leading up to the Second World War. The intervening years saw the highly unstable period of the Weimar Republic, marked by the proliferation of adamantly opposed political groupings, profound economic difficulties, and, notwithstanding the vibrant modernist culture focused in particular on the major urban centers, the constant threat of political and societal disintegration. When the National Socialist German Workers Party (NSDAP) under the leadership of Adolf Hitler presented itself as the solution to the political and economic crisis of the early 1930s, it did so on an ideological platform that drew extensively on an antimodernist rhetoric of cultural decadence and decline that by then was well-established in the German-language tradition.[41] Political fragmentation and threatened social dissolution were to be opposed by a collective version of a traditional "masculine" identity: Germany was to become a unified and autonomous nation, directed by the willpower, physical self-discipline, and virile aggression of its leadership and special forces.

There are many aspects of the National Socialists' ideological program that make the movement appear to be in reaction against the general cultural currents of modernity, and these include its policies on gender. Roger Griffin, among fascism's most authoritative theorists today, warns against seeing the fascist movements of the 1930s in simplistically antimodernist terms, however, stressing "Fascism's essentially palingenetic, and hence anticonservative, thrust toward a *new* type of society [. . .]. It thus represents an alternative modernism rather than a rejection of it."[42] This is of crucial importance to what came later, since it is precisely because fascism could be interpreted, not as a break with Enlightenment modernity, but as a historical phenomenon that brought to the surface in extreme form its underlying trends, that the postwar and post-Holocaust critique of modernity could take as its target not just fascism, but the entire history of the construction of human subjectivity since the Enlightenment. With this in mind, it is valuable to consider briefly the way in which National Socialist ideology constructed gender roles and their cultural significations.

Woman was, for the Nazis, above all subsumed by the maternal role. As mother, she was projected back into the domestic sphere, where she had been in the bourgeois era, and once again entrusted with the task of providing children with the moral upbringing that would fit them for their later social functions. But, crucially, the home was much more open to the public sphere than it had been. Motherhood was now constructed as an overtly *national* task, and women were enabled to conceive of their contribution to society — both in terms of childbearing and -rearing and in other ways — in broadly nationalist terms.[43] Moreover, girls and women as much as boys and men were provided with organizations and movements intended to integrate them mentally and physically into the national collective. This was not a complete return to the dependency of the bourgeois era, nor by any means a total banishment of women from the public arena. In this sense, the ideal type of the National Socialist woman was a canny mix of traditional maternity and the masculinized "new woman."

What was quite *absent* from the Nazi image of woman was any hint of the erotic or sensual. Sexuality was openly acknowledged, for both sexes, in a way that contrasted quite strongly with the bourgeois era's concern to keep all physical processes out of sight, but it was oddly anaesthetized and de-eroticized. The Nazi obsession with race and breeding translated into a highly rationalized conceptualization of sexual relations,[44] and extended to state sponsorship of the rearing of racially approved children, for example in a project run by Heinrich Himmler under the name Leb-ensborn.[45] This rationalistic approach represents a distinct continuity with Enlightenment modernity's stress on science as the driver of social prog-ress. Sensuality and eroticism, bodily nature and desire, meanwhile, once the preserve of the abstracted "feminine" vis-à-vis the nineteenth-century bourgeois male subject, became lodged with the image of the Jew as the embodiment of everything that threatened the physical discipline and mental control of the Aryan German (of either sex). In effect, the concept of the *German* inherited the characteristics of the specifically *male* subject of the bourgeois era, while the Other was constructed in similarly racist, as opposed to gendered, terms. This conceptual move was possible because of the established connection between the "feminine" and Jewishness in the anti-Semitic writings of the fin de siècle — the same cultural history of anti-Semitism that had enabled Weininger to associate the two. This also meant that the opposition of the same range of characteristics as had pre-viously characterized the masculine-feminine dichotomy — the power of the mind versus physical nature, the disciplined body under the command of the will versus the sensuous body unrestrainedly indulging its desires, and, rather less obviously, modern rationality, technical mastery, and sci-ence versus the vestigial premodern influences of the aesthetic and the spiritual — could now be represented in terms of an opposition between different types of masculinity, rather than as an opposition of the sexes. The predominant image of the Jew in Nazi propaganda is, one notes, of the grotesquely self-indulgent and often overtly sexualized *male* body. It is a token of National Socialism's interest above all in the construction of masculinity that its central ideology should be staged as a contest of con-trasting male types.

For at the very heart of fascist ideology was its image of ideal mascu-linity. Mosse states: "Never before or since the appearance of fascism was masculinity elevated to such heights: the hopes placed upon it, the impor-tance of manliness as a national symbol and as a living example played a vital role in all fascist regimes" (155). Yet, as he also points out, "fascism merely expanded and embellished aspects of masculinity that had always been present" in the image of man created in the modern era (155). The fascist ideal drew its inspiration from Greek classical statuary: this was a beautiful, although expressly de-eroticized male body,[46] a body that sym-bolized the moral discipline of the mind that controlled it, a trained, fit, and self-evidently healthy body, representing the health and vigor not just of the individual but of the entire nation. Striking, too, in the National Socialist ideal of masculinity is the way it appealed — or was designed to appeal — to the "longings both instinctual and transcendental" (Izen-berg 3) that a purely economically driven modernity had failed to satisfy in its construction of the ideal type of the male subject. National Social-ism offered release from the atomized and anonymous individuality of modern mass society in the collective emotional swell of national belonging. The NSDAP's carefully staged rallies and public shows used coordinated mass physical movement and elements such as national emblems, light effects, music, rhetoric, and the placement of significant figureheads both to generate and then to channel mass psychic energy.[47] The constraints of an autonomous selfhood based on *intellectual* self-discipline was replaced by a model in which the boundaries between selves were erased, not in terms of an erotic encounter or "feminization," but in sublimated, quasi-religious form: as self-dedication and self-sacrifice to the nation — and to its self-made "genius" figure, the singular, all-powerful, and charismatic *Führer*. As Hitler's later propaganda chief, Joseph Goebbels, wrote in a semiautobiographical novel published in 1931: "What constitutes the modern German is not so much cleverness and intellect, as the new principle, the ability to give oneself to a cause unreservedly, to sacrifice oneself, to devote oneself to one's people."[48]

The "eternal longing for redemption from the intellect" of which Goebbels also writes in this passage (121) was answered above all, though, in the construction of the ideal type of National Socialist man as a warrior whose will was to be imposed on the vicissitudes of "nature" through primordial, brutal, physical force. This was a suitably masculine version of the Dionysian destructive energy that had so attracted the imagination of Nietzsche as a necessary precondition for the founding of a new social order. Nietzsche's writings, selectively edited and bowdlerized, were among those deployed by the National Socialists to give philosophical cachet to their vision.[49] In National Socialist ideology, all physical and emotional vulnerabilities or weaknesses were presented as a blight to be eradicated, whether encountered in the responses of the individual to the challenges of founding this new imperial state or as embodied by the victims selected by the regime to figure degeneracy: Jews, gypsies, homosexuals, the mentally and physically disabled, and so on. The mass psychology of National Socialism, the question of why this brutal and violent construction of what might be termed the national subject was appealing enough to generate the support that kept Hitler and his henchmen in power and that duly resulted in the annihilation of millions of victims, remains the subject of reflection and analysis, and probably no single answer will ever fully explain the phenomenon. Striking, though, is the structural continuity in fascist thinking with the central concern of the intellectual revolution of the Enlightenment: the exertion of human control over the material forces of nature and the combating of weaknesses and vulnerabilities rooted in the human condition in order finally to achieve a perfected society. Yet as National Socialism revealed with greater clarity than at any previous point in the history of Enlightenment modernity, the ultimate logic of this pursuit of the control of internal and external nature could only be the annihilation of life itself.

In other words, in terms of the Enlightenment construction of human selfhood, the logical trajectory of the conceptually "masculine" subject, who is socially endorsed only insofar as he transcends his physical and material nature and his emotional vulnerabilities, is the ineluctable return to that which he set out to defeat: death. It is precisely this paradox that is at the heart of Max Horkheimer's and Theodor W. Adorno's analysis of Enlightenment subjectivity in the *Dialektik der Aufklärung* (Dialectic of Enlightenment), the work that more than any other laid the theoretical ground for the renewed German-language critique of modernity in the post-1945 period.

Notes

[1] Georg Simmel, "Female Culture," in Simmel, *On Women, Sexuality, and Love,* ed. and trans. Guy Oakes (New Haven and London: Yale UP, 1984), 65–101, here 67. Subsequent references appear as parenthetical page numbers in the text.

[2] The women's rights activist Helene Lange referred to Simmel in *Die Frauen-bewegung in ihren modernen Problemen* (1908), for example. For commentary on the influence of Simmel, see Marianne Ulmi, *Frauenfragen — Männergedanken: Zu Georg Simmels Philosophie und Soziologie der Geschlechter* (Zurich: eFeF, 1989).

[3] Simmel, "Female Culture," 88. The translation has been significantly modi-fied in order to restore Simmel's sentence construction: compare Georg Simmel, "Weibliche Kultur," in Simmel, *Aufsätze und Abhandlungen 1909–1918,* vol. 1 (*Gesamtausgabe,* vol. 12), ed. Rüdiger Kramme and Angela Rammstedt (Frank-furt am Main: Suhrkamp, 2001), 274–75.

[4] Georg Simmel, "Philosophie der Geschlechter. Fragmente," in Simmel, *Aufsä-tze und Abhandlungen 1901–1908,* vol. 2 (*Gesamtausgabe,* vol. 8), ed. Alessandro Cavalli and Volkhard Krech (Frankfurt am Main: Suhrkamp, 1993), 74–75.

[5] This term is used to denote the fact that the values and assumptions charac-teristic of the eighteenth-century intellectual revolution in Europe and beyond and that are summed up in the term "Enlightenment" — broadly speaking, the movement toward the secularization of the social order, the centrality of scientific inquiry as a means of bettering the human condition and of commercialization as a means of raising social living standards, together with the emphasis, new to the Enlightenment period, on the individual subject, invested with rights and disci-plined by obligations — have remained the underlying values and assumptions of the entire modern period in the West and still persist today. I shall be distinguish-ing, however, between different phases in the period of Enlightenment moder-nity: the bourgeois era (late eighteenth century to the turn of the nineteenth to the twentieth), the era of mass society (from the enfranchisement of the working classes at the start of the twentieth century to the 1960s), and the "late modern" or postmodern era (from the late 1960s onwards).

[6] See Lynn Abrams, *The Making of Modern Woman: Europe 1789–1918* (London: Longman, 2002), 160–63 on the "new woman" and chapter 10 on "First-wave Feminism." See also her account of the new patterns of employment for women

brought about by changes in the economy at the end of the nineteenth century, 205–8. Subsequent references to this work appear in the text as parenthetical page numbers, identified when necessary as Abrams.

[7] See Richard J. Evans, *The Feminist Movement in Germany 1894–1933* (London and Beverly Hills: Sage, 1976), 75–77.

[8] See Evans, *The Feminist Movement in Germany,* 177, and Ute Frevert's discussion of the defenders of exclusively male voting rights in *"Mann und Weib, und Weib und Mann": Geschlechter-Differenzen in der Moderne* (Munich: C. H. Beck, 1995), 109–25. Subsequent references to this work appear in the text as parenthetical page numbers, identified when necessary as Frevert. Variations on the derogatory "Man-Woman" (*Mannweib* or *Männin*) appear in speeches cited by Frevert, 111, 117.

[9] Richard von Krafft-Ebing's *Psychopathia Sexualis* (1886) was among the earliest of these works on sexual deviancy. Also important were: Iwan Bloch, *Das Sexualleben unserer Zeit in seinen Beziehungen zur modernen Kultur* (1907) and Magnus Hirschfeld, *Die Homosexualität des Mannes und des Weibes* (1914) and his three-volume magnum opus *Sexualpathologie* (first edition 1916).

[10] Andreas Huyssen, *After the Great Divide: Modernism, Mass Culture, Postmodernism* (Basingstoke and London: Macmillan, 1988), 45.

[11] See George L. Mosse, *Nationalism and Sexuality: Respectability and Abnormal Sexuality in Modern Europe* (New York: H. Fertig, 1985).

[12] Rita Felski, *The Gender of Modernity* (Cambridge, MA and London: Harvard UP, 1995), 1. Subsequent references appear in the text as parenthetical page numbers, identified when necessary as Felski.

[13] Jacques Le Rider, *Modernity and Crises of Identity: Culture and Society in Fin-de-Siècle Vienna* [first published 1990], trans. Rosemary Morris (New York: Continuum, 1993). Subsequent references appear in the text as parenthetical page numbers, identified as Le Rider.

[14] Gerald N. Izenberg, *Modernism and Masculinity: Mann, Wedekind, Kandinsky through World War I* (Chicago and London: U of Chicago P, 2000), 4. The modernist quest to unite within the male artistic subject both the feminine and the masculine elements marks a point of connection with German Romanticism; see Izenberg 220–21 for a discussion of the parallels and distinctions between the two movements. Subsequent references appear in the text as parenthetical page numbers, identified when necessary as Izenberg.

[15] Introduction to *Mother Right,* in *Myth, Religion, and Mother Right: Selected Writings of J. J. Bachofen,* intro. Joseph Campbell, trans. Ralph Manheim (Princeton: Princeton UP, 1992), 109.

[16] See Le Rider, *Modernity and Crises of Identity,* 104–5, 112.

[17] Le Rider, *Modernity and Crises of Identity,* 106. This proved of interest to the intellectual battle of the sexes in post-1968 France; see Jacques Derrida, *Éperons. Les styles de Nietzsche* (1978), in which Derrida suggested that Nietzsche identified with woman, and Luce Irigaray, *Amante marine. De Friedrich Nietzsche* (1980).

[18] See Izenberg's chapter "Thomas Mann and the Feminine Passion for Transcendence," *Modernism and Masculinity,* 97–159.

[19] For a variety of responses to Nietzsche's views on gender, and in particular on woman, see Peter J. Burgard, ed., *Nietzsche and the Feminine* (Charlottesville and London: UP of Virginia, 1994).

[20] John E. Toews, "Refashioning the Masculine Subject in Early Modernism: Narratives of Self-Dissolution and Self-Construction in Psychoanalysis and Literature, 1900–1914," *Modernism/Modernity* 4.1 (1997): 31–67, here 32.

[21] Chandak Sengoopta, *Otto Weininger: Sex, Science, and Self in Imperial Vienna* (Chicago and London: U of Chicago P, 2000), 24–25. The quotation within this passage is from Ernst Mach, *The Analysis of the Sensations and the Relation of the Physical to the Psychical,* trans. C. M. Williams and Sydney Waterlow (New York: Dover, 1959), 17. See also John T. Blackmore, *Ernst Mach: His Work, Life and Influence* (Berkeley: U of California P, 1972).

[22] Ernst Mach, *Analyse der Empfindungen und das Verhältnis des Physischen zum Psychischen* (Jena: Fischer, 4th edn. 1903), 20. The translation given here is Sengoopta's (25).

[23] Sengoopta, *Otto Weininger: Sex, Science, and Self,* 55. Sengoopta notes that Weininger's conversion from Judaism to Protestant Christianity is in keeping with his turn to the German Idealist tradition in his philosophy.

[24] Otto Weininger, *Geschlecht und Charakter* (Munich: Matthes & Seitz, 1980), 440–41. The translation is Sengoopta's (64).

[25] On the ideology of separate spheres, see Abrams, *The Making of Modern Woman,* 30.

[26] See George L. Mosse, *The Image of Man: The Creation of Modern Masculinity* (New York and Oxford: Oxford UP, 1996), for a wide-ranging discussion of the ideal of masculinity in European modernity.

[27] See Mosse, *The Image of Man,* especially chapters 2 and 6. Subsequent references to the work appear in the text as parenthetical page numbers, identified when necessary as Mosse.

[28] There were, needless to say, all of these things in reality, and it became one of the self-appointed tasks of literature to explore the "heart of darkness" concealed behind the bourgeois façade.

[29] Jean-Jacques Rousseau, *Émile* [first published 1762] (London, 1993), 388, cited from Abrams, *The Making of Modern Woman,* 20.

[30] Izenberg, *Modernism and Masculinity,* 7. He refers in this passage to Frevert's *"Mann und Weib, und Weib und Mann,"* which includes an illuminating chapter on the delegation of the pursuit of aesthetic culture to the sphere of the feminine within the bourgeois division of labor; see her "Kulturfrauen und Geschäftsmänner. Soziale Identitäten im deutschen Bürgertum des 19. Jahrhunderts," 133–65.

[31] Toews's account of the narratives of self-dissolution and self-construction in texts by Freud, Schnitzler, and Musil is illuminating in this respect (Toews, "Refashioning the Masculine Subject in Early Modernism." For details see note 20 above).

32 Quoted by Silvia Bovenschen in *Die imaginierte Weiblichkeit: Exemplarische Untersuchungen zu kulturgeschichtlichen und literarischen Präsentationsformen des Weiblichen* (Frankfurt am Main: Suhrkamp, 1979), 28.

33 This would prove to be a conceptual double bind, since these characteristics of "femininity" can easily be seen as an inheritance from women's status as cultural objects. It is a problem that would repeat itself in 1970s French feminist theory, as women thinkers sought to occupy the contemporary meanings of the "feminine" for the advantage of the women's movement. See discussion in chapter 2.

34 Toews, "Refashioning the Masculine Subject," 32.

35 This is, in a nutshell, Izenberg's thesis in his readings of the three male modernists who form the subject of his study.

36 Felski, *The Gender of Modernity,* 112, 114, italics added. See also Christine Battersby's insightful examination of the historical construction of genius as a necessarily male attribute which appropriates the "feminine" in the course of its self-construction: *Gender and Genius: Towards a Feminist Aesthetics* (London: The Women's Press, 1989).

37 Virginia Woolf, *A Room of One's Own* (London: Granada, 1977), 98.

38 Fredric Jameson has analyzed the ideological construction of bourgeois identity and its relation to what it represses by interpreting the traces (for example, of the bourgeois fear of working-class physicality) legible in some of the great writers of the bourgeois era; see his thoroughly illuminating, if theoretically idiosyncratic work *The Political Unconscious: Narrative as a Socially Symbolic Act* (1981).

39 See Mosse, *The Image of Man:* "The First World War added no new feature to the stereotype of modern manhood, but it deepened certain aspects" (109), and subsequent discussion.

40 Ernst Jünger, *Der Kampf als inneres Erlebnis* (1929), quoted from Roger Griffin, ed., *Fascism* (Oxford: Oxford UP, 1995), 109.

41 Oswald Spengler's *Der Untergang des Abendlandes* (The Decline of the West) (2 volumes, 1918–23) was influential in the post-1918 period. But he drew on a long-standing tradition, going back to Schopenhauer, Eduard von Hartmann, Nietzsche, and others; see Michael Pauen, *Pessimismus: Geschichtsphilosophie, Metaphysik und Moderne von Nietzsche bis Spengler* (Berlin: Akademie Verlag, 1997). Pauen demonstrates the connection between Spengler's thought and Nazism (209–10).

42 Roger Griffin, *The Nature of Fascism* (London: Routledge, 1993), 47.

43 See Paula Siber, "The New German Woman" (translated extract from "Die Frauenfrage und ihre Lösung durch den Nationalsozialismus," 1933), in Griffin, ed., *Fascism,* 136–37. One notes in this text, apart from the emphasis on motherhood, including "motherhood of the soul," the recourse, too, to the association of women with the mythical past: "The mother is also the intermediary for the people and national culture [*Volkstum*] to which she and her child belong. For she is the custodian of its culture, which she provides her child with through fairy-tales, legends, games, and customs in a way which is decisive for the whole relationship which he will later have to his people."

[44] See Dagmar Herzog's account of Nazi policies on sexuality in "Hubris and Hypocrisy, Incitement and Disavowal," in Herzog, ed., *Sexuality and German Fascism* (New York, Oxford: Berghahn, 2005), 1–21.

[45] On Himmler's Lebensborn project, see Georg Lilienthal, *Der Lebensborn e. V.: Ein Instrument nationalsozialistischer Rassenpolitik* (Stuttgart, New York: Gustav Fischer Verlag, 1985), and Catrine Clay and Michael Leapman, *Master Race: The Lebensborn Experiment in Nazi Germany* (London: Hodder & Stoughton, 1995).

[46] See the discussion of Nazism's efforts to minimize the erotic implications of the male nudity favored in its iconography in Mosse, *The Image of Man*, 172–73.

[47] See Griffin, *The Nature of Fascism*, 96, on the degree of calculation in Nazi handling of mass psychology.

[48] Joseph Goebbels, *Michael: Ein deutsches Schicksal in Tagebuchblättern*, quoted from Griffin, ed., *Fascism*, 120. Subsequent references appear in the text as parenthetical page numbers.

[49] See Mosse's discussion of the interest in Nietzsche in the Italian and German fascist movements in *The Image of Man*, 157–58, 163.

2: The Post-1945 Crisis of Enlightenment and the Emergence of the "Other" Sex

Gender and the Post-Holocaust Crisis of Enlightenment

"HUMANITY HAD TO INFLICT TERRIBLE INJURIES on itself before the self — the identical, purpose-directed, *masculine* character of human beings — was created, and something of this process is repeated in every childhood," wrote Max Horkheimer and Theodor W. Adorno in the *Dialectic of Enlightenment*.[1] It has been generally rather little acknowledged that Horkheimer and Adorno's post-Holocaust analysis of the disaster that had engulfed the historical and cultural project of the Enlightenment is couched quite specifically as a critique of the *masculine* traits that had come to define the concept of human subjectivity in European modernity. At the center of the *Dialectic of Enlightenment* is an explicitly gendered critique of a form of rationality that, seeking at every stage to dominate and transcend nature in the interests of human self-preservation and progress, leads with fatal inevitability to the destruction both of the rational capacity and of selfhood itself. Horkheimer and Adorno wrote their book of "philosophical fragments" in the United States as Jews in exile from Germany during the latter phases of the Second World War.[2] In this respect, the phenomenon of fascism was key to their studies and lent their critique of Enlightenment a particular political urgency. However, fascism, as they saw it, was more than a mere historical interlude. For them, it displayed a logic underlying the entire trajectory of Enlightenment modernity and indeed, given their analysis of the genesis of masculine subjectivity via a reading of Homer's *Odyssey*, of the recorded history of patriarchal civilization in the West.

In launching their attack on the fetishization of instrumental rationality and on the alienation of the modern self from external and internal nature, they revived motifs from the masculinity crisis of the turn of the century. By the mid-1940s, however, as knowledge of the National Socialists' concentration camps spread, that culturally endemic "too-exclusive affirmation of values connected with the masculine element" (Le Rider 90) — scientific and technical rationality, self-mastery, and mastery of the object — that had been the issue of concern for artists and intellectuals at the earlier period, now appeared to them to be directly linked to the collapse of Enlightenment into barbarism. Their project, then, was a critique that would expose the mechanisms of power and the concomitant psychological distortions at work beneath the surface of the Enlightenment construction of the subject.

The essay on the *Odyssey* that forms one section of the *Dialectic* treats the narrative of Homer's eponymous hero as a representation of the identity formation of the prototype Enlightenment subject. It opens with a contrast between myth, as the heterogeneous material handed down by popular tradition, and epic, as the narrative organization of this diverse material into the story of the singular individual. *Mythos* and *epos* are posited as the representatives in *formal* terms of the dialectic of manifold nature on the one hand and the autonomous and unified rational self who is intent on mastering nature on the other, which they identify as the *Odyssey*'s subject matter. As their dialectical approach makes clear, it is only through the conflict with and triumph over the mythical forces that the unified self can be generated (H-A 25). In ways that are not always obvious, then, the self is in fact dependent on the resistant materiality of nature, including his own, as the basis — Horkheimer and Adorno call it the "substrate" (H-A 87) — of his own identity formation as coherent and unified. At the same time, since rational selfhood, as embodied by the cunning Odysseus, realizes itself through the triumph over not only external but also internal nature, it is paradoxically *also* a form of self-annihilation:

> The human being's mastery of itself, on which the self is founded, practically always involves the annihilation of the subject in whose service that mastery is maintained, because the substance which is mastered, suppressed, and disintegrated by self-preservation is nothing other than the living entity, of which the achievements of self-preservation can only be defined as functions — in other words, self-preservation destroys the very thing which is to be preserved. (H-A 43)

Within the schema of identity formation presented in the Odysseus chapter, woman is placed on the other side of the dialectic and identified with the forces of nature that are to be mastered. The foremost personification of this aspect of woman is the sorceress Circe, who transforms the men who succumb to her seductions into pigs, thus reversing the cultural process by which men have created a distinction between themselves and animal nature (H-A 54–55). As Horkheimer and Adorno stress, this does not necessarily imply the annihilation of the self. Rather, the story preserves "an older form of life" in which self-mastery and self-denial were not yet the foundation of subjectivity. In Odysseus' resistance of Circe, the transition to a new order is represented in which self-discipline becomes the key to masculine power (H-A 56). From this point onwards, they argue, to love is to demonstrate one's inability to rule over one's own passions, and while society may glorify the one who loves, it simultaneously requires that he be punished: "The inability to master himself and others demonstrated by his love is reason enough to deny him fulfillment" (H-A 57). The defeat of Circe's power marks the moment of the reversal in the power relationship between man and woman, and ushers in the era of patriarchy as the era of the transcendence of nature: "Circe's power, which subjugates men as her slaves, gives way to her enslavement to the man who, through renunciation, has refused to submit" (H-A 57).

The continued association with nature in the cultural imagination nevertheless gives woman a particular symbolic status. "As a representative of nature, woman in bourgeois society has become an enigma of irresistibility and powerlessness. Thus she reflects back the vain lie of power, which substitutes the mastery over nature for reconciliation with it" (H-A 56). Woman, in other words, reflects back to the male subject the irresistible forces that he himself has overcome, embodying in his perception therefore both the allure of nature and nature's powerlessness. In the excursus entitled "Juliette or Enlightenment and Morality," Horkheimer and Adorno go on to consider the underlying cultural justification of the destruction and exploitation of the powerless (aligned with nature) by the powerful (the executors of culture) in Enlightenment thought. Intercutting passages from Nietzsche's *Geneologie der Moral* (Genealogy of Morals) and the works of the Marquis de Sade, they demonstrate the affinities between the Nietzschean *Übermensch* and the Sadeian libertine, highlighting the positions of both as expressions of the logic of Enlightenment. In terms of their central theme of the Enlightenment subject's domination and transcendence of nature, de Sade's work in particular might appear to reverse the self-disciplined containment of the sexual drives that underpins Enlightenment subjectivity. In Horkheimer and Adorno's reading, however, the indulged sexual impulses of the Sadeian libertine represent the return of repressed nature in *distorted* form (whereby distortion is understood, with Freud, as a modality of the language of the unconscious). The point is not a reconciliation of subjectivity with nature, but rather the intensified assertion of the self via the affront to the social order, the deliberate exposure of its moral laws as rationally untenable: Juliette embodies "the joy of defeating civilization with its own weapons" (H-A 74). In this sense, the destructive, sadistic activities of de Sade's protagonists represent the intensification of the Enlightenment principle by which subjective power is asserted via the mastery of nature and through the objectification and exploitation of all those weaker others who reflect nature back to the self.

Of these weaker others, Horkheimer and Adorno give privileged consideration to the position occupied by woman in the hierarchy of cultural power, but notably they also read across from her to the objectification of racial others: "Woman bears the stigma of weakness; her weakness places her in a minority even when she is numerically superior to men. As with the subjugated original inhabitants in early forms of state, the indigenous population of colonies, who lack the organization and weapons of their conquerors, as with Jews among Aryans, her defencelessness legitimizes her oppression" (H-A 86). From this "natural" weakness there results also the occupation of woman by the meanings ascribed to her by the culturally dominant male:

> Man as ruler refuses to do woman the honor of individualizing her. Socially, the individual woman is an example of the species, a representative of her sex, and thus, wholly encompassed by male logic, she stands for nature, the substrate of never-ending subsumption on the plane of ideas and of never-ending subjection on that of reality. Woman as an allegedly natural being is a product of history, which denatures her. (H-A 87)

In representing within the male-generated culture both the idea of nature and the principle of "powerlessness" and "subjection," woman becomes the object of a hatred that is in fact pathological, a violence that seeks to avenge the subject's own fear of regression to nature: "To eradicate utterly the hated but overwhelming temptation to lapse back into nature — that is the cruelty which stems from failed civilization; it is barbarism, the other side of culture" (H-A 87–88). This observation provides the authors with the link from their discussion of the symbolic position of woman within Enlightenment culture to that of the Jews as the victims of torture in the fascist concentration camps in one of the *Dialectic*'s most passionate passages:

> The signs of powerlessness, hasty uncoordinated movements, animal fear, swarming masses, provoke the lust for murder. The explanation for the hatred of woman as the weaker in mental and physical power, who bears the mark of domination on her brow, is the same as for the hatred of the Jews. Women and Jews show visible evidence of not having ruled for thousands of years. They live, although they could be eliminated, and their fear and weakness, the greater affinity to nature produced in them by perennial oppression, is the element in which they live. In the strong, who pay for their strength with their strained remoteness from nature and must forever forbid themselves fear, this incites blind fury. They identify themselves with nature by calling forth from their victims, multiplied a thousand times, the cry they may not utter themselves. (H-A 88)[3]

Here, the parallelism of Jews and women in their culturally symbolic alignment with the body, with sensuality, and with nature, encountered earlier in the work of Otto Weininger, reappears. Now, though, it forms part of a critique of a construction of human subjectivity founded on the pathological repression of and alienation from nature and a too-exclusive emphasis on rationality and control.

In an illuminating engagement with the work of the Frankfurt School in her book *Woman, Nature, and Psyche*, Patricia Jagentowicz Mills takes Horkheimer and Adorno to task for their failure to consider a specifically female perspective on the cultural issues that they raise.[4] While the criticism has some justification, Mills underplays the extent to which their critique of Enlightenment subjectivity *has* to be formulated in terms of the critique of male subjectivity, since the root of the malaise that afflicts the Enlightenment project from their perspective is the conflation of selfhood with "masculinity." In revisiting themes that had already found expression in the fin-de-siècle crisis of masculinity — the alienation of the male subject from material nature as also from the older layers of memory reaching back to the archaic history of humanity, his entrapment and reduction as a self by the demands made of him as an agent of cultural progress under the conditions of modernity — Horkheimer and Adorno repeat the opposition inherent in the construction of the Enlightenment subject of the "masculine" as the bearer of culture and the "feminine" as its designated Other. But they are providing a diagnosis rather than exhibiting a masculinist bias. Within the terms of the Enlightenment conceptualization of the subject they illuminate the logic of this subject's collapse back into barbarism as it seeks vengeance for its own self-alienation on those whom it has chosen to represent nature to itself. The crisis of Enlightenment is thus identified as a crisis of the claim to universal subjecthood of the partial psychic dynamic designated by "masculinity": the drive to individuation, to rational autonomy, and to mastery.

Horkheimer and Adorno famously do not consider in any detail a way of resolving the cultural malaise that they diagnose in the *Dialectic*. They hint at points at the possibility of reconciliation (*Versöhnung*) with nature, attainable through the "remembrance [*Eingedenken*] of nature within the subject" (H-A 32) and the abolition (*Aufhebung*) of the "false absolute, the principle of blind power" (H-A 33) that they imagine as the precondition of the Enlightenment project's reorientation.[5] They remain essentially wedded to a negative form of dialectics, however. Nietzsche and de Sade ultimately earn praise since they, as the "dark writers of the bourgeoisie, unlike its apologists, did not seek to avert the consequences of the Enlightenment with harmonistic doctrines" (H-A 92). The coldness with which these writers pursued the logic of Enlightenment rationality to the point at which its destructive potential is made transparent is, in Horkheimer and Adorno's reading, the precondition for the dialectical reversal that brings into view "the utopia of a humanity which, itself no longer distorted, no longer needs distortion" (H-A 93). Exactly how humanity is to regain an undistorted relation to its origin in nature is left indeterminate, however.[6]

In the analogous situation at the turn of the century, writers and artists concerned to generate an altered conception of the male subject turned to the symbolic figure of woman in their search for those elements of the psyche and of human psychic history that had been excluded and repressed in the narrowly rationalistic construction of modern subject-hood. In *Woman, Nature, and Psyche*, Mills traces the way in which the critical theorists of the Frankfurt School likewise, in works that appeared subsequently to the *Dialectic*, drew on conceptualizations and figurations of the "feminine" in the attempt to formulate an alternative to the destructive momentum of Enlightenment modernity. In Horkheimer's work, for example, she observes the attempt to posit the maternal principle as offering a critical utopian potential vis-à-vis the functionalization of the (male) individual in modern society, pursuing a line in his thought from a prewar essay entitled "Authority and the Family" (1936) to his postwar review of the situation of the family in "Authoritarianism and the Family Today" (1949) to an essay of 1957 entitled "The Concept of Man." Common to all of these essays is an argument concerning the potentiality of woman, and in particular the mother, to represent to man "a principle other than reality,"[7] preserving through her love for him his sense of himself as a "definite, irreplaceable, and distinct individual" in contrast to his representation in the public sphere as "a certain function, the neutral incorporation of a service, a replaceable cog in a great machine."[8] In the postwar works, this maternal role is seen as threatened, even lost, because of the integration of woman into the labor force: "Women have paid for their limited admission into the economic world of the male by taking over the behavior patterns of a thoroughly reified society."[9] Yet the nostalgia for the utopian potential contained in the figure of the bourgeois woman as the guardian of the home continues to surface even in the latest of the three essays:

> [Woman's] nature, unlike that of man, was not shaped by activity in the labor market and adapted to circumstances outside the home. Yet her passive role, which nothing could justify, also enabled her to avoid reduction to object-status and thus to represent, amid an evil society, another possibility. In the passage from the old serfdom to the new she could be regarded as a representation of nature, which eluded utilitarian calculation. This element, regardless of whether woman was opposing society or submitting to it, determined her image for the bourgeois era.[10]

There are, as Mills points out, a number of problems with Horkheimer's analyses of women's role. In the first place, these essays exhibit a distinct gender bias that assesses the cultural position of women solely in terms of the psychological benefit to the male individual's identity formation (148). There is no consideration at all of the issue of women's individuality or agency or the benefit *to women* of their greater access to civil society. Second, the essays display a distinct class bias. Focused as he is on the bourgeois model of the family, Horkheimer is blind to the cultural role of the working-class woman who, as Mills discusses, "was an active economic subject in the nineteenth century" already (111). In short, Horkheimer is looking back to an idealized maternal role entirely characteristic of nineteenth-century bourgeois ideology. Moreover, he fails to take into account the *ambivalence* that characterizes the male subject's relation to the mother and, by extension, to woman, an aspect that was so signally acknowledged in the *Dialectic*. As a figure representing within culture the nature that the male subject transcends, woman functions not only as a mediatrix of his potential reconciliation with nature, but also — as the *Dialectic* argued — as an embodiment of the nature that he seeks to dominate. As Mills states: "The patriarchal concept of woman *as* nature and the socioeconomic legitimation of the domination *of* nature combine to form the basis of abstract patriarchy" (100).

A more concerted attempt at generating a model for the reconciliation of culture and nature is found in the work of Herbert Marcuse, who is also interested in the "feminine" as a site within culture at which "a principle other than reality" (Horkheimer[11]) has been preserved. Marcuse was a member of the Institute for Social Research in exile who chose *not* to return from the United States to Germany after the war. Nevertheless, his work, written and published first in English, was to prove an important source of intellectual inspiration for the revolutionary generation of 1968 in Germany. His *Eros and Civilization,* published in 1955 and reissued in 1966, is subtitled *A Philosophical Inquiry into Freud.* In it, Marcuse returns to the Frankfurt School's central theme of the domination of nature, but now the Freudian influences that implicitly underpinned the arguments of the *Dialectic* are brought to the surface. He takes as his starting point Freud's argument that cultural attainment and progress is necessarily predicated upon the repression of the instinctual drives and the sublimation of the pleasure principle's impulse toward instinctual gratification. Like Horkheimer and Adorno in the *Dialectic,* though, Marcuse questions the objective benefit to humankind of a "reality principle" founded on repression, and like them, he makes an explicit connection between the rational domination of nature and the destructiveness inherent in the culture of modernity.[12] But whereas Horkheimer and Adorno did not pursue an analysis of how the reconciliation with nature was to be achieved, Marcuse is concerned to generate a positive counter-model, a map for the progression of human society "beyond the reality principle."[13] Given the advanced development of industrial civilization, in which human material needs are now in large part provided for and automation looks set to replace human labor, he sees the civilizatory possibility of a "dialectical regression," envisaged as the "emergence of a non-repressive reality principle involving instinctual liberation [that] would *regress* behind the attained level of civilized rationality" (143). Key to the "remembrance of nature" (H-A 32) that would form the basis of such a dialectical regression is the figure of the mother, here projected as the source of an abstracted "maternal Eros"[14] that, albeit in sublimated form, would replace the repressive principle of the paternal *Logos*.

In *Counterrevolution and Revolt*, published in 1972 at a time when second wave feminism was emerging as a social force in the United States and Western Europe, Marcuse retracted his theorization of the maternal principle with an apologetic acknowledgement of the latter's provenance in a repressive ideology: "The image of woman as mother is itself repressive; it transforms a biological fact into an ethical and cultural value and thus it supports and justifies her social repression."[15] However, his reformulation of his theory of Eros in this work reveals how wedded he remains to the conceptual potential of the "feminine" as a source of cultural reform. Here, the notion of the maternal is replaced by that of a "feminine principle" that is to be activated as a cultural force in both women *and* men, although Marcuse notes that the history of civilization to date means that the particular behavioral characteristics he is looking for have been fostered more effectively in women. Mills summarizes:

> Here, characteristics that have been designated feminine in the onto-genetic and phylogenetic processes of civilization are seen as necessary to the overturning of the repressive domination of nature: "The faculty of being 'receptive,' 'passive,' is a precondition of freedom: it is the ability to see things in their own right, to experience the joy enclosed in them, the erotic energy of nature — an energy which is there to be liberated; nature, too, awaits the revolution!" Passivity and receptivity, tenderness, and sensitivity — all traditional feminine traits — are essential to the vision of liberation. Here it is woman's *distance* from civil society, her embeddedness in the specific logic of the family, that allows her to represent a vision of liberation: "Isolation (separation) from the alienated work world of capitalism enabled the woman to remain less brutalized by the Performance Principle, to remain closer to her sensibility: more human than men."[16]

We seem to have come full circle. Not only is this reminiscent of Hork-heimer's class-biased idealization of the ability of woman "to represent, amid an evil society, another possibility."[17] It also significantly recalls Gerald N. Izenberg's analysis of the position of bourgeois women as an object of the male imagination at the fin de siècle: "In part because they were confined to the domestic sphere, women could pursue the spiritual inwardness that made them the humanistic and Romantic 'whole beings' that men aspired to be but that their worldly striving made all but impossible to achieve."[18] However, as Horkheimer's postwar reflections on women's greater participation in the labor market indicate, women in the postwar epoch were no longer reliably at home representing to their alienated sons and husbands the dream of another form of being. In the Frankfurt School's terms, they were, insofar as they were entering the world of men, entering into the same alienation. In short, the positive utopian function of the figure of woman in the perspective of the male writers and theorists proves to be predicated upon the confinement of women in the domestic sphere characteristic of the nineteenth-century division of labor within the bourgeois class. The positive values that Marcuse associates with the feminine and sees as "essential to the vision of liberation" are, then, no less the product of women's objectification than was the function he ascribed to maternal Eros.[19]

There is a further aspect to this shift in women's social positioning that is of central importance to the arguments that will follow in the chapters of textual readings in this book. As a comparative consideration of the symbolic function of woman at the fin de siècle and in the post-1945 period reveals, the change in the civil status and social positioning of women significantly altered the *ownership* of the culturally symbolic values of the "feminine." As long as women were confined in the home and excluded from the public sphere, they were, so to speak, passively available for symbolic occupation by male intellectuals and artists, who interpreted the symbolic material of the "feminine" as they wished for their own conceptual purposes, whether in a positive or negative vein. Under conditions in which women were much more significantly present in the public sphere, this function of the "feminine" is compromised. The male subject in the latter half of the twentieth century is confronted by a female figure whose social position is now changing to become not dissimilar to his own. Economically active and thus potentially independent, increasingly self-assertive, mobile, and a subject in her own right, she no longer serves so easily as the embodiment of the "ideal feminine" whose energies can be subsumed by the transcendent male author/subject into the project of his own identity formation. Nevertheless, the draw toward the "feminine" as the symbolic site of the potential solution to the crisis of male subjectivity remains. As will become evident from the textual readings below, there is a prevailing tendency among the *male* writers to turn to the figure of woman, or at least to elements conventionally associated with the "feminine" — eroticism, immediacy, liquidity, flow, the destruction of boundaries, and so on — in their search for the redemption of the self or of history. But, in contrast to the state of affairs at the turn of the century, the "feminine" is no longer passively available for male appropriation and incorporation into a reconceptualized masculine identity. Rather, the male protagonists struggle with a new state of affairs in which woman, having become an active figure in her own right, has in large part abandoned the male to his own irredeemability. Meanwhile, it is in the works of the *female* writers that we find the most concerted efforts to generate utopian potential from the symbolic significations of the "feminine." In short, in the post-1945 period, women are taking possession of the cultural significance of the "feminine" for themselves.

The next section of this chapter will examine both the cultural preconditions and some of the conceptual repercussions of this move. First, though, a note of caution from the Frankfurt School critic whose post-*Dialectic* position has so far not been considered in this discussion. Adorno remained unconvinced of the "feminine" as an authentic cultural position and maintained that the return of repressed "nature" was only possible in distorted form. In *Minima Moralia,* a collection of short reflective pieces begun after the completion of the *Dialectic* and eventually published in 1951 after his return to Germany, he wrote:

> The feminine character, and the ideal of femininity on which it is modeled, are products of masculine society. The image of undistorted nature arises only from distortion, as its opposite. Where it claims to be humane, masculine society imperiously breeds in woman its own corrective, and shows itself through this limitation implacably the master. The feminine character is a negative imprint of domination [*Der weibliche Charakter ist ein Abdruck des Positivs der Herrschaft*]. But therefore equally bad. [. . .] The glorification of the feminine character implies the humiliation of all who bear it.[20]

This astute, but negative, assessment of the conditions of possibility for the signification of the feminine conceptually discounts the value of the "feminine" as a positive platform for an emergent female cultural subject position in the post-1945 period. What it means is that the female author/subject who seeks to deploy the cultural meanings attached to her femininity to cultural-critical ends is effectively still entrapped in the definitions imposed upon her by a male-generated cultural order; in other words, she is still an object within the patriarchal system that has created the opposition between masculinity and femininity as one between domination and nature. We do not have to accept the implication of Adorno's argument that this excludes from cultural agency a subjectivity that is distinctively marked as female, in particular since, as the textual readings will show, the male subject position itself no longer functions so reliably as a configuration of domination in the context of the conceptual shifts taking place in the post-1945 period. Nonetheless, Adorno's caveat concerning femininity does draw attention to the conceptual complexities that attend women's aspiration to a gender-differentiated subject position as the female sex moves more vigorously into the limelight of the public sphere in the postwar epoch.

The Emergence of the "Other" Sex

In *Le Deuxième Sexe* (The Second Sex, 1949), Simone de Beauvoir wrote: "In truth women have never set up female values in opposition to male values; it is man who, desirous of maintaining masculine prerogatives, has invented that divergence."[21] Horkheimer and Adorno's *Dialectic of Enlightenment* established a basis for the post-1945 German-language critique of the inherently "masculine" construction of human subjectivity, but it was de Beauvoir's *The Second Sex* that provided a conceptual framework for women's bid to subjectivity on equal terms with men in the post-1945 phase of the European and North American feminist movements. De Beauvoir's understanding of the relative cultural positions of the sexes is remarkably close to the one put forward in the *Dialectic*. For de Beauvoir, as for Horkheimer and Adorno, the age of belief in the essential natures of the two sexes belongs to the past. Gender difference is, as it was for them, a product of culture, and the terms in which gender has come to be understood are the product of a culture dominated by men. The category of the human being has historically become occupied by the male sex ("man represents both the positive and the neutral, as is indicated by the common use of *man* to designate human beings in general," writes de Beauvoir [15]), and this has permitted man to define women in relation to himself: "[Woman] is defined and differentiated with reference to man and not he with reference to her; she is the incidental, the inessential as opposed to the essential. He is the Subject, he is the Absolute — she is the Other" (16).

How, though, did this domination of one sex by the other come about historically? The key factor, in de Beauvoir's account, is woman's reproductive function. It was this that from the outset tied her to her biology and enforced her dependence on the males of her social group for protection and food during pregnancy, childbirth, and menstruation (94). As human culture developed, this *natural* function entrapped women in what de Beauvoir calls "immanence":[22]

> The woman who gave birth, therefore, did not know the pride of creation; she felt herself the plaything of obscure forces [. . .]. But in any case giving birth and suckling are not *activities*, they are natural functions; no project is involved; and that is why woman found in them no reason for a lofty affirmation of her existence — she submitted passively to her biological fate. The domestic labours that fell to her lot because they were reconcilable with the cares of maternity imprisoned her in repetition and immanence; they were repeated from day to day in an identical form, which was perpetuated almost without change from century to century; they produced nothing new. (94–95)

This is contrasted with the male's ability to transcend his animal existence through cultural activity:

> Man's case was radically different; he furnished support for the group, not in the manner of worker bees by a simple vital process, through biological behaviour, but by means of acts that transcended his animal nature. *Homo faber* has from the beginning of time been an inventor: the stick and the club with which he armed himself to knock down fruits and to slaughter animals became forthwith instruments for enlarging his grasp upon the world. He did not limit himself to bringing home the fish he caught in the sea: first he had to conquer the watery realm by means of the dugout canoe fashioned from a tree-trunk; to get at the riches of the world he annexed the world itself. In this activity he put his power to the test; he set up goals and opened up roads towards them; in brief, he found self-realization as an existent. To maintain, he created; he burst out of the present, he opened the future. (95)

Since the transcendence of animal nature comes to define what it is to be human, it is therefore man who represents all that is properly understood as humanity: "It is male activity that in creating values has made of existence itself a value; this activity has prevailed over the confused sources of life; it has subdued Nature and Woman" (97). In this account, we can discern the central features of the ideological construction of the difference between the sexes characteristic of Enlightenment modernity.

Where de Beauvoir differs from Horkheimer and Adorno is in her consideration of the perspective of women on this cultural history of gender differentiation. She proceeds from the assumption that women have been complicit in the maintenance of male domination, and that in general terms women affirm the goals of the culture that has been shaped by men: "In setting himself up as sovereign, [man] is supported by the complicity of woman herself. For she, too, is an existent, she feels the urge to surpass, and her project is not mere repetition but transcendence toward a different future — in her heart of hearts she finds confirmation of the masculine pretensions" (96). In claiming their right to be regarded as human beings on equivalent terms to those that apply to men, women are, then, asserting their desire for transcendence: "What [women] demand today is to be recognized as existents by the same right as men and not to subordinate existence to life, the human being to its animality" (97). They are seeking, in other words, to become more like men.

At first sight, this may seem a logical contradiction. For if woman has been so thoroughly circumscribed by the definitions that man, in his sovereignty, has imposed upon her, how is it that women have, by de Beauvoir's day, attained sufficient autonomy to demand recognition as "existents"? The answer lies in the emancipatory trajectory of Enlightenment modernity.

Up until now in the discussion, the emphasis has been on the coercive character of Enlightenment, its imposition of constraints upon individuals disciplined to rational self-mastery and the renunciation of instinctual longings. But Enlightenment originated in a socially revolutionary and essentially libertarian movement. At its heart is the concept of the rational individual, the *thinking* individual, who lays claim to the inalienable right of each and every human being to develop to the limit of his natural capacity, a vision that in turn sets the basis for the progress of the entire of humanity toward future perfection. The eighteenth-century Enlightenment's declaration of human rights justified the rebellion against the established hierarchies of social power and the principle of absolutist monarchy, and began the historical drive toward government by parliamentary representation of the people. Moreover, since the philosophy of the Enlightenment defined human subjectivity in terms of autonomy of *mind,* there was, as many Enlightenment thinkers acknowledged, no conceptual reason for excluding women from the notion of autonomous individuality.[23] It is certainly no historical coincidence that two of the major foundational texts for the later women's emancipation movement, Olympe de Gouges's *Declaration of the Rights of Woman and Citizen* (1789)[24] and Mary Wollstonecraft's *Vindication of the Rights of Woman* (1792), were written during the overtly revolutionary phase of the Enlightenment, prior to the remythologization of woman-as-nature that would underpin the ideology of separate spheres.

However, from very early on, Enlightenment thought displayed a fear of the uncontrollable and potentially disintegrative social force of its own intellectual revolution. In *A Sociology of Modernity,* Peter Wagner notes the move, following the French Revolution's descent into the Terror, to re-impose limits on the potentially "boundary-less" nature of the Enlightenment's central categories of humanity and autonomy. This was achieved by the exclusion from universal subjecthood of those considered lacking in reason and civilization, "most importantly the *lower, working classes,* the *women* and the *mad.*"[25] The subsequent history of Enlightenment modernity has been an almost continual contest to renegotiate the boundaries that separated the self-defined subjects of modernity and their posited Others — not just the working classes, women, and the mad, but also those excluded from the status of subject or compromised in it by their race or ethnicity or by their religion: the enslaved and the colonized, the nomadic, and a whole range of religious peoples of whom the Jews are only the most prominent in European historical memory. In the event, the emancipatory logic of the Enlightenment proved a more powerful impulse than the attempts to contain and limit the applicability of its original propositions. The ideologies generated to justify containment, however, both spawned a profound resentment of the ideologues among the eventually emancipated and also, importantly, delivered the terms in which this resentment is articulated.

This is evident in the history of women's emancipation. Women's claim to equal rights with men, conceptually justified in the Enlightenment's own terms, was effectively repulsed by means of the nineteenth century's ideology of separate spheres. As shown in chapter 1, the definitions of masculinity and femininity on which the division of labor between the public and the private spheres was founded were oriented toward the specific social and economic interests of the bourgeois class. They do not withstand scrutiny in the universal terms projected; the claims made concerning the differential "nature" of men and women can be seen, for example, to be not applicable to working-class men and women at the same period. However, in upholding a *universal* distinction between two sexes whose "nature" predisposes them to contrasting social functions, and in determining on this basis that all human cultural achievements are solely the achievement of the publicly active sex, the ideology of separate spheres delivers both the terms by which women were able to construct themselves as a distinctive sex with its own collective emancipatory agenda and the grounds on which members of this sex could, once emancipated, distance themselves qua sex from the history of that earlier cultural achievement. To return to de Beauvoir: despite the fact that she acknowledges women's historical "complicity" in the male pursuit of transcendent cultural aims, such aims remain for her distinctively marked as belonging to the realm of male activity alone from which women, entrapped qua sex in "immanence," have historically been excluded. In this sense, her arguments are still dependent to a discernible degree on the ideology of separate spheres. At the same time, the claim or belief that human culture has hitherto been the creation of the male sex alone establishes the conceptual ground for an emancipated female sex to set itself apart from that history of cultural achievement if it suits its political or theoretical purposes to do so. To cite an incisive thought-image from Virginia Woolf's *A Room of One's Own:* "If one is a woman one is often surprised by a sudden splitting off of consciousness, say in walking down Whitehall, when from being the natural inheritor of that civilization, she becomes, on the contrary, alien and critical."[26] This "alien and critical" stance was to prove an immensely powerful political and theoretical platform in the post-1945 history of feminism. Based on the assumption of the *exclusion* of women from cultural agency up until this period, a feminist vision could arise in which women's active contribution to the development of "humanity" would indeed act as a significant "corrective" (Adorno[27]) to the malaise seen to be affecting a culture structured around "masculine" characteristics — rather as Simmel had suggested at the beginning of the century. Moreover, the feminist position emerged all the more powerfully as a platform for cultural critique because a crucial new phase in the social and civil emancipation of women in Western societies coincided with a further decisive crisis of modernization, which came to a head in the latter part of the 1960s.

Peter Wagner identifies 1968 as a pivotal date in what he terms the "second crisis of modernity,"[28] following a first crisis dated at the turn of the nineteenth to the twentieth century.[29] The crisis of modernity at the fin de siècle was characterized, in this account, by the breakdown of those conceptual boundaries erected to limit the libertarian rights of the Enlightenment in the bourgeois era (a period Wagner terms "restricted liberal modernity"). The second is created by what Wagner diagnoses as an almost complete systemic closure in the organization of social practices in modern mass society (which he terms "organized modernity"). On this understanding, the period from the turn of the century reveals a consistent underlying trend that reaches its limit at around 1960:

> The achievements of organized modernity were to transform the disembedding and uncertainties of the late nineteenth century into a new coherence of practices and orientations. Nation, class and state were the main conceptual ingredients to this achievement, which provided the substance for the building of collective identities and the setting of boundaries. [. . .] Organized modernity was characterized by the integration of all individuals inside certain boundaries into comprehensively organized practices. [. . .] This configuration achieved a certain coherence, or closure, at about 1960, in terms of the various institutions, their specific embodiments of collective agency, their interlinkages, and their respective reaches. It appeared as a naturally "interlocking order." (118–19)

The student revolt and the emergence of the new women's movement in the late 1960s are, in Wagner's reading, phenomena related to a more general "de-conventionalization" (123) of social practices in the face of a cultural order that had become once again too restrictive, too coercive. As such, they heralded a period of renewed dynamism within the historical development of modern Western societies — and one that, for a time at least, was fired by an anticapitalist energy. This aspect was particularly prominent in Germany, where the generation of 1968 became forcefully associated in the national imagination with an anti-establishment political agenda as well as the revolt against the generation of the fathers who had been tainted by their involvement with National Socialism.[30] From the perspective of cultural as opposed to social historians, it is significant that this period saw the re-issue of key works from earlier in the post-1945 period that fed into the current of social protest, forming the basis of the conviction that what was in fact a relatively limited rebellion against established conventions of social organization was a wholesale revolt against the social order.[31] Thus Horkheimer and Adorno's *Dialectic of Enlightenment*, which, as Wiggershaus points out, had received little attention after its first publication (344), was re-issued in 1969; Marcuse's *Eros and Civilization*, first published in 1955, was re-issued in 1966, although it was his 1964 work, *One-Dimensional Man,* that more significantly influenced the theoretical positions of the student movement in both the English-speaking West and in Germany; de Beauvoir's *The Second Sex* attained its international status as the foundational text for the new women's movement at this time; and, indeed, Woolf's 1929 essay *A Room of One's Own* was also widely re-issued and read by a new generation of feminists. These works were joined by theoretical initiatives that would set the intellectual agenda for the coming decades. Most important among these was a wealth of writings coming out of France that were broadly critical of the established conventions of knowledge, social organization, and language. Particularly worthy of note among these in the context of the present discussion are Michel Foucault's influential analyses of historical practices of categorization and social demarcation, starting with *Folie et déraison* (Madness and Civilization, 1961), and of what he termed "discourse" as the social instrument by which identities, institutions, and systems of knowledge were organized;[32] Jacques Derrida's "deconstruction" of the philosophical foundations of Enlightenment modernity and its signifying practices, starting with *L'écriture et la différence* (Writing and Difference, 1967) and *De la grammatologie* (Of Grammatology, 1967); Jacques Lacan's linguistic reformulation of Freudian psychoanalysis, in fact dating back to the 1950s but coming into its own as a major theoretical force from the mid-1960s onwards with the publication of his *Écrits* (1966); Gilles Deleuze and Félix Guattari's *L'Anti-Oedipe* (Anti-Oedipus: Capitalism and Schizophrenia, 1972), a "political analysis of desire as it is expressed and repressed in Western Culture";[33] and the work of Roland Barthes, whose revolutionary approach to the study and interpretation of literature in "La mort de l'auteur" (The Death of the Author, 1968) and espousal of the analysis of popular cultural forms in *Mythologies* (Mythologies, 1957) was theoretically influential internationally, while his departure from the conventions of academic and analytical style injected energies generally associated with imaginative literature into the interpretation of cultural phenomena. It would be risky indeed to try to summarize what all these very diverse theoretical projects had in common, but certainly a prevalent concern among them was to subject to critical scrutiny established systems of thought, categorization, and organization, and in particular the role played by language and signification in producing and underpinning such systems, and to reflect in a highly self-aware manner on the mechanisms of exclusion and repression (the conceptual apparatus of psychoanalysis was key to all of them) that enabled the erection of apparently coherent and unified systems and entities. What it all added up to was a sustained critical assault on notions of coherence, unity, self-identity, rational mastery, intentional meaning, and will, and on the social institutions and regulations that uphold these, and at the same time a raising to critical awareness and reflection of the repressed "unconscious" ground of such cultural attainments, the underlying manifold of desire and of things, the flux and flow of corporeal and psychical energies that culture "organizes" in order to create the illusion of stability — in effect, in Horkheimer and Adorno's terms, a "remembrance of nature."

Given the correlation between "nature," the "repressed," and the "feminine" observed throughout the discussion so far, it is unsurprising that women theorists, often involved in emergent collective feminist projects during this period, seized upon the conceptual opportunities opened up by the general revolt against fixity to generate a new feminist *theoretical* politics. I emphasize *theoretical* since a distinction needs to be drawn between a feminist politics with pragmatic social goals — such as eliciting from the state an acknowledgement of women's rights to equal recognition as civil subjects, raising issues of women's control of their own bodies and fertility, their right to legal protection from domestic and other violence, and a host of questions to do with education, work, equal pay, tax status, and childcare provision — and a theoretical feminist politics targeted at conceptualizations of subjectivity, the body, and the relation of human culture to the natural world, and intent on questioning a metaphysical tradition generated out of an exclusively male worldview. Feminist work in these theoretical fields appeared in the form of interventions aimed not only at breaking the hold of male writers and thinkers on how human cultural activity and subjectivity is defined and evaluated, but also at taking possession of the symbolic meanings attached to the "feminine" in the interests of generating a form of cultural subjectivity marked as distinctively different from established, masculine-inflected concepts.

This is, at any rate, an apt way of describing the work of the feminist theorists who made the greatest impact internationally on the development of theoretical feminism in the 1970s and who serve here as exemplars of the feminist theoretical activity of the period, the French writers Hélène Cixous and Luce Irigaray.[34] The Bulgarian emigrée Julia Kristeva, a Lacanian psychoanalyst whose reformulation of Lacan's linguistic theory of subject formation also proved hugely influential, remained theoretically far more ambivalent about the possibility of conceptualizing a female subjectivity as such, and so is less immediately relevant in this context, though her work offers useful stimuli for thinking about matters of representation (as will become evident in chapter 3). Hélène Cixous became renowned above all in the context of the 1970s feminist movements for her espousal of *l'écriture féminine* (feminine writing). A teacher and scholar of literature rather than a psychoanalyst (though her readings of psychoanalysis were crucial to her work on and with texts), Cixous's interest was in the energy, playfulness, and semantic multiplicity of literary and poetic language, but also emphatically in the political potential of such language and textuality. Strongly influenced by Derrida's thought and writing, her texts are, like his, full of verbal play and double entendres, demonstrably and deliberately refuting the claims of theoretical language to unified and singular meaning and "system," and enacting instead an exuberant and ever-proliferating *différance;* radiating, moreover, a kinetic energy that, in the texts' "arguments," are drawn into the association with the body and its rhythms and desires, with nervous excitation, and with voice. In this sense, her textual gesture is reminiscent of the semiotic *chora* analyzed by Kristeva as "an essentially mobile and extremely provisional articulation constituted by movements and their ephemeral stases," a modality "analogous only to vocal or kinetic rhythm" understood as breaking into and disrupting the symbolic order of regulated syntax in poetic language.[35]

Cixous's understanding of gender oscillates between the symbolic and the apparently essentialist. In the essay "Sorties" from *La Jeune Née* (The Newly Born Woman, 1975), one of her two most renowned programmatic pieces alongside "Le Rire de la Méduse" (The Laugh of the Medusa, 1975), Cixous indicates that she does not wish the qualifiers "masculine" and "feminine" to be confused with the biological categories "man" and "woman."[36] As Verena Andermatt Conley explains, the terms are for Cixous socially produced and metaphorical: "The (political) economy of masculine and feminine is organized by different needs and constraints which, when they become socialized and metaphorized, produce signs, relations of power and production, a whole immense system of cultural inscriptions."[37] Moreover, underlying this system of socialized gender is, Cixous argues, a bisexuality inherent in every subject, "that is to say the location within oneself of the presence of both sexes, evident and insistent in different ways according to the individual" (C-C 85).

However, as Cixous realizes, to posit "masculinity" and "femininity" as a set of culturally inscribed characteristics or behaviors, accessible to persons of either sex, since all are in psychic terms bisexual, is to foreclose the *political* potential of the equation of the "feminine" and "woman." The point is that if the "feminine," implicitly validated as a stance that is "alien and critical" (Woolf 93) within this cultural-historical environment of critical-theoretical rebellion, can be *categorically* extended to "woman," it can become the focal point of an identity politics aimed at forcefully reconceptualizing and reorganizing social relations. This is what Cixous sets out to do, in a virtuoso textual performance that takes *the desiring female body* as its point of departure:

> If there is a self proper to woman, paradoxically it is her capacity to depropriate herself without self-interest: endless body, without "end," without principal "parts"; if she is a whole, it is a whole made up of parts that are wholes, not simple, partial objects but varied entirety, moving and boundless change, a cosmos where eros never stops traveling, vast astral space. She doesn't revolve around a sun that is more star than the stars.

That doesn't mean that she is undifferentiated magma; it means that she doesn't create a monarchy of her body or her desire. Let masculine sexuality gravitate around the penis, engendering this centralized body (political anatomy) under the party dictatorship. Woman does not perform on herself this regionalization that profits the couple head-sex, that only inscribes itself within frontiers. Her libido is cosmic, just as her unconscious is worldwide: her writing also can go on and on, without ever inscribing or distinguishing contours [. . .]. (C-C 87–88)

Moreover, since woman is posited as having a privileged access to the differences within herself, she also represents more effectively than man the subject's inherent bisexuality: "In a certain way *woman is bisexual* — man having been trained to aim for glorious phallic monosexuality" (C-C 85, italics in the original).

This is an interesting and paradoxical move. Although part of Cixous's project is to dismantle the binary oppositions that she identifies as underpinning the (by inference Western) philosophical tradition, there is a sense in which she also reinforces the binary oppositions man/woman and masculine/feminine. She does this by identifying woman with a positively encoded plurality and multiplicity that oppose the culturally destructive and deathly unity and self-sameness of the "masculine," now equated with man. At the same time, precisely because "woman" figures plurality and multiplicity, including the acknowledgement of the "masculine" *within itself*, it becomes the site at which the erasure of the binary is enacted. In this way, "man" becomes equated with the binary system underpinning Western metaphysics and "woman" with a multiplicity that has the potential to supersede the strictly oppositional system of Self versus Other — a figuration, perhaps, of a reconciliation with nature?

A similar valorization of woman takes place in the writing of Luce Irigaray. Her feminist project, too, demonstrates its debt to Derrida, in that it was launched in her *Speculum de l'autre femme* (Speculum of the Other Woman, 1974) with an energetic deconstructive critique of a sequence of pivotal authors and texts from the Western philosophical tradition, starting with an exposure of Freud's masculine bias in his theoretical accounts of femininity, and moving back through Hegel, Kant, and Descartes to Aristotle and Plato. Irigaray's approach to the assault on the male-generated philosophical tradition is, on the one hand, "to interrogate the *conditions under which systematicity itself is possible:* what the coherence of the discursive utterance conceals of the conditions under which it is produced." She conceives of this project above all in terms of the retrieval of the *material* conditions and contiguity of a discourse that lays claim to the status of universal truth. On the other hand, she embarks on a linguistically oriented psychoanalytical investigation of the "procedures of repression" operating within each philosophy, "the structuration of language that shores up its representations, separating the true from the false, the meaningful from the meaningless, and so forth."[38] The issue is, as she avows at one point, "not one of elaborating a new theory of which woman would be the *subject* or the *object*, but of jamming the theoretical machinery itself, of suspending its pretension to the production of a truth and of a meaning that are excessively univocal." Women should, she argues, not seek to define what woman is, "but rather, repeating/interpreting the way in which, within discourse, the feminine finds itself defined as lack, deficiency, or as imitation and negative image of the subject, they should signify that with respect to this logic a *disruptive excess* is possible on the feminine side" (Irigaray "Power" 78, italics in the original).

However, at the same time as pursuing this course of "mimicry," of "assum[ing] the feminine role deliberately" in order to "convert a form of subordination into an affirmation, and thus to begin to thwart it" (Irigaray "Power" 76), Irigaray is also to be found making what look like truth statements concerning "women" that create implicit contrasts with the traditions of male thought at which her deconstructive practice is aimed. In the title essay of her 1977 volume *Ce Sexe qui n'en est pas un* (This Sex Which Is Not One), she famously presents her characteristic conceptualization of the feminine as tactile, simultaneous, fluid in the *anatomical* figure of woman's "two lips in continuous contact." This becomes in turn the basis for a conceptualization of subjectivity that resists definition in established "masculine" terms: "Whence the mystery that woman represents in a culture claiming to count everything, to number everything by units, to inventory everything as individualities. *She is neither one nor two.* Rigorously speaking, she cannot be identified either as one person, or as two. She resists all adequate definition."[39] From here, she proceeds to develop the suggestive possibilities of such an intrinsically plural form of subjectivity, including hints at its wider sociocultural implications: "Her sexuality, always at least double, goes even further: it is *plural.* Is this the way culture is seeking to characterize itself now?" (Irigaray "Sex" 28). Like Cixous, then, Irigaray seeks to generate alternative ways of thinking about subjectivity, social order, and signification from the "ground" of the term "woman." "Woman" becomes a figure, as it were, for *différance* itself.

My point in pursuing a discussion of Cixous and Irigaray here has been to demonstrate, with reference to two of the foremost theorists to emerge from 1970s new-wave feminism, how women writers of the period moved to occupy and to transform inherited significations of the "feminine," in their case derived in particular from psychoanalytical models of subject formation: as multiplicity and simultaneity, as fluidity and flow, as desire, as corporeality and materiality, and so on. They did so at a period of more general intellectual revolt against the philosophical tradition of the West and its systems of social regulation and discipline. By conflating the "feminine" with "woman," they projected a form of gender-specific subjectivity capable of overturning the cultural assumptions characteristic of millenia of male-dominated and male-generated culture. Their work encouraged a vibrant sense of women at last entering history on their own terms.

To what extent were the terms their own, however? The theoretical trajectory of Cixous's and Irigaray's work, and that of the scholars, critics, and artists who followed their lead, undoubtedly had the merit of mobilizing those aspects of human culture and the human psyche repressed in the course of a philosophical and cultural tradition that has persistently privileged mind over matter, and unity, coherence, and certain forms of rationality over multiplicity, simultaneity, and affect. Yet the conflation of "woman" with the unconscious of this tradition[40] potentially entrapped women and their writing within a set of significations that has consistently defined the "feminine" within Western modernity and that can be traced back to the Western tradition's classical origins. This is one reason why the critical response among feminist scholars to Cixous and Irigaray so frequently turned on those moments in their writing that betrayed an apparent essentialism. Their defenders reflected on the political benefits of the "risk" of essentialism and argued that what seemed essentialist, for example in Irigaray's arguments, was in actuality strategic and combative. Elizabeth Grosz states, for example:

> Contrary to the objection that she is describing an essential, natural or innate femininity, unearthing it from under its patriarchal burial, Irigaray's project can be interpreted as a contestation of patriarchal representations *at the level of cultural representation itself.* The two lips is a manoeuvre to develop a *different* image or model of female sexuality, one which may inscribe female bodies according to interests outside or beyond phallocentrism, while at the same time contesting the representational terrain that phallocentrism has hitherto annexed.[41]

To their detractors, however, the risk was that "woman" was back where she had always been, figuring the Eternal Feminine. Toril Moi, reading Irigaray, objects: "The mimicry fails because it is no longer merely a mockery of the absurdities of the male, but a perfect reproduction of the logic of the Same."[42] Moreover, detractors argued, this theorization of "woman" (in the archetypal singular, notably also used by de Beauvoir) effaced differences between women (in the plural), thus positing a white Western bourgeois intellectual understanding of "woman" as a universal in a way that was remarkably similar to the positing of white Western bourgeois male subjectivity as the universal norm in the Enlightenment tradition. This was an issue that came increasingly to the fore of the women's movement as the inflections of race, ethnicity, class, sexual orientation, and varying culturally determined "identities" were brought into the debate. Moreover, the work of Cixous and Irigaray was held by its materialist feminist critics to be ultimately so focused on the sphere of *representation* that it failed to deliver any kind of model for women's agency in the social and political spheres.

More crucial from the point of view of the project of this book is to draw attention to the relation between them and the work of male writers and thinkers from their direct cultural environment. Cixous acknowledged the proximity of her theoretical project to Derrida's, though she claimed to be able to distinguish between his "masculine" and her own "feminine" slant on the projects of deconstruction. However, on the whole, feminist thinkers and writers of this period tended to erase the degree to which their work was methodologically and stylistically dependent on, or at least enabled by, the work of contemporary male writers and thinkers also intent on questioning and subverting established conventions of thought. Just as crucial to the *political* dimension of the feminist theoretical project as the annexing of the dynamic multiplicity, the flux and flow of the "feminine" for the attempted construction of a social identity of "woman" was its erasure of the extent to which the Enlightenment male-subject-as-norm in all his unity, coherence, and rational self-identity was under intense scrutiny at this period, and as a result not nearly as unremittingly phallic or gloriously monosexual as the feminist theoreticians would have had us believe. This in turn raises questions about the cultural reach of the feminist theoretical project. To what extent were the feminine-inflected forms of subjectivity projected by Cixous's and Irigaray's writings (and, by extension, those that appear in the literary texts to be examined in the following chapters of this book) no more than an occupation of the meanings of "femininity" that, in Adorno's terms, masculine society had imperiously bred as "its own corrective," and that thus were already conceptually provided for, as the "negative imprint of domination," within the systems of thought critiqued? Do they, as the skeptics thought, fail to break out of the definitions of the "feminine" in which women had been confined for almost the entire modern period? Or, alternatively, should the feminist theoretical activity of the 1970s be seen as what Irigaray herself termed "an initial phase" (Irigaray "Power" 76), in which the significations of the feminine were to be mimetically occupied in order that women could begin to generate, not the form of subjectivity in the public sphere that bore the recognizable stamp of the "masculine," but a distinctively *different* (*différant*) form of subjectivity able to challenge it, so that, again in Irigaray's words, "the masculine would no longer be 'everything'" (Irigaray "Power" 80)? In essence, this is also a question about women's historical *agency* — one of the central problems to emerge from the representations of the female would-be-subject in the fictions to be considered in this book.

Two Figures

The sketch of the theoretical activity on the part of both male and female thinkers of the post-1945 period undertaken above sets the frame for the textual readings that will follow in part II of this book. The discussion has, in the first place, drawn attention to the degree to which the critique of modernity pursued by the theorists of the Frankfurt School builds on figurations of gender that already from the turn of the nineteenth to the twentieth century had led to the equation of the conceptualization of human subjectivity characteristic of Enlightenment modernity with "masculinity." Under this system, "woman" and the "feminine" came to figure those aspects of the human psyche and of human cultural memory, and, indeed, the environment in which human culture is lived out ("nature"), which had been projected away from the culturally constructed "identical, purpose-directed, *masculine* character of human beings" (H-A 26). What Peter Wagner calls the "first crisis of modernity" at the turn of the nineteenth to the twentieth century coincided with a variety of cultural phenomena that scholars have scrutinized as evidence of a "crisis of masculinity." As Felski, Le Rider, and Izenberg show, this "crisis of masculinity" was symptomatically linked to a crisis of social and economic modernization, and made symbolically possible precisely because of the conflation of "masculinity" with the conceptualization of what it means to be a human subject and historical agent. The "second crisis of modernity" has not hitherto been examined in these terms. Yet when we turn to the readings of the texts written by male authors of the post-1945 period, we will find them full of the signs of a collapse in masculine identities. The causes of this collapse are various. In part, it is sparked by the movement of the female figures into the sphere of independence from the male, reflecting a decisive shift in social relations between the sexes in the postwar period: this will be investigated in relation to Max Frisch's *Mein Name sei Gantenbein* (chapter 4). A further factor is historical guilt: the association of the male figures with the destructive implications of Enlightenment modernity's fetishization of instrumental rationality, as in Frisch's *Homo faber* (chapter 5), or with the violence conducted in the name of ideologically driven societal reform, as in Heiner Müller's contemplation of the history of socialism in *Die Hamletmaschine* (chapter 7). Finally, masculine identity crisis arises from the refusal of the inherited model of human subjectivity and the social regulation and discipline implied in it. This refusal is characteristic of the postmodern phase of Western Enlightenment, and will be explored in the reading of Rainald Goetz's *Irre* (chapter 6). Horkheimer and Adorno's *gendering* of their critique of modernity and the modern construction of the self in the *Dialectic of Enlightenment* transpires, then, to offer the key to the first of the symbolic figures to pervade the fictions examined: the male subject in crisis.

As we have seen, both at the fin de siècle and again in the post-1945 period, the questioning of the "masculine" attributes of the modern subject — self-identity, rationality, purposiveness, and so on — occasioned a turn in theoretical writing as well as in literature and in art toward the "ideal feminine" or to abstract figurations of woman in her avowed capacity "to represent, amid an evil society, another possibility" (Horkheimer[43]). Since woman's culturally inscribed alignment with nature arises above all from her childbearing function, this makes the mother a privileged figure when it comes to envisaging a potential reconciliation with nature or dialectical regression "behind the attained level of civilized rationality" (Marcuse 143). But also as the object of men's sexual desire, woman offers to the male imagination both the promise of liberation from the constraints of the public role and the dream of the potential reconciliation with nature, while at the same time, as a creature kept apparently pure by her historical exclusion from the public sphere, she may embody humane values and moral wisdom untainted by the concerns of life in a competitive, commercial society. The meanings of "woman" are, in other words, highly unstable and varying, and if in her person she challenges masculine narcissism too gravely, she may in an instant be transformed back from an idealized object into a derided, inadequate figure, the unscientific housewife, the bad driver, the perennial actress, devoid of all true identity, who serves as the foil for the restitution of the male subject's imagined unity, coherence, and rationality, as we shall see when we come to the reading of Frisch's *Gantenbein* novel (chapter 4). Nevertheless, the texts by male writers examined in this book are fascinated by the figure of woman, and the central male character persistently seeks from his female counterpart the solutions to his own crisis of identity. The sole exception considered in this study is Goetz's *Irre*. Here, the homosexuality of the central male subject in crisis is hinted at, and he seeks a solution in a breaching of boundaries that nevertheless permits a continuing masculine self-identification (chapter 6).

The turn of the male subject in crisis toward figurations of woman — as lost partner, as moral guide, as one less contaminated than he by the guilt of historical agency, or as the victim of the history enacted by himself — opens up a signifying space into which the women writers move, seeking to occupy the meanings attached to woman and the feminine for the purposes of their own authorial projects. This turns out to be a complex and ambivalent undertaking, however. From the works of the women writers it emerges with some clarity that they are struggling against the weight of a cultural tradition in which agency and authorship are conceived in masculine terms. To stake a claim to authorship is, then, to seek to occupy a cultural position of which one is conscious that it is conventionally the preserve of men; it is, possibly, to take on characteristics traditionally thought of as "masculine" or strategically to erect a masculine persona; in the extreme case, it is to masquerade as master. At the same time, the project of female authorship, in particular in the period of second-wave feminism, is staked on the *difference* set into cultural motion by the sex of the author. The author's status as a woman offers a productive critical platform, that "alien and critical" stance that sets her apart from a cultural tradition generated by men in the interests of men. "Femininity" can thus also serve as the covering term for a range of alternative values and concepts, not least of which is that of a form of subjectivity not constituted by the strict demarcation of Self from Other nor by the severance of itself from its origins in nature, for this is how "woman" appears culturally — admittedly in the perspective of a tradition that has projected woman as the Other to man. And that is the problem. To what extent *can* such an occupation of the significations of the feminine by women writers provide the basis for a revolution in the conceptualization of subjectivity, since the terms are delivered by the very tradition that is supposedly to be overcome? This, as the discussions that follow will show, is a problem that all of the works by female writers ultimately come up against.

The complexity of the position of the female author within the dialectic of Enlightenment is reflected in the presence in all the fictions by women examined in this book, and in some of those by men, of variations upon the second of this study's pervasive symbolic figures, what I am going to call the "double-gendered" or, more simply, the "doubled" female figure. This is a figure who, while self-evidently a woman in terms of her sex and social self-understanding, nevertheless perceives herself or is perceived by others as combining characteristics of both genders, or alternatively, containing within her own subjectivity personae specifically identified as masculine — whether the introjected form of a beloved male person or an extrojected "identity" created in order to concretize the masculine-connoted aspects of the self. Frequently, this coexistence within the self of different selves gives rise to tensions, problems, self-misunderstandings. Undoubtedly, in probing the meanings of this "double-gendering," women writers are working toward an understanding of their own position as female subjects entering a cultural tradition that long denied the conceptual possibility of the "female subject."

"[In] a certain way *woman is bisexual*," Cixous claimed, meaning that woman, less wedded to a form of subjectivity that "annihilates differences" within itself, is more open to the bisexuality conceived as underlying all human sexual identity (C-C 85). Certainly, it does emerge as a striking contrast between the texts by men and the texts by women considered in this study that the female writers seem as a matter of course to have a sense of interrogating the presence of the "masculine" within themselves, whereas for the male writers, the "feminine" is always Other, always external to the male subject, always a reflecting surface in which the male subject's self-restitution is sought. I do not wish to use Cixous's term "bisexual" to denote the double-gendered female figure in these fictions, however, since it bears too distinctive a connotation of sexual orientation, which distracts from the figurative sense of the coexistence precisely of different *genders* within the self. Nor do I want to use the term "androgyne," which implies a harmonious coexistence of differently gendered aspects and attributes in a being that may transcend sexed identity altogether. It is the disharmonious, apparently self-contradictory nature of the term "double-gendered female" that in actuality most accurately conveys the disharmonious and self-contradictory, or at any rate *problematic* qualities that are represented and puzzled over in the figures so designated.

In an essay on the problems of the representability of the position of "woman" within the dialectic of Enlightenment, Sigrid Weigel reflects on the conceptual complexities attending the entry of women as subjects into a history in which what woman is has been so largely defined and determined in the interests and from the perspective of men:

> The position of the *female subject* is not only far more complicated than that of the male one, it also introduces a *doubly reversed* perspective into the dialectic: namely, the perception and speech of the second sex which wishes to occupy the position of the first, but which cannot simply shake off its provenance from the dark reverse side — and which is anyway not altogether certain how desirable that position, so long denied it, really is. The complexity of this constellation seems constantly to elude conceptual articulation.[44]

This finding is reminiscent of Simone de Beauvoir's analysis, made some fifty years earlier, in the closing pages of *The Second Sex:* "woman is opaque in her very being; she stands before man not as a subject but as an object paradoxically endued with subjectivity; she takes herself simultaneously as *self* and as *other,* a contradiction that entails baffling consequences" (727). Weigel's answer to the difficulties of conceptualizing the female subject is to look to the possibilities of literary representation. Her model for an adequately complex, manifold, and polyvalent representation of the position of women and the function of the feminine within the dialectic of Enlightenment is the Austrian writer Ingeborg Bachmann's 1971 novel *Malina.* It is with this work that the sequence of textual readings in part II begins.

Notes

[1] Max Horkheimer and Theodor W. Adorno, *Dialectic of Enlightenment: Philosophical Fragments,* ed. Gunzelin Schmid Noerr, trans. Edmund Jephcott (Stanford: Stanford UP, 2002), 26, italics added. Subsequent references appear the text as parenthetical page numbers, identified as H-A.

2 The fragmentary form is evidence for the need they felt to produce the book quickly. It was first published in 1944 in a mimeographed edition by the Institute of Social Research in New York and in book form, with the addition of the last of the theses on anti-Semitism, by Querido in Amsterdam in 1947.

3 The German original speaks of "der Starke" at the end of this passage, "the strong man," rather than "the strong" as an ungendered plural: "Das reizt den Starken, der die Stärke mit der angespannten Distanzierung zur Natur bezahlt und ewig sich die Angst verbieten muß, zu blinder Wut. Er identifiziert sich mit Natur, indem er den Schrei, den er selbst nicht ausstoßen darf, in seinen Opfern tausendfach erzeugt." — Horkheimer and Adorno, *Dialektik der Aufklärung* (Frankfurt am Main: Fischer Taschenbuch Verlag, 1988), 120.

4 Patricia Jagentowicz Mills, *Woman, Nature, and Psyche* (New Haven and London: Yale UP, 1987). Subsequent references appear in the text as parenthetical page numbers.

5 See Rolf Wiggershaus's commentary on the *Dialectic* in Wiggershaus, *The Frankfurt School: Its History, Theories and Political Significance*, trans. Michael Robertson (Cambridge: Polity Press, 1984), 326–44.

6 Joel Whitebrook discusses this problem, which he sees as solvable only through a coherent theory of sublimation, in "The *Urgeschichte* of Subjectivity Reconsidered," *New German Critique* 81 (Fall 2000), 125–41.

7 Max Horkheimer, "Authoritarianism and the Family Today" [1949] in *The Family: Its Function and Destiny,* ed. Ruth Anshen (New York: Harper & Brothers, 1949), 367. Compare the passage on the role of maternal and sisterly love within the family as a counterweight to the dehumanizing impulses of contemporary society in Horkheimer, "Authority and the Family" [1936], in *Critical Theory: Selected Essays,* trans. Matthew J. O'Connell et al. (New York: Continuum, 1992), 47–128, here 114–18. In this passage, woman is, on the authority of Hegel, symbolically associated with the "principle of love for the whole" (117) as opposed to the tendency within the patriarchal, authoritarian social order to reduce the individual to an object (118). See Mills's discussion in *Woman, Nature and Psyche*, 100–113.

8 Erich Fromm, Max Horkheimer, Herbert Marcuse et al., *Studien über Autorität und Familie* (English abstracts; Paris: Felix Alcan, 1936), 906, cited from Mills, 102.

9 Horkheimer, "Authoritarianism and the Family Today," 366.

10 Max Horkheimer, "The Concept of Man" [1957], in Horkheimer, *Critique of Instrumental Reason,* trans. Matthew O'Connell et al. (New York: Seabury Press, 1974), 1–33, here 16. See also Mills, *Woman, Nature, and Psyche,* 109–10.

11 Horkheimer, "Authoritarianism and the Family Today," 367 (see note 7 above).

12 Herbert Marcuse, *Eros and Civilization: A Philosophical Inquiry into Freud* (London: Abacus, 1972), 23. Subsequent references appear in the text as parenthetical page numbers, identified when necessary as Marcuse.

13 "Beyond the Reality Principle" is the title of part II of *Eros and Civilization.*

14 Marcuse, *Eros and Civilization,* 162. See Mills, *Woman, Nature, and Psyche,* 155–61 for an account of Marcuse's theorization of maternal Eros.

[15] Herbert Marcuse, *Counterrevolution and Revolt* (London: Allen Lane The Penguin Press, 1972), 75.

[16] Mills, *Woman, Nature, and Psyche,* 161–62. The quotations are from Marcuse, *Counterrevolution and Revolt,* 74, 77. The Performance Principle is a term coined by Marcuse to refer to a heightened form of the repressive reality principle characteristic of the advanced capitalist mode of production, "a Reality principle based on the efficiency and prowess in the fulfilment of competitive economic and acquisitive functions." — Herbert Marcuse, "Marxism and Feminism," *Women's Studies* 2 (1974): 279.

[17] Horkheimer, "The Concept of Man," 16 (for details see note 10 above).

[18] Gerald N. Izenberg, *Modernism and Masculinity: Mann, Wedekind, Kandinsky through World War I* (Chicago and London: U of Chicago P, 2000), 7.

[19] This is a point made by Silvia Bovenschen in a landmark essay for 1970s feminism in Germany, "Über die Frage: gibt es eine 'weibliche' Ästhetik?," first published in *Ästhetik und Kommunikation* 7.25 (September 1976): 60–76, in which she takes issue with Marcuse's essay "Marxism and Feminism" of 1974. I discuss her refutation of Marcuse's vision of the liberating potential of the "feminine" in chapter 6.

[20] Theodor W. Adorno, *Minima Moralia: Reflections from a Damaged Life,* trans. E. F. N. Jephcott (London: New Left Books, 1974), 95–96, translation modified. Compare Theodor W. Adorno, *Minima Moralia: Reflexionen aus dem beschädigten Leben* (Berlin and Frankfurt am Main: Suhrkamp, 2001), 168, 170.

[21] Simone de Beauvoir, *The Second Sex,* trans. H. M. Parshley (Harmondsworth: Penguin, 1983), 96. Subsequent references appear in the text as parenthetical page numbers.

[22] The term belongs to her Existentialist vocabulary: "immanence," signifying confinement in animal nature or restriction to the fulfilment of repetitive tasks that are not culturally innovative, contrasts with "transcendence," which signifies cultural achievement over and above animal existence in which the individuality of the "existent" — de Beauvoir's habitual term for the subject — is affirmed. See also translator's footnote, de Beauvoir, *The Second Sex,* 94.

[23] See Thomas Laqueur, *Making Sex: Body and Gender from the Greeks to Freud* (Cambridge, MA and London: Harvard UP, 1990), 156: "Political theorists beginning with Hobbes had argued that there is no basis in nature, in divine law, or in a transcendent cosmic order for any specific sort of authority — of king over subject, of slaveholder over slave, or, it followed, of man over woman" and subsequent discussion.

[24] De Gouges wrote her tract in direct response to the *Declaration of the Rights of Man and of the Citizen* approved by the revolutionary National Assembly of France in 1789, asserting (among other things) that "the only limits on the exercise of the natural rights of woman are perpetual male tyranny" (Article IV); see Darline Gay Levy, Harriet Branson Applewhite, and Mary Durham Johnson, eds., *Women in Revolutionary Paris, 1789–1795* (Urbana: U of Illinois P, 1980), 87–96.

[25] Peter Wagner, *A Sociology of Modernity: Liberty and Discipline* (London and New York: Routledge, 1994), 39, italics in the original. Subsequent references appear in the text as parenthetical page numbers.

[26] Virginia Woolf, *A Room of One's Own* (London: Granada, 1977), 93.

[27] Adorno, *Minima Moralia*, 95 (see note 20 above).

[28] Wagner, *A Sociology of Modernity*, 18, and part IV "The second crisis of modernity," 121–71. On the significance of 1968, see 141.

[29] Wagner, *A Sociology of Modernity*, 16, and chapter 4 "Crisis and transformation of modernity," 55–69.

[30] See Rob Burns and Wilfried van der Will, *Protest and Democracy in West Germany: Extra-parliamentary Opposition and the Democratic Agenda* (Basingstoke: Macmillan, 1988), and Nick Thomas, *Protest Movements in 1960s West Germany: A Social History of Dissent and Democracy* (Oxford: Berg, 2003).

[31] Wagner is interesting in his analysis of the differences between the actual results of the 1968 students' revolt and what the "contestants" (as well as the political elites who opposed them) thought they were looking to achieve — see Wagner, 141–45.

[32] See *Naissance de la clinique* (The Birth of the Clinic: An Archaeology of Medical Perception, 1963), *Les mots et les choses* (The Order of Things, 1966), *L'archéologie du savoir* (The Archaeology of Knowledge, 1969), *Surveiller et punir* (Discipline and Punish, 1975), and the three-volume *Histoire de la sexualité* (History of Sexuality, 1976–1984).

[33] Back cover blurb, Gilles Deleuze and Félix Guattari, *Anti-Oedipus: Capitalism and Schizophrenia*, trans. Robert Hurley, Mark Seem, and Helen R. Lane, preface by Michel Foucault (London, New York: Continuum, 2003).

[34] A special double edition of the literary journal *alternative* following the "Treffen schreibender Frauen" (Meeting of Women Writers) in Munich in May 1976 marked the first appearance in German translation of essays by the French feminists who would become so influential in the development of feminist theories internationally; see *alternative* 108/109 (1976): *Das Lächeln der Medusa.*

[35] See Julia Kristeva, *Revolution in Poetic Language* [1974], trans. Margaret Waller (New York: Columbia UP, 1984), 25, 26.

[36] Hélène Cixous and Catherine Clément, *The Newly Born Woman*, trans. Betsy Wing, intro. Sandra M. Gilbert. Theory and History of Literature, volume 24 (Manchester: Manchester UP, 1986), 81. Subsequent references appear in the text as parenthetical page numbers, identified as C-C.

[37] Verena Andermatt Conley, *Hélène Cixous: Writing the Feminine* (Lincoln and London: U of Nebraska P, expanded edition 1991), 57. See Cixous and Clément, 80–81, 83.

[38] Luce Irigaray, "The Power of Discourse and the Subordination of the Feminine," in *This Sex Which Is Not One*, trans. Catherine Porter with Carolyn Burke (Ithaca, NY: Cornell UP, 1985), 74–75. "The Power of Discourse" is an interview first published in the journal *Dialectiques* in 1975, following the 1974 publication of her first major work, *Speculum de l'autre femme* (Speculum of the Other

Woman). Subsequent references appear in the text as parenthetical page numbers, identified as Irigaray "Power."

[39] Irigaray, "This Sex Which Is Not One," in *This Sex Which Is Not One*, 26, italics in the original. Subsequent references appear in the text as parenthetical page numbers, identified as Irigaray "Sex."

[40] "Thus we might wonder whether certain properties attributed to the unconscious may not, in part, be ascribed to the female sex, which is censured by the logic of consciousness. Whether the feminine *has* an unconscious or whether it *is* the unconscious." — Irigaray, "The Power of Discourse," 73.

[41] Elizabeth Grosz, *Sexual Subversions: Three French Feminists* (St. Leonards: Allen & Unwin, 1989), 116, italics in the original. See also Diana J. Fuss, "'Essentially Speaking': Luce Irigaray's Language of Essence," in *Revaluing French Feminisms: Critical Essays on Difference, Agency and Culture*, ed. Nancy Fraser and Sandra Lee Bartky (Bloomington: Indiana UP, 1992), 94–112; and "The Risk of Essence," in Fuss, *Essentially Speaking: Feminism, Nature and Difference* (London: Routledge, 1990), 1–21.

[42] Toril Moi, *Sexual/Textual Politics: Feminist Literary Theory* (London and New York: Routledge, 1988), 142. See also Monique Plaza's coruscating critique, reproduced in Moi, 146.

[43] Horkheimer, "The Concept of Man," 16 (see note 10 above).

[44] Sigrid Weigel, "Towards a Female Dialectic of Enlightenment: Julia Kristeva and Walter Benjamin," in Weigel, *Body- and Image-Space: Re-reading Walter Benjamin*, trans. Georgina Paul with Rachel McNicholl and Jeremy Gaines (London: Routledge, 1996), 68, italics in the original.

Part II: Readings in Post-1945 German Literature

3: Challenging Masculine Subjectivity: Ingeborg Bachmann's *Malina*

SINCE ITS PUBLICATION IN 1971, the Austrian writer Ingeborg Bach-mann's *Malina* has come to be regarded as a classic, perhaps even *the* classic representation of the problematics of gender identity and gender relations in post-Holocaust German-language literature. This formally highly innovative novel (if it can be called a novel at all)[1] presents the story of a female character *Ich*,[2] who inhabits the continuous present of *heute* (today). *Ich*'s existence is played out in the tension between two male characters, her lover, Ivan, and the enigmatic Malina with whom she shares her apartment. Appearing at first to be *Ich*'s husband or partner, Malina emerges as the narrative progresses with ever-greater clarity as her male double or complement. The text is structured in three chapters, preceded by a scene-setting prologue. The first chapter, "Glücklich mit Ivan" (Happy with Ivan), focuses on the relationship between *Ich* and Ivan, and also gradually constructs a profile of *Ich*, a renowned writer living in Vienna, in her daily life of letter-writing and magazine interviews and creative composition. The third, "Von letzten Dingen" (Of Last Things), chronicles the changing relationship of the female-male pair *Ich* and Malina as the love affair with Ivan fades and *Ich* is gradually eliminated as a character position. In between, and anticipating the trajectory of the third chapter, there is a chapter of nightmares, "Der dritte Mann" (The Third Man), revealing *Ich* in a symbiotic relationship of violation and victimhood with a figure identified in her dreams as her "father" and at the end of the chapter as her "murderer." These dream sequences are punctuated by dialogues, reminiscent of those between analyst and analysand in psychoanalysis, in which Malina probes *Ich* for the meaning of what she dreams. At the novel's close, *Ich* disappears into a crack in the wall of the apartment. It is this famous scene of eradication, together with the resonant last sentence "Es war Mord" ("It was murder"), that have become paradigmatic moments within German feminist literary-critical discussions of the history of the feminine in the Western cultural tradition.

Publication and Reception: A Brief History

When *Malina* was published, ten years had passed since the appearance of Bachmann's previous work of fiction, the short prose collection *Das dreißigste Jahr* (The Thirtieth Year, 1961). She had spent the intervening decade at work on a complex sequence of narrative elaborations that she gradually came to conceptualize as a cycle of novels under the collective title *Todesarten* (Modes of Death/Death Styles/Ways of Dying). *Malina,* as the latest novel upon which she embarked, but the first to appear (and, in the event, the only one to be completed before her death in 1973), was, as she stated in interviews at the time of publication, to be the "overture"[3] to the *Todesarten* cycle. Moreover, Malina, as the sole remaining figure on the novel's mental stage at its close, was intended to become the narrator of the subsequent works.[4]

The year 1971 was, of course, prior to the emergence, from the mid-1970s onwards, of the feminist literature of the new women's movement and well ahead of the establishment of a corpus of feminist cultural-theoretical writing that was later to provide so important an interpretative frame. *Malina*'s unprecedented narrative form posed a considerable challenge to its first critics, and initial responses tended to privilege the reading of the novel as a pathological case study or a kind of hysterical autobiography, starting the trend (which has proved persistent) of collapsing the distinction between the fictional character *Ich* and the person of the author herself.[5] The publication of the first major edition of Bachmann's works in 1978,[6] in which *Malina* appeared grouped with substantial fragments from two other *Todesarten* narratives from the 1960s, entitled here *Der Fall Franza* (The Franza Case)[7] and *Requiem für Fanny Goldmann* (Requiem for Fanny Goldmann), plus drafts featuring the character Malina, allowed a sense to emerge of the place of the first novel in relation to the themes of the conceptual cycle. Moreover, with the arrival on the German feminist theoretical scene, from 1976 onwards, of the first translations of French feminist poststructuralist theory,[8] a new phase of reading *Malina* and the *Todesarten* fragments was initiated, with a 1984 volume of the journal *Text + Kritik* under the guest editorship of Sigrid Weigel marking a pivotal moment in the history of Bachmann interpretation. In this new light, *Malina* was seen as a remarkable anticipatory work: as a condemnation of "phallogocentric" patriarchy, with the father of the dream chapter now seen as the *père symbolique* of Lacanian theory, and as an acute account of the violent erasure of the "feminine" in the symbolic order of the Western tradition.[9] Though this seam of criticism has since been exhausted, the publication, in a controversial edition, of the extant manuscripts of the whole *Todesarten* project in 1995[10] gave new impetus to the perennial critical fascination with Bachmann and her work. Most recently, Bachmann criticism has become dominated by two contrasting strands: one largely biographically motivated, generated by scholars editing material from the late author's estate in the archive in Vienna;[11] the other theoretically motivated, pursuing links between Bachmann and the Jewish thinkers of the Frankfurt School and with literary friends and colleagues such as Paul Celan for valuable illumination of Bachmann's political position post-Holocaust.[12]

My interest here is to return to the issue of gender in *Malina,* and to some extent in the other *Todesarten* fragments, but in a changed context. The renowned status of the novel as a representation of a gender dialectic makes it an obvious entry point into the study of how gender functions as a symbolic category in German-language literary texts of the post-1945 period. In this context, the interrogation of what it is that gender is being made to *mean* and how the tension between notions of the masculine and the feminine are organized in relation to each other within the text opens up new perspectives on the issue of the erasure of "the feminine" within a male-dominated culture as well as on the novel's representation of masculine-connoted subjectivity.

Form in the *Todesarten* Cycle: The Gendering of Narration

In an interview given in the context of the publicity activity surrounding *Malina*'s publication, Bachmann hinted at the long prehistory of the novel and explicitly addressed the issue of gender and narration. It is among the most frequently quoted passages from Bachmann's published interviews:

> Für mich ist das eine der ältesten, wenn auch fast verschütteten Erinnerungen: daß ich immer gewußt habe, ich muß dieses Buch schreiben — schon sehr früh, noch während ich Gedichte geschrieben habe. Daß ich immerzu nach dieser Hauptperson gesucht habe. Daß ich wußte: sie wird männlich sein. *Daß ich nur von einer männlichen Position aus erzählen kann.* Aber ich habe mich oft gefragt: warum eigentlich? Ich habe es nicht verstanden, auch in den Erzählungen nicht, warum ich so oft das männliche Ich nehmen mußte. Es war nun für mich wie das Finden meiner Person, nämlich dieses weibliche Ich nicht zu verleugnen und trotzdem das Gewicht auf das männliche Ich zu legen.[13]

> [For me it is one of the oldest, albeit almost submerged memories: that I always knew I must write this book — already very early on, at the time when I was still writing poetry. That I was always searching for this central character. That I knew: he will be male. *That I can only narrate from a male point of view.* But I've often asked myself: Why exactly? I didn't understand, not in the short prose either, why I so often had to adopt the male "I." So it was for me like the discovery of my own person, not to deny the female "I" and yet still to give the emphasis to the male "I."]

Before the publication of the *Todesarten* manuscripts this statement tended to be read as referring to the dominance of male narrators and narrative perspectives in *The Thirtieth Year*. Since 1995, however, the edition of the *Todesarten* drafts has made as legible as it probably ever will be Bachmann's struggle throughout the 1960s to find an adequate form for her narrative intentions and the emergence of a gender logic within her thematic framework.

The editors trace the origins of her search for her protagonist back to the period 1954–57, to a sequence of fragments featuring a male figure, Eugen, which they group together under the heading "Eugen-Roman I" (Eugen Novel, I). In 1962–63, following the completion of *The Thirtieth Year*, Eugen reappears as the central figure of the first drafts of a novel with the title *Todesarten*, subtitled by the editors "Eugen-Roman II" (Eugen Novel, II). Through this figure, identifiable as a precursor of Malina,[14] Bachmann addresses what will become a central motif of the *Todesarten* project: the split between the "normal" surface appearance of the restored Viennese society of the postwar years and a subterranean domain of anxiety and (historical) trauma concealed beneath the public façade as reflected within the individual consciousness. This split passes through the psyche of the character Eugen, who on the one hand moves normally through his social world, but on the other privately suffers symptoms of a profound anxiety, already in this early draft associated with the fear of being "murdered."[15] The scenes of Eugen's anxiety attacks, now reallocated to the male double Malina, will be recalled by *Ich* in a dialogue scene between them in the 1971 novel, the only point in the book where Malina loses his characteristic analytical cool-headedness.[16] Interestingly, the "Eugen" drafts are narrated by a female first-person narrator; and it seems to be this to which the later figure Malina refers when he tells *Ich:* "Ich bin oft im Dunkeln geblieben. Du standst ja damals im Licht" ("I often stayed in the dark. You were in the light back then"; *M* 289/191).

In Bachmann's second phase of work on the *Todesarten* novel in 1964, the theme of surface (public) normality versus concealed (private) trauma has switched to the sphere of literature, with the plot of a female figure called Fanny who is "murdered" — in her case, destroyed psychologically — in that her private life is used as material for a book, and so sold into the public domain, by her younger lover, Toni Marek.[17] These drafts constitute the earliest form of the Fanny Goldmann plot, one of the two central narratives of the *Todesarten* project as it evolves in the course of the 1960s. Initially the drafts are cast as perspectival third-person narrative, adopting Fanny's point of view, a form that is retained in the work phase of spring and summer 1966.[18] However, in the later phase of work on this plot, from 1966–67 through to 1970 (parallel to the writing of the *Malina* novel), the still predominantly third-person narration adopts the perspective of Malina,[19] in this context a writer figure who has the overview of all the stories and subplots recounted. Malina takes shape here as the projected "master narrator" of the *Todesarten* cycle.

The second major narrative strand emerged following a journey by Bachmann to Egypt in the spring of 1964. This is the plot of Franziska Ranner-Jordan who is "zugrunde gerichtet" (destroyed) by her husband, the renowned psychiatrist Leo Jordan. He observes her as a case study akin to his psychiatric case studies of the female survivors of Nazi medical experiments — hence the title *The Franza Case* — eventually inducing a nervous breakdown. Having fled from a psychiatric clinic back to her childhood home at the beginning of the novel, Franza embarks on a journey through the deserts of Egypt with her brother Martin. It becomes a metaphorical "Reise durch eine Krankheit" ("journey through an illness").[20] The earliest drafts of a text concerned with the Egyptian journey, conceived of by Bachmann in the first instance as a project separate from the novel *Todesarten* and provisionally entitled "Wüstenbuch" (Desert Book),[21] are cast as first-person narrative. To read these intense reflections arising out of a journey both actual and mental through the desert and the encounters with the traces of ancient Egyptian culture is to read a text that seems very close to the diary form — the narrating "I" reads as a directly authorial persona. However, as the "Desert Book" is transformed into a novel centered on the fictional character of Franza in the course of 1965, the narration reverts to the third person, adopting the perspective of Franza's brother Martin as the one who must attempt to "read" his traumatized sister. As a result, some of the scenes in Egypt originally cast in the first person reappear in the conceptual third chapter of the *Franza* novel, "Die ägyptische Finsternis" (The Egyptian Darkness), in the third-person form, with Franza narrated from outside rather than from within her consciousness.[22]

To summarize the findings of this brief review: the earliest *Todesarten* character, Eugen, bears the split within himself between public "normal appearances" on the one hand and private anxiety and trauma on the other, and is narrated by a female first-person narrator. She, in pointing out that her male heroes "weinen wie unsereins" (weep as the likes of us do),[23] moreover implies the "femininity" of displaying trauma. This is, significantly, in keeping with the findings of scholars who have investigated the literary representation by male writers of trauma in men in the post-1945 period, since "for men, the 'meaning' of traumatization [. . .] may only be reconstituted as a form of femininity, precisely because it does not fit within culturally accepted models of masculinity [. . .]. Trauma remains split off from the self in the form of femininity."[24] As the *Todesarten* project develops, however, the experiences of victimization, of "being murdered," and thus of sickness, madness, and trauma, come to be expressed through female characters (Fanny Goldmann, Franziska Ranner, and later a third female character, Eka Kottwitz/Aga Rottwitz, whose story adds a second strand to the Fanny Goldmann plot). The narrative perspective, meanwhile, moves progressively from the first person or that of the female central character as revealed through third-person perspectival narration, to the impersonal third person, and finally to a male figure (Malina, Martin). Both of these male focalizers have the function of retaining analytical rationality and objectivity as the prerequisites for an organized narrative account — it is a significant aspect of their characterization that both are trained scientists. But each of them also has a sister who is "murdered": Malina's is an actress named Maria Malina, whose death provides a foundational motif in the later stages of the development of the Fanny Goldmann plot.[25] Given the importance within the *Franza* plot of the allusion, via Robert Musil, to the ancient Egyptian brother-sister deity Isis and Osiris,[26] a lost cultural alternative to the Father God of the Christian West, the death of the sister can be seen as signifying the male figure's damaging loss of the "feminine" principle that balances and complements his own "masculine" principle.[27] In this sense, Malina's and Martin's narratives, for all that they retain their surface objectivity and scientific detachment,[28] are also works of mourning for the lost "feminine" *within themselves.* This in turn means that both Malina and Martin can be understood as male doubles, behind whose controlled and publicly acceptable façade the long-since-disappeared female "I" of the early drafts is still resonating.

It is, as Weigel points out, a matter for speculation why Bachmann abruptly broke off work on the *Franza* book — at that stage the furthest progressed of the *Todesarten* novels — in late 1966.[29] But the observations so far of the evolution of the detached, objective "masculine" narrative perspective in both of the central *Todesarten* plots, compared with the very different, indeed entirely revolutionary narrative form Bachmann generated *after* this caesura, forcibly suggest that it was a perception of the loss of the intensity and immediacy of the first-person experience, as manifest in the "Desert Book," for example, that made her once again reconceive the project and embark on the writing of *Malina.* The "insight" of which Bachmann wrote in the letter to her publisher explaining why she was breaking off work on the *Franza* book[30] may thus be understandable as some form of realization that, in the words of Hannah Arendt, the "reification and materialization, without which no thought can become a tangible thing, is always paid for, and that the price is life itself: it is always the 'dead letter' in which the 'living spirit' must survive."[31] This meant that the cycle needed to begin with an overture that revealed the originary "murder": that of the intensity of lived experience — and here particularly the heightened intensity of the "feminine" experience of trauma — in the dead, objectifying word of the (male-) narrated text.[32] Thus *Malina* is conceived as an intrinsically paradoxical enterprise: that of representing excitation and anxiety within the present moment *prior to* its representation and reification in retrospective narrative form. The aim is to raise to a level of conscious awareness the *absence* of living immediacy in the more conventionally narrated novels that would make up the remainder of the cycle, and to arrive at a point from which, as it were, the echo of what has been eliminated will resonate through the entire subsequent narrative.

The *Todesarten:* Levels of Exegesis

Before considering how Bachmann addressed the paradoxical challenge of representing in *Malina* the excitation and immediacy that precedes coherent narrative representation, it is useful to consider a little further the way in which gender is functioning within the texts of the *Todesarten* cycle, and how it is to be read symbolically. The hypothesis is that the categories of "masculine" and "feminine," "male" and "female," as applied to perspective and character respectively, stand at the head of, and thus function as a kind of shorthand for, a complex sequence of further oppositional pairings that may be seen to correspond to different levels of textual exegesis. At the level of the representation of individual subjectivity or the individual psyche, rational and objective (scientific) contemplation of states of affairs and the reconstruction of the history that has preceded and produced these states of affairs (i.e., narration) come to be gendered masculine (Martin Ranner, Malina). So, in a separate category, does violence and the pursuit of public power (Toni Marek, Leo Jordan, eventually the "father" of the dream chapter in *Malina*). Anxiety and trauma, and later, in *Ich,* also the intensity of being in love, the ingredients of excitation in the present, meanwhile come to be gendered feminine, as does victimization at the hands of the power-hungry and the consequent will to self-destruction (Fanny Goldmann, Franziska Ranner, *Ich*). Taken in connection with the theme of trauma and its concealment, the metaphors of darkness and light (as in Malina's "I often stayed in the dark. You were in the light back then"), or elsewhere of depth and surface appearance,[33] create a link between the conceptualization of the individual psyche and the social sphere. What is deemed publicly acceptable appearance on the one hand and what the individual must strive to keep out of the public spotlight on the other is subject to social regulation. In this respect, it is significant that the characters of the *Todesarten* cycle, even if they do not start out as such, evolve into figures who are in the public eye: Fanny Goldmann is a famous actress, Aga Rottwitz a well-known journalist, Franza the wife of an eminent scientist, *Ich,* like her author, a writer whose prominence is publicly acknowledged.[34] What their plots in part address is the conflict between their traumatized internal states on the one hand and the need to conform outwardly to the rules of socially acceptable behavior on the other, proceeding from the assumption that to display trauma, or indeed their own victimization, is *not* socially acceptable. Here the "masculine" becomes the equivalent of the public façade, while the "feminine" is what is concealed in the darkness of the private emotions. If the "feminine" aspects are able to find a form of expression at all, it tends to be in the form of mute bodily symptoms or pathological behaviors (Fanny Goldmann's alcoholism, Aga Rottwitz's suicide attempt, and so on) — symptoms that in a psychoanalytical reading indicate the return of the repressed.

This conceptualization of the social sphere links to a second level of exegesis: a historically specific critique of postwar society in which the violence and destruction so recently displayed in the public arena of fascist society has, as it were, gone underground, withdrawing into the private sphere of relationships where it is no longer immediately publicly visible.[35] On this level, the private relationship between man and woman, whether husband and wife or lovers, becomes the domain of the perpetration of violence now suppressed from the public sphere, but that the text associatively connects to the structures of fascism. Thus the reputation of the psychiatrist Leo Jordan is based on his work on the "Spätschäden" (delayed harmful effects) observable in the female victims of medical experimentation in the Nazi concentration camps, while the dream chapter in *Malina* brings into play a series of images readable as abbreviations of the Holocaust (the gas chamber, the electrified barbed-wire fence, the SS uniform) that are associated with the figure of the father/murderer. On this level of exegesis, then, the male characters figure as the perpetrators, while the female characters are the victims — although it is worth noting that in *Malina* the male figure of the "dark stranger," who is also the archetypal lover in *Ich*'s dreams, is identified as Jewish[36] and associated with images drawn from the poetry of Paul Celan,[37] so that the allocation of the roles in the drama of violator and violated does not take place within a strict gender binary. Rather, the feminine and the Jew are brought into association with one another, an established metonymical link in German-language culture, as shown in chapters 1 and 2.[38]

The critique of the ascendancy of the "masculine" principle of violence that characterized the fascist public sphere and is found to be operating still in the private domain of postwar society is historically specific in its coordinates. However, the terms according to which the gender positions are elaborated — public-private, surface-depth, light-dark, rationality-trauma, and so on — and very particularly the motif of the double in its various figurations (Martin-Franza=Osiris-Isis, Malina-*Ich*), point toward a cultural history of far longer duration and thus to a third level of exegesis. Since the motif of the double enables a reading of the male-female couple as a complementary pairing, the ascendancy of the male figure, not only as violator, but also as the only possible narrator of the story, at the expense of the "murdered" sister or female double, reenacts a cultural-historical trajectory through which a particular model of human subjectivity, defined by characteristics that this same cultural history calls "masculine," has come to be generated at the expense of, and thus victimizing, the so-called "feminine" characteristics. While the "masculine" characteristics have come to define the public and social norms of subjectivity and historical agency, the "feminine" characteristics of the subject have been repressed into the private sphere or allocated to women in the course of the cultural construction of femininity. The violence of the archetypal male subject toward the female figures is thus legible as a symptom of the repressive force through which the rational, analytical, self-contained and -controlled male self has been culturally produced. This cultural-historical narrative contained within the *Todesarten* project corresponds closely to, and was indubitably influenced by, the account of the generation of human subjectivity and historical agency within the Western tradition set out by Max Horkheimer and Theodor W. Adorno in the *Dialectic of Enlightenment*. While on the one hand appearing to address universal issues, the *Dialectic* is, like Bachmann's project, suffused with an urgent need to lay bare the structures within the Western tradition that have led inexorably to fascism, the ultimate ascendancy of the "masculine."[39]

At each of these levels of exegesis — personal/psychological, social, cultural-historical — Bachmann's project of bringing into the light that which has been private, concealed, and in darkness, and ultimately of revealing the shadow side of the dialectic of Enlightenment[40] is to be understood as a profound political and philosophical challenge to the cultural status quo, as a call for the reconceptualization of the subject and for the restoration of the violated "feminine" in the interests of the health of the individual psyche, the body social, and the culture as a whole. And with *Malina*, the last of the *Todesarten* plots to be embarked upon, but the conceptual forerunner of the entire cycle, Bachmann extends the critique of the norms of Western culture contained within the earlier narratives to the norms of representational language and thus of narrative itself.

Ich: "The voice of excitation in the Today"

In a sense, Bachmann's puzzlement at her difficulty in narrating from anything other than a male point of view is understandable in terms of the legacy of the established models of intellectual and literary discourse she inherited as a writer. In her 1959 Frankfurt Poetics Lectures, in the context of a sequence of reflections on "Das schreibende Ich" (The Writing I), Bachmann considers the process of reading (understood as the prerequisite of writing) as one of finding in the literary works of the past the "I" that is both another person's "I" and yet magically able to speak for and to one's own experience. She describes this in terms of the *Besetzung* or occupation of one's own "I" by other "I"s: "und dann kamen andere

Bücher und andere Gedichte, also andere Ich, und die taten es auch, besetzten immer wieder unser eigenes Ich" (and then came other books and other poems, and so other "I"s, and they did it too, occupied again and again our own "I").[41] Twice in *Malina* there are scenes that display the works that make up *Ich*'s personal library, readable as the archive of "I"s that occupy her or have gone into the formation of her. It is striking that these works embody a tradition of male, not female, authorship.[42]

How is the woman writer to create for herself a voice that can be apprehended as distinctively gendered in the face of the male-authored tradition that precedes her, how achieve the mark of *difference* in her writing that denotes the cultural difference of her sex? This was a problem that preoccupied the feminist theorists who came into the public eye through the new women's movement in the 1970s. Access to language and signifying systems was seen as regulated according to the structures of patriarchal power, which denied woman the status of subject. Sigrid Weigel wrote:

> That the stories in the volume "The Thirtieth Year" are for the most part written from the male perspective is an expression of the fact that woman, as Lacan says, is excluded from the symbolic order or, as Irigaray and Cixous formulate it from the woman's perspective, that she has no place in the dominant cultural order.[43]

Since, in the Lacanian system, woman cannot be conceptualized as a subject in her own right, as a woman, theoretically she has no access to symbolic speech. As Elizabeth Grosz notes, summarizing Lacan's position: "when she speaks as an 'I' it is never clear that she speaks (of or as) herself. She speaks in a mode of masquerade, in imitation of the masculine, phallic subject."[44] Luce Irigaray, however, Lacan's disobedient student, seized on a breach in his system in order to generate an alternative speaking position. If psychoanalysis situates "woman" on the side of the unconscious, then she can stage her entry into history as a return of what has been repressed in the construction of masculine subjectivity and of a cultural history invested with male interests. The result is a dramatized counter-subjectivity, marked by its provenance in the unconscious, which returns as a disruptive force in the disordered and fragmentary articulations of hysteria and madness.

It is precisely in this guise that the "feminine" appears in the second of Bachmann's *Todesarten* narratives of the 1960s, the story of Franziska Ranner. Franza, the escaped inmate of a psychiatric clinic, is a "case" produced by her violation at the hands of her scientist husband. When she narrates in her own voice, as she does for quite large sections of the conceptual second chapter of the novel, "Die Jordanische Zeit" (Jordanian Time), in which she works through the experiences of her marriage to Leo Jordan, it is in the excitable, hysterical form that will later reappear, albeit somewhat modified, in *Ich*'s self-narration in *Malina*. But Franza's inner turmoil makes her incapable of producing a coherent account of herself; her fragmentary discourse demonstrates the limits of her ability to communicate. This is what necessitates the presence of her brother as the one who, detached to a degree and always still rational, can frame and so contain the chaos of her articulations. In other words, if Franza's story is to be told, then she needs to be narrated by someone else. Meanwhile, both she and Martin are contained by third-person narrative in the conventional retrospective preterite, the equivalent on the formal level of the objectifying analysis represented as a characteristic of the male figure Martin. It is this impersonal, authorial narrator who, in accordance with the conventions of realist narration, also establishes at the outset the coordinates of time and space that serve to fix and frame the activity of the novelistic imagination.

If the challenge of the "overture" to the cycle, as conceived by Bachmann from late 1966, was to find a form through which paradoxically to represent the excitation in the present that *precedes* retrospective narrative organization (as it were, the psyche in its state of incoherence and multiplicity, prior to its disciplining by social regulation and time), then a formal solution had to be found to the concomitant problem of framing the chaotic and alogical articulations of the traumatized "feminine" in the absence of the analytical male narrator figure and the retrospective narrative preterite. The solution that Bachmann arrived at is the list of dramatis personae with which *Malina* opens, a convention drawn from the genre of drama rather than of narrative prose fiction. With this stroke of genius, Bachmann contrived a maximally abbreviated substitution for the conventional novelistic opening. The first page and a half creates, by naming them, the character positions for the fiction that will follow, and also establishes the coordinates of the fictional time and space: "Zeit Heute / Ort Wien" ("Time: Today / Place: Vienna"; *M* 12/2). Just as importantly, the use of a convention from drama allows the conceptualization of *Ich* as a speaking voice, as opposed to a written position. This is underpinned by the references to musical notation in the novel, that is, to a conventional notation that provides a "script" for the realization of sound: the quotation of bars of music (from Arnold Schönberg's *Pierrot Lunaire*: *M* 15, 319/4, 212), and the markings ("diminuendo," "presto, agitato," and so on) given to *Ich*'s voice, but not Malina's, in their dialogues in chapter 3. The use of different forms of dialogue in the novel — the telephone conversations between *Ich* and Ivan, the script of the magazine interview with Herr Mühlbauer, and the "interior dialogues" between *Ich* and Malina — further points to Bachmann's interest in emphasizing voice as opposed to written narrative.

Crucial to the characterization of *Ich* are the modulations of her "speech," as conveyed from the outset by the extraordinary syntax of the prologue. In the list of dramatis personae, *Ich* is described according to the conventions of the passport ("Augen br., Haare bl., geboren in Klagenfurt" / "Eyes — br., Hair — blnd.; born in Klagenfurt"; *M* 12/1), a strictly legal circumscription of a person that tells us nothing of her character. As soon as the voice begins to speak, however, the reader is swept into the flow of the long, rhythmically ruptured sentences, the tangible, sensational movement of a nervous mind:

> denn durch dieses Heute kann ich nur in höchster Angst und fliegender Eile kommen und davon schreiben, oder nur sagen, in dieser höchsten Angst, was sich zuträgt, denn vernichten müßte man es sofort, was über dieses Heute geschrieben wird, wie man die wirklichen Briefe zerreißt, zerknüllt, nicht beendet, nicht abschickt, weil sie von heute sind und weil sie in keinem Heute mehr ankommen werden. (*M* 12)

> [for it is only in the greatest anxiety and flying haste that I can get through this Today and write about it, or just say, in this greatest anxiety, what is happening, since everything written about today should be destroyed immediately, just as it is with the letters that really matter, which one tears up, screws into a ball, doesn't finish, doesn't send, because they are of today and because they won't arrive today any more. (*M* 2, translation modified)][45]

Quite apart from the prologue's alogical leaps on the semantic level, characteristic of a mind in a state of high tension, and the thematic focus on the Now that knows no past or future, it is the *rhythm* that conveys intensity, excitation, the immediacy of presence, "the voice of excitation in the Today," as Weigel calls *Ich*.[46] This is not the conventional narrative prose of the novel, but a poetic, even corporeal rhythm, readable in terms of Julia Kristeva's reformulation of Lacanian theory in her *Revolution in Poetic Language:* as the return of what she calls the semiotic *chora*, a pre-symbolic modality that "precedes and underlies figuration and thus specularization, and is analogous only to vocal or kinetic rhythm"[47] and that she (in keeping with Lacan's psychoanalytical narrative that asserts the link between the symbolic and the father) connects to the maternal body.[48]

Whereas Franza's articulations in the earlier phase of the *Todesarten* are strictly speaking to be understood as *hysterical,* the obsessive renarration of the moments in her marriage to Jordan in which her distress originated, *Ich*'s are a purer expression of *trauma,* since they circle around a central "memory" that she cannot recall, a "verschwiegene Erinnerung" ("silent reminiscence" or, better, suppressed memory; *M* 23/9) by which her other recollections are disturbed.[49] This suggests an originary moment to *Ich*'s anxiety that is blocked from conscious memory, and that the dreams of the second chapter approach through repetition in distorted form, that is: in the language of the unconscious. Kristeva's distinction between the hysteric and the "subject in process" are helpful in this context:

> The instinctual *chora*, in its very displacement, transgresses representation, memory, the sign. In contrast to the hysteric, the subject in process/on trial [*subjet en procès*] does not suffer from reminiscences, but rather from obstacles that tend to transform the facilitation, the "affective charge," and the "excitation" into reminiscences. Unlike hysteria, where the subject visualizes past experience and represents those "memories . . . in vivid visual pictures," this process breaks up the totality of the envisioned object and invests it with fragments (colors, lines, forms). Such fragments are themselves linked to sounds, words, and significations, which the process rearranges in a new combination.[50]

Moreover:

> This combinatory moment, which accompanies the destructive process and makes it a *practice*, is always produced with reference to a moment of stasis, a boundary, a symbolic barrier. Without this temporary resistance, which is viewed as if it were insurmountable, the process would never become a practice and would founder instead in an opaque and unconscious organicity.[51]

The function of (in Kristeva's terms) the boundary or symbolic barrier is fulfilled in Bachmann's novel by Malina, the stable figure who ultimately ensures that a form of narration emerges from *Ich*'s fragmentary speech: "mich selber vor allem muß und kann ich nur vor ihm klären" ("above all I must and can explain myself, but only to him"; *M* 23/9).

Ich's excitation, the central characteristic of her "speech," is explicable with reference to the obstacle to her reminiscing, the implied source of her traumatized state that she cannot recall directly, but only circumscribe, and that remains an enigma at the heart of the novel. To this, however, Bachmann adds a further element, new within the genesis of the *Todesarten* cycle. It is, in cultural-historical terms, the ultimate in "feminine" experience: the intensity, even madness, of being in love, an experience that Horkheimer and Adorno, in the *Dialectic*, identify as signaling the loss of self-mastery and so as a form of punishable offense under the terms of Enlightenment rationality.[52] *Ich*'s passion for, her obsessive focus on Ivan, is connected in twofold manner to her characterization as traumatized. On the one hand, she invests an inordinate hope in the potential of the relationship to redeem her from the evils of the past: "Aber weil Ivan mich zu heilen anfängt, kann es nicht mehr ganz schlimm sein auf Erden" ("But since Ivan is beginning to cure me, things can't be all that bad on earth"; *M* 33/15). On the other hand, Ivan's indifference, his

inability to love her in return — "Das wirst du wohl schon verstanden
haben. Ich liebe niemand. Die Kinder selbstverständlich ja, aber sonst niemand" ("I'm sure you've already understood. I don't love anyone. Except
my children, of course, but no one else"; *M* 58/33) — point toward the
fact that *Ich*'s love for him is the expression of a repetition compulsion:
she, as a person, but also as the personification of the intensity of passion,
is destined to be destroyed by his indifference to her, just as she has been
destroyed already by the "murderer" for whom the father figure in her
dreams stands.[53]

Among the many different forms employed by Bachmann to articulate the *Ich*, one form in particular stands out in the text as *not* spoken,
namely the letters that *Ich* writes at night, but never sends, and that bear
the signature "Eine Unbekannte" (An unknown woman). The inclusion
of these "Letters from an Unknown Woman" (surely also an allusion to
Stefan Zweig's 1922 novel of the same name) draw attention to the nature
of the unsent and unsendable letter as a form of writing that can have no
life in the sphere of the publicly acceptable, i.e., is not understandable
as a letter in any conventional sense. These nighttime letters are juxta-
posed within the novel with the bland official letters written by *Ich*'s sec-
retary, Fräulein Jellinek, who represents an acceptable and conventional
"feminine" role and who acts as a filter between the actual thoughts of
Ich and what may be conveyed into the public sphere. The juxtaposition
highlights the exceptional nature of the nighttime letters: as notations of
private thoughts, written in moods of intensity and irrationality, which
may be eradicated, once expressed (*Ich* tears up some of these letters after
writing them). This reference within the text to a form of writing that has
no public validity (together with the Mühlbauer interview, a comical pastiche of the conventional magazine interview that simultaneously draws
attention to the status of *Ich*'s answers as unprintable) provides a frame
of interpretation for the entire text of the novel: a written text, of course
and after all, but a text that is the notation of the voice of excitation
rather than the voice of conventional and permissible day-to-day speech
as figured in the contrastive, clichéd and helplessly broken sentences of
the telephone conversations between *Ich* and Ivan. The signature "An
unknown woman" conveys the habitual exclusion of this form of writing
from the cognizability of the public domain.

Preconditions for the Appearance
of the "Feminine": Configurations

The aspects of voice and musicality within *Ich*'s characteristic syntax, and
the suggestion of trauma underlying her articulations, give body to those
aspects identified earlier as "feminine." However, the precondition for the
appearance of the feminine remains the contrastive structure that defines

the feminine in relation to the masculine that it is not. It is a common-place of feminist theorizing since de Beauvoir that the "feminine" is the artificial creation of a system of binary oppositions in which that which is defined as "masculine" can only be secured in the contrast with a cultur-ally devalued "feminine." Yet it is also the case that the meanings allocated to woman or "the feminine" in the process of feminist theoretical activity have been similarly reliant on an oppositional contrast with often-mono-lithic notions of what constitutes masculinity. The terms "masculine" and "feminine," "male" and "female" remain irretrievably caught in a struc-ture of relationality.

In embarking on a project to bring the concealed "feminine," in the entire range of the possible meanings of the term, into appearance in the public domain, Bachmann is therefore bound to work with a contrastive structure. The enabling device that allows the appearance of the feminine *Ich* in principle is the invention of the figure of Malina, in whom Bach-mann, as it were, siphons off the conventionally "masculine" characteristics within the psyche — rationality, objectivity, analysis, and thus self-contain-ment — leaving the *Ich* as the counter-field of the "feminine" — excitation, emotion, and thus self-dissipation: "Auch das Gesetz der Erhaltung der Energie ist nicht anwendbar auf mich. Ich bin die erste vollkommene Ver-geudung, ekstatisch und unfähig, einen vernünftigen Gebrauch von der Welt zu machen," as *Ich* says of herself ("Nor does the law of the energy conservation apply to me. I am the first perfect extravagance, ecstatic and incapable of putting the world to any reasonable use"; *M* 251/165). It is important, however (and strangely difficult, as much of the secondary literature on *Malina* reveals), to remember that *Ich* and Malina are a con-ceptual single entity. Their relationship enacts the dialectic between con-trasting and complementary principles within the individual psyche (and within society, and within our given cultural history).[54]

The dialectical drama between *Ich* and Malina, the conceptual feminine and the conceptual masculine within the psyche, can only be set in motion by a third position external to this psyche to which it responds. Bachmann posits this in the figure of Ivan, who is, then, the catalyst for the novel's "plot." Ivan's figuration as the Lover, or, in Weigel's phrase, as "[the Other], by whom the 'I' desires to be desired,"[55] enables the revelation of *Ich,* the feminine, in the obverse of the traditional love plot of the Western tradition in which the male writer/poet creates himself as cultural subject in relation to the (objectified) Beloved.[56] Moreover, the constellation *Ich*-Ivan, as the motivating framework for *Ich*'s self-revelations in the novel's first chapter, allows the "feminine" to appear in rare ascendancy — as open-ness to the other and as the principle of *relational* construction of subjectiv-ity: selfhood as simultaneous self-loss, the diametric opposite of Malina's self-containment. The concomitant vulnerability of this "feminine" posi-tion is progressively revealed as the novel unfolds.

In the chapter "Happy with Ivan," the love relationship is constructed in dual form: on the one hand as utopian desire in the legend that *Ich* composes for Ivan, the "Geheimnisse der Prinzessin von Kagran" (The Mysteries of the Princess of Kagran), and on the other as the real-existing relationship between the two. While the legend projects the relationship as one of mutual recognition across the vicissitudes of history and thus of a realized — or at least realizable — redemption, the actuality of their meetings is a destructive imbalance, for *Ich*'s exclusive orientation toward Ivan, her faith in their mutuality, runs up against the block of his indifference and inability to love, the principle of self-preservation that he shares with Malina. His self-containment is perhaps most evident in his counter-conceptualization of their relationship as a "Spiel" or "Game" (also figured in his chess-playing), in which each is allocated stereotypical gender roles:

> Man kann nur fesseln mit einem Vorbehalt, mit kleinen Rückzügen, mit Taktiken, mit dem, was Ivan das Spiel nennt. Er fordert mich auf, im Spiel zu bleiben, denn er weiß nicht, daß es für mich kein Spiel mehr gibt, daß das Spiel eben aus ist. [. . .] Er sagt auch: Ich muß doch dir nachlaufen, sorg dafür, du darfst mir nie nachlaufen, du brauchst dringend einen Nachhilfeunterricht, wer hat es denn versäumt, dir den Elementarunterricht zu geben? [. . .] Du bist zu durchsichtig, sagt Ivan, man sieht ja in jedem Moment, was los ist mit dir, spiel doch, spiel mir etwas vor! [. . .] Hast du denn das Gesetz nicht verstanden? (*M* 84–86)

> [One can only captivate by keeping something back, by strategically withdrawing, by using tactics, by playing what Ivan calls the Game. He challenges me to stay in the Game, because he doesn't realize that it no longer exists for me, that the Game is over. [. . .] He also says: I should be the one to run after you, you better not ever run after me, you're in bad need of some private tutoring, who was it that didn't teach you the basics? [. . .] You're too transparent says Ivan, I can see what's going on with you at every minute, you have to play the Game, so play something for me! [. . .] Don't you understand the rules? (*M* 50–52, translation modified)]

The role-play envisaged by Ivan represents a mechanical reproduction of a traditionally conceived male-female relationship, a defensive mechanism that allows (a form of) relationship without self-risk. It marks Ivan's inability or unwillingness to acknowledge *Ich* in her totality or to enter into the relationship as she desires it. For a time, *Ich* manages to sustain the relationship from the energy of her own desire. Once this desire has consumed itself, though, it is the other aspect of the psyche, the masculine Malina, who characteristically acts to re-establish the boundaries of the self, exhorting his feminine double: "Töte ihn! töte ihn!" ("Kill him! Kill him!"; *M* 305/202).

The third male position in relation to which the "feminine" is articulated in the novel is that of the father/murderer of the dream chapter. Unlike Malina and Ivan, who occupy with *Ich* the unmediated present of Today, the father of *Ich*'s dreams embodies a simultaneously historical *and* timeless dimension to the relationships figured elsewhere. It is the temporality of the unconscious. Malina's question, in the first of the analytical dialogues with which the chapter is punctuated, as to the identity of the "father" — "Aber sag mir endlich: Wer ist dein Vater?" ("But will you finally tell me who your father is?"; *M* 179/116) — is an early warning not to read this figure too narrowly or literally. Rather, the "father" is to be seen as a symbolic condensation of the principle of psychological/social/cultural-historical power: he is the One who directs, dictates, abuses, destroys.[57] That he is necessarily a male figure is in conformity with the cultural history of patriarchy, and what the dreams repeatedly enact is the devaluation, humiliation, objectification, and ultimately destruction of the female figures: of *Ich* as daughter, but also of the subordinated figures of the mother, sister, and, in a rather different way, of the woman who willingly acts in consort with male power, Melanie.[58] In this way, the dream chapter both shockingly reveals the origins of *Ich*'s "sickness"[59] and sets out the cultural-historical conditions of impossibility of *Ich*'s as a viable alternative subject position to Malina's.

The thirty-five dream scenes are punctuated by seven scenes of dialogue between the terrorized *Ich* and the detached, analytical Malina, plus two interludes depicting *Ich* awake in the night, which frame and therefore lend a certain weight to the "deportation" dream (*Ich* and the "dark stranger" as victims of the Holocaust). The analytical dialogues interact with the dream images produced by *Ich*'s unconscious, so that there is a progression in the sequence. Central to the analytical procedure initiated by Malina is the question of *Ich*'s complicity with the structures of violence embodied in the figure of the father:

ICH:	Ich habe die Spuren verwischt, falsch ausgesagt, das gehört sich doch, nicht wahr?
MALINA:	Warum hast du ihn gedeckt?
[. . .]	
MALINA:	Warum hast du es getan?
ICH:	Ich weiß nicht. Ich habe es getan. Damals war es richtig für mich, es zu tun. (*M* 207–8)

[ME:	I covered up all the tracks, I gave false testimony, that's what you're supposed to do, isn't it?
MALINA:	Why did you cover up for him?
[. . .]	
MALINA:	Why did you do that?

Me: I don't know. I just did. It was the right thing for me to
        do at the time. (*M* 135–36)][60]

Here the theme, central to the *Todesarten* cycle, of the need to uphold an
acceptable public façade is reprised.[61] Under the force of Malina's questioning as to why *Ich* allowed the abusive structures of power to prevail —
"Gewußt hast du es vielleicht nicht, aber du warst einverstanden"; "Wie
einverstanden aber muß man sein?" ("Maybe you didn't know, but you con-
sented to it"; "But how much consent is required?"; *M* 222–23/145–46,
translation modified) — *Ich* begins to liberate herself from the power that her
own sense of the bond between them lends to the father, culminating in two
successive dreams in which *Ich* attacks him. Repeating a gesture used by the
father against her earlier in the sequence, where he throws first glass (Dream
VI, 182/118–19), then flower pots full of earth (Dream XIX, 204/134) at
her, *Ich* here throws heavy ashtrays made of glass (Dream XXXIV, 231/152)
and of marble (Dream XXXV, 234/153) at him: "Jetzt weiß er, daß ich
kein Gefühl mehr habe für ihn, und daß ich ihn töten könnte" ("He now
knows that I no longer have any feelings for him and that I could kill him";
M 234/153). It is a particularly interesting moment for the consideration of
gender symbolism in the novel, as it is precisely at this point, where *Ich* takes
the power of violence into her own hands, that the gender of the father figure
becomes unstable. In both of the dreams in which *Ich* attacks him, the father
appears *also* as *Ich*'s mother. It is a reminder that what we are dealing with is a
symbolic gender scenario of power versus powerlessness, violence versus violation that is not necessarily attached to biological sex as such. It also proves to
be the turning point in *Ich*'s reading of the dream images:

> ich weiß nie genau, wann er mein Vater und wann er meine Mutter
> ist, dann verdichtet sich der Verdacht, und ich weiß, daß er keiner
> von beiden ist, sondern etwas Drittes. (*M* 233)

> [I don't know exactly when he is my father and when he is my
> mother, then the suspicion takes shape, and I know he's not either
> one, but a third thing. (*M* 153)]

In the dialogue between *Ich* and Malina that concludes the chapter, she
arrives at the insight: "Es ist nicht mein Vater. Es ist mein Mörder" ("It's not
my father. It's my murderer"; *M* 235/154). With this, she must acknowledge an eternal principle of violence in which she, too, is implicated:

Malina: Du wirst also nie mehr sagen: Krieg und Frieden.
Ich: Nie mehr.
            Es ist immer Krieg.
            Hier ist immer Gewalt.
            Hier ist immer Kampf.
            Es ist der ewige Krieg. (*M* 236)

[MALINA: So you'll never again say: War and Peace.
ME: Never again.
        It's always war.
        Here there is always violence.
        Here there is always struggle.
        It is the eternal war. (*M* 155)]

But in what sense, exactly, is this figure in whom is condensed "everything that is terrible that happens in this time"[62] to be understood as *Ich*'s murderer? Above all, surely, in that, as the distillation of a historical reality — a public social order based on the aggressive pursuit of self-interest, and on the exploitation and objectification of others — he is the embodiment of everything that makes the emotional, open, vulnerable, would-be relational self that is figured in *Ich* unviable. In this sense he is the origin of her traumatized state. In relation to him, or rather, the public social order abbreviated in him, this *Ich* can only ever be a victim or, should she take recourse to self-defense and kill in herself the vulnerability that exposes her to his force, lose herself by *becoming like him*. This is revealed in *Ich*'s final dreams. The salvation of a "feminine" inflection of subjectivity must, then, be achieved in some other way.

Articulate Absence: The Conclusion of the Novel

MALINA: Du mußt auf der Stelle bleiben. Es muß deine Stelle sein. Du sollst nicht vordringen und nicht zurückgehen. Dann wirst du, auf dieser Stelle, auf der einzigen, auf die du gehörst, siegen.
ICH: (con brio) Siegen! Wer spricht denn hier noch von siegen, wenn das Zeichen verloren ist, in dem man siegen könnte.
MALINA: Es heißt immer noch: siegen. Es wird dir ohne einen einzigen Kunstgriff gelingen und ohne Gewalt. Du wirst aber auch nicht mit deinem Ich siegen, sondern —
ICH: (allegro) Sondern — siehst du?
MALINA: Du wirst es nicht mit deinem Ich tun. [. . .] An der richtigen Stelle hast du nichts mehr zu wollen. Du wirst dort so sehr du sein, daß du dein Ich aufgeben kannst. Es wird die erste Stelle sein, auf der die Welt von jemand geheilt ist. (*M* 312–13)

[MALINA: You have to remain in one place. It has to be your place. You should neither press forward nor retreat. Because then you shall conquer, in this place, the only place where you belong.
ME: (con brio) Conquer! Who said anything about conquering, now that the sign is lost in which to conquer.

MALINA: Nevertheless the word is: conquer. You will succeed without a single trick and without force. Furthermore you will
not conquer with your "I," but rather —
ME: (allegro) But rather — you see?
MALINA: Not with your "I." [. . .] In the proper place you will
have nothing more to want. There you will be yourself
so much that you'll be able to give up your "I." It will be
the first place where someone has healed the world. (*M*
207–8, translation modified)]

This passage from the exchanges between *Ich* and Malina in the final
chapter, "Of Last Things," prefigures the end of the novel, when *Ich*
comes to a resting point, the place in which she ceases to be an "I," in
the crack in the wall. As Ivan progressively withdraws in this part of the
novel, *Ich* is deprived of the focus of her intensity and suffers a diminu-
tion of energy and purpose. The final pages chart the gradual elimination of the "feminine" position figured in her, until only the male double
Malina remains. Yet the eradication of *Ich* as a position enacted at the
novel's close must be read together with Malina's earlier description of
this state of affairs as a form of total self-fulfillment — "There you will be
yourself so much that you'll be able to give up your 'I'" — and simultaneously with the lapidary final words: "Es war Mord" ("It was murder";
M 337/225). The effect is profoundly paradoxical, so that the ending of
the novel leaves the reader with a host of questions. Has *Ich* chosen this
course, is it to be read, then, as a form of suicide? Was she murdered? And
if so, by whom? By Malina? By Ivan? But what of her assurances "Es war
nicht Herr Malina, es war auch nicht Ivan" ("It was not Herr Malina,
nor was it Ivan"; *M* 329/219)? And who speaks the words "It was murder"? *Ich* herself, despite the fact that it is a wall "aus der nie mehr etwas
laut werden kann" ("from which nothing can ever be heard again"; *M*
337/225)? Malina? Another narrator? In short, Bachmann has succeeded
in attaining a form of narrative closure that simultaneously refuses closure. As Eva Lindemann perspicaciously observes:

The wall, the old wall has [. . .] a crack in it which has preoccupied
the fantasy of the "I" for a long time already. This crack in the wall
[*Sprung in der Wand*], the opening in what is closed, the hope of
the shattering of the idea of closure, is a hope for the truthfulness of
that which is fragmentary.[63]

The ending can, in other words, be read as an affirmation of the openness
and fragmentation figured throughout the novel through Bachmann's
complex compositional technique, the network of allusions and cross-references, leitmotivs and puzzles that forever elude interpretative closure
and are thus the essence of the work's continued energy: its symbolic

"femininity" as opposed to a "masculinity" based on self-containment and coherent unity. As such, it is indeed the completely fitting culmination of all that *Ich* has been and, in the state of suspension (*Aufhebung*) in which she is held at the close, in effect still is.

At the same time, in the story of the elimination of *Ich* and all that she stands for — trauma, excitation, self-dissipation, the principle of love and thus of the relational construction of subjectivity — that leaves the rational, analytical Malina as the embodiment of self-preservation alone at the close, Bachmann has written a history of the construction of the male-subject-as-norm in the terms of the Western tradition. In doing so, she has made that history tangible. Had *Malina* in fact been followed by a succession of novels narrated by *Ich*'s male double (and even though it was not, the fact that Bachmann spoke of the intention has served to construct the *Todesarten* cycle as an object of the imagination), the absent *Ich* and the accusation, "It was murder," would have haunted the remainder of the narratives. As in the often-quoted passage from the *Franza* fragments in which Martin Ranner records the reaction of his sister Franza to the visibly expunged image of the Queen Hatscheput in her temple in Dêr el-Bahari in Egypt, the eradicated *Ich* at the end of the novel is an articulate absence: "Siehst du, sagte sie, aber er hat vergessen, daß an der Stelle, wo er sie getilgt hat, doch sie stehengeblieben ist. Sie ist abzulesen, weil da nichts ist, wo sie sein soll" ("Look, she said, but the pharaoh forgot that though he eradicated her, she is still there. She is legible, because nothing is there where she should be").[64] If Bachmann started with the question why she had always found it so difficult to narrate from the female perspective, why she had so often adopted the male perspective in her writing, *Malina* comes up with an explanation of the difficulty that is simultaneously an inscription of the lost "feminine."

The Position of the Female Author in the Dialectic of Enlightenment

As already noted, the account of the formation of the rational, analytical, self-contained male-subject-as-norm that underlies Bachmann's novel corresponds closely to the account of the Enlightenment subject presented in Horkheimer and Adorno's *Dialectic of Enlightenment*.[65] The complex dialectic set out by them between Enlightenment and pre-Hellenic or premodern myth, between logical positivism and objectified nature, between a subjectivity reliant on reason and self-preservation on the one hand and the suppression of the chaotic passions and desires that endanger the self-discipline necessary for that subjectivity on the other bears a clear relation to the gender dialectic represented by Bachmann. This is especially evident since Horkheimer and Adorno themselves write

a gender plot into their cultural narrative: "Humanity had to inflict terrible injuries on itself before the self — the identical, purpose-directed,
masculine character of human beings — was created, and something of
this process is repeated in every childhood" (H-A 26, italics added).
They also acknowledge the structures of power that permitted the cultural creation of woman as the embodiment of objectified nature (i.e.,
that which Enlightenment strives against):

> Man as ruler refuses to do woman the honor of individualizing her.
> Socially, the individual woman is an example of the species, a repre-
> sentative of her sex, and thus, wholly encompassed by male logic,
> she stands for nature, the substrate of never-ending subsumption on
> the plane of ideas and of never-ending subjection on that of reality.
> (H-A 87)

Here, the mechanism is made transparent whereby sexual difference has
historically been used by the dominant male sex as the basis of a projection: "femininity" becomes the site in which is lodged all that masculinized subjectivity has had to repress in the course of socialization. This
functions both on the cultural-historical plane, and on the individual psychological one, as their phrase "something of this process is repeated in
every childhood" acknowledges. The unconscious aspect of the relationship to the projected "feminine" motivates the male subject's psychological attraction to it, as well as his violence toward women as those who
embody to him what is impermissible in himself.

There are further traces that link Bachmann's text to Horkheimer
and Adorno's assessment of the internal logic of Enlightenment. The
theme of "la prostitution universelle," for example, introduced into the
novel in connection with a reference to de Sade (*M* 78–79/46–47) and
later developing into a critique of the objectification of others in postwar
sexual relations in Vienna, corresponds with Horkheimer and Adorno's
excursus on the work of de Sade and Nietzsche as revealing the underlying moral code of Enlightenment, its (on the surface never acknowledged) endorsement of the instrumentalization of the weaker other.[66]
Similarly, Bachmann's critique of the development, out of the black market of postwar Vienna, of "ein universeller schwarzer Markt" ("a universal
black market"; *M* 262/173) of department stores and supermarkets and
her pastiche of advertising slogans promising the substitute emotional
stimuli of consumer culture (*M* 252/166) have something in common
with Horkheimer and Adorno's assessment of the totalitarian economics
of contemporary Enlightenment and the objective of ideological control
that motivates its "Culture Industry."[67]

Horkheimer and Adorno's is an extremely negative account of
Enlightenment modernity that is intent on bringing to the surface the
price of the Age of Reason in terms of the suppression and distortion of

human instincts and personality, its catastrophic construction of the relation between human subjectivity and nature, and its logical development toward the mechanization and economic functionalization of those placed in subordinate positions in society's power hierarchy. The negativity of their assessment is based on the urgent perception of continuities between the historical trajectory of Enlightenment and the fascist social order, and as such, their work founds a postwar tradition that reads German Nazism and the Holocaust not as a demonic aberration from the goals of Enlightenment, but as an extreme articulation of trends inherent in enlightened modernity.[68] Bachmann's *Todesarten* project is likewise a post-Holocaust work, as revealed through the multiple references to fascism and images drawn from the archive of Holocaust memory, notably in *Malina*'s dream chapter. And Bachmann shares with Horkheimer and Adorno the purpose of revealing the dark side of Enlightenment, the structures of violence and violation that underlie it, in order to open up a space for the conceptualization of an alternative order, "the utopia of a humanity which, itself no longer distorted, no longer needs distortion" (H-A 93).

The difference between Horkheimer and Adorno and Bachmann is that she articulates in their terms from the culturally symbolic position of the disempowered, objectified, and violated within the dialectic of Enlightenment, because she writes as a woman. In other words, Bachmann occupies the position that, if their cultural analysis is accurate, is denied individuation and subjecthood. This is a paradox that the complex structure and polyvalent meanings of Bachmann's novel strive to express. Yet the fact is that postwar social and cultural developments had changed the position of the woman writer. Bachmann, as a doctor of philosophy who wrote her dissertation on Martin Heidegger and as a highly sophisticated intellectual reader, was herself the product of the emancipatory trajectory of Enlightenment, which by the middle of the twentieth century was permitting women access to the universities in a manner unimaginable a century or even half-century before, thereby giving them the basis on which to participate actively in the shaping of the public cultural sphere. Her character *Ich*, a female writer like her author, is probably the first female figure in fiction to be endowed not only with the memory of the solemn admission into the academic community (*M* 187, 308/122, 204), but also with a biography of reading that encompasses all the seminal works of the Western philosophical and literary tradition (*M* 80–81, 183–84/48–49, 119–20). At the same time, the dialectic between *Ich* and Malina articulates a tension of *difference* in the relationship of the female author to the inherited tradition. The fictional configuration suggests that Bachmann experienced herself as both subject and object, as both "masculine" persona — a "Malina" generated to protect her personal vulnerability and to guarantee her agency in the public sphere — and as the embodiment, through the very fact of her sex, of all that has been objectified and demoted in the course of the cultural-historical construction of the male-subject-as-norm. In short, we see in this quasi-autobiographical text[69] a particularly vivid expression of the consciousness of being double, of being both subject and nonsubject in cultural-historical and individual psychological terms — and this is articulated in the double gendering of the figure of Malina-*Ich*. This doubling informs much of the writing by women to be explored in this study, and is a mark of the way in which women writers through the very fact of their sex tend to bear the legacy of the cultural-historical construction of the "feminine," although through writing they are seeking to take possession of the meanings attached to it. If finding a way to say "I" was, for Bachmann, "like the discovery of my own person," it was also a way to transform the position of culture's Other into a position of active protest against that culture's murderous propensities and to open up a gap in the system for the "Ahnung" or "anticipation"[70] of another way of being.

Notes

[1] See Sigrid Weigel, *Ingeborg Bachmann: Hinterlassenschaften unter Wahrung des Briefgeheimnisses* (Vienna: Paul Zsolnay, 1999), 527: "The genre categorization is only partially applicable to the text," and subsequent discussion.

[2] The manner of *Ich*'s introduction into the narrative, which will be discussed below, puts a question mark over the appropriateness of referring to her in conventional terms as a first-person narrator; she is, rather, a character who is designated as "I," whereby "Ich" has the advantage in German of being both a first-person pronoun and usable as a noun, "das Ich" (the ego), comprehensible as a persona within the individual psyche. In what follows, therefore, I shall use *Ich* as if it were the character's proper name, modifying the English translation where necessary for the purposes of consistency.

[3] Ingeborg Bachmann, *Wir müssen wahre Sätze finden: Gespräche und Interviews*, ed. Christine Koschel and Inge von Weidenbaum (Munich, Zurich: Piper, 1983), 95 (Interview with Toni Kienlechner, 9 April 1971).

[4] See Bachmann, *Wir müssen wahre Sätze finden*, 96: "Malina wird uns erzählen können, was ihm der andere Teil seiner Person, das Ich, hinterlassen hat" (Malina will be able to tell us what the other part of his person, the I, has left behind).

[5] See Irmela von der Lühe's opening discussion in "Erinnerung und Identität in Ingeborg Bachmanns Roman 'Malina,'" in *Ingeborg Bachmann. Text + Kritik Sonderband*, ed. Heinz Ludwig Arnold (Munich: edition text + kritik, 1984), 132–49, here notably 132–33.

[6] Ingeborg Bachmann, *Werke*, ed. Christine Koschel, Inge von Weidenbaum, and Clemens Münster (Munich, Zurich: Piper, 1978), 4 vols.

[7] Later editorial work has suggested that Bachmann came to refer to the work as *Das Buch Franza*, which is the title used as the basis for the English translation: *The Book of Franza & Requiem for Fanny Goldmann*, trans. Peter Filkins (Evanston, IL: Northwestern UP, 1999).

[8] The double issue of *alternative* 108/109 (1976): *Das Lächeln der Medusa* was the first entry point into German of the work of the 1970s French feminist theorists.

[9] See especially the contributions of Weigel and Birgit Vanderbeke to the *Text + Kritik Sonderband*.

[10] Ingeborg Bachmann, *"Todesarten"-Projekt: Kritische Ausgabe*, ed. Monika Albrecht and Dirk Göttsche (Munich, Zurich: Piper, 1995), 4 vols.

[11] Ingeborg Bachmann, *Letzte, unveröffentlichte Gedichte, Entwürfe und Fassungen*, ed. Hans Höller (Frankfurt am Main: Suhrkamp, 1998); Ingeborg Bachmann, *Ich weiss keine bessere Welt: unveröffentlichte Gedichte*, ed. Isolde Moser, Heinz Bachmann, Christian Moser (Munich: Piper, 2000); Ingeborg Bachmann, *Kritische Schriften*, ed. Dirk Göttsche and Monika Albrecht (Munich: Piper, 2005). For an insightful survey of scholarship on Bachmann, see Dirk Göttsche and Monika Albrecht, eds., *Bachmann-Handbuch: Leben, Werk, Wirkung* (Stuttgart: Metzler, 2002).

[12] See especially Sigrid Weigel's magnum opus *Ingeborg Bachmann: Hinterlassenschaften unter Wahrung des Briefgeheimnisses* of 1999 (details in note 1, above), and Bernhard Boschenstein and Sigrid Weigel, eds., *Ingeborg Bachmann und Paul Celan: Poetische Korrespondenzen. Vierzehn Beiträge* (Frankfurt am Main: Suhrkamp, 1997). The relationship between Bachmann and Celan has been further illuminated by the publication of their correspondence: *Herzzeit: Ingeborg Bachmann — Paul Celan. Der Briefwechsel*, ed. Bertrand Badiou, Hans Höller, Andrea Stoll, and Barbara Wiedemann (Frankfurt am Main: Suhrkamp, 2008).

[13] Bachmann, *Wir müssen wahre Sätze finden*, 99–100 (Interview with Toni Kienlechner, 9 April 1971), italics added.

[14] The "Stadtpark" fragment included under the heading "Eugen-Roman I" (*"Todesarten"-Projekt*, vol. 1, 45–46) corresponds with the scene at the tram stop in the prologue of *Malina* in which *Ich* claims she nearly met Malina years earlier, suggesting a link between the two figures; see *Werke*, vol. 3, 18 / *Malina*, trans. Philip Boehm (New York, London: Holmes & Meier, 1990), 5.

[15] *"Todesarten"-Projekt*, vol. 1, 104.

[16] Compare *"Todesarten"-Projekt*, vol. 1, 107–11 and *Werke*, vol. 3, 288–89 / *Malina*, trans. Boehm, 190–91. At the conclusion of the dialogue, Malina turns physically violent, taking *Ich* by the shoulders and shaking her, possibly even hitting her (cf. her "schlag mich nicht, bitte nicht schlagen" / "don't hit me, please don't hit me," 290/191). Subsequent references to *Malina* appear in the text, identified as *M* (in German to the *Werke* edition, in English to the Boehm translation).

[17] See "Arbeitsphase 1964" (Work phase 1964), *"Todesarten"-Projekt*, vol. 1, 117–67, and here especially the fragment headed "Die gestohlenen Jahre" (The Stolen Years), 117–26.

[18] See section entitled "Requiem für Fanny Goldmann," *"Todesarten"-Projekt*, vol. 1, 285–333.

[19] See drafts in section entitled "<Goldmann/Rottwitz-Roman>," *"Todesarten"-Projekt*, vol. 1, 337–99.

[20] See "[Vorrede] Entwurf," *Werke*, vol. 3, 341, also *"Todesarten"-Projekt*, vol. 2, 77 / *The Book of Franza*, 3.

[21] *"Todesarten"-Projekt*, vol. 1, 237–83. That this was a project which Bachmann intended at one point for publication is indicated in an interview with Harald Grass, 1 May 1965; see *Wir müssen wahre Sätze finden*, 57–58.

[22] *"Todesarten"-Projekt*, vol. 2 traces the stages of the composition of the *Franza* book.

[23] *"Todesarten"-Projekt*, vol. 1, 85.

[24] Roy Jerome, "Introduction," in Jerome, ed., *Conceptions of Postwar German Masculinity* (Albany: SUNY Press, 2001), 7.

[25] The actress Maria Malina appears first in the 1966 development of the Fanny Goldmann plot; see *"Todesarten"-Projekt*, vol. 1, 294–96. Her death is a sensational one: she is (purportedly) eaten by a shark during a sailing trip off Greece (347). The prologue to *Malina* contains a cross-reference to this other plot; compare *Malina*, 19–20 and *"Todesarten"-Projekt*, vol. 1, 342–43.

[26] Musil's poem "Isis und Osiris" is quoted in a radio essay on Musil written by Bachmann ca. December 1952: *Werke*, vol. 4, 98–99. For Franza and Martin in the *Franza* book, the poem provides a reference point for their relationship; compare *Werke*, vol. 3, 357, 397, 469 / *The Book of Franza*, 19, 58, 141.

[27] See Maria Behre, "'Das Ich, weiblich': 'Malina' im Chor der Stimmen zur 'Erfindung' des Weiblichen im Menschen," in Andrea Stoll, ed., *Ingeborg Bachmanns "Malina"* (Frankfurt am Main: Suhrkamp, 1992), 210–32 for an illuminating account of the conceptualization of the masculine and feminine principles in, for example, the works of Musil and Nietzsche, important influences on Bachmann.

[28] In the drafts, both figures are characterized as "leidenschaftlich gleichgültig" (passionately indifferent); see *"Todesarten"-Projekt*, vol. 1, 330, 337.

[29] Weigel, *Hinterlassenschaften*, 525. The editors of the *"Todesarten"-Projekt* cite letters from Bachmann to her publisher, Klaus Piper, and her *Lektor*, Otto Best, dated 20 and 25 November 1966 respectively, which describe the author's "shock" on reading the *Franza* manuscripts for the purposes of revision: the manuscript, writes Bachmann, seems to her "a helpless allusion to something that has yet to be written": *"Todesarten"-Projekt*, vol. 2, 397.

[30] *"Todesarten"-Projekt*, vol. 2, 397.

[31] Hannah Arendt, *The Human Condition* (Chicago and London: U of Chicago P, second edition 1998), 169.

[32] The editors of the *"Todesarten"-Projekt* note that the earliest drafts relating to the *Malina* novel, after the interruption of work on the *Franza* book in late 1966, focus on issues of the conduct of the narrative and the search for a narrator figure; see *"Todesarten"-Projekt*, vol. 3.2, 788. Weigel sees the novel *Malina* as the "*Bildungsroman* of the narrator": "In order for the narrator to become the master in the house of the 'I,' his co-habitant, the voice of excitation in the Today, must disappear or be sacrificed": Weigel, *Hinterlassenschaften*, 528.

[33] See references to "Abgründigkeit und Hintergründigkeit" (profound and cryptic quality) versus "Schein" (appearance), *"Todesarten"-Projekt*, vol. 2, 16–17.

[34] Stephanie Bird addresses the female characters' public prominence and fear of public humiliation in *Women Writers and National Identity: Bachmann, Duden, Özdamar* (Cambridge: Cambridge UP, 2003), 54.

[35] See the "[Vorrede] Entwurf" to *Der Fall Franza, Werke*, vol. 3, 341 / *The Book of Franza*, 3–4: "I've often wondered, and perhaps it has passed through your minds as well, just where the virus of crime escaped to — it cannot have simply disappeared from our world twenty years ago just because murder is no longer praised, desired, decorated with medals, and promoted."

[36] See *Malina*, 69/40: "*Der Fremde lächelte: Mein Volk ist älter als alle Völker der Welt und es ist in alle Winde zerstreut*" ("*The stranger smiled: My people is older than all the peoples of the world and is scattered in the four winds*"); and the deportation dream in chapter 2 (193–95/126–27).

[37] Weigel provides a table of cross-references between *Malina* and the poetry of Paul Celan; see *Hinterlassenschaften*, 420–23.

[38] Bird comments: "The direct identification of the oppression of women in patriarchy with the persecution of the Jews is a worrying feature in the book": *Women Writers and National Identity*, 90. It is, however, surely derived from Bachmann's reading of Horkheimer and Adorno; see discussion of the traces of the *Dialectic of Enlightenment* in Bachmann's novel in the final section of this chapter.

[39] See discussion in chapter 2.

[40] In *Malina, Ich* describes herself as "eine unvermeidliche dunkle Geschichte, die seine [Malinas] Geschichte begleitet, ergänzen will, die er aber von seiner klaren Geschichte absondert und abgrenzt" ("an unavoidable dark tale accompanying and hoping to supplement his [Malina's] own bright story, a tale which he, however, detaches and delimits"; *M* 22–3/8–9).

[41] Bachmann, "Das schreibende Ich" ["Frankfurter Vorlesungen," III], in *Werke*, vol. 4, 221.

[42] See *Malina*, 80–82/48–49, which constructs a history of *Ich*'s reading, and 182–84/119–20, in the dream chapter, where the father figure orders the destruction of *Ich*'s library. In both of these scenes, only the works of male authors are named.

[43] Sigrid Weigel, "'Ein Ende mit der Schrift. Ein andrer Anfang.' Zur Entwicklung von Ingeborg Bachmanns Schreibweise," in *Ingeborg Bachmann. Text + Kritik Sonderband*, 58–92, here 73.

[44] Elizabeth Grosz, *Jacques Lacan: A feminist introduction* (London and New York: Routledge, 1990), 72.

[45] Boehm shortens Bachmann's very long sentences in this opening passage, which entails the sacrifice of the syntactical rhythms crucial in establishing her nervous character.

[46] Weigel, *Hinterlassenschaften*, 528.

[47] Julia Kristeva, *Revolution in Poetic Language* [1974], trans. Margaret Waller (New York: Columbia UP, 1984), 26.

[48] See Kristeva, *Revolution in Poetic Language*, 27: "Drives involve pre-Oedipal semiotic functions and energy discharges that connect and orient the body to the mother."

49 See the motif "es stört mich alles in meiner Erinnerung" ("it all upsets me, in my remembering"; *M* 27/11) — and its variations throughout the novel.

50 Kristeva, *Revolution in Poetic Language,* 102. The phrases given in quotation marks in this passage are from Freud and Breuer, "Studies in Hysteria," *Standard Edition,* vol. 2, 7, 53. It is, of course, remarkable that Bachmann's novel *precedes* the publication of Kristeva's *La revolution du langage poétique* by three years and yet formally anticipates its findings.

51 Kristeva, *Revolution in Poetic Language,* 102.

52 Max Horkheimer and Theodor W. Adorno, *Dialectic of Enlightenment: Philosophical Fragments,* ed. Gunzelin Schmid Noerr, trans. Edmund Jephcott (Stanford: Stanford UP, 2002), 57. Subsequent references appear in the text, identified as H-A.

53 It is worth considering whether the status of Ivan as divorced, and the absence of a mother to his children, is a hint that Ivan is another version of a male subject, alongside Malina at the novel's close, in whom the "feminine" impulse (for example, his ability to open himself to the Other in the love relationship) has been eradicated. The text opens up a space to pursue this interpretation at the point at which *Ich* says: "Ivan muß eine Geschichte hinter sich haben, in einem Zyklon gewesen sein" ("Ivan must have some history behind him, must have been in a cyclone"; *M* 279/184). The German word "Zyklon" creates an association with the gas "Zyklon B," which was used in the concentration camps.

54 See the editors' commentary on the "dialectical constellation" of *Ich* and Malina in *"Todesarten"-Projekt,* vol. 3.2, 790.

55 Weigel, *Hinterlassenschaften,* 531.

56 There is a thread of a tradition of the depiction of the love relationship from the point of view of the (discarded) woman: *Ich* alludes to Gaspara Stampa, a sixteenth-century Venetian poet, as a forerunner, or sister, (slightly mis-) quoting her line "viver ardendo e non sentire il male" (*M* 214/140); compare Gaspara Stampa, *Selected Poems,* trans. Laura Anna Stortoni and Mary Prentice Lillie (New York: Italica Press, 1994), 160 [sonnet 208]. See also Bachmann's references to Gaspara Stampa and the *Letters of a Portuguese Nun* in *Wir müssen wahre Sätze finden,* 110 (interview with Ilse Heim, 5 May 1971).

57 Compare the characterization of Leo Jordan (here clearly a precursor to the father figure in *Malina*) in the *Franza* drafts, *"Todesarten"-Projekt,* vol. 2, 230: "er ist das Exemplar, das heute regiert, das heute Erfolg hat, das angreift und darum lebt, nie hab ich einen Menschen mit soviel Aggression gesehen" (he is the type that rules today, that succeeds today, that attacks and lives to do so, for I've never seen a person with so much aggression); compare *Werke,* vol. 3, 412 / *The Book of Franza,* 79.

58 Her name is, of course, tantalizingly close to Malina's, and forms part of the riddle of names in the novel. *Ich*'s housekeeper, who also appears in the dream chapter, is called Lina, and at one point "meine Lina" ("my Lina"; *M* 218/143).

59 In an interview, Bachmann described the sickness of *Ich* in the novel as "die Krankheit unserer Zeit für mich" (for me, the sickness of our time): *Wir müssen wahre Sätze finden,* 72 (interview with Dieter Zilligen, 22 March 1971).

[60] Weigel reads the suggested aspect of complicity as a trace of the aftermath of the Shoah in the second generation on the perpetrator side; see *Hinterlassenschaften*, 539–42. Stephanie Bird is also interested in the aspect of complicity: *Women and National Identity*, 76–78.

[61] See also Eva Lindemann's study of the leitmotif phrase "es ist nichts" ("it's nothing") in Bachmann's work: Lindemann, *Über die Grenze: Zur späten Prosa Ingeborg Bachmanns* (Würzburg: Königshausen & Neumann, 2000), 42–54.

[62] *Wir müssen wahre Sätze finden*, 70 (interview with Dieter Zilligen, 22 March 1971).

[63] Lindemann, *Über die Grenze*, 31. The word "Sprung," meaning crack, also resonates with the meaning "jump" or "leap," so that it figures not just an opening, but a decisive movement to a different order of thought.

[64] "Der Fall Franza. Unvollendeter Roman," *Werke*, vol. 3, 436 / *The Book of Franza*, 109, translation modified (Filkins unfortunately erases the gender-specificity in his translation).

[65] Weigel (*Hinterlassenschaften*, 531) and Hans Höller, in *Ingeborg Bachmann. Das Werk. Von den frühesten Gedichten bis zum "Todesarten"-Zyklus* [Frankfurt am Main: Anton Hain (Athenäums Programm], 1987), 264, note the proximity of aspects of *Malina* to ideas contained in the *Dialectic of Enlightenment*, while Göttsche and Albrecht devote a section to the influence of Critical Theory and sociology on Bachmann's thought in their *Bachmann-Handbuch*, 216–18.

[66] Horkheimer and Adorno, *Dialectic of Enlightenment*, "Excursus II: Juliette or Enlightenment and Morality," 63–93.

[67] Horkheimer and Adorno, *Dialectic of Enlightenment*, "The Culture Industry: Enlightenment as Mass Deception," 94–136.

[68] See, for example, Zygmunt Bauman, *Modernity and the Holocaust* (Cambridge: Polity Press, 1991). Peter Wagner concurs with Baumann's analysis, seeing the Holocaust as "an extreme exemplification of organized modernity rather than as a terrible deviation from otherwise benevolent rule": Wagner, *A Sociology of Modernity*, 69. The constitutive practices of "organized modernity" are analysed in his chapters 5, 6 and 7.

[69] Bachmann referred in interview to *Malina* as "autobiography, but not in the traditional sense": *Wir müssen wahre Sätze finden*, 71.

[70] In a 1952 radio essay on Robert Musil, Bachmann inscribes her understanding of the function of the "utopia [of the] 'other state of being'" as figured, notably, in the brother-sister relationship Ulrich-Agathe in *The Man Without Qualities*: "And yet this utopia, as an image which gives direction [*als Richtbild*], is the precondition for another such image which is capable of freeing the human being from the clutches of ideology. For is it not the case that Ulrich, after his journey into the thousand-year empire has come to nothing, retains from it precisely *the anticipation [Ahnung], in which the movement of the spirit is kept constantly watchful and ready*?" — Bachmann, "Der Mann ohne Eigenschaften," *Werke*, vol. 4, 101–2, italics added. Göttsche and Albrecht discuss the influence of Musil on Bachmann's concept of utopia in the *Bachmann-Handbuch*, 220–22.

4: From His Point of View: Max Frisch's *Mein Name sei Gantenbein*

M ORE THAN ANY OTHER GERMAN-LANGUAGE WRITER of the 1950s and 1960s, the Swiss writer Max Frisch is identified with the representation of the problems of masculine identity in the period of societal restoration following the end of the Second World War. His reputation in this respect is based above all on three prose works: *Stiller* (1954), *Homo faber* (1957), and *Mein Name sei Gantenbein* (1964). The subject of this chapter is the last and, in terms of its narrative structure, most complex of these works, read both on its own terms and as a partner-text to Bachmann's *Malina* for its illumination from the alternative perspective of the male writer of issues of subjectivity and gender in the postwar period.

Malina and *Gantenbein*: An Established Pairing

A shared history links the composition of Bachmann's *Malina* to Frisch's *Mein Name sei Gantenbein* (literally, Let my Name be Gantenbein),[1] so that coming to Frisch's chronologically earlier novel *after* the consideration of Bachmann's not only enables a contrastive examination of differing gender perspectives on questions of subjectivity, but also adds a further layer to the reading of *Malina* given in the previous chapter. In 1974, almost immediately after Bachmann's death, Lore Toman published a short article in which she proposed that the two novels were to be seen as "two sides of the same life."[2] The basis for her claim was the perceived connection to the intimate personal relationship between Bachmann and Frisch that began in 1958 and ended, with a great deal of injury on both sides, in 1962. Frisch, she suggested, had used the relationship as material for his *Gantenbein* novel, in which the central female character was purportedly recognizable to those who knew the couple as a portrait of Bachmann. Toman reads *Malina* as Bachmann's revenge. The traces left by the personal relationship in the literary work were subsequently pursued in some depth by Monika Albrecht. In a 1989 book-length study and in a contribution to a volume of essays published in 1992, Albrecht argues the case for perceiving a network of allusions to Frisch's work, including the *Gantenbein* novel, in the *Todesarten* cycle. In addition, she supplies a body of evidence to support the claim that the "verschwiegene Erinnerung" (suppressed memory), the central lacuna around which *Ich*'s narration is constructed in *Malina,* corresponds to the period of the relationship between Bachmann and Frisch. In this reading, the relationship is understood as the key to the fictional *Ich*'s trauma.[3]

The publication of the *Todesarten* manuscripts in 1995 potentially brought into play a great deal more material with which to extend Albrecht's thesis. In particular, Bachmann's switch in 1964 from the plot centered on the male figure, Eugen, to the prototype Fanny Goldmann plot with its central theme of the exploitation of the female character as the material of a literary work by her author-lover becomes legible in this context as a direct response to the publication of Frisch's *Gantenbein* novel in the same year, although as co-editor of the *"Todesarten"-Projekt,* Albrecht did not pursue this point in her editorial commentary.[4] Read in the light of Albrecht's earlier contributions, however, the *Todesarten* drafts reveal the extent to which Bachmann was concerned precisely to *eliminate* overtly personal aspects before she would release her work into the public sphere. The publications of "unauthorized" poems from Bachmann's literary estate in 1998 and 2000 appear problematic for this reason. While publication was justified on the basis of the light thrown on her creative process and poetological development in the course of the 1960s, the draft poems and fragments in the volume *Ich weiß keine bessere Welt* in particular were reviewed primarily in prurient terms, as a source of information on Bachmann's personal problems in the mid-1960s.[5] The publication that *was* authorized by Bachmann, the novel *Malina,* undoubtedly contains within its complex fabric a number of messages intended for Frisch. As a work of literature that rises out of, but also above, the personal life of the author, however, it engages at a structurally highly complex level with supra-personal issues of human subjectivity, interrelationship, and cultural history. Emphasizing the concealed personal vendetta as the novel's primary concern detracts from the status of the novel *as literature,* since it closes down the simultaneity of multiple layers of meaning that is the novel's particular aesthetic merit.

In this chapter, the concern is not with the real-life relationship between the two authors, nor is it the intention to elaborate further on literary-historical issues of influence. Rather, the interest here is in structural and thematic parallels and contrasts between the two works that serve to illuminate them as alternative approaches to the issue of the construction of masculine subjectivity within the specific historical moment of post-1945 European modernity. More precisely, the overtly self-reflexive nature of the narrative construction in both novels, and the correlation they both assert between modes of narration and the conceptualization of selfhood, enable conclusions to be drawn about the historical pressures being brought to bear on traditional, bourgeois notions of masculinity in this period. At the same time, the distinctively different handling of the relationality of gendered positions within the respective narratives highlights the differential investment of the male as opposed to the female author in the maintenance of the parameters of subjectivity as inherited from the bourgeois Enlightenment tradition.

It is widely recognized that Max Frisch's prose works characteristically circle around the themes of personal identity and of relations between the sexes as a site in which personal identity is created and contested, and the secondary literature to date has considered these aspects extensively. There are also a number of studies of the images of women in Frisch's work, a theme that has been favored particularly by female scholars.[6] However, the crisis in the male subject position underlying *Gantenbein* has not hitherto been adequately investigated in historical and categorical terms, that is, in its relevance to masculine subjectivity per se in the post-World War II era, nor the gender relations represented in the novel sufficiently understood as the nexus in which the narrator attempts to retrieve a fundamentally endangered masculine selfhood. It is on these aspects that the reading of the novel that follows is focused.

Narration in *Mein Name sei Gantenbein*: Reflexive Self-Identity in Late Modernity

Like Bachmann's *Malina*, Frisch's *Mein Name sei Gantenbein* appears on first reading to be a profoundly subjective work, dealing not with the political and social issues that motivated much German-language writing in the 1960s but rather with self-identity and personal relationship. This is justified within the novel's narrative in the following bracketed aside:

> (Manchmal scheint auch mir, daß jedes Buch, so es sich nicht befaßt mit der Verhinderung des Kriegs, mit der Schaffung einer besseren Gesellschaft und so weiter, sinnlos ist, müßig, unverantwortlich, langweilig, nicht wert, daß man es liest, unstatthaft. Es ist nicht die Zeit für Ich-Geschichten. Und doch vollzieht sich das menschliche Leben oder verfehlt sich am einzelnen Ich, nirgends sonst.)

> [(I, too, often have the feeling that any book which isn't concerned with the prevention of war, with the creation of a better society and so on, is senseless, futile, irresponsible, tedious, not worth reading, inadmissible. This is no time for ego stories [*Ich-Geschichten*]. And yet human life is fulfilled or goes wrong in the individual ego, nowhere else.)][7]

At the center of the novel, then, is "the individual ego," in the person of an unnamed male first-person narrator, an "I" who does not, however, relate his own story (with the exception of a few key episodes), but rather generates a network of narrative fragments grouped around named fictional character-positions.

The basic premise of the chosen form of narration has customarily been explained in the terms of Frisch's own reflections on the relation between language and identity in his *Tagebuch 1946–1949* (Sketchbook 1946–1949):

> Was wichtig ist: das Unsagbare, das Weiße zwischen den Worten, und immer reden diese Worte von den Nebensachen, die wir eigentlich nicht meinen. Unser Anliegen, das eigentliche, läßt sich bestenfalls umschreiben, und das heißt ganz wörtlich: man schreibt darum herum. Man umstellt es. Man gibt Aussagen, die nie unser eigentliches Erlebnis enthalten, das unsagbar bleibt; sie können es nur umgrenzen, möglichst nahe und genau, und das Eigentliche, das Unsagbare, erscheint bestenfalls als Spannung zwischen diesen Aussagen.

> [What is important is what cannot be said, the white space between the words. The words themselves always express the incidentals, which is not what we really mean. What we are really concerned with can only, at best, be written about, and that means, quite literally, we write around it. We encompass it. We make statements which never contain the whole true experience: that cannot be described. All the statements can do is encircle it, as tightly and closely as possible: the true, the inexpressible experience emerges at best as the tension between these statements.][8]

This frequently quoted passage reveals Frisch's fundamental distrust of language's ability to articulate experience, reality, what is "true" (*das Eigentliche*). Elsewhere he indicates his belief in the inexpressibility of the self, which can only be deciphered from the characteristic movement of one's concretized thoughts: "Wir können nur, indem wir den Zickzack unsrer jeweiligen Gedanken bezeugen und sichtbar machen, unser Wesen kennenlernen [. . .], seine Wahrheit, die wir unmittelbar nicht aussagen können" ("All we can do, by bringing to light and recording the zigzag course of our successive thoughts, is to recognize our own nature [. . .], its truth, which we cannot directly attest"; *T* 361/12). Despite the skepticism as to the possibility of expressing the truth of experience or of the self except in oblique form, it is nonetheless recognized that the *impulse* to narrate, in order to construct a sense of self or in order to come to terms with one's experiences (or both), is also fundamental. Thus the starting point of the narrative of *Gantenbein* is the need to find a story that is in accordance with the (unspoken and unspeakable) experience of the narrator in order to secure existence:

> Ein Mann hat eine Erfahrung gemacht, jetzt sucht er die Geschichte dazu — *man kann nicht leben mit einer Erfahrung, die ohne Geschichte bleibt, scheint es,* und manchmal stelle ich mir vor, ein andrer habe genau die Geschichte meiner Erfahrung. (*G* 11, italics added)

[A man has been through an experience, now he is looking for the story to go with it — *you can't live with an experience that remains without a story, it seems,* and I often imagine that someone else has exactly the story to fit my experience. (*G* 11, translation modified, italics added)]

In the light of the diary reflections and on the terms of the novel itself, the project of the narrative thus appears to be to *circumscribe* the experience of the narrator, which remains an absence at the novel's center, through the projection of narrative "roles." These are explicitly identified as the narrator's imaginings, via the repeating motif "Ich stelle mir vor" ("I imagine"), or as self-projection, via the initiation of a self-invention, as in "Mein Name sei Gantenbein" ("Let my name be Gantenbein"; *G* 25/24).[9]

Three main roles emerge in the course of the novel: Enderlin, an academic who has just been awarded a chair at Harvard University, an honor that fills him with dread at the prospect of having to fulfill the expectations leveled at him by this publicly prominent post, and whom we also see becoming involved in an affair with the wife of an associate; Svoboda, the sometime husband of the woman with whom Enderlin becomes involved, by profession an architect; and, as the predominant and preferred role, the eponymous Gantenbein, who though sighted pretends to be blind, and who is married to a famous actress he suspects of deceiving him with other men. In all three role-plays, the female figure remains recognizably the same and, as such, representative of archetypal Woman. In the Gantenbein plot she is given the name Lila, which signals her status as dependent on the perception of the male character, since "lila" (lilac) is the color taken on by the world as seen through Gantenbein's blind man's spectacles. Where Svoboda reacts to Lila's extramarital affair with jealous rage that leads to the break-up of his marriage, Gantenbein's role-play as a blind man constrains him to pretend that he does not see her deceptions, thus enabling the preservation of their marriage. The narratives featuring these major roles are supplemented by a multitude of minor stories inserted into the novel's fabric — told by the narrator to a barman, or by Gantenbein to the secondary female character Camilla Huber, or divulged directly to the reader.

The relation between the narrator's unspoken "experience" and the fictions he generates is addressed within the narrative via the metaphor of clothing with which the narrator seeks to cover his "naked" experience: "Ich probiere Geschichten an wie Kleider!" ("I try on stories like clothes!"; *G* 22/21). On the one hand, the identity of the experiencing self will be revealed through the fact that the clothes — that is, the fictional roles adopted — will always develop creases in the same places:

Ich werde mir neue Kleider kaufen, dabei weiß ich: es hilft nichts, nur im Schaufenster erscheinen sie anders. [. . .] Schon die Minuten, während der Schneider mit dem Stecknadelkissen am Arm sich dienerisch in die Hocke läßt und fachmännisch mit Kreide markiert, wie weit ich von der Konfektion abweiche, sind Pein. Ob billig oder teuer, englisch oder italienisch oder einheimisch, bleibt einerlei; immer entstehen die gleichen Falten am gleichen Ort, ich weiß es. (*G* 20–21)

[I shall buy new clothes, but all the time I know it won't help; it's only in the shop-window that they look different. [. . .] Even the minutes during which the tailor with the pin-cushion on his arm crouches down subserviently and with a professional air marks with the chalk how much I deviate from the standard measurements are agony. Whether it is cheap or dear, English or Italian or native makes no odds; the same creases always develop in the same places, I know that. (*G* 20, translation modified)]

On the other hand, however, these "stories" appear in the telling as *alternatives,* with the Gantenbein story in particular emerging as one that promises to endow freedom and thus enable escape from the a priori "experience":

Ich stelle mir vor:
Sein Leben fortan, indem er den Blinden spielt auch unter vier Augen, sein Umgang mit Menschen, die nicht wissen, daß er sie sieht, seine gesellschaftlichen Möglichkeiten, seine beruflichen Möglichkeiten dadurch, daß er nie sagt, was er sieht, ein Leben als Spiel, seine Freiheit kraft eines Geheimnisses usw.
Sein Name sei Gantenbein. (*G* 21)

[I imagine:
His life henceforth, as he plays the blind man even in private, his dealings with people who don't know that he can see, his social possibilities, his professional possibilities due to the fact that he never says what he sees, a life as a game, his freedom by virtue of a secret and so on.
Let his name be Gantenbein. (*G* 21, translation modified)]

As for the primary "experience," hinted at but nowhere explicitly related: the prime candidate for the key to this experience, identified as such by the majority of commentators on the novel, is to be found in a recurring scene of desertion and desolation. The narrator sits alone in his empty apartment, remnants of food rotting or gone hard in the fridge, mold floating on the wine in an abandoned open bottle, the furniture covered with dust sheets. In the wardrobe hang clothes that indicate that the former inhabitants were a man and a woman, a couple, of which the female partner has left:

> Von den Personen, die hier dereinst gelebt haben, steht fest: eine männlich, eine weiblich. Ich sehe Blusen im Schrank, etwas Damenwäsche, die nicht mehr in den Koffer paßte oder nicht mehr Mode ist. (G 19)

> [As to the people who once lived here, it is clear that one was male and one female. I see blouses in the cupboard, some lady's underwear that wouldn't go into the case or is no longer fashionable. (G 19)]

This points to the break-up of a relationship that has left the narrator alone. The fact that the stories of Enderlin, Svoboda, and Gantenbein all revolve around adultery, deception, jealousy, and loss (or in the case of Gantenbein, the prevention of loss through self-control) supports the thesis that the central crisis of the text has to do with the male narrator's loss of the relationship with his female partner.

The reading presented here sets a rather different emphasis. The endangered state of the male-female relationship undoubtedly forms a prominent strand within the overall weave of the narrative, and the scene of desertion and its relevance to the conceptualization of male-female relationship in the novel will be discussed in due course. However, my argument is that it needs to be seen, as the novel itself constructs it, within the work's broader exploration of issues of self-identity.

Two distinct models of self-identity are addressed within the novel. On the one hand, it is the effect of an "Ich-Geschichte" (literally, an "I-story") or narrative of the self that serves to establish an individual's sense of who he is and also to locate himself in the world.[10] This model is problematic for the first-person narrator, since his own highly articulated self-consciousness means that he cannot help seeing such narratives of the self as fictional constructs with no ultimate claim to truth. This is revealed in a poetologically motivated scene between the first-person narrator and a barman early in the novel:

> Ich sitze in einer Bar, Nachmittag, daher allein mit dem Barmann, der mir sein Leben erzählt. Ein trefflicher Erzähler! Ich warte auf jemand. Während er die Gläser spült, sagt er: So war das! Ich trinke. Eine wahre Geschichte also. Ich glaub's! sage ich. Er trocknet die gespülten Gläser. Ja, sagt er noch einmal, so war das! Ich trinke und beneide ihn — nicht um seine russische Gefangenschaft, aber um sein zweifelloses Verhältnis zu seiner Geschichte . . .
> [. . .]
> "Jede Geschichte ist eine Erfindung," sage ich nach einer Weile, ohne deswegen an den Schrecknissen seiner russischen Gefangenschaft zu zweifeln, grundsätzlich: "jedes Ich, das sich ausspricht, ist eine Rolle — ." (G 48)

[I'm sitting in a bar, afternoon, so I'm alone with the barman, who is telling me his life-story. A first-class raconteur! I'm waiting for someone. As he rinses the glasses he says: That's how it was. I drink. So it was a true story. I believe you, I say. He dries the rinsed glasses. Yes, he says again, that's how it was. I drink and envy him — not for having been a prisoner of war in Russia, but for his doubt-free relationship to his story . . .
[. . .]
"Every story is an invention," I say after a while, without on that account doubting the horrors of being a prisoner of war in Russia, as a general principle: "every ego [*Ich*] that expresses itself in words is a role — ." (*G* 46)]

For the narrator, the phenomenon of self-narration is fundamentally to be understood as a form of *social* identity-creation: "'Man kann sich selbst nicht sehen, das ist's, Geschichten gibt es nur von außen,' sage ich" ("'One can't see oneself, that's the trouble, stories only exist from outside,' I say"; *G* 49/46–47). His counter-proposal for the conceptualization of self-identity — and this will provide the basis for the conduct of self-narration in the novel — is as an "Erlebnismuster" or "pattern of experience" that emerges from an albeit intrinsically limited series of accounts:

> "— vielleicht sind's zwei oder drei Erfahrungen, was einer hat," sage ich, "zwei oder drei Erfahrungen, wenn's hochkommt, das ist's, was einer hat, wenn er von sich erzählt, überhaupt wenn er erzählt: Erlebnismuster — aber keine Geschichte," sage ich, "keine Geschichte." (*G* 49)

> ["— perhaps a man has two or three experiences," I say, "two or three experiences at the outside, that's what a man has had when he tells stories about himself, when he tells stories at all: a pattern of experience — but not a story," I say, "not a story." (*G* 46)]

The proposition is that the recurrent patterns within self-narration, or narration in general, enable identity to be discerned, but specifically as a tension between varying stories or statements rather than in the falsifying fixity of the "Ich-Geschichte" or story of the self.

A recurrent theme in the novel, however, and thus, as it were, an element in the "pattern of experience," or, more accurately, pattern of thought revealed by the narrator's multiple stories, is the need for such a fiction of the self in order to function *as* a self. It is here that an uncomfortable gap is opened up: between, on the one hand, the role or fiction of the self with its contingent demand for relative consistency and coherence and, on the other, the larger reality of the self as in excess of the limitations of coherent self-narration. This gap poses a challenge to the individual of highly developed self-awareness who must live out this selfhood — hence the narrator's envy of the barman, since the latter apparently is not troubled in this way. The problem is elaborated in several narrative variants placed toward the beginning of the novel, most extensively in the story of Enderlin.

Enderlin exists in a state of painful division within himself. Moving as normal among his friends, accepting their congratulations on his appointment to a chair at Harvard, and upholding the correct front, he is not sufficiently at one with the role being thrust upon him to be confident of being able to sustain it:

> Die Vorlesung, die Enderlin in Harvard halten sollte, hat er. Und er brauchte sie bloß in den Koffer zu packen. Aber er kann nicht. Was überzeugt, sind nicht Leistungen, sondern die Rolle, die einer spielt. Das ist's, was Enderlin spürt, was ihn erschreckt. Krank werden, um nicht nach Harvard fahren zu können, wäre das Einfachste. Enderlin kann keine Rolle spielen — (*G* 118)

> [The lecture which Enderlin is supposed to deliver at Harvard is already written. All he has to do is to pack it in his case. But he can't. What convinces is not a person's achievements, but the role he plays. This is what Enderlin feels, what scares him. To fall ill, so that he can't go to Harvard, would be the simplest thing. Enderlin can't play any role. (*G* 113)]

Enderlin's professional failure of nerve is contrasted with the counter-story of an ambassador, a man who similarly sees through his own role: "Er hat eingesehen, daß er gar nicht die Exzellenz ist, für die ihn die Welt, unter Kronleuchtern empfangen, zu halten vorgibt" ("He has realized that he is not the Excellency for which the world, attending receptions beneath chandeliers, pretends to take him"; *G* 119/113, translation modified). Unlike Enderlin, though, the ambassador chooses to uphold his role:

> Er wählt das Größere: die Rolle. Seine Selbsterkenntnis bleibt sein Geheimnis. Er erfüllt sein Amt. [. . .] Und es geschieht, was aussieht wie ein Wunder: indem er eigentlich bloß spielt, leistet er nicht nur Ordentliches wie bisher, sondern Außerordentliches. [. . .] Er meistert seine Rolle, die somit die Rolle eines Hochstaplers ist, kraft des Geheimnisses, das er nicht preisgibt, nie, auch nicht unter vier Augen. (*G* 119)

> [He chooses that which is greater: the role. His self-knowledge remains his secret. He fulfils his office. [. . .] And something happens that looks like a miracle: while he is really only acting a part he not only achieves good solid results as heretofore, but exceptional

results. [. . .] He masters his role, which is that of a confidence trick-
ster, by virtue of the secret which he does not give away, never, not
even in a tête-à-tête. (*G* 113–14)]

Through his role-play, the ambassador makes history: he saves a city from
bombing, his name enters the history books, after his death streets are named
after him. Historical agency (traditionally a male preserve) is here presented
as the product of role-play successfully upheld in spite of potentially paralyz-
ing insight into its fictionality, the product, then, of self-mastery.

The inherent precariousness of identity as (social) role-play is
approached from another angle in the incidental narrative (recounted by
the first-person narrator to the barman) of Otto, a milkman and solid citizen who, having delivered milk for twenty-one years without any adverse
incident, suddenly experiences a breakdown:

"Es war ein Abend im Frühling, ein Sonnabend, als der Otto, seine
Pfeife rauchend wie all die Jahre, auf dem Balkon seines Reihenei-
genheims stand, das zwar an der Dorfstraße gelegen war, jedoch
mit so viel Gärtlein versehen, daß die Scherben niemand gefährden
konnten. Nämlich aus Gründen, die ihm selbst verschlossen blie-
ben, nahm der Otto plötzlich einen Blumentopf, Geranium, wenn
ich nicht irre, und schmetterte denselben ziemlich senkrecht in das
Gärtlein hinunter, was sofort nicht nur Scherben, sondern Aufsehen
verursachte. [. . .] Dieses öffentliche Aufsehen, scheint es, verdroß
unseren Milchmann dermaßen, daß er sämtliche Blumentöpfe,
siebzehn an der Zahl, in das Gärtlein hinunterschmetterte [. . .]. Seit-
her galt der Otto als verrückt. [. . .] sein Ich hatte sich verbraucht,
das kann's geben, und ein anderes fiel ihm nicht ein. Es war entsetz-
lich." (*G* 50–51)

["It was one evening in spring, a Saturday, as Otto, smoking his pipe
as all through the years, was standing on the balcony of his detached
house, which, although it was on the village street, had so much
little garden round it that the pieces couldn't hurt anybody. You see,
for reasons unknown even to himself, Otto suddenly seized a flower
pot, a geranium if I'm not mistaken, and threw it pretty well verti-
cally down into his little garden, which immediately caused not only
broken pieces, but also a sensation. [. . .] This public sensation, it
seems, so vexed our milkman that he hurled all the flowerpots, sev-
enteen in number, down into the little garden [. . .]. After that Otto
was considered mad. [. . .] his ego [*Ich*] was worn out, that can happen, and he couldn't think of another one. It was horrible." (*G* 48)]

The recurrent motif of throwing objects (encountered already in the previous chapter, in the dream chapter in *Malina*) — here flower pots,
elsewhere in the novel whisky glasses and bottles — is a signal throughout

the work for the exhaustion of the adopted role, and the return of what has been repressed in the process of the construction of publicly accepted and acceptable identity and self-mastery. This is in marked contrast to the reading of such gestures in Bachmann's text, where they function as the violent assertion of power and terrorize the object of the assault.

Notwithstanding this point of contrast, certain parallels with the conceptualization of identity in Bachmann's *Malina* have, perhaps surprisingly, become apparent here: surprisingly, since on the basis of the male figures in Bachmann's text — Malina, Ivan, and the father/murderer — one might have expected the masculine identity to be less reflexive, more confidently and un-self-consciously coherent and unified. Counter to such an expectation, the model of selfhood in Frisch's novel is closer to *Ich*'s. The construction of the identity and experience of the first-person narrator out of the patterns common to, but also the tensions of difference between, the multiple role-plays and subsidiary narratives points to a conceptualization of the self as inherently fragmentary and potentially contradictory, and thus as reduced by the fixity of the coherent publicly accepted and acceptable role. The public or social identity, meanwhile, is posited as a construction from which inconsistent, spontaneous, immediate, and therefore vulnerable, elements have been eliminated, just as it is with Malina, the publicly acceptable face of the *Ich*/Malina self and the "identity" that remains at the close of Bachmann's novel. The potentially debilitating gap between public role and the interiority of the private self, meanwhile, addressed in particular in the Enderlin narrative, has some features strikingly in common with the characterization of Eugen in the 1962–63 phase of Bachmann's work on the *Todesarten* project. A marked difference between the two texts is that Frisch's novel does not posit a differential gendering of the two poles, public versus private, of selfhood. The narrating "ich" and the fragmentary roles he projects in order to approach, via elaborate circumscription, the underlying reality of the self are all male. It is only for the female author that the entry into the public sphere and the accession into its regulatory practices of self-containment and -control can be represented in terms of the generation of a "masculine" double, and she retains a sense of her femininity as inserting a distance between herself and the public "role." In Frisch's text, by contrast, the gender opposition functions not as a way of symbolizing the tension between the fragmentary and alogical totality of the self versus the construction of coherent self-identity, but, as will be demonstrated, as the site in which the fragmenting male self seeks once again to secure his masculine identity vis-à-vis the female Other.

The structural parallels between the two texts' approach to the issue of self-identity are an indication that both are responding symptomatically to a shift taking place in the broader conceptualization of identity and selfhood within the localized theoretical and philosophical environment of this period. And indeed, the premise that social and personal identity is a reflexively constructed role, and that to function as a subject in contemporary Western and westernized society requires the strength of mind to uphold a narrative self-construction that is perceived as such, corresponds in remarkable detail to the account of self-identity in late modernity proposed by Anthony Giddens.[11] One of the key features of the late-modern age, according to Giddens, is its institutional reflexivity. Understood as "a post-traditional order, but not one in which the sureties of tradition and habit have been replaced by the certitude of rational knowledge" (2–3) as the Enlightenment thinkers who initiated the modern historical dynamic anticipated (21), late modernity — "our present-day world" — "institutionalises the principle of radical doubt and insists that all knowledge takes the form of hypotheses: claims which may very well be true, but which are in principle always open to revision and may have at some point to be abandoned" (3). Within this inherently dynamic and unstable cultural environment, the self, too, becomes subject to reflexive organization, as opposed to being guaranteed as an inherited position within a traditional social order: "The reflexive project of the self, which consists in the sustaining of coherent, yet continuously revised, biographical narratives, takes place in the context of multiple choice as filtered through abstract systems" (3).

However, if a person's identity is to be found, as Giddens claims, "in the capacity *to keep a particular narrative going*" (54, italics in the original), the "project" of self-identity is, as already indicated, potentially threatened by the reflexive awareness that the narrative of the self *is* narrative, that is: a form of fiction.[12] Frisch's text displays multiple symptoms of the debilitating effect of self-reflexive awareness. In the first place, there is the sense of entrapment in one's role. This is conveyed most acutely in the narrator's hospital dream of a horse's head emerging from a granite wall, "ein Lebewesen, es hat aus dem Granit herauszuspringen versucht, was im ersten Anlauf nicht gelungen ist und nie, ich seh's, nie gelingen wird" ("a living creature, it has tried to jump out of the granite, which it didn't succeed in doing at the first attempt and, I can see, will never succeed in doing"; G 12/11). This dream is later passed on to Enderlin:

> aus diesem Granit heraus, wie ein Schrei, aber lautlos, plötzlich ein Pferdekopf mit roter Mähne, aufwiehernd, aber lautlos, Schaum im Gebiß, aber der Leib bleibt drin, nur der Kopf ist heraus, die Augen groß und irr, Gnade suchend. (*G* 153–54)

> [out of this granite, like a scream, but silent, suddenly a horse's head with a red mane, neighing, but soundlessly, foam on its teeth, but its body remains inside, only the head is out, the eyes big and mad, seeking mercy. (*G* 146)]

The horse's head comes to symbolize the entrapment of the "living creature" that is the individual self in the constrictions of the "I"[13] that, as the contrast in these passages between head (*Kopf*) and body (*Leib*) suddenly make apparent, is so very much a product of rational self-control at the expense of the corporeal. It seems that what Enderlin seeks in his spontaneous sexual encounter with the text's central female character is precisely a suspension of self-consciousness in the *bodily* experience of immediacy in the present — "Sie wollten, was nur einmal möglich ist: das Jetzt" ("They wanted what is possible only once: the now"; *G* 73/69). In this sense, the dimension of spontaneous desiring in this text corresponds to the temporality of the "feminine" *Ich* in Bachmann's *Malina*. Yet desire's extension of the singular encounter in the Now into longer term relationship (a possibility played out by the narrator in imagination, *G* 133–37/127–30) threatens the return of narrative, social embeddedness, and a Nietzschean eternal repetition of the same: " — denn die Zukunft, das wußte er, das bin ich, ihr Gatte, ich bin die Wiederholung, die Geschichte, die Endlichkeit und der Fluch in allem, ich bin das Altern von Minute zu Minute" (" — because the future, he knew, that's me, her husband, I am the repetition, the story, the finitude and the curse in everything, I am the process of ageing minute by minute"; *G* 73/70). The underlying fear of repetition and the concomitant existential ennui that afflicts the narrator, as indicated by the leitmotiv of his boredom (*Langeweile*) throughout the novel, translates itself into a death-wish: the swift death at the wheel of a car that opens the novel is described by the narrator as "ein Tod wie gewünscht" ("the sort of death anyone would like to have"), for the corpse "braucht keine Geschichte [*sic*] mehr wie Kleider" ("doesn't need stories like clothes any more"; 8/8); and the novel's penultimate scene again focuses on a corpse that *almost* succeeds in floating away without a story (*G* 319/303).

According to this reading, Frisch's novel is — with its characteristically oblique methods — addressing a failure in the Enlightenment conceptualization of (male) subjectivity. Rationality and self-reflexivity, instead of being the instruments of widespread social improvement and the source of the male subject's self-confidence, have become a source of crippling self-alienation. "Identity" has become a role-play, and the cultural over-investment in rational self-control and self-containment makes of the role a straitjacket. If the Enlightenment's revolution in thought promised individuality to all, or at any rate to all bourgeois male citizens, what it has delivered is the requirement for predictable, calculable behavior that effectually entraps the individual subject in a role from which his escape "will never succeed." The *conscious awareness* of such entrapment paralyzes the energy to live, as is played out above all in the Enderlin plot. The object of Frisch's critique appears here in broad terms as the social order of late modernity: the social order damned by Horkheimer and Adorno for its devastating reduction of human multiplicity and for its underlying principle, the "mimesis: of death."[14] This is in keeping with Frisch's negative representation of the imprisoning trends in the social construction of identity elsewhere in his work, notably in the 1954 novel *Stiller*.[15] At the same time, the novel's central interest in the moment of collapse of the male-female relationship points to another, more specific cause of the male narrator's existential malaise: the catastrophic self-repetition that leads to the destruction of relationship as the site of the ontological security that, in Giddens's account of self-identity, is the necessary counterbalance to the intrinsic insecurity of life in late-modern society.

The Male-Female Relationship: The Nexus of Masculine Identity

The recurring scene in the deserted apartment (*G* 18–20, 198, 313–14/18–20, 188–89, 298) may be read on at least two levels. Taken as a key to the "experience" of the narrator as an individual, it appears in strictly personal terms. The narrator has been left by his female partner, and the "pattern of experience" that emerges from the novel's multiple role-plays and subsidiary narratives points to the narrator's inability (nowhere directly and explicitly acknowledged) to deal with his partner's affairs with other men or to control his jealous anger. There are two key moments in the novel in which the narrator's fictional role-plays, Svoboda on one occasion and Gantenbein during a confession of his pretense of blindness on the other, lose their self-control, become violent toward her and smash glass (*G* 165, 231/157, 219). This signifies, as in the story of Otto the milkman, the exhaustion of their social role — and perhaps a more general destructive desire, a reassertion of atavistic masculinity, like the father's in *Malina's* dream chapter.[16] In this reading, the novel's narrative process can be understood in personal therapeutic terms. The role-plays of Enderlin (through which the motivation for entering into the erotic relationship is explored) and of Svoboda and Gantenbein (which focus on the inability to master jealousy) by implication permit the narrator to work through the prehistory of the scene of his desertion at a distance from himself. This reading is borne out by the fact that in the negative plots, the first-person narrator appears in a commentating, analytical relationship to the named fictional character positions. So, for example, where Enderlin, caught up by desire, chooses to miss the flight that would carry him away from further involvement with "Lila" and, in returning to her, initiates the eternal repetition of the same that is established relationship, the narrator has the strength (and coldness) to allow the sexual encounter to remain singular and takes the flight (*G* 129–33/123–27). In relation to Svoboda, meanwhile, the narrator sets himself at a distance, both by reverting himself at this point to the

Enderlin role (i.e., to the role as "other man" as opposed to the deceived husband) and via his repeated assertion "Ich möchte nicht Svoboda sein" ("I shouldn't like to be Svoboda"; *G* 233, 240/221, 228). The role-play of Gantenbein as pretend blind man, by contrast, emerges as an alternative narrative of the self that offers a strategy for self-discipline — and thus also a parallel in the private sphere of relationship to the public role successfully upheld by the ambassador. The role is intrinsically self-reflexive, since there is a difficult pretense to uphold, and here the acting self and the analytical self are conceptualized as a single entity, as the first-person pronoun and the named character position merge: "*Mein* Name sei Gantenbein" ("Let *my* name be Gantenbein"). The self-discipline imposed by the requirement to maintain the pretense of blindness enables the narrator-as-Gantenbein to avoid the shame of regression into the atavism of jealous temper, albeit at the price of genuine relationship, of being known by the other.[17]

On a second level, the scene of desertion lends itself to a reading in cultural-historical terms, which also brings into view the historical specificity of the male-female relationship as represented in the novel as the nexus of the now-problematic construction of masculine identity. The presence in the description of the deserted apartment of the ancient symbols of bread and wine in a state of decay (*G* 18–19/18) signal the status of the scene as symbolic of the decay of the home. It is, moreover, explicitly identified not as a joint home, but as the home of the male narrator/subject: "Ich sitze in einer Wohnung: — meiner Wohnung" ("I'm sitting in a flat — my flat"; *G* 18/18). The desertion of the home by the female partner has its correlation in the refusal of the text's female characters of the traditional domestic role as housewife. Thus Camilla Huber, as the first female figure to appear in the narrative, insists that she is "keine Hausfrau" ("no housewife"; *G* 36/34), while Lila, usually presented as an actress, is emphatically not placed in a subservient domestic role even in the passage in which the narrator removes her profession: "Sie ist eine Frau, aber kein Untertan, also durchaus eine Frau von heute" ("She is a woman, but not a subservient being, thus entirely a woman of today"; *G* 220/209). These female figures are, moreover, represented as independently mobile, a characteristic of the modern subject. Camilla enters the novel as the albeit unskilled driver of the symbolically named Karmann automobile (*G* 29/28), while Lila is variously the owner of an Austin sports car (*G* 184/175), a car of her own (*G* 220/209), and above all associated with airports, to which she is repeatedly presented as returning from travel elsewhere. This contrasts with the male narrator's symbolically significant temporary immobility following a driving accident on black ice in the frame narrative (*G* 22–25/21–24).

The mobility of the female characters and their preoccupation with their own (social) roles (Lila as actress!) poses a cultural-historical challenge to the text's male characters: to reinvent a masculine subjectivity that has traditionally defined itself in opposition to an immobile, domesticated, essentially subordinate woman who, in her very subordination, takes on the properties of a mirror reflecting back to the male his own superiority. As Virginia Woolf described in her 1928 essay *A Room of One's Own:* "Women have served all these centuries as looking-glasses possessing the magic and delicious power of reflecting the figure of man at twice its natural size. Without that power probably the earth would still be swamp and jungle."[18] Seen in this light, the motif of jealousy, like that of the narrator in Proust's *La Prisonnière,* with which the Gantenbein-Lila plot bears a certain resemblance, becomes understandable as the male subject's anxiety vis-à-vis the increasing independence of woman and her evasion of his control. This anxiety, furthermore, is generated out of the analogy with his own quest as subject for the renewing vitality of desire for other Others: thus Gantenbein draws his fantasies of Lila's deceptions of him "aus dem Arsenal meiner eignen Geheimnisse" ("from the arsenal of my own secrets"; *G* 183/174). In this context, it is striking that the one scene in which a declaration of love for Lila is made is one in which she is observed asleep — in other words, immobile, controllable by the male gaze (*G* 192/182–83).[19]

In this cultural-historical reading, in which the male narrator figures as the personification of the male subject within a social order in which the female Other has become independently mobile, the different role-plays appear as the testing-ground for viable male/masculine subject positions. If the Enderlin plot serves to state the problem — a subjectivity that has become divided within itself, vacillating, instinctually attracted to the female, seeking in the sexual encounter with her the corporeal experience of the Now, yet afraid of entrapment in the (self-) repetition of long-term relationship — the plots of Svoboda and Gantenbein when *not* pretending to be blind play out the collapse of the role-play of male subjectivity into violence and destructive rage. Klaus-Jürgen Bruder's comments in an essay on "Masculinity and Sexual Abuse" are illuminating here:

> He [the abusive male] knows that he does not become a man by employing violence but rather through the possibility of employing violence and his control of this possibility. The concept of (self-) control belongs to the (self-) image of the man, and, with that, responsibility. His doubt in his ability to control himself, to remain in control of the situation, places his masculinity in question.[20]

What remains at the conclusion of these plots is not only desertion, but the male characters' shame at having lost their self-control. Gantenbein, as long as he upholds the pretense of being blind, emerges by contrast as a model of self-mastery, as well as being attractive in narrative terms for the comical self-irony that his role offers the narrator. But beneath the comedy, more is at stake. On the surface, Gantenbein solves the problem of male subjectivity vis-à-vis the mobility and independence (also economic) of modern woman by accepting a reversal of roles. Thus as Lila's supposedly blind husband, it is he who stays at home and takes care of the household, concealing his labor, moreover, in keeping with the traditional role of the bourgeois housewife.[21] Lila, meanwhile, is the breadwinner who picks up the bills and provides him with pin money for clothes and gifts. In this way, the potential for conflict in a relationship in which both partners earn, while it is still only the male who is publicly treated as the earner, is avoided (*G* 88/84).

From the internal perspective, however, the Gantenbein role offers the possibility of shoring up a traditional masculine identity as controlling master. In the first place, the female characters are presented as variously incompetent. Camilla Huber, for example, is a poor driver, and Gantenbein's superiority is presented in categorical terms:

> Er [Gantenbein] ahnte schon die täglichen Schwierigkeiten seiner Rolle, beispielsweise neben einer Frau zu sitzen, die steuert, und dabei kein Wort zu sagen, keine Seufzer zu atmen, keine männlichen Lehren zu erteilen, nicht einmal zu zucken, wenn er sieht, was sie übersieht, einen Lastwagen von rechts, und freundlich zu bleiben, wenn sie, ohne ihren Fehler zu merken, tatsächlich noch einmal vorbeikommt. (*G* 31)

> [He [Gantenbein] was already getting an inkling of the daily difficulties of his role, for example to sit next to a woman who is driving and not to say a word, not to breathe a sigh, not to impart masculine instruction, not even to wince when he sees something she misses, a lorry coming from the right, and to remain friendly when she, not noticing her mistakes, actually gets by once again. (*G* 30)]

Lila, meanwhile, is disorganized (like *Ich* in Bachmann's novel), neither fully in control of her finances nor of the household — she mislays things in the kitchen, and leaves the shower hanging over the bath, thereby causing a flood. She is, moreover, a deceiver in more senses than just the sexual: in a scene placed late in the novel, she takes over the role of housewife to delight her guests at a party that Gantenbein has largely prepared (*G* 218–19/206–8). She conforms, in short, to the image of desirable femininity created by a male-oriented culture: attractive, glamorous, a prestigious object who reflects well on her husband, and simultaneously capricious, chaotic, inferior — not a man. In the second place, Gantenbein can register all of this because he is, of course, not blind, but sighted, merely concealing his capacity to see. It became a commonplace of the feminist theory of the 1970s that male-generated, phallocentric accounts of the subject (notably those generated by psychoanalysis) privileged sight or vision in the construction of self-other relations, as Elizabeth Grosz summarizes:

Of all the senses, vision remains the one which most readily confirms the separation of subject from object. Vision performs a distancing function, leaving the looker unimplicated in or uncontaminated by its object. With all of the other senses, there is a contiguity between subject and object, if not an internalization and incorporation of the object by the subject. [. . .] As Sartre (1974) recognized, the look is the domain of domination and mastery; it provides access to its object without necessarily being in contact with it.[22]

Moreover, Luce Irigaray's comments on the displacement of (male) potency into the gaze in Freud's account of femininity reads as acutely relevant to what is going on in Frisch's narrator's construction of the Gantenbein role: "So Freud will see, without being seen? Without being seen seeing? Without even being questioned about the potency of his gaze?"[23] For what the pretense of blindness permits is the greater knowledge of the one who sees without being seen seeing. Thinking her husband blind, Lila makes no effort to conceal the lovers with whom she betrays him; he sees all — or thinks he does. The Gantenbein role is a fantasy of knowledge and control, of a mastery that rescues itself from the threat of castration and self-loss.

It is not until quite late in the novel that the narrator arrives at the realization that the attractive (self-) mastery represented by the Gantenbein role paradoxically has deception as its precondition. Thus, while the conclusion of the fairy-tale narrative of Ali and Alil (*G* 161–63/153–55), told by Gantenbein to Camilla Huber, seems to express a wish-fantasy — the male as longing for love and affirmation of himself even when he loses his self in wounded rage and violence — the pattern of the narrative play in the novel as a whole reveals that what the male subject *really* desires is paradoxically the material resistance of the other, encapsulated in the word "Verrat" (betrayal), in the mastery of which he confirms his selfhood to himself:

> Ich lechze nach Verrat. Ich möchte wissen, daß ich bin. Was mich nicht verrät, verfällt dem Verdacht, daß es nur in meiner Einbildung lebt, und ich möchte aus meiner Einbildung heraus, ich möchte in der Welt sein. Ich möchte im Innersten verraten sein. Das ist merkwürdig. (*G* 270)

> [I am hankering after betrayal. I want to know that I exist. That which does not betray me is subject to the suspicion that it exists only in my imagination, and I want to come out from my imagination, I want to be in the world. I want to be betrayed in my innermost being. That's odd. (*G* 256, translation modified)]

In terms of the male-female relationship, this means that Gantenbein/the narrator *requires* Lila to deceive him — hence the fact that her deception is among the first characteristics ascribed to her (*G* 82/78) — since in controlling her deception, if not in actuality, then at least in his visual mastery of it, he confirms his identity as master to himself.[24] If she does not deceive him, he is robbed of his role: "Lila betrügt ihn nicht. / Dafür hat er keine Rolle" ("Lila isn't deceiving him. / For these circumstances he has no role"; *G* 311/296). Notably, it is at the point of this latter realization that the Gantenbein narrative comes to a halt. In other words, the "role" of male selfhood has no basis, no motivation if the "feminine" is not conceived of as resistant matter to be mastered.[25] We are, in effect, back with Ivan and his demand for an evasive "femininity" through which his masculinity is affirmed, telling *Ich* that she can only captivate by using tactics and playing what Ivan calls the Game (*Malina* 84/50). The risk of real relationship is nowhere in sight.

Malina and *Mein Name sei Gantenbein*: Two Versions of the Subject under the Conditions of Late Modernity

Reading Bachmann's *Malina* and Frisch's *Mein Name sei Gantenbein* alongside each other on the terms delineated here brings them into view as alternative versions of the construction of inherently masculine-connoted subjectivity, with certain of the differences between them traceable to a differential investment, according to the sex of the author, in the gendered positions within a cultural-historically established symbolic order. As versions of the construction of subjectivity, both works are symptomatic of a historical moment — termed here, with Giddens, "late modernity" — in which the conditions of selfhood have become exposed to self-conscious intellectual awareness, so that the "project of the self" (Giddens) has become self-reflexive. In both works, identity within society and within language as the medium of social communication — one's existence as an "Ich" or "I"[26] — is understood as a narrative construction or role, of which it is socially required that it be coherent, unified, internally consistent. However, both also reveal a conception of the self underlying social identity as a far more complex, manifold, fragmentary, alogical material base.

The differences between them are marked, however. The work of the male author Max Frisch displays the strains under which the bourgeois male subject has come with the development of an increasingly self-reflexive social order. The traditional role of historical agent has become exposed as just that: a role. Self-consciousness has opened up a potentially debilitating gap between the interiority of the self — the reflecting mind — and the capacity for action in the public arena. In continuation of a central theme of the pre–Second World War modernist novel,[27] the interior selfhood of the male subject in Frisch's novel is conceived of as highly complex, beyond the grasp of the linear constructions of conventional narrative. The publicly accepted and acceptable identity, by contrast, is felt by the individual to be a "role" imposed (among other things by language) and confining, albeit necessary in order to function as a self within society at all. Prominent is the fear of the "role" as an eternal repetition of the same.

Particularly endangering under these circumstances is the shift taking place in the social construction of the relationship to the female Other as the latter leaves her formerly static and contained position in the symbolic order and becomes mobile. Frisch's novel reveals the extent to which male subjectivity relies on the otherness of woman as the guarantee of selfhood, and an underlying motivation of the novel's narrative play is the reconstruction of masculine (self-) mastery vis-à-vis persistently devalued "femininity." The narrative's quest for a viable masculine identity breaks off at the point at which the narrator sees through this motivation.[28] That Lila is a *projection*, a female/feminine Other generated from within the male psyche as its counterpart is only partially acknowledged, notably through the trace of her name. However, in marked contrast with the conceptualization of the relationship between the feminine *Ich* and the masculine Malina as complementary principles *within* the individual psyche in Bachmann's novel, Lila as archetypal Woman remains irreducibly Other in relation to the male roles generated by Frisch's narrator: she is projected beyond the male subject's psyche to become a position opposed to it.

In the female author Ingeborg Bachmann's representation, the publicly accepted and acceptable coherent identity is only conceivable in masculine terms — as rational, analytical, and self-contained — and as a male persona: Malina. However, by denoting the time of the novel as Today, the temporality of immediacy in the present prior to the narrative construction of the coherent self, she is able to generate a position named *Ich* with which she can identify as author, but which does not conform to the conventional expectations of self-identity. Rather, the pronoun "I" serves as a referent that holds together a mass of fragmented and alogical thoughts and impulses, with *Ich*'s "speech" traversed by kinetic rhythm and musicality. That this position is feminine serves both to thematize the difficult relationship of woman to the symbolic order that, as figured in the violent patriarchal figure of the father/murderer, denies her subjectivity, and simultaneously to reveal a history of the male-subject-as-norm, personified by Malina, which is achieved via the repression, the jettisoning as the "feminine" of the polyvalence and corporeality underlying this subject. Where the male subject represented by Frisch's narrator ultimately appears narcissistic and self-absorbed, so intent on retrieving his masculinity-as-mastery that he remains largely blind to the conditions of his own subject formation,[29] Bachmann's complex conceptualization of the tension of opposing principles within the psyche carries the greater self-knowledge, though the far-more-fluid and would-be *relational* self figured in *Ich* remains stymied by the lack of response from the male Other, Ivan.

The incompatibility of the "masculine" self, wedded by the imperatives of cultural history to his singularity and self-sameness, and the "feminine" relational self, predisposed to construct herself anew in each new relationship, is the focus of the passages that are the most obvious point of cross-referential contact between Bachmann's novel and Frisch's. It is given to the deceived husband Svoboda in Frisch's text to articulate the male's disquiet at the adaptability of woman:

> Der naturhafte und durch keine Gleichberechtigung tilgbare Unterschied zwischen Mann und Frau bestehe darin, daß es immer der Mann ist, der in der Umarmung handelt. *Er bleibt er selbst,* und das weiß die Frau; sie kennt ihn. [. . .] Umgekehrt weiß der Mann keineswegs, was eine Frau, wenn sie weg geht, in der Umarmung mit einem andern ist; er kann es überhaupt nicht erraten. *Die Frau ist ungeheuer durch ihre fast grenzenlose Anpassung,* und wenn sie von einem andern kommt, ist sie nicht dieselbe. (*G* 284, italics added)

> [The natural difference between man and woman, which no equality of rights can do away with, lies in the fact that it is always the man who acts during lovemaking. *He remains himself,* and the woman knows that; she knows him. [. . .] On the other hand, the man doesn't know at all what a woman, when she goes away, is like in the embrace of another man; he can't guess at all. *The woman is monstrous in her almost limitless adaptability,* and when she comes from another man she is not the same. (*G* 269–70, italics added)]

The opinions are clichéd and, to be fair, are presented with a degree of irony. But they betray an investment in the masculine self-image as singular and constant, and the fear of the monstrous changeability of the female Other. Bachmann's retort[30] is ruthlessly satirical:

> Es muß ja einen Menschen schon in die Krankheit führen, wenn er selber so wenig Neues erlebt, sich immerzu wiederholen muß, ein Mann zum Beispiel beißt mich ins Ohrläppchen, aber nicht weil es mein Ohrläppchen ist oder weil er, vernarrt in das Ohrläppchen, unbedingt hineinbeißen muß, sondern er beißt, weil er alle anderen Frauen auch in die Ohrläppchen gebissen hat, in kleine oder größere, in rotblaue, in blasse, in fühllose, in gefühlvolle, es ist ihm völlig gleich, was die Ohrläppchen dazu meinen. [. . .] Für ihn ist es ja leicht, wenig an die Frauen zu denken, denn sein krankes System ist unfehlbar, er wiederholt, er hat sich wiederholt, er wird sich wiederholen. [. . .] von einem Mann zum andern muß sich ein Frauenkörper alles abgewöhnen und wieder an etwas ganz Neues gewöhnen.

Aber ein Mann zieht mit seinen Gewohnheiten friedlich weiter, manchmal hat er eben Glück damit, meistens keines. (*M* 269–71)

[It must make a person sick to have so few new experiences that he has to constantly repeat himself, for example a man bites my earlobe, but not because it's my earlobe or because he's crazy about earlobes and feels a compulsion to bite them, he bites them because he's bitten the earlobes of all the other women, whether small or large, purple, pale, sensitive or numb, he doesn't care what the earlobes think about it. [. . .] It's easy for him to think so little about women, for his diseased system is infallible, he repeats, he has repeated, he will repeat. [. . .] from one man to another a woman's body has to forget everything and get accustomed to something entirely new. But a man goes quite peaceably from one to another with all his established habits, sometimes he gets lucky, mostly he doesn't. (*M* 177–78, translation modified)][31]

At this point of exchange, the two novels seem to embody the impasse of an age-old mutual hatred between the sexes that is exacerbated by their mutual dependency.

However, a recent article by Carl Pietzker offers a more sympathetic analysis of the state of play with regard to male subjectivity at this point in late modernity. Under the title "The Motif of the Man, Who, Although He Loves, Goes to War: On the History of the Construction of Masculinity in the European Tradition," Pietzker begins by investigating classical narratives concerning the emasculation of the male in the love relationship — "Such a love means the loss of masculine-phallic activities that profoundly shape the civilizing of the world"[32] — and the retrieval of masculine identity in the desertion of woman for heroic male activity. He offers a psychoanalytical reading, whereby the reconstruction of masculinity is achieved with the aid of "triangulating" figures such as military commanders (the male psyche's perspective on the *père symbolique* perhaps). Such figures are, however, absent from narratives of the modern period, such as *Faust*, where the male figure's reconstitution of masculine identity is achieved internally, but at the price of guilt at the desertion. In the post-1945 period, Pietzker notes, "the motif has reversed itself: the man is left by the woman and exposed in his dependency and desertedness" (159). Peter Handke's *Die Stunde der wahren Empfindung* (A Moment of True Feeling, 1975) and *Die linkshändige Frau* (The Left-Handed Woman, 1976), and Botho Strauß's *Rumor* (Tumult, 1980) are adduced as examples. Pietzker's speculative reading of this as wish-fantasy is surely questionable: "Presumably, the male author thus fulfils his wish that the woman keep her distance from a man who is uncertain about himself, and that she no longer threaten him" (160). But the conclusion he draws is intriguing and undoubtedly relevant to a reading of the similar constellation in Frisch's *Gantenbein*. Noting the growing visibility in contemporary fiction of "man's many-tiered ambivalence" toward woman, "his oscillation between love, even enchantment, fear, hate, and flight," Pietzker diagnoses "the end of old phallic-dominating identity":

> This end also is an opportunity. Were a man to subject himself to his ambivalences and still remain close to a woman, a concrete woman could emerge from behind the mother-images. Perhaps a new masculine identity would become possible, which no longer binds itself to the early drama of dis-identification [from the mother] and no longer requires forced, fearful phallic activity or triangulating duty. Could empathy, recognition of the woman as an Other, and reciprocity increase? (161)

As a conclusion, this points to the challenge to be faced by the male subject in our possibly transitional time: to renounce his attachment to phallic power in the interests both of sustainable relationship with the individualized other and of his own psychical completeness. It is striking, in the light of the comparative readings of Bachmann and Frisch presented here, that the emergent female subject, with so much less of an investment in phallic identity, has the advantage over the male in terms of her predisposition to the relational construction of subjectivity and her greater openness to the internal ambivalences and tensions between "masculine" and "feminine" aspects of the psyche.[33] She also, on the evidence at least of these two novels, has the greater sense of the cultural urgency of the transformation of the determinants of identity and subjectivity. Her disadvantage is that she remains largely disempowered by a still patriarchal social order.

Notes

[1] First published in English as *A Wilderness of Mirrors* (1965), re-issued as *Gantenbein*, trans. Michael Bullock (London: Methuen, 1982).

[2] Lore Toman, "Bachmanns *Malina* und Frischs *Mein Name sei Gantenbein*: Zwei Seiten des gleichen Lebens," in *Literatur und Kritik* 12 (1977): 274–78 (first publ. in *Die Tat* [Zurich], 24 August 1974). The link between the female character Lila in *Mein Name sei Gantenbein* and Frisch's former partner Ingeborg Bachmann is addressed explicitly by Frisch in his prose work *Montauk*, published in 1975 (notably again after Bachmann's death), in an apparent effort to justify his position.

[3] Monika Albrecht, *Die andere Seite: Untersuchungen zur Bedeutung von Werk und Person Max Frischs in Ingeborg Bachmanns "Todesarten"* (Würzburg: Königshausen & Neumann, 1989); Albrecht, "Mein Name sei Gantenbein — mein Name? Malina: Zum intertextuellen Verfahren der 'imaginären Autobiographie' *Malina*," in *Ingeborg Bachmanns 'Malina,'* ed. Andrea Stoll (Frankfurt/Main:

Suhrkamp, 1992), 265–87. For further discussion of the Bachmann-Frisch and/or *Malina-Gantenbein* connection, see Gerhard F. Probst, "Mein Name sei Malina: Nachdenken über Ingeborg Bachmann," *Modern Austrian Literature* 11, no. 1 (1978): 103–19; Manfred Jurgensen, *Ingeborg Bachmann: Die neue Sprache* (Bern: Peter Lang, 1981), 100ff; J. Jabłkowska, "Ingeborg Bachmanns *Malina* und Max Frischs *Mein Name sei Gantenbein* — Varianten derselben Geschichte," *Acta Universitatis Lodziensis: Folia Litteraria* 11 (1984): 69–84; the chapter on the "literarischen Dialog Max Frischs mit Ingeborg Bachmann," in Walter Schmitz, *Max Frisch: Das Spätwerk (1962–1982). Eine Einführung* (Tübingen: Francke, 1985).

[4] In an article in the *Neue Zürcher Zeitung* in 2003, Franz Haas scolds Bachmann scholars (with the exception of Albrecht and Hans Höller) for avoiding commentary on the relevance of the Frisch-Bachmann relationship to the work, and calls for an end to such discretion; see Haas, "Fechten vor verhängten Spiegeln. Ingeborg Bachmann, Max Frisch und die diskrete Germanistik," *Neue Zürcher Zeitung*, 8 March 2003.

[5] See in particular the double review by Peter Hamm and Reinhard Baumgart in *Die Zeit*, 5 October 2000, 61, and Franz Haas, "Die Schnäppchenjäger," *Neue Zürcher Zeitung (Internationale Ausgabe)*, 16 November 2000, 35.

[6] Doris Fulda Merrifield, *Das Bild der Frau bei Max Frisch* (Freiburg im Breisgau: Universitätsverlag Becksmann, 1971); Ursula Haupt, *Weiblichkeit in Romanen Max Frischs* (Frankfurt am Main: Peter Lang, 1996); Liette Bohler, *Der Mythos der Weiblichkeit im Werke Max Frischs* (New York: Peter Lang, 1998). All of these studies are doctoral theses and all suffer from argumentative limitations. The most perceptive work on Frisch's women figures is that of Mona Knapp; since she is particularly interested in the figure of Hanna Piper in *Homo faber*, I shall be referring to her readings in the next chapter.

[7] Max Frisch, *Mein Name sei Gantenbein*, quoted from Frisch, *Gesammelte Werke in zeitlicher Folge*, ed. Hans Mayer with the cooperation of Walter Schmitz (Frankfurt am Main: Suhrkamp, 1976), vol. 5, 68 / *Gantenbein*, trans. Bullock, 65. Subsequent references appear in the text, identified as *G* (in German to the *Werke* edition, in English to the Bullock translation).

[8] Max Frisch, *Tagebuch 1946–1949*, quoted from Frisch, *Gesammelte Werke in zeitlicher Folge*, vol. 2, 378–79 / *Sketchbook 1946–1949*, trans. Geoffrey Skelton (New York and London: Harcourt Brace Jovanovich, 1977), 25. Subsequent references appear in the text, identified as *T*.

[9] These aspects are considered in some detail by Chloe E. M. Paver in *Narrative and Fantasy in the Post-War German Novel: A Study of Novels by Johnson, Frisch, Wolf, Becker, and Grass* (Oxford: Clarendon Press, 1999), chapter 3.

[10] I use the generic masculine here deliberately because the novel's narrator does not conceive of this process of self-creation as being something embarked upon by the female characters, with the possible exception of Camilla Huber whose public role as a manicurist is a cover for her presumed concealed activity as a prostitute.

[11] Anthony Giddens, *Modernity and Self-Identity: Self and Society in the Late Modern Age* (Cambridge: Polity Press, 1991). Subsequent references appear in the text as parenthetical page references.

[12] Jacques Lacan's theorem of the "mirror-stage" as a phase in the formation of the identity of the self is surely also symptomatic of the reflexive organization of selfhood in late modernity. Lacan's essay on the mirror stage moreover acknowledges correspondences between the imago of the coherent self in the mirror and fictional role-play; see Jacques Lacan, "The Mirror Stage as Formative of the Function of the I as Revealed in Psychoanalytic Experience" [1949], in Lacan, *Écrits: A Selection*, trans. Alan Sheridan (London: Routledge, 2001), 1–6. At the moment in which the theorem is formulated, however, it holds up a mirror, as it were, to the formation of identity before the mirror, introducing a double-reflexivity into the process. In brief, the formation of identity under the conditions of late modernity becomes an increasingly self-conscious and therefore potentially destabilizing process for the intellectual subject. This is reflected in the complexity of the construction of identity in Frisch's novel.

[13] See Paver's commentary on the motif of the horse's head, "generally taken to symbolize an unsuccessful attempt to break out of social roles," in *Narrative and Fantasy in the Post-War German Novel*, 49.

[14] Max Horkheimer and Theodor W. Adorno, *Dialectic of Enlightenment: Philosophical Fragments*, ed. Gunzelin Schmid Noerr, trans. Edmund Jephcott (Stanford: Stanford UP, 2002), 44.

[15] See also Giddens's account, via Christopher Lasch, of the narcissistic personality, "chronically bored, restlessly in search of instantaneous intimacy — of emotional titillation without involvement and dependence," and the link to contemporary socioeconomic order: "Consumer capitalism, with its efforts to standardize consumption and to shapes [*sic*] tastes through advertising, plays a basic role in furthering narcissism": Giddens, *Modernity and Self-Identity*, 172. The first passage quoted is from Christopher Lasch, *The Culture of Narcissism* (London: Abacus, 1980), 85.

[16] The collapse of the rational subject into violence, as the symptomatic expression of the violence by which the nonrational aspects of the self have been repressed, is analysed by Horkheimer and Adorno vis-à-vis the violence of fascism in the *Dialectic*; see discussion in chapter 2.

[17] On shame as a correlate of the requirements of upholding the narrative of self-identity, as "anxiety about the adequacy of the narrative by means of which the individual sustains a coherent biography," see Giddens, *Modernity and Self-Identity*, 64–69.

[18] Virginia Woolf, *A Room of One's Own* (London: Granada, 1977), 35.

[19] In Frisch's 1967 play *Biographie: Ein Spiel* (Biography: A Game), which is thematically very close to the *Gantenbein* novel, the male player, Kürmann, takes the game a step further, and immobilizes the female player Antoinette by shooting her dead.

[20] Klaus-Jürgen Bruder, "Masculinity and Sexual Abuse in Postwar German Society," in *Conceptions of Postwar German Masculinity*, ed. Jerome (Albany: SUNY Press, 2001), 113.

[21] See the discussion in chapter 1 of the demand placed on nineteenth-century bourgeois housewives to maintain "a façade of nonwork while at the same time

consolidating their reputation as good housewives and household managers": Lynn Abrams, *The Making of Modern Woman*, 132–33.

[22] Elizabeth Grosz, *Jacques Lacan: A Feminist Introduction* (London and New York: Routledge, 1990), 38.

[23] Luce Irigaray, *Speculum of the Other Woman*, trans. Gillian C. Gill (Ithaca, NY: Cornell UP, 1985), 47.

[24] This is strikingly similar to the relation of Proust's narrator to the elusive Albertine, the narration of which is sustained over many hundreds of pages in a manner inconceivable were she more tractable.

[25] Compare the consideration in chapter 2 of on the formation of the self out of material resistance, examined in the context of the discussion of Horkheimer and Adorno's *Dialectic of Enlightenment*.

[26] Giddens discusses the use of the first-person pronoun as the precondition for self-awareness: *Modernity and Self-Identity*, 52–53.

[27] For a consideration of Frisch's relation to the modernist tradition in literature, see Helmut Heissenbüttel, "Max Frisch oder Die Kunst des Schreibens in dieser Zeit" [1958], in *Über Max Frisch I*, ed. Thomas Beckermann (Frankfurt am Main: Suhrkamp, 1971), 54–68.

[28] The abandonment of the narrative play with "roles" at the point at which it is acknowledged that "Gantenbein" is reliant on Lila's deception is followed in the narrative only by the framing device, corresponding to the novel's opening scene, of the story of the corpse who nearly manages to get away without a (hi)story, and then by a final paragraph beginning "Alles ist wie nicht geschehen" ("Everything as if it had never happened"; *G* 319–20/303–4). The scene is temporally located in the immediacy of the present ("alles ist Gegenwart" / "everything is the present"), features a first-person plural "we," from which the reader deduces that the narrator is once again partnered, and, interestingly, the elements of the reconstitution of the home: bread and wine. The scene is one of travel, however: an Etruscan landscape is suggested, and there is mention of the narrator's car, grey with dust and burning hot, beneath an olive tree. The narrator, we must infer, has escaped from the immobility in which he was entrapped by the accident on ice, and has reconstructed selfhood, partnership, and "home" in mobile, modern terms.

[29] "Ich bin blind. Ich weiß es nicht immer, aber manchmal" ("I'm blind. I don't always know it, but sometimes I do"; *G* 314/298), the narrator acknowledges as the novel draws to a close.

[30] "Du hast aber dein altes Buch nicht sehr klug versteckt," *Ich* says ("you didn't do a very good job hiding your old book"): Ingeborg Bachmann, *Malina*, in *Werke*, vol. 3, 268 / *Malina*, trans. Philip Boehm (New York, London: Holmes & Meier, 1990), 177). Subsequent references appear in the text, identified as *M* (in German to the *Werke* edition, in English to the Boehm translation).

[31] Dieter Zilligen attempts to draw Bachmann out on this passage in his 1971 interview with her, and is bested, rather as Herr Mühlbauer is in his attempts to interview *Ich* in the novel; see Bachmann, *Wir müssen wahre Sätze finden*, 70–71 (interview with Dieter Zilligen, 22 March 1971).

[32] Carl Pietzker, "The Motif of the Man, Who, Although He Loves, Goes to War: On the History of the Construction of Masculinity in the European Tradition," in *Conceptions of Postwar German Masculinity*, ed. Jerome, 133–70, here 134. Subsequent references appear in the text as parenthetical page numbers.

[33] This corresponds with Hélène Cixous's analysis as discussed in chapter 2.

5: The Critique of Instrumental Reason: Max Frisch's *Homo faber* and Christa Wolf's *Störfall*

WHILE MAX FRISCH'S 1964 NOVEL *Mein Name sei Gantenbein* reveals the continuing investment of the bourgeois male author/subject in a form of subjectivity based on phallic control and (self-) mastery, a rather earlier work by Frisch, the 1957 novel *Homo faber*, adopts a more critical and more effectively ironic stance on the fantasies of mastery — both of self and of the natural world — underpinning the Enlightenment construction of the de facto male/masculine subject. This chapter looks at Frisch's *Homo faber* alongside a later work, Christa Wolf's 1987 novel *Störfall*, written in response to the nuclear reactor explosion at Chernobyl in 1986, in order to examine the way in which gender functions symbolically in the critique of Enlightenment instrumental rationality in these texts. The readings of Frisch and Wolf are preceded by a brief consideration of the tradition of critical ambivalence vis-à-vis the achievements of modernity in German culture, in order to illuminate the way in which gender maps symbolically onto the negative assessment of modern scientific and technological endeavor in these texts.

Enlightenment and Its Shadow: The Ambivalence of Modernity

The privileging of the human faculty of reason and of the notion that humankind could, through reason, achieve mastery over the forces of nature to which it had hitherto been subject lay at the heart of the eighteenth-century Enlightenment thinking in which the self-understanding of Western modernity has its roots. The hero of enlightened modernity was — and in many respects still is — the human subject who, through the active submission of the forces of nature within and outside of himself to rational control, aims to wrest freedom from the realm of necessity. As Karl Marx stated in *Das Kapital*, freedom in the social sphere could only be attained by "socialized men, the associated producers, rationally regulating their interchange with Nature, bringing it under their common control, instead of being ruled by it as by the blind forces of Nature; and achieving this with the least expenditure of energy and under conditions most favorable to, and worthy of, their human nature."[1] Through the conceptualization of human subjecthood as rational mastery, the modern age as an age of industrialization has seen advances unprecedented in earlier phases of human history in science and technology, making the collectivity of human beings, at least in the developed countries of the West, lords as never before of the world around and within them.

Yet Enlightenment also has its dark side. The Enlightenment thinkers of the eighteenth century may have been propelled by the vision of perfectible human community, but the historical course of the development of the Enlightenment project has successively confronted their heirs with unforeseen and unforeseeable outcomes: the devastating destructiveness in terms of human life of the drive toward modernization, the expanded potential for conflict that brings forth wars on a global scale, environmental depredation, psychological alienation — the list could be extended ad infinitum. Cultural unease at the destructive aspects of Enlightenment modernity is a central theme in Marshall Berman's classic study *All That Is Solid Melts Into Air*, which, starting with Goethe's *Faust*, explores the tensions between modernization in the sociopolitical and economic spheres and the contemplation of its human costs in modernist art and literature.[2]

Skepticism about the advantages of modernization has accompanied economic, scientific, and technological progress at every stage of the history of Western modernity, but forms a particularly strong thread in the German-language intellectual tradition. Rita Felski has put this down to the combination in German culture of "a long-standing tradition of Romantic organicism" with "a relatively late and rapid experience of industrialization" that encouraged "a profound ambivalence vis-à-vis the supposed benefits and values of the modern."[3] In chapter 1, I discussed the way in which Felski and scholars such as Jacques Le Rider and Gerald N. Izenberg have analyzed the perceived "crisis of masculinity" in the arts at the turn of the nineteenth to the twentieth centuries as a symptom of a "crisis of modernization, interpreted and experienced as a too-exclusive affirmation of values connected with the masculine element."[4] The analysis of the negative impact of modernization continued to be a feature of German intellectual culture in the early part of the twentieth century, notably as technological advances radically transformed social organization and working life in the high modernist period. Thus while the German modernist movements of the 1910s and 1920s optimistically and energetically sought in new technologies the key to the reshaping of human personality and society, it was in particular in the aftermath of the First World War that a marked cultural pessimism began to assert itself.[5] Among the most influential works of cultural philosophy of this period was Oswald Spengler's *Der Untergang des Abendlandes* (The Decline of the West, 1918–23). In the context of an overarching theory of the organicism of cultures, their cyclical growth and decline, Spengler set out a historical narrative of Western culture in which the "nordic-Faustian human being," driven by the will to power, applies his intellectual capacity (*Geist*) to the creation and production of technologies that, though they raise him above his origins in nature, end by enslaving him. Ludwig Klages, in *Der Geist als Widersacher der Seele* (The Intellect as Adversary of the Soul, 1929–32), similarly identifies in man's intellect the motor behind his alienation from nature. Since, for Klages, nature is the source of vital energies, the alienation of the machine age is life-destroying over the long term, and this sick civilization can, in his view, only be redeemed via the return to the origins. On the left of the political spectrum, meanwhile, Karl Jaspers, in *Die geistige Situation der Zeit* (Man in the Modern Age, 1931), initiated what would become an important trend in sociological analysis after the war with his consideration of the effects of the technological age on human consciousness. His findings constitute a gloomy diagnosis for human personality: "The individual is merged in the function. Being is objectified, for positivism [*Sachlichkeit*] would be violated if individuality remained conspicuous."[6]

In a sense, the cultural-historical analysis undertaken by Max Horkheimer and Theodor W. Adorno in their *Dialectic of Enlightenment* (1944/47) marks a continuation in the postwar era of this intellectual tradition of skepticism vis-à-vis modernization and its effects on human personality and social organization. While both politically and intellectually they share precious little common ground with either Spengler or Klages, it is striking that their arguments are still structured by the opposition between, on the one hand, rational thought and, on the other, nature (internal as well as external) as that from which the human individual has become alienated under the conditions of modernity. Like the earlier writers, they see the exclusive pursuit of instrumental reason as culminating in the catastrophic loss of what constitutes the human being. Moreover, through their perceptions, especially in the "Culture Industry" essay, of the parallels between German National Socialism and the structures of the U.S. society in which they were in exile, they laid the foundation for the postwar critique of U.S. business and commercial culture that was to come to play such an influential role in the development of European societies in the period after 1945.

The cultural-critical impulses of the 1920s and 1930s enjoyed a striking renaissance in Germany in the 1950s. Notable in a range of publications from this decade is the recurrent concern with the impact of mechanization and with the moral repercussions for human social existence of the predominance in contemporary life of the *homo faber:* man as fabricator and inventor. Friedrich Georg Jünger's *Die Perfektion der Technik* (The Perfection of Technology, written 1939, first published 1946) and *Maschine und Eigentum* (Machine and Property, 1949), Hans Freyer's

Theorie des gegenwärtigen Zeitalters (Theory of the Contemporary Age, 1955), and the first volume of Günther Anders's *Die Antiquiertheit des Menschen* (The Antiquation of Humanity), entitled *Über die Seele im Zeitalter der zweiten industriellen Revolution* (The Soul in the Age of the Second Industrial Revolution, 1956) are among the works that fed debate about the negative impact on human society and personality of the technological revolution. Anders, as perhaps the most radical of the critics of mechanization (and notably one whose arguments again had their basis in his observations of American society during his wartime exile), opens his study with the consideration that machines were now outstripping their inventors, generating a world of products with which human beings could no longer keep pace.[7] He goes on to develop his hypothesis of a "Promethean shame" afflicting the contemporary human being: a shame at being born, at being the product of the "blind and uncalculated, the veritably antiquated process of procreation and birth" as opposed to being made (24).

Hannah Arendt, one of the German-Jewish exiles to remain in the United States after the end of the war (she and Anders were married from 1929 to 1937), opened her major 1958 work *The Human Condition* with a not-dissimilar argument. Writing under the dual impact of the launch of the first satellite into space and the advent of automation in manufacture, she begins with the surmise that human scientific and technological endeavor was being propelled by "a rebellion against human existence as it has been given" (2). Her book was intended as a counter-gesture to the thoughtlessness with which, as she perceived it, scientific and technological progress was being embraced:

> If it should turn out to be true that knowledge (in the modern sense of know-how) and thought have parted company for good, then we would indeed become the helpless slaves, not so much of our machines as of our know-how, thoughtless creatures at the mercy of every gadget which is technically possible, no matter how murderous it is. (3)

Crucial to the restoration of properly human thought was, she argued, the countering of the purely utilitarian values of the *homo faber:*

> Man, in so far as he is *homo faber*, instrumentalizes, and his instrumentalization implies a degradation of all things into means, their loss of intrinsic and independent value, so that eventually not only the objects of fabrication but also the "earth in general and all the forces of nature," which clearly came into being without the help of man and have an existence independent of the human world, lose their "value because [they] do not present the reification which comes from work."[8]

This passage gives some insight into the way in which the arguments against the technological, utilitarian, and instrumentalizing worldview lend themselves to being mapped onto conventional notions of gender and so to representation in terms of gendered oppositions. It is not simply that the familiar conflation of masculine subjectivity with human subjectivity per se supports the grammatical use of the generic masculine pronoun. It is also that the pitting of *homo faber* against the earth and the forces of nature falls in with the schema of binary oppositions, inherited from the ancients and re-activated during the Enlightenment, whereby man is understood as the active, rational, thinking, shaping force, while the feminine denotes the material that is wrought, corporeality, the passive, natural matter. Misgivings as to the ultimate implications of the reification and instrumentalization of the natural world and of cultural aspirations to overcome entirely those aspects of the human being that are rooted in his (or her) status as a creature of nature — and taken to their extreme, such aspirations always lead to visions of the physical annihilation of humanity altogether[9] — can therefore readily be expressed in terms of a need to recast the balance between the masculine and the feminine element in culture.

In chapter 2 I discussed the impulse in the work of the Frankfurt School thinkers in the 1950s and 1960s to look to the "feminine" for the solution to perceived cultural malaise. In the work of Max Horkheimer and later of Herbert Marcuse, though, the impact was noted of the changing social position of women in the post-1945 period on the symbolic capacity of woman to represent, for man, an alternative to his own alienated state. Symbolically, as addressed in the reading of Frisch's *Mein Name sei Gantenbein* in the previous chapter, man was left alone, abandoned by his female counterpart as she became a cultural subject in her own right. It is in these changed historical circumstances that Max Frisch's *Homo faber* is located, a novel that turns to gender as a symbolic category in its fictional critique of the U.S.-led, technologically oriented postwar socioeconomic order.

Homo faber: The Truncated Masculine Subject

The central protagonist, and also the narrator, of Frisch's 1957 novel is Walter Faber, an engineer who works for UNESCO in the area of technical aid for underdeveloped countries.[10] In him, Frisch created the exaggerated type of modern rationalist and technological man.[11] What Faber most respects in himself and in others is *Sachlichkeit*: objectivity, factuality, the detached and unemotional viewpoint. He repudiates mythical structures of thought, preferring to see life in terms of scientific principles, mathematical probabilities, and statistics. And he surrounds himself with technology: wherever he goes he is accompanied by his Baby

Hermes typewriter (*HF* 29/33) and his cine-camera (*HF* 23/26), the tools that mediate his perceptions and lend them durability, and by his electric shaver (*HF* 9/12) on which he relies to fend off any reminder of the residual degree to which he is still a creature of nature:

> Ich fühle mich nicht wohl, wenn unrasiert; nicht wegen der Leute, sondern meinetwegen. Ich habe dann das Gefühl, ich werde etwas wie eine Pflanze, wenn ich nicht rasiert bin, und ich greife unwillkürlich an mein Kinn. (*HF* 27)

> [I don't feel comfortable when unshaven; not on account of other people, but on my own account. Not being shaved gives me the feeling I'm some sort of plant and I keep involuntarily feeling my chin. (*HF* 30)]

Though he travels the globe by those means of transport devised by rational mankind to defeat distance — airplanes, ocean-going liners, or motor vehicles whose engines he is able to dismantle and reassemble at will — he is ordinarily resident (albeit in a rented apartment that he gives up in the course of the novel) in central New York City, the metropolis that epitomizes more than any other in the twentieth-century European imagination both the fascination of modernity and also its perversion of traditional values.[12] At the outset of the novel he is involved in an intermittent personal relationship with Ivy, an American woman already married, who embodies stereotypically the kind of artificial femininity produced by the modern consumer economy — she is a model by profession and is characterized in consumerist terms: "sie wählte ihre Kleider nach der Wagenfarbe, glaube ich, die Wagenfarbe nach ihrem Lippenstift oder umgekehrt, ich weiß es nicht" ("she chose her clothes according to the colour of the car, I think, and the colour of the car according to her lipstick or the other way round, I'm not sure which it was"; *HF* 31/34). In this sense, Ivy is a recasting in 1950s terms of a figure prominent in the modernist cultural imagination of the 1900s to the 1920s, that of the consuming woman,[13] with an admixture of the likewise characteristically modernist, sexually manipulative prostitute:[14] she is represented, for example, as seducing Faber against his will (*HF* 62, 66/67, 71). As such, she figures as the female counterpart to the modern, technologically oriented *homo faber* of 1950s culture. Representing to Faber emotional entanglement versus his own avowed preference to be alone as "Mann unter Männern" ("a man among men"; *HF* 64/69) and a sexuality perceived by him as "absurd" versus his ideal of self-contained rationality (an aspect reminiscent of Otto Weininger's theories, as discussed in chapter 1), she fits unproblematically into the rigid hierarchical dualities that structure his mental universe: not only self-containment versus burdensome relationship, but also technology versus nature, science versus the arts, reason and predictability versus superstition and fatalism, male versus female.[15]

Faber's narrative is concerned, however, with a series of challenges to his rationally ordered life, his carefully preserved distance from nature, and his reliance on technology. During a flight to Caracas where he is due to oversee the installation of turbines in a power plant, the airplane in which he is traveling is forced by an engine failure to make an emergency landing, which leaves him and his fellow-passengers stranded in the Mexican desert for four days. This temporary immobility creates the conditions for the formation of relationship that Faber otherwise eschews.[16] He discovers in Herbert, who was seated next to him in the airplane, the brother of his closest friend from his youth in Zurich, Joachim, with whom he had lost touch over twenty years before. Once they are mobile again, he decides uncharacteristically to divert from his own business to accompany Herbert on the search for Joachim in the depths of the Latin American jungle. Unaccustomed to such proximity to nature, Faber experiences this environment as rampant and threatening, fertile and sexualized: "Tümpel im Morgenrot wie Tümpel von schmutzigem Blut, Monatsblut, Tümpel voller Molche, nichts als schwarze Köpfe mit zuckenden Schwänzchen wie ein Gewimmel von Spermatozoen, genau so — grauenhaft" ("pools in the red of dawn like pools of filthy blood, menstrual blood, pools full of newts, nothing but black heads with jerking tails like a seething mass of spermatozoa, just like that — horrible"; *HF* 68/73–74). At the same time, it appears to him as deathly: his narrative stresses the presence of vultures on the watch for carrion, and when they reach Joachim, they find that he has hanged himself. The engine failure, the acquaintance with Herbert, and the discovery of the dead Joachim initiate a sequence of fateful chances that propel the narrative to its doom-laden conclusion. Yet even before the emergency landing, there is an ominous portent: in the airport toilet before take-off, Faber has a fainting-spell that transpires to be a first intimation of a fatal illness. By the end of the novel it is clear that he has been dying of stomach cancer throughout. *Homo faber*, who would control the world and overcome nature by technical prowess, is confronted in this narrative with his mortality, the aspect of human nature that is beyond his rational control.

Faber's journey toward death is also a journey back into the past: culturally, in that his narrative takes him via France to Greece, ending in Athens, where Western culture has its origins; personally, in that the series of encounters that begins with Herbert and the dead Joachim continues with a meeting on a ship sailing for Europe with his daughter by the lover of his youth, Hanna. Ultimately he is lead back to Hanna herself. He had left Hanna behind in Zurich in 1936 after she, a half-Jew, refused his offer of marriage, made in order to protect her in the unstable political climate of the prewar years. She refused him, it seems, because of his failure to acknowledge the emotional bond between them, as figured above all in their unborn child to which he referred as "dein Kind" ("your child") rather than "unser Kind" ("our child"; 48, 202/53, 218). Leaving in order to take up a job contract in Baghdad (i.e., prioritizing his career), he assumed that she would go ahead with the abortion as they had discussed and so does not know that he has a daughter. He becomes involved with the young girl Elisabeth, whose name he abbreviates to Sabeth, in part because she reminds him of Hanna (*HF* 78, 94/84, 100), in part, it is implied, because her youthfulness offers him renewed life and vitality at the moment he becomes haunted by ageing and death.[17] Through his ignorance of his daughter's existence, which is the legacy of a too-cavalier attitude toward the ties of human relationship, but also through his wilful overlooking of the hints that she is indeed his daughter, he enters into an incestuous relationship with his child that ends in her death through fatal accident — as always with the death of a child in literature, the symbolic destruction of the future.

Frisch skilfully constructs the first-person narration in his novel in order to reveal both the characteristic thought-patterns of his protagonist and simultaneously his profound self-delusion. This begins with the designation of the narrative as a "Bericht" or "report" that conveys Faber's aspiration to objectivity in the account of his actions that he writes after Sabeth's death. Despite the features of his narrative that correspond to those of the scientific protocol,[18] there are notable moments of insistent rhetorical denial that betray the repressive mechanisms at work in Faber's psyche.[19] For example, when he collapses in the airport toilet, he attempts to diminish his fear by representing the experience as harmless: "es war ein Schweißanfall, nichts weiter, Schweißanfall mit Schwindel" ("It was a sweating attack, that was all, a sweating attack accompanied by dizziness"; *HF* 11/14). Shortly afterwards, he has a dream — that is, the language of the unconscious provides the scrambled images of what his conscious mind refuses to acknowledge — that features among its elements his former teacher, Professor O., who will figure in the narrative as a mirror-image of Faber's own physical deterioration, and that concludes with the crumbling of his teeth, suggesting an anxiety about his loss of virility.[20] A further prominent, because lengthy, example of rhetorical denial occurs when Faber recounts a night stranded in the desert. This passage juxtaposes Faber's insistent stress on what it is that he can see — "Ich bin Techniker und gewohnt, die Dinge zu sehen, wie sie sind" ("I'm a technologist and accustomed to seeing things as they are"; *HF* 24/27) — and what appear as the involuntary promptings of his imagination, for example:

> Ich weiß nicht, wie verdammte Seelen aussehen; vielleicht wie schwarze Agaven in der nächtlichen Wüste. Was ich sehe, das sind Agaven, eine Pflanze, die ein einziges Mal blüht und dann abstirbt. Ferner weiß ich, daß ich nicht (wenn es im Augenblick auch so aussieht) der erste oder letzte Mensch auf der Erde bin; und ich kann mich von der bloßen

Vorstellung, der letzte Mensch zu sein, nicht erschüttern lassen, denn es ist nicht so. Wozu hysterisch sein? (*HF* 24)

[I don't know what the souls of the damned look like; perhaps like black agaves in the desert at night. What I see are agaves, a plant that blooms once only and then dies. Furthermore, I know (however it may look at the moment) that I am not the last or the first man on earth; and I can't be moved by the mere idea that I am the last man, because it isn't true. Why get hysterical? (*HF* 27–28)]

This scene, in which Faber both rejects and paradoxically creates the desert landscape as a mythical scene prefiguring his imminent death, concludes: "Ich weigere mich, Angst zu haben aus bloßer Fantasie, beziehungsweise fantastisch zu werden aus bloßer Angst, geradezu mystisch" ("I refuse to feel afraid simply because of an over-active imagination, or to start imagining things simply because I feel afraid. It was altogether too mystical for me"; *HF* 25/28).

As the narrative goes on, the reader becomes accustomed to deciphering the moments at which Faber becomes overly insistent as indicative of the extent to which his clear-cut sense of identity is threatened by what is happening to him (or, from his perspective as the author of his report, has already happened). As in the scene quoted above, in which for all his denials it is "imagination" and "mysticism" that patently afflict him, Faber consistently seeks to shore up his identity through recourse to a hierarchized system of binary oppositions that affirms his sense of his own superiority. The gender binary is particularly prominent. Thus while Faber appears to himself as the epitome of masculinity — "Ich stehe auf dem Standpunkt, daß der Beruf des Technikers, der mit den Tatsachen fertig wird, immerhin ein männlicher Beruf ist, wenn nicht der einzigmännliche überhaupt" ("I took the standpoint that the profession of technologist, a man who masters matter, is a masculine profession, if not the only masculine profession there is"; *HF* 77/82) — the repudiated "fantasy" and "mysticism" are feminized, dismissed not only as "hysterical," but also as "weibisch" ("womanish"; *HF* 24/27). So, too, are the native Indians Faber encounters in the jungle settlement at Palenque, whose adaptation of their life rhythm to their natural environment also appears *uncanny* (*unheimlich*) to him: "Abende lang hocken sie in ihren weißen Strohhüten auf der Erde, reglos wie Pilze, zufrieden ohne Licht, still. Sonne und Mond sind ihnen Licht genug, ein *weibisches* Volk, unheimlich, dabei harmlos" ("They squatted for whole evenings in their white straw hats on the earth, motionless as toadstools, content without light, silent. The sun and moon were enough light for them, a *womanish* people, uncanny, though innocuous"; *HF* 38/42, translation modified, italics added). In Freudian theory, the uncanny is the return in distorted form of what is close and familiar to us.[21] It is, then, not coincidental that this remark of

Faber's comes at a point when he has just acknowledged that apathy is the only possible reaction to the tropical climate. He is, in effect, delegating his own behavior to the racial Other in order to retrieve his identity as the white, colonial-style male, intent on getting the use of a motor vehicle with which to penetrate the jungle.

Ultimately feminized, too, is the similarly uncanny jungle environment once he, Herbert, and the French-speaking amateur anthropologist Marcel set off into it. What Faber sees is a natural cycle of fertility and death that mirrors his own mortal existence, but his reaction is one of horror and disgust, as to something irreducibly other and alien. Moreover, while his disturbance at the puddles shining red in the dawn light and alive with newts is revealed in his imagery of menstrual blood and spermatozoa (*HF* 68/73–74), the masculine element is discarded as he leaps to approve Marcel's phrase "Tu sais que la mort est femme! [. . .] et que la terre est femme!" (*HF* 69/74). Marcel himself is not feminized, although his disquisition on "The American Way of Life," an important element in the novel's implicit critique of Faber's lifestyle, is dismissed by Faber as "Künstlerquatsch!" ("Highbrow tripe," or more literally: arty nonsense; *HF* 50/55). The opposition of science/technology versus the human sciences/arts that is established via Faber's antagonism to Marcel at this point will play a central role in the major male-female relationships (Faber-Sabeth and Faber-Hanna) in the plot. In the context of those relationships, the interest in art and knowledge of ancient cultures and myth *is* feminized through the association with Sabeth and above all Hanna. What Frisch's ironic conduct of his protagonist's self-narration is doing, then, is displaying a cultural procedure addressed in previous chapters: the jettisoning of aspects of human experience and behavior, or indeed the natural environment, as "the feminine" in order to sustain the identity of the (here white, bourgeois, modern, both European *and* Americanized) male subject as cultural agent. At the same time, the self-narration displays Faber's self-delusion, and consequently the precariousness and spiritual poverty of his selfhood.

What appears in Faber's story as fate, despite or because of his strenuous denials — "Ich glaube nicht an Fügung und Schicksal, als Techniker bin ich gewohnt mit den Formeln der Wahrscheinlichkeit zu rechnen. Wieso Fügung?" ("I don't believe in providence and fate, as a technologist I am used to reckoning with the formulae of probability. What has providence to do with it?"; *HF* 22/25) — is in essence to be understood as the return of the repressed,[22] which is why it takes on such mythical dimensions.[23] For the ancient Greek myths express the law, perceived anew in the modern science of psychoanalysis, that what is put away out of sight — the infant exposed on the hillside, like Oedipus or Paris, for example — will come back to wreak havoc in due course. From the intimation of mortality that initiates the narrative, everything that happens to Faber is an actualization of what he has denied and repressed in the course of becoming who he is. His life has been based on his denial of his existence as a creature of nature, subject to the limits of beginning and ending and to the arc of youth and of ageing in between. He has chosen to ignore the need for deep human bonds and for a sense of belonging, whether to a place or to a chosen partner. He has underrated the importance of rootedness in the past, and the relation between one's own and the next generation. To the extent that his life, conveyed by the attitudes he expresses and in the scenes in New York, is typical — exaggerated, but suggestive — of life in an Americanized late-modern society, Frisch's novel is to be understood as a critique of a social order characterized, in Marcel's phrase, by "Lebensstandard als Ersatz für Lebenssinn" ("living standards a substitute for a purpose in living"; *HF* 50/55) and of the kind of reduced human personality it has both created and depends upon.

Hanna: The Counter-Figure to Faber

Although Faber is shown in relationship to three female figures in the course of the novel, it is Hanna who functions as the active counter-pole to Faber within the narrative's symbolic structure. In the first place, she is resident in Athens, the city most strongly associated with the origins of Western culture as New York is the paradigmatic city of twentieth-century modernity. Second, she is a philologist who works at an archaeological institute (*HF* 111/119) and has interests in mythology and art history, as can be seen from the knowledge she has passed on to her daughter. As such, she figures as the embodiment of the humanities vis-à-vis Faber's science and technology, and reactivates the association of the "feminine" with archaic human memory that, as discussed in chapter 1, was a prominent trope in the cultural critique of modernity from the fin de siècle onward. Moreover, Faber's narration successively associates her with all of his categories of otherness. Recalling the Hanna of their Zurich years, Faber writes: "Hanna hatte einerseits einen Hang zum Kommunistischen, was ich nicht vertrug, und andererseits zum Mystischen, um nicht zu sagen: zum Hysterischen" ("on the one hand Hanna had Communist leanings, which I couldn't bear, and on the other a tendency to mysticism, or to put it less kindly, hysteria"; *HF* 47/51, translation modified). On first seeing her face at the moment of their renewed encounter in the Athens hospital, Faber comments: "es könnte, abgesehen von ihren blauen Augen, das Gesicht von einem alten Indio sein" ("apart from the blue eyes it might have been the face of an old South American Indian"; *HF* 126/133). At moments she appears to him, too, as the embodiment of age and the corporeal, shown, for example, in his uncannily detailed description of her hand as:

nervös und schlaff, häßlich, eigentlich gar keine Hand, sondern etwas
Verstümmeltes, weich und knochig und welk, Wachs mit Sommer-
sprossen, eigentlich nicht häßlich, im Gegenteil, etwas Liebes, aber
etwas Fremdes, etwas Entsetzliches, etwas Trauriges, etwas Blindes
[. . .]. (*HF* 141)

[tense and slack, ugly, really not a hand at all, but something maimed,
soft and bony and flabby, wax with freckles, not really ugly, on the
contrary, something sweet, but something alien, something horrible,
something sad, something blind [. . .]. (*HF* 148–49)]

The narrative insistently constructs them as a pair, caught in a symbiotic opposition, but as Faber begins, albeit not altogether consciously,
to confront his own mortality, she appears to him in his thoughts as his
true partner, lost to the life decisions he made as a young man: "Nur
mit Hanna ist es nie absurd gewesen" ("Only with Hanna was it never
absurd"; *HF* 100/106).

In the narrative's final phase, in which Faber writes no longer on the
typewriter, but by hand, as he awaits the operation on what he anticipates will prove to be an inoperable cancer, a number of factors emerge
that seem to cast Hanna as a similarly negative figure to Faber, because
representative of the opposite extreme, and to allot her a share of the
guilt in the catastrophe that has been brought upon their child. Her stub-
born pride is stressed, and her too-exclusive grasp on her daughter, which
has denied Elisabeth a father figure. A number of commentators have
developed the theme of Hanna's culpability,[24] while overlooking that it is
Hanna herself who concedes her part in the tragedy that has befallen her
"family" following a significant change of her outer attire. As Faber's end
draws near, she appears at his bedside dressed in white (*HF* 182/196). It
is from this point that she begins to reveal herself to him, thereby allevi-
ating his sense of sole guilt for Sabeth's death. Thus Hanna confesses to
Faber that it was only after he left for Baghdad in 1936 that she discov-
ered that she wanted a child without a father, not their child, but hers
alone (*HF* 201/216). Her determined self-sufficiency and consequent
rejection of men also forms part of her confession as Faber lies dying: she
recalls her oath never to love a man, made after she had been defeated in
a wrestling match with her brother in her late childhood (*HF* 182/196).
In the terms of this work of the late 1950s, her refusal to love and depend
upon a man makes her as much in rebellion against her nature as a woman
as Faber is against his nature as a mortal being. A 1959 article by Gerhard
Kaiser serves to remind us of this now. Nevertheless, the vehemence of
Kaiser's condemnation of Hanna is striking:

Because she rejects the man and wishes to exclude him from the
deepest levels of her existence, she can also not be a real woman, but

only an anti-man weighed down with resentment. Her apparently superior stance toward Faber rests in reality, both as far as her much-emphasised competence and also her maternal egoism and antipathy toward technology are concerned, on a concealed inferiority complex, on a lack.[25]

The text holds open another possible interpretation. Faber's enthusiasm for technology and his preference for self-containment is portrayed in terms of his repression of his physical nature: "*Überhaupt der ganze Mensch! — als Konstruktion möglich, aber das Material ist verfehlt: Fleisch ist kein Material, sondern ein Fluch*" ("*It's the same with the whole of man — the construction is passable, but the material is no good: flesh is not a material, but a curse*"; 171/184, italics here indicate that Faber's text is hand-written).[26] Hanna's feminist independence, by contrast, is presented as a culturally understandable rebellion against the persistent subordination of woman in the male-female pairing:

> Der Mann sieht sich als Herr der Welt, die Frau nur als seinen Spiegel. Der Herr ist nicht gezwungen, die Sprache der Unterdrückten zu lernen; die Frau ist gezwungen, doch es nützt ihr nichts, die Sprache ihres Herrn zu lernen, im Gegenteil, sie lernt nur eine Sprache, die ihr immer unrecht gibt. [. . .] Solange Gott ein Mann ist, nicht ein Paar, kann das Leben einer Frau, laut Hanna, nur so bleiben, wie es heute ist, nämlich erbärmlich, die Frau als Proletarier der Schöpfung, wenn auch noch so elegant verkleidet. (*HF* 140)

> [The man sees himself as master of the world and the woman only as his mirror. The master is not compelled to learn the language of the oppressed; the woman is compelled, though it does her no good, to learn the language of the master, she merely learns a language that always puts her in the wrong. [. . .] As long as God is a man, not a couple, the life of a woman, according to Hanna, is bound to remain as it is now, namely wretched, with woman as the proletarian of Creation, however smartly dressed. (*HF* 147)]

Faber dismisses this as teenage philosophizing (*HF* 140/147), "rightly so" in Kaiser's opinion.[27] Recalling the motif of the ancient Egyptian brother-sister deity Isis and Osiris in Bachmann's *Franza* book, however, the vision of god as a male-female pair deserves to be taken more seriously as an incitement to think about how differently the cultural tradition would have developed if male and female had been consistently conceived as complementary principles, rather than as a hierarchical relationship. This is further encouraged by the fact that, because the death of Sabeth (and so of the future) arises out of an unreconciled opposition between her parents, the *ideal* projected by the text appears as a relationship or balance between the two extremes, imaginable as a reciprocal interaction of masculine and feminine principles, of modern technological know-how tempered by respect for tradition, imagination, and the natural cycle of life, as figured in the marriage of male and female.[28]

Since both partners are guilty of missing their chance to create this reciprocal relationship at its proper moment, the burden of figuring the ideal falls on the unnatural relationship between Faber and his daughter — unnatural not only because incestuous, but also because asynchronous, the ageing father's attempt to live the lost relationship with his true female partner, but with the simulacrum of his partner at the time he left her.[29] Thus Sabeth is open to his interest in technology as Hanna by implication was not, while Faber's burgeoning love for Sabeth draws him into going to the opera and visiting art galleries and archaeological sites with her, against his earlier custom. At the most perfect moment of their relationship, a night spent in the open before the catastrophe of Sabeth's accident, this reciprocality between the text's masculine and feminine principles is figured in their language game, where each suggests similes for what they see in the landscape, Faber from the realm of science and technology, Sabeth from the realm of the arts (*HF* 150–52/158–60).[30] The impact of this creative interaction is shown as Faber plays the game again in his imagination after Sabeth's death (*HF* 195–96/210–11), a symptom of his new desire to experience the world more directly, with more intense awareness, no longer mediated and kept at a distance by technology.

Yet Hanna is not as unambiguously cast as the opposite and so equally culpable and undesirable extreme to Faber as commentators on the novel have tended to argue, for she is also invested with considerable moral authority in the text. Where Faber's self-narration betrays his emotional ignorance and blindness to his own needs and desires, Hanna's insights offer a compelling commentary on his moral malaise, so that she appears wise where he continues to be evasive, seeing where he is blind:

> "Das ist nun einmal so," sagt sie [Hanna], "wir können das Leben nicht in unseren Armen behalten, Walter, auch du nicht."
> "Ich weiß!" sage ich.
> "Warum versuchst du es denn?" fragt sie.
> Ich verstand Hanna nicht immer.
> "Das Leben geht mit den Kindern," sagt sie —
> Ich hatte mich nach ihrer Arbeit erkundigt.
> "Das ist nun einmal so," sagt sie, "wir können uns nicht mit unseren Kindern nochmals verheiraten." (138–39)

> ["That's the way things are," she [Hanna] said, "we can't keep life in our arms, Walter, you can't either."
> "I know," I said.
> "Then why do you try?" she asked.
> I couldn't always understand what Hanna meant.

"Life goes with the children," she said.
I had enquired about her work.
"That's the way things are," she said. "We can't marry again
through our children." (*HF* 146)]

Moreover, Hanna's generalizations from Faber's particular case in the
course of the narrative's so-called "Second Station," embedded within
the novel itself as if to provide an interpretative guide,[31] offer the most
provocative and acute reading of Faber's story as a moral tale for the tech-
nologically-obsessed postwar modern social order:

> *Diskussion mit Hanna! — über Technik (laut Hanna) als Kniff, die*
> *Welt so einzurichten, daß wir sie nicht erleben müssen. Manie des Tech-*
> *nikers, die Schöpfung nutzbar zu machen, weil er sie als Partner nicht*
> *aushält, nichts mit ihr anfangen kann; Technik als Kniff, die Welt als*
> *Widerstand aus der Welt zu schaffen, beispielsweise durch. Tempo zu*
> *verdünnen, damit wir sie nicht erleben müssen. (Was Hanna damit*
> *meint, weiß ich nicht.)* [. . .] *Mein Irrtum: daß wir Techniker ver-*
> *suchen, ohne den Tod zu leben. Wörtlich: Du behandelst das Leben nicht*
> *als Gestalt, sondern als bloße Addition, daher kein Verhältnis zur Zeit,*
> *weil kein Verhältnis zum Tod. Leben sei Gestalt in der Zeit. Hanna gibt*
> *zu, daß sie nicht erklären kann, was sie meint. Leben ist nicht Stoff,*
> *nicht mit Technik zu bewältigen. Mein Irrtum mit Sabeth: Repetition,*
> *ich habe mich so verhalten, als gebe es kein Alter, daher widernatürlich.*
> *Wir können nicht das Alter aufheben, indem wir weiter addieren,*
> *indem wir unsere eigenen Kinder heiraten.* (*HF* 170–71, italics here
> indicate that Faber's text is hand-written)

> [*Discussion with Hanna — about technology (according to Hanna) as*
> *the knack of so arranging the world that we don't have to experience it.*
> *The technologist's mania for putting Creation to a use, because he can't*
> *tolerate it as a partner, can't do anything with it; technology as the*
> *knack of eliminating the world as resistance, for example, of diluting*
> *it by speed, so that we don't have to experience it. (I don't know what*
> *Hanna means by this.)* [. . .] *My mistake lay in the fact that we tech-*
> *nologists try to live without death. Her own words: "You don't treat life*
> *as form, but as mere addition, hence you have no relationship to time,*
> *because you have no relationship to death." Life is form in time. Hanna*
> *admits that she can't explain what she means. Life is not matter and*
> *cannot be mastered by technology. My mistake with Sabeth: repetition. I*
> *behaved as though age did not exist, and hence contrary to nature. We*
> *cannot do away with age by further addition, by marrying our own*
> *children.* (*HF* 182–83, translation modified; italics here indicate that
> Faber's text is hand-written)][32]

Hanna's status as moral authority in the latter stages of the text is
underpinned by the representation of her as an independent subject. Far

from being figured in stereotypical "feminine" terms, as the emotional, feeling, capricious Other in relation to "masculine" rationality that Faber's early reminiscences of her (*HF* 46–47/51) might have led us to expect, the mature Hanna is an academic, an intellectual who earns her own living, although interestingly she is not portrayed as lacking in "femininity" because of it: "Dabei kann man nicht einmal sagen, Hanna sei unfraulich. Es steht ihr, eine Arbeit zu haben" ("Moreover, you couldn't even say Hanna was unwomanly. Having a job suited her"; *HF* 143/151). But if she is not "unwomanly," she can also be quite masculine in Faber's terms: "Hanna überhaupt sehr sachlich. [. . .] Ich staunte über Hanna; ein Mann, ein Freund, hätte nicht sachlicher fragen können" ("Hanna was altogether very matter-of-fact. [. . .] I was astounded at Hanna; a man, a [male] friend couldn't have asked in a more matter-of-fact tone"), as he notes at their first meeting after Sabeth's accident (*HF* 127/133–34). The presence of what are, in the text's system of oppositions, "masculine" elements is also noticeable in Faber's description of Hanna's apartment:

> Ihre Wohnung: wie bei einem Gelehrten (auch das habe ich offenbar gesagt; später hat Hanna, in irgendeinem Gespräch über Männer, meinen damaligen Ausspruch von der Gelehrten-Wohnung zitiert als Beweis dafür, daß auch ich die Wissenschaft für ein männliches Monopol halte, überhaupt den Geist), — alle Wände voller Bücher, ein Schreibtisch voller Scherben mit Etiketten versehen, im übrigen fand ich auf den ersten Blick *nichts Antiquarisches*, im Gegenteil, *die Möbel waren durchaus modern*, was mich bei Hanna wunderte. "Hanna," sage ich, "*du bist ja fortschrittlich geworden!*" (*HF* 133, italics added)

> [Her flat. Like a [male] scholar's (I evidently told her that, too; later, in the course of a conversation about men, Hanna quoted my remark about a scholar's flat as proof that I, too, considered science a masculine monopoly, all intellectual activity in fact); all the walls were covered with books, there was a desk covered with fragments of pottery bearing labels, but apart from this I saw, at first glance, *nothing antiquarian*, on the contrary, *the furniture was thoroughly modern*, which surprised me where Hanna was concerned. "Hanna," I said, "*how progressive you've become!*" (*HF* 140, italics added)][33]

The function within the novel of these unexpectedly masculine-connoted elements in Hanna is undoubtedly to challenge the complacency of Faber's habitual binary thinking. But it is nevertheless striking that if the text's unspoken ideal is a balance between masculine and feminine principles, we find this balance figured not only in the relationship between Faber and Sabeth (as the unnatural version of the rightful relationship between Faber and Hanna), *but also in the single figure of Hanna*. This is of interest because in this text that well precedes the feminist theory of the post-1968 period, this is readable as a gesture, in the work of a male author, toward a new kind of female figure, not incorporated by but distinct from the male subject, in whose double gender the apprehension of a form of solution to a perceived cultural malaise might be found. In short, an answer to the malaise of the Enlightenment project, the too-exclusive focus on reason and the subordination of nature, is looked for in the strange dual position of the modern intellectual woman as a cultural *subject* who, unlike her male counterpart, retains the connection to nature (figured in her maternity), tradition, and intuitive insight that is the legacy of her status as cultural *object* or Other. In this *symbolic* position — and it cannot be emphasized enough that it is a symbolic position, with only a suggestive connection to real women's lives — the balance of intellect and intuitive insight, mind and (maternal) body, can be achieved in a way that is denied to a male subject too caught up in the cultural history of rationality and of political and technological domination. The male author at this point abrogates, as it were, the aspiration noted in the works of the fin-de-siècle of the male author/subject to appropriate the feminine in order to represent "whole being," and passes it to the symbolic figure of woman. This element of the characterization marks a very significant difference between Frisch's *Homo faber* and his *Mein Name sei Gantenbein*. One might speculate that it is the difference between a work about a male subject who feels his masculinity to be under threat, and a more abstract narrative in which the characters function within a framework of historical allegory. At any rate, the figure of Hanna in Frisch's 1957 text *Homo faber* can be seen in the context of the arguments of this book as an anticipatory figure, whose double gendering looks forward to the interest within the feminist theory of the 1970s in what Cixous would call the "bisexuality" of woman as the basis for utopian projection. Less wedded than the male subject to "glorious phallic monosexuality,"[34] woman has the potential, in Cixous's vision, to figure the coexistence within the individual subject of characteristics of both genders simultaneously, thus exploding the inherently oppositional binary structure of the subject-object, self-other model inherited from the male-authored philosophical tradition. It is this that permits her, as discussed in chapter 2, to become, at least in theory, the figurative embodiment of the reconciliation of human culture with nature.

Christa Wolf's *Störfall*: Gender and the Critique of Instrumental Reason

This is a good point at which to turn to Christa Wolf's *Störfall* (Accident). Published in 1987, it comes at the end of a sequence of texts written by Wolf under the influence of feminist thinking that promote the "doubled" modern female consciousness as potentially culturally redemptive. In *Kein Ort. Nirgends* (No Place on Earth, 1979), the figure of Karoline von Günderrode functions in a not dissimilar way to Hanna as I have been reading her in Frisch's *Homo faber.* She combines a "masculine" intellect and cultural subjecthood (she is a poet, a writer) with a "feminine" intuition and insight that is presented as giving her a greater moral acuity than her male counterpart, Heinrich von Kleist, whose fragmentation under the pressures of expectation leveled at, and internalized by, the male subject she is able to perceive where he is not: "Ihr [Männer] werdet durch den Gang der Geschäfte, die euch obliegen, in Stücke zerteilt, die kaum miteinander zusammenhängen. Wir [Frauen] sind auf den ganzen Menschen aus und können ihn nicht finden" ("The constant round of responsibilities you men must deal with cut you into pieces which scarcely bear any relation to each other. We women are looking for a whole human being, and we cannot find him").[35] Her doubled gender is encapsulated in the neologism "Jünglingin" (*KO* 24), the word for a male youth with a feminine suffix added, which is applied to her by the observing Kleist.[36] He displays an interesting unease at the term he himself has generated: "Kleist unterdrückt das Wort, das ihm zu passen scheint. Dem Widerwillen gegen Zwitterhaftes geht er nicht auf den Grund" ("Kleist suppresses the word which seems to him suitable. He does not enquire into the roots of his antipathy to the hermaphroditic"; *KO* 24/19). Again, a repressive mechanism seems to be at work here, since Kleist himself will be represented in the text in androgynous terms. Where he will not own his "doubled" psyche, the female character is at least able to acknowledge the masculine as a part of herself: "Sie zerreißt sich in drei Personen, darunter einen Mann" ("She dismembers herself, making herself into three persons, one of them a man"; *KO* 103/117).

The eponymous Kassandra in Wolf's 1983 novel appears similarly "doubled." She is presented in a biographical progression from hysteric, shaken bodily by her intuitive insights into the malaise of her native Trojan culture but only able to articulate herself in the form of shrieking prophecy (the familiar figure of Kassandra from the ancient Greek sources), to the measured narrator of her own life story and that of her society's decline at the moment of her death. In the course of this progression she is shown as achieving the balance of, on the one hand, intuition and feeling and, on the other, the intellectual grasp of her own position. In this way she emerges by the end of the novel as the model for an alternative to the still self-alienated heroism of the male characters, with its implied destructive tendency. That there are nevertheless problematic aspects in the symbolic position she represents will be discussed when this text is examined in detail in chapter 7.

Störfall, constructed as a sequence of stream-of-consciousness reflections embedded in the narration of a day in the life of the author following the Chernobyl nuclear reactor explosion in April 1986, in many respects continues in this line, extending Wolf's feminist critique of male-dominated culture from the destructiveness of the cult of warfare and aggression as represented in the Western heroic tradition to the destructiveness of instrumental reason, similarly gendered masculine. The female narrator, "doubled" in that she is both author and shown embedded in the domestic sphere, unfolds her reflections upon the way in which the cultural privileging of instrumental reason and the pursuit of abstract knowledge has acted to alienate human beings from the relationship to nature and to sensory perception, and ultimately, then, from moral responsibility.

The realm of "Wissenschaft und Technik" (science and technology)[37] is portrayed in Wolf's text, as it is in *Homo faber,* as an exclusively male realm. The implications in terms of the text's surface gender symbolism emerge with particular clarity from the passage that narrates the story of a modern-day Faust named Peter Hagelstein. Hagelstein is a scientist working at the Livermore laboratory in the United States on the "Star Wars" project, the defense program initiated by the Reagan administration in the mid-1980s with the aim of developing the capacity to intercept nuclear attack in space. The Livermore environment is presented as the ultimate extreme of modernized society. The human individuals, all male, who work there are instrumentalized, in that their only function is to pursue the technical solutions to the specific problems set before them. For the sake of maximum efficiency, they are cut off from all normal human relationships, and their emotional needs are redirected to the technological device of the personal computer. They are fed on fast food — and one notes the negative characterization, as in Frisch's *Homo faber,* of American culture as the paradigm of the alienating trends within modernity:

Wenn sie dort ankommen, in ihrem Sternkriegslaboratorium Livermore [. . .], dann ist es wahrscheinlich schon um sie geschehen. Sie kennen, habe ich gelesen, nicht Vater noch Mutter. Nicht Bruder noch Schwester. Nicht Frau noch Kind (es gibt dort keine Frauen [. . .]). Was sie kennen, diese halben Kinder mit ihren hochtrainierten Gehirnen, mit ihrer ruhelosen, Tag und Nacht fieberhaft arbeitenden linken Gehirnhälfte — was sie kennen, ist ihre Maschine. Ihr lieber geliebter Computer. An den sie gebunden, gefesselt sind, wie nur je ein Sklave an seine Galeere. Ernährung: Erdnußbutterbrote. Hamburger mit Tomatenketchup. Cola aus dem Kühlschrank. Was sie kennen, ist das Ziel, den atomgetriebenen Röntgenlaser zu konstruieren, das Kernstück jener Phantasie von einem total sicheren Amerika durch die Verlegung künftiger Atomwaffenschlachten in den Weltraum. (*S* 68–69)

[By the time of their arrival [. . .] at their Star Wars laboratory, Livermore, they are probably already done for. They know not father nor mother, I have read. Not brother nor sister. Not woman nor child (there are no women there [. . .]). What they do know, these mere children with their highly trained brains, with the restless left hemispheres of their brains working feverishly night and day — what they do know is their machine. Their lovely, beloved computers. To which they are bound, shackled, as only ever a slave to his galley. Nourishment: peanut-butter sandwiches. Hamburgers with ketchup. Coke from the fridge. What they do know is the objective to construct the nuclear-powered X-ray laser at the core of that fantasy of an America rendered totally secure through the relocation of future nuclear battles to outer space. (*S* 62–63)]

Peter Hagelstein's female counterpart is his girlfriend, Josie Stein, a peace-movement activist who attempts to support Hagelstein's uneasy conscience vis-à-vis his work and his wish to escape his environment — "Ein Gretchen, das, anstatt an ihm zugrunde zu gehen, ihn erlösen will" ("A Gretchen who wishes rather to redeem him than be destroyed by him"; 71/65). In a coda to this story, Wolf's narrator learns of Hagelstein's defection, which she reads as a victory for moral feeling: "Einer hat es geschafft. Nichts ist endgültig. Ich muß erneut über die Schicksale und Entscheidungen des modernen Faust nachdenken" ("Somebody made it. Nothing is final. I'll have to reconsider the destinies and decisions of modern Faust"; *S* 97/93).

The "male" realm of the pursuit of science as an end in itself, blind to or simply unable to divert from its own destructive potential, is contrasted within the text with the "female" realm of domestic labor and child-rearing. The opposition is reminiscent of Simone de Beauvoir's schema in *The Second Sex,* where the male realm of the *homo faber* is described in terms of the active shaping of the world, the setting of goals that open out the future, while the female realm is characterized by the passive endurance of an eternal repetition of the same:

> The domestic labours that fell to her lot because they were reconcilable with the cares of maternity imprisoned her in repetition and immanence; they were repeated from day to day in an identical form, which was perpetuated almost without change from century to century; they produced nothing new.[38]

In Wolf's text, though, the project of the *homo faber* has become associated not with the opening out of the future, but with the threat of its long-term pollution (in this instance by radioactivity) or even its eradication (through the link between the civil and military utilization of the discoveries of nuclear physics). The realm of immanence and repetition, by contrast, provides the ground for a relationship to life's cyclical continuity and, through childcare, to the future of humanity:

Liste der Tätigkeiten, die jene Männer von Wissenschaft und Technik vermutlich nicht ausüben oder die sie, dazu gezwungen, als Zeitvergeudung ansehen würden: Einen Säugling trockenlegen, Kochen, einkaufen gehn, mit einem Kind auf dem Arm oder im Kinderwagen. Wäsche waschen, aufhängen, abnehmen, zusammenlegen, bügeln, ausbessern. Fußböden fegen, wischen, bohnern, staubsaugen. Staubwischen. Nähen. Stricken. Häkeln. Sticken. Geschirr abwaschen. Geschirr abwaschen. Geschirr abwaschen. Ein krankes Kind pflegen. Ihm Geschichten erfinden. Lieder singen. (*S* 39)

[A list of the activities which these men of science and technology presumably do not pursue or which, if forced upon them, they would consider a waste of time: Changing a baby's diapers. Cooking, shopping with a child on one's arm or in the baby carriage. Doing the laundry, hanging it up to dry, taking it down, folding it, ironing it, darning it. Sweeping the floor, mopping it, polishing it, vacuuming it. Dusting. Sewing. Knitting. Crocheting. Embroidering. Doing the dishes. Doing the dishes. Doing the dishes. Taking care of a sick child. Thinking up stories to tell. Singing songs. (*S* 31)]

Since the narrator is presented in the domestic sphere, pursuing activities such as making meals and doing shopping, chatting to shopkeepers, working in the garden, and telephoning with friends and family — and indeed singing a number of songs — it appears in the first instance that this is emphatically the narrative of a woman who uses her own cultural position as a platform on which to adopt a morally critical stance on the male pursuit of abstract science. The destructive potential of the latter is encapsulated in the news of the nuclear explosion, with its fallout no longer directly perceptible by the human senses, and its danger in particular for children who must grow up in a polluted environment.

To read the text in this way is, however, to overlook the way in which it simultaneously works to undermine the clarity of its own gender schema. In the first place, this day in the aftermath of the nuclear reactor explosion is also the day in which the narrator's brother undergoes an operation to remove a brain tumor. Negatively perceived science is balanced, then, by positively perceived science in which the mechanistic procedures of sawing a hole in the skull (*S* 17/7), draining the fluid from the brain (*S* 44/36), and displacing the brain mass in order to access the tumor (*S* 28/19) must be accompanied by the skill and corporeal sensitivity of the human practitioner, the "Fingerspitzengefühl deines Chirurgen" ("fine sense of touch of your surgeon"; *S* 20/10, translation modified). Moreover, the brother himself is both a scientist to the narrator's artist — "Er ist das genaue Gegenteil von mir, habe ich gesagt. Er steht mir nahe" ("He's the exact opposite of me, I said. We're close"; *S* 60/54) — and the addressee of much of her stream-of-consciousness reflection, the "you" to her "I." The relationship functions on a dual level: as that between an actual brother and sister within the fiction as presented, but also as symbolically suggestive, conjuring up the male-female bond within culture as that between siblings, a less antagonistic variant, perhaps, than the sexual partnership,[39] as seen, for example, in the relationship between Martin and Franza in Bachmann's *Todesarten* project.[40] The actualization of the sibling relationship in the imaginary address in *Störfall* indicates the closeness between the two individuals, but also suggests the other as an aspect of the self, internalized through shared childhood and upbringing. And it is in a recollected dialogue with the brother that the narrator retreats from her delegation of the destructive aspects of the human imagination to the scientist as Other in order to acknowledge the parallels with her own activity as a writer. She begins by expressing her alienation from the scientists' motivation: "Ganz, sagte ich, würde ich diesen Kitzel wohl niemals verstehen, der jene Handvoll höchstbegabter Physiker und Chemiker vor einem halben Jahrhundert, in einem anderen Zeitalter, dazu verführte, weiterzumachen" ("I would never entirely understand the titillation which had seduced that handful of most highly gifted physicists and chemists into forging ahead half a century ago, in another age, I said"; *S* 54/47). But her brother's remembered riposte generates parallels in the text between the realm of technology, or more specifically of warfare, and the realm of intellectual work:

> Ich solle lieber an mich selber denken. Ob ich denn innehalten könnte. Ob ich nicht mal zu ihm gesagt habe, Worte könnten treffen, sogar zerstören wie Projektile; ob ich denn immer abzuwägen wisse — immer bereit sei, abzuwägen — , wann meine Worte verletzend, vielleicht zerstörend würden? Vor welchem Grad von Zerstörung ich zurückschrecken würde? Nicht mehr sagen, was ich sagen könnte? Lieber in Schweigen verfallen? (*S* 55)

> [I should rather think of myself. Whether I would be able to stop. Whether I hadn't once told him that words could wound, even destroy, like projectiles; whether I was always able to judge — always willing to judge — when my words would wound, perhaps destroy? At what level of destruction I would back down? No longer say what I could? Opt for silence? (*S* 48)]

As always in Wolf's texts, the self-narration contains a progression. At the outset, the tendency is to blame some nameless Other for the rationalist pursuit of solutions to technical problems that, with the reactor explosion, has transpired to put human beings at risk — "*Die* lernen doch nichts, hat meine jüngere Tochter gesagt. *Die* sind doch alle krank" ("*They'll* never ever learn, said my youngest daughter. *They're* all sick"; *S* 25/16, italics added). However, by its conclusion the narrative has arrived, via its reflections on the structure of the brain and the parallels between quite distinct spheres of human activity, at the crucial insight into the human tendency to project negatively connoted aspects of the self onto the Other and the moral obligation not to pursue this psychological course:

> warum solle es nicht eine Chance für eine ganze Kultur sein, wenn möglichst viele ihrer Mitglieder wagen können, der eigenen Wahrheit ohne Angst ins Gesicht zu sehen? Was ja heiße, die Bedrohung nicht dem äußeren Feind aufzubürden, sondern sie da zu lassen, wo sie hingehöre, im eigenen Innern. (*S* 98–99)

> [why shouldn't there be a chance for an entire civilization if as many of its members as possible can dare to look their own truth in the eyes without fear? Which meant not burdening the outside enemy with the threat, but leaving it where it belonged, in one's own inner self. (*S* 94, translation modified)]

In terms of the text's gender symbolism, this can be interpreted as challenging the feminist tendency displayed within the novel itself to jettison as "masculine" those aspects of the psyche that do not fit in with the female figure's desired self-image as morally superior — the reverse psychological mechanism to the one Frisch ironically exposes in his male narrator in *Homo faber.* Thus it is a symptom of the impulse to self-knowledge that the aforementioned "list of activities" supposedly regarded as a waste of time by the men of science and technology *ends* with the admission: "Und wieviele dieser Tätigkeiten sehe ich selbst als Zeitvergeudung an?" ("And how many of these activities do I myself consider a waste of time?"; S 39/31)[41]

In this sense, Wolf's text can be understood as a mature and complex reflection on the extent to which the feminist identification of "male" culture as the source of cultural destructiveness functions as a projection through which "masculine" rationality and science is constructed as Other to the "feminine" relation to the domestic sphere, to childcare, to nature, in a way that does not necessarily bear a relation to the actual behavior of real, flesh-and-blood men and women. For *we* — and the text uses the first person plural frequently in its passages reflecting on the nature of human civilization[42] — whether men *or* women, are equally implicated, in our different and individual ways, in the structures of our culture and the means by which we pursue self-realization within these structures.[43] In drawing away from the view that women per se hold the key to countering the negative and destructive trends inherent in scientific and technological progress, Wolf makes a move in this text toward taking leave of the symbolic figure of Woman as culturally redemptive. Rather, it is the morally responsible, and above all self-aware, *individual* who provides the implicit positive model here — the individual, whether man or woman, who sees through the cultural mechanism of projecting "Others," and looks straight into the heart of darkness[44] within him- or herself.

On the other hand, this female narrator, who owns up to the traits initially projected onto the male figure of the scientist, can be seen as a further variation of the "doubled" female figure appearing in the literature of our period. The gesture of acknowledging her "Mitverantwortung" ("shared responsibility"; *S* 61/54, translation modified) for the aspects of contemporary culture that alarm her is structurally similar to Hanna's acceptance of her share of the guilt at the end of *Homo faber*: in both cases, the gesture displays a profound sense of moral accountability, precisely that characteristic that tends, according to the findings of this study so far, to be associated with the female side in the gendering of post-1945 modernity in the literary text. Furthermore, a number of commentators on *Störfall* have noted the importance of dialogue within the process of self-recognition within the novel: "only through a dialogue, a multiplicity of voices, can one see beyond the darkness in which one speaks," as Russell West observes, and he goes on: "The narrator addresses her brother as "Bruderherz" [brother-heart], installing a dialogue which links persons, founds communication, binds bodies together."[45] This summons up the vision of the relational subject that we found projected in Bachmann's text. Yet it is notable that the dialogues of moral import that actually take place within the novel tend to be between the narrator and female interlocutors, whether her two daughters (*S* 24–27, 97–101/16–19, 93–97) or female friends (*S* 30–31, 60–61, 84–85 and 87–88/22–23, 53–54, 79–81 and 82–83). The symbolically significant dialogue with the brother takes place in the imagination, as does the "dialogue" with the male author Joseph Conrad within the text's closing pages. In order for the relationship between male and female to be realized, reassurance is needed that the symbolic brother within contemporary culture will respond to the sister's offer of communication. Will he enter into the risk of the relationship? Will he be able to?

The nightmare narrated at the very end of the text offers a cluster of symbolic images that convey the perceived need for a technologically oriented modernity to reinstate its relationship to the abstract symbolic feminine:

> Soeben war in meinem Traum ein riesengroßer, naher, ekelhaft in Zersetzung übergegangener Mond sehr schnell hinter dem Horizont versunken. Am nachtdunklen Himmel war ein großes Foto meiner toten Mutter befestigt gewesen. Ich schrie. (*S* 112)

> [Just then, very close to me, in my dream, a giant, nauseatingly putrescent moon had swiftly sunk down below the horizon. A large

photograph of my dead mother had been fastened to the dark night sky. I screamed. (*S* 109)]

The putrescent moon is not, as Anna K. Kuhn reads it, "symbolic of our own planet that we are destroying"[46] so much as a figure for the decay of the feminine principle in our culture: the moon is an ancient symbol of the feminine. The photograph of the dead mother, meanwhile, suggests a technologically mediated relationship to the matter (the *mater*, the *materia*) from which human life springs; the image is deceptive, though, if what it captures is dead. Interestingly, both of these symbols — the moon and the technically reproduced image of a dead woman — appear also in Frisch's *Homo faber*. The sexual consummation of the relationship between father and daughter, fatal in its consequences, takes place during an eclipse of the moon (*HF* 124–25/131–32), when the guardian maternal spirit, as it were, is in abeyance. And one of Faber's most traumatic moments is when he watches his cine film of Sabeth after her death. The film images of the vital, living Sabeth are akin to nightmare images, in that they summon up a presence now entirely lost:

> Ich habe nichts mehr zu sehen. Ihre zwei Hände, die es nirgends mehr gibt, ihre Bewegung, wenn sie das Haar in den Nacken wirft oder sich kämmt, ihre Zähne, ihre Lippen, ihre Augen, die es nirgends mehr gibt, ihre Stirn: wo soll ich sie suchen? Ich möchte bloß, ich wäre nie gewesen. (*HF* 192)

> [I had nothing more to see. Her two hands, that no longer existed anywhere, her movements as she tossed the pony-tail towards the back of her head or combed her hair, her teeth, her lips, her eyes that no longer existed anywhere, her forehead — where could I look for them? All I wished was that I had never existed. (*HF* 206, translation modified)]

In her introduction to *The Human Condition*, Hannah Arendt poses the question:

> Should the emancipation and secularization of the modern age, which began with a turning-away, not necessarily from God, but from a god who was the Father of men in heaven, end with an even more fateful repudiation of an Earth who was the Mother of all living creatures under the sky? (Arendt 2)

In this question is expressed, in archetypal gendered terms, the anxiety of many postwar critics of untrammelled modern technological and scientific progress. Wolf's closing word in *Störfall* is in this tradition: "Wie schwer, Bruder, würde es sein, von dieser Erde Abschied zu nehmen" ("How difficult it would be, brother, to take leave of this earth"; *S* 112/109).

Notes

[1] Karl Marx, *Capital* (New York: International Publishers, 1977), vol. 3, 820. He further notes that, while the realm of production remains a realm of necessity, beyond it begins "that development of human energy which is an end in itself, the true realm of freedom, which, however, can blossom forth only with this realm of necessity as its basis." But contrast Hannah Arendt's examination of the contradictions inherent in Marx's oppositional construction of necessity and freedom in *The Human Condition* (Chicago and London: U of Chicago P, second edition 1998), 104–5, and her more life-affirming dialectical vision of "the fertility of the human metabolism with nature," 106 and following. Subsequent references to *The Human Condition* appear in the text, identified as Arendt.

[2] Marshall Berman, *All That Is Solid Melts Into Air: The Experience of Modernity* (London, New York: Verso, 1983).

[3] Rita Felski, *The Gender of Modernity* (Cambridge, MA and London: Harvard UP, 1995), 50. See discussion in chapter 1 above.

[4] Jacques Le Rider, *Modernity and Crises of Identity: Culture and Society in Fin-de-Siècle Vienna* [first published 1990], trans. Rosemary Morris (New York: Continuum, 1993), 90.

[5] Walter Schmitz offers a useful overview account of the debates that accompanied the technological revolution, increasing mechanization in production, and the functionalization of labor, and of the opposition of "technology and intellect" in twentieth-century literature and theoretical writing in *Max Frisch. Homo faber. Materialien, Kommentar* (Munich, Vienna: Carl Hanser, 1977), 32–48. The account that follows draws in part on Schmitz's.

[6] Karl Jaspers, *Man in the Modern Age*, trans. Eden and Cedar Paul (London: Routledge & Kegan Paul, 1951), 49. It is notable that this book, first published in 1931, was reprinted in both Britain and Germany in the early 1950s.

[7] Günther Anders, *Die Antiquiertheit des Menschen*, vol. 1: *Über die Seele im Zeitalter der zweiten industriellen Revolution* (Munich: C. H. Beck, 2nd edition 2002), 17–18.

[8] Arendt, *The Human Condition*, 155, 156. Arendt is quoting here from Marx's *Capital*.

[9] See discussion of Otto Weininger in chapter 1. Günther Anders's book ends with an essay on the "Annihilismus" (304) expressed by the atom bomb, as the ultimate instrument created by human beings that they may no longer have the moral strength to resist using. Arendt notes this essay approvingly: 150 n. 13.

[10] Max Frisch, *Homo faber. Ein Bericht*, quoted from Frisch, *Gesammelte Werke in zeitlicher Folge*, ed. Hans Mayer with the cooperation of Walter Schmitz (Frankfurt am Main: Suhrkamp, 1976), vol. 4, 10 / *Homo faber: A Report*, trans. Michael Bullock (Harmondsworth: Penguin, 1974), 12–13. Further references appear in the text, identified as *HF* (in German to the *Werke* edition, in English to the Bullock translation).

[11] See Gerhard Kaiser's comment that in Faber "the individual personality shows features typical of the time which make of the figure a representative one": "The

engineer Walter Faber is the *homo faber*, the prototype of the technological human being, whereby this term denotes not just the technologist in particular, but quite generally the human being shaped by the world of technology and, whether consciously or unconsciously, accepting of its categories." Kaiser, "Max Frischs 'Homo faber'" [1959], in *Max Frisch: Beiträge zur Wirkungsgeschichte*, ed. Albrecht Schau (Freiburg im Breisgau: Universitätsverlag Becksmann, 1971), 80–89, here 86.

[12] The United States of America is as a nation the product of the Enlightenment, and as its global economic influence increased in the course of the twentieth century, it became both in its own self-understanding and in the view of the other nations of the world, the paradigm, in both good and bad aspects, of the modern. See Schmitz's discussion "Zum Amerika-Bild" in *Materialien, Kommentar*, 58–61, and his bibliography on this theme, 161–63.

[13] See Felski's commentary in *The Gender of Modernity*, chapter 3: "Imagined Pleasures: The Erotics and Aesthetics of Consumption." On the representation and cultural significance of the postwar consuming woman in the Federal Republic of Germany, see Erica Carter, *How German is She?: Postwar West German Reconstruction and the Consuming Woman* (Ann Arbor, MI: U of Michigan P, 1997).

[14] See Lynn Abrams on the symbolic status of the prostitute in *The Making of Modern Woman*, 152–57, here 154: "the disorderly, diseased, corrupt body of the prostitute was used as a metaphor for fears about urban decay, national decline, and transgressions across class, gender and racial borders." For a useful discussion of a variety of issues to do with the representation of the prostitute in specifically German culture, see Christiane Schönfeld, ed., *Commodities of Desire: The Prostitute in Modern German Literature* (Rochester, NY: Camden House, 2000).

[15] See Alan D. Latta, "Die Verwandlung des Lebens in eine Allegorie: Eine Lektüre von Max Frischs Roman *Homo faber*," in *Frischs "Homo faber,"* ed. Walter Schmitz (Frankfurt am Main: Suhrkamp, 1983), 79–100, and on Faber's dualistic worldview, especially 80–86.

[16] See the character markers placed early in the narrative: "Ich war froh, allein zu sein" ("I was glad to be alone"; *HF* 7/9); "Menschen sind anstrengend" ("People are tiring"; *HF* 8/10).

[17] In the course of the narrative, Faber celebrates his fiftieth birthday; Sabeth is just twenty. It is, however, too little emphasized in the secondary literature that Faber generally seems to prefer relationships with younger women: Ivy is twenty-six (*HF* 61/66).

[18] See Hans Geulen, "Max Frischs *Homo faber*," in *Frischs "Homo Faber,"* ed. Schmitz, 101–32, here 119: "Noticeable in the first instance in Faber's report are precisely those protocol statements which regularly contain the following data: coordinates of time, coordinates of space, circumstances, the description of phenomena. The report is full of facts."

[19] See also the section on "Die sprachlich manifeste Eigendynamik der Psyche" in Schmitz, *Materialien, Kommentar*, 26–28.

[20] On the relation between teeth and castration anxiety in dreams, see Sigmund Freud, *The Standard Edition of the Complete Psychological Works*, ed. James

Strachey et al., vol. V: *The Interpretation of Dreams* (London: Hogarth Press, 1953), 387 n. 1. This note added in 1914 supplements the main text's theory that loss of teeth in dreams is related to male masturbation. Faber very frequently comments on other people's teeth throughout his narrative.

[21] Sigmund Freud, "The 'Uncanny'" [1919], *Standard Edition*, Vol. XVII: *An Infantile Neurosis and Other Works* (London: Hogarth Press, 1955), 217–52, here 220.

[22] See Walter Schmitz's assertion that "the economy of the *homo faber* conforms to the law of repression": Schmitz, "Max Frischs Roman *Homo faber*. Eine Interpretation," in *Frischs "Homo Faber,"* ed. Schmitz, 208–39, here 214.

[23] Allusions to Greek myth within the novel (notably to the Oedipus myth, *HF* 192/207, and the murder of Agamemnon by Klytemnestra, *HF* 136/143) have led a number of commentators to see the chain of events in which Faber becomes involved in terms of a mythical "plot." Schmitz sees Frisch's use of myth as more ironically intended; see *Materialien, Kommentar*, 57–58.

[24] Prominent cases in point are Gerhard Kaiser, in "Max Frischs 'Homo faber'" (for details see note 11 above), whose 1959 reading proved influential for subsequent interpretations of the figure of Hanna, and Michael Butler in *The Novels of Max Frisch* (London: Oswald Wolff, 1976). Both stress that Hanna's characteristics are as negative as Faber's.

[25] Kaiser, "Max Frischs 'Homo faber,'" 87. See Mona Knapp's rebuttal of Kaiser in her essay "'Eine Frau, aber mehr als das, eine Persönlichkeit, aber mehr als das: eine Frau': The Structural Function of the Female Characters in the Novels of Max Frisch," in *Beyond the Eternal Feminine: Critical Essays on Women and German Literature*, ed. Susan L. Cocalis and Kay Goodman (Stuttgart: Akademischer Verlag Hans-Dieter Heinz, 1982), 261–89, especially 273–75.

[26] This is a clear allusion to Günther Anders and marks Frisch's reception of Anders's book; see Anders's commentary on an overheard remark about the human being as a "faulty construction" (*Fehlkonstruktion*) in *Die Antiquiertheit des Menschen*, 31–35.

[27] Kaiser, "Max Frischs 'Homo faber,'" 87.

[28] Butler suggests that the model of synthesis is to be found in Sabeth, but in setting out why he thinks so, he in fact describes her relationship with Faber. He is also at this point not giving sufficient emphasis to the fact that, in the relationship with Faber, Sabeth figures as a kind of repetition of Hanna, and notably the narrative discards her once Faber and Hanna are reunited: *The Novels of Max Frisch*, 104.

[29] See Karl Jaspers's comment on the "levelling of the various ages of life" as an effect of "technical mass-order": *Man in the Modern Age*, 50.

[30] Michael Butler concurs with my interpretation here in seeing the night on Akrokorinth, and in particular the language game played by Faber and Sabeth, as figuring an ideal synthesis: *The Novels of Max Frisch*, 95. Walter Schmitz, however, is in clear disagreement, since in his view "metaphor in Frisch's poetology is the epitome of untruthful speech and creates connections without unifying. Thus Faber's and Sabeth's game of metaphors on Akrokorinth also demonstrates that

they are seeking one another, not that they — as a couple — had found and recognized each other": Schmitz, "Eine Interpretation," 230.

[31] Schmitz goes so far as to state: "Her ideas of time and transience [. . .] must be understood as authorial commentary": *Materialien, Kommentar,* 120 n. 151.

[32] Kaiser, as the commentator who most openly dislikes Hanna, quotes this analysis of Faber's behavior and concedes: "These accusations of Hanna's do indeed hit the nail on the head as far as fundamental behavioral patterns of the technological human being are concerned"; however, in the next paragraph, as he turns to the critique of Hanna's way of life, he finds that Hanna "de-naturalizes [. . .] the feminine principle by making it into a mere counter-ideology, into irrationalism. This is demonstrated already in her protest in principle against technology which exhausts itself in negation and has not the power to subsume the possibilities of technological behavior into a higher conception of the human being in any fruitful manner": Kaiser, "Max Frischs 'Homo faber,'" 86–87.

[33] Both Kaiser and Butler are keen to stress Hanna's antiquarianism, and so choose to overlook the signifiers that indicate that she is also modern in certain respects.

[34] Hélène Cixous and Catherine Clément, *The Newly Born Woman,* trans. Betsy Wing, intro. Sandra M. Gilbert. Theory and History of Literature, volume 24 (Manchester: Manchester UP, 1986), 85. See discussion in chapter 2.

[35] Christa Wolf, *Kein Ort. Nirgends,* in Wolf, *Werke,* ed. Sonja Hilzinger (Munich: Luchterhand, 2000), vol. 6, 84 / *No Place on Earth,* trans. Jan van Heurck (London: Virago, 1995), 93. Subsequent references appear in the text, identified as *KO* (in German to the *Werke* edition, in English to the van Heurck translation).

[36] The word defies translation; van Heurck comes up with "Youth-maiden" (19).

[37] Christa Wolf, *Störfall: Nachrichten eines Tages,* in Wolf, *Werke,* ed. Hilzinger, vol. 9, 29 and passim / *Accident: A Day's News,* trans. Heike Schwarzbauer and Rick Takvorian (London: Virago, 1989), 21. Subsequent references appear in the text, identified as *S* (in German to the *Werke* edition, in English to the Schwarzbauer/ Takvorian translation).

[38] Simone de Beauvoir, *The Second Sex,* trans. H. M. Parshley (Harmondsworth: Penguin, 1983), 94–95; see discussion in chapter 2 above. See also the further set of cultural oppositions: "The religion of woman was bound to the reign of agriculture, the reign of irreducible duration, of contingency, of chance, of waiting, of mystery; the reign of *Homo faber* is the reign of time manageable as space, of necessary consequences, of the project, of action, of reason" (107).

[39] For an insightful analysis of the symbolic construction of the brother-sister relationship, see Ursula Ziller, "Christa Wolf: *Störfall. Nachrichten eines Tages,*" in *Erzählen, Erinnern. Deutsche Prosa der Gegenwart. Interpretationen,* ed. Herbert Kaiser and Gerhard Köpf (Frankfurt am Main: Diesterweg, 1992), 354–71, especially 357–60.

[40] See chapter 3 above.

[41] The "list of activities" is very frequently quoted in the secondary literature, but this concluding sentence very seldom.

[42] William H. Rey, comparing this novel with the *Voraussetzungen einer Erzählung* (*Conditions of a Narrative*) that formed part of the *Kassandra* project, comments approvingly: "The accusatory 'they' has been replaced by the responsible 'we' which of course also includes the 'I' of the author": Rey, "Blitze im Herzen der Finsternis: Die neue Anthropologie in Christa Wolfs *Störfall*," *German Quarterly* 62.3 (1989): 373–83, here 373. In fact the transition from "they" to "we" takes place in the course of the novel, as I have shown here.

[43] Weigel has consistently argued that women are not *only* to be seen as the victims and the oppressed of history, as early feminist theory tended to claim, but are *also* implicated in the structures of the culture they inhabit; on this point see especially the concluding section of her essay "Towards a female dialectic of enlightenment: Julia Kristeva and Walter Benjamin," in Weigel, *Body- and Image-Space*, 78–79.

[44] In the closing pages of the novel (*S* 109–11/106–8), the narrator begins to read Joseph Conrad's novel *Heart of Darkness*. For commentaries on the significance of the references to Conrad, see Russell West, "Christa Wolf reads Joseph Conrad: *Störfall* and *Heart of Darkness*," *German Life and Letters* 50, no. 2 (April 1997): 254–65; Dieter Saalmann, "Elective Affinities: Christa Wolf's *Störfall* and Joseph Conrad's *Heart of Darkness*," *Comparative Literary Studies* 29, no. 3 (1992): 238–58; Saalmann, "Christa Wolf's *Störfall* and Joseph Conrad's *Heart of Darkness:* The Curse of the 'Blind Spot,'" *Neophilologus* 76, no. 1 (January 1992): 19–28; and Brigid Haines, "The Reader, the Writer, Her Narrator and Their Text(s): Intertextuality in Christa Wolf's *Störfall*," in, *Christa Wolf in Perspective,* ed. Ian Wallace (Amsterdam, Atlanta, GA: Rodopi, 1994), 157–72, especially 169.

[45] West, "Christa Wolf reads Joseph Conrad," 265.

[46] Anna K. Kuhn, *Christa Wolf's Utopian Vision: From Marxism to Feminism* (Cambridge: Cambridge UP, 1988), 225.

6: Pathologies: Elfriede Jelinek's *Die Klavierspielerin* and Rainald Goetz's *Irre*

ELFRIEDE JELINEK'S *DIE KLAVIERSPIELERIN* (The Piano Teacher) and Rainald Goetz's *Irre* (Crazy) were both published in 1983. As literary products of the early 1980s, they are exemplary of an intensified phase in the questioning of the Enlightenment conceptualization of selfhood and social order in the aftermath of the 1968 movement and the rise of the new feminism in the 1970s. The decade and a half before their publication was characterized by an extraordinary wave of critical-theoretical activity in Western Europe and the United States, corresponding in the intellectual arena to what Peter Wagner terms the "de-conventionalization" of social practices.[1] Two features of the very diverse theoretical work of the late 1960s and the 1970s are important to note. One is the rebellious turn among a broadly defined intellectual left in the West against the perceived totalitarian character of international capitalism and its ideological control of the masses, both via the false promises of consumerism and through its institutionalized regulation of social power and knowledge. The second is the key aspect of the critique of language — both as the sum of social signifying practices and as institutionalized discourse — as that by which social reality is produced and organized. On the one hand, this emphasis on language acts finally to unseat the Enlightenment subject from its central position as the agent of history, at any rate theoretically. Individual subjectivity and agency become a chimera, since the "individual" must be acknowledged, too, as the product of signifying practices and as always already determined by pre-existing orders of discourse.[2] On the other hand, the theoretical focus on signifying practices as the site of the production of social reality means that subversive and disruptive play with language becomes explicitly politicized, a means of destabilizing regulatory social or philosophical systems through undercutting the certainties of their meanings, revealing what has been excluded or repressed in order for them to function as systems at all, or making transparent the ideological purpose of their signs.

The aspect of subversive linguistic play as political practice became increasingly important within continental European feminist writing (perhaps rather less so in Anglo-American feminism, which retained a more pragmatic political attitude oriented toward the gaining of rights and social liberties for women). An early focus of feminist theorizing on the Franco-German axis in the 1970s was the quest for an authentic femininity, supposedly to be found expressed in aesthetic forms specific to women,[3] as opposed to a femininity defined and determined by its symbolic position in the masculine-feminine binary. This soon transpired to be a logical cul-de-sac, in that attempts to define this "femininity" invariably returned to terms derived from the patriarchal tradition. In an important essay for the mid-1970s German-language feminist theoretical scene, "Über die Frage: gibt es eine 'weibliche' Ästhetik?" (On the question: is there a "female" aesthetic?, 1976), Silvia Bovenschen addressed a range of contemporary attempts to conceptualize the authentic feminine and argued their limited usefulness. Read today, her essay gives insight into the ideas that were current in German feminist circles at the time. There was no point, she argued, in trying to connect back to a matriarchal past via the recourse to mythical figures, since there could be no direct link to the experiences of women in the twentieth century.[4] Nor was there any such thing as a consistent female counter-culture in history that could form the basis for the conceptualization of feminine language and art forms. Notions of women's "nature" were derived from male thinking; trying to turn them to positive account was simply to perpetuate the binary model. On this basis, Bovenschen is dismissive of Herbert Marcuse's contemporary vision of women's revolutionary potential, consisting in the "realisation of qualities which in the long history of patriarchal society have been attributed rather to women than to men," qualities such as "receptivity, sensitivity, non-violence, tenderness," in which Marcuse saw the potential to "undermine" the repressive rationality and work ethic of the capitalist order.[5] Bovenschen acknowledges the utopian lure of these qualities associated with femininity, but points out that they are symptomatic of women's historical subordination (95). In order to assert themselves against the constraints of patriarchal organization — in the family, professionally, or in the sphere of artistic practice — women were, by contrast, going to have to develop "new forms of productivity, of rationality and, if necessary, and it *is* necessary, of aggression" (95). As for the question of the "female aesthetic," Bovenschen is clear that the socialization of women, their historical exclusion from large areas of production and public life, as well as their traditional responsibility for biological and social reproduction, have shaped a different awareness and perspective. In what manner this difference will articulate itself in artistic forms cannot, however, be anticipated in a preemptive theory of "the feminine." Rather, according to Bovenschen, it must emerge from women's artistic practice that engages, as all artistic practice does, with the pre-existing tradition and its characteristic languages: "The critical engagement with the forms of language, the sign systems and the image-worlds, the symbols and the forms of behavior and communication is a piece of work which has only just begun and which will require considerable tenacity" (96).

Elfriede Jelinek: Strategies of Subversion

For a discussion of the literary text as a locus of linguistic violence and an aggressive, subversive, politically motivated play with pre-existing signifying systems, there can hardly be a more fitting object than the work of the Austrian writer Elfriede Jelinek. Having made her debut as a novelist in 1970, she achieved literary prominence with the publication in 1975 of *Die Liebhaberinnen* (Women as Lovers), a send-up of the Austrian *Heimatroman* that offers a glitteringly cynical analysis of the economic interests underlying romantic love. While Jelinek's exposé of the entrapment of working-class women within a merciless social and economic machinery seemed to place this novel within the literature of the women's movement, Jelinek proved a controversial figure in feminist circles since her work ran so counter to the mid-1970s trend of autobiographical, self-exploratory writing and the representation of positive emancipatory models. In an interview of the early 1990s, Jelinek explained the antagonism she had experienced from feminist readers as caused by the fact that she had never portrayed women as better and higher beings, which, she claimed, was how the women's movement wanted to see them, but rather as the distorted caricature (*Zerrbild*) produced by patriarchal society, which ultimately adapts its slaves to its own purposes.[6]

The target of Jelinek's writing was not only patriarchal society, but also the capitalist social order. As a Marxist feminist, she believed the emancipation of women to be impossible within the present capitalist system since their subjugation and objectification is inherent in its structures.[7] Under these circumstances, political action must necessarily be conceived of as a practice of negation of the existing structures. The word *Zerrbild* used in the interview referred to above offers a good clue to her textual strategy. Jelinek's method is to work with established linguistic patterns — the language of the media, of popular literary forms, of pornography, or, in work of the late 1980s onwards, even the higher register language of philosophy or the nineteenth-century German poetic tradition[8] — and through montage, extreme juxtapositions, or jumps in register (such as the unexpected introduction of the imagery of capitalist consumption or of fascist politics) to distort, grotesquely to exaggerate, or to undercut meanings, exposing the interests of the socioeconomic order in shaping and controlling its human objects.[9] Her target is language as an instrument of social domination, her aim to jam its functioning:

> Ich schlage sozusagen mit der Axt drein, damit kein Gras mehr wächst, wo meine Figuren hingetreten sind [. . .]. Meine Arbeitsweise funktioniert, wenn es mir gelingt, die Sprache zum Sprechen zu bringen, durch Montage von Sätzen, die verschiedene Sprachen miteinander konfrontiert, aber auch durch Veränderung von Worten oder Buchstaben, die im Idiom verhüllte Aussagen entlarvt.[10]

[I attack with an axe, so to speak, so that not a blade of grass can grow any more on the ground my figures have stepped on [. . .]. My method works when I succeed in getting language itself to speak, through the montage of sentences which confront different kinds of language with each other, but also through changes to words or single letters which expose the meanings hidden in familiar idioms.]

Die Klavierspielerin is generally regarded as something of an exception in her oeuvre, in that it is Jelinek's only work to have an acknowledged autobiographical basis[11] and on account of its fuller-than-usual psychological portraiture.[12] Given Jelinek's claim that she writes not about real people, but about persons as they are materialized in the form of linguistic templates or verbal patterns,[13] one should hesitate to see this text as in any way realist, however. The reading presented here will emphasize the dramatization in this novel, too, of linguistic registers and social significations.

Erika Kohut: The "Doubled" Female Figure as Pathological Case

The narrative of Jelinek's *Die Klavierspielerin* (1983) is concerned with Erika Kohut, the piano player of the novel's title. Her father having been sent to a sanatorium for the mentally ill during her childhood, she has since lived as the companion — as it were, the substitute husband — of her mother. It is her mother who has consistently promoted her talent as a pianist, hoping in the first instance that she would succeed in becoming an internationally recognized concert musician, while simultaneously inculcating in her a fear of sexual involvement with men. As the narrative makes plain, Frau Kohut senior is not so much interested in Erika's own independence and well-being as in the benefit to herself, in particular financial, of her daughter's career and status. By the time the narrative takes up Erika's story, she is a piano teacher at a conservatory of music, in her late thirties and yet still living in a small rented apartment with her mother with whom she even shares a bed. She has had a small number of short-lived relationships with men, by whom she has always been rapidly discarded. Erika's attempted rebellion against her domineering mother is expressed through sprees of buying fashionable clothes of which her mother disapproves — not only because they represent Erika's residual aspiration to femininity, but also because they divert money from her mother's goal of saving for an apartment of their own. In fact, Erika seldom wears these clothes, keeping them in the wardrobe as a form of fantasy, while preferring her spinsterish garb for her everyday working life. Erika's suppressed sexuality, meanwhile, has its only outlet in visits to peep shows and porn cinemas in Vienna's more insalubrious suburbs or in nocturnal wanderings across the Praterauen — Vienna's central park — where she spies on couples having sex in the bushes under the cover of darkness. Unable to live out her own sexuality, she has become a voyeur.

In the course of the narrative, however, she becomes the object of the sexual attentions of one of her pupils, the vigorous youth Walter Klemmer. Klemmer can, in the terms of this narrative, have no genuine romantic regard for Erika. Rather, he sees her as a means to an end, the older woman who will provide him with the sexual experience that will smooth his path to self-confident male subjecthood:

> Einmal muß jeder anfangen. Er wird bald die Anfängerstufe verlassen können, genau wie der Anfänger beim Autofahren sich zuerst ein gebrauchtes Kleinauto kauft und dann, beherrscht er es einmal, auf ein größeres und neues Modell umsteigt. [. . .] Lernen möchte er im Umgang mit einer um vieles älteren Frau — mit der sorgsam umzugehen nicht mehr nötig ist — , wie man mit jungen Mädchen umspringt, die sich weniger gefallen lassen. Könnte dies mit Zivilisation zu tun haben? [. . .] Er wird ihr alles behutsam beibringen, was sie für die Liebe benötigt, doch anschließend wird er sich lohnenderen Zielen und schwierigeren Aufgaben zuwenden, was das Rätsel Frau betrifft. Das ewige Rätsel. Nun wird einmal er ihr Lehrer sein.

> [Everyone has to start sooner or later. Soon he will be able to leave the beginner's level behind him, just like a new driver, who first buys a small secondhand car, then replaces it with a new and bigger model as soon as he becomes an experienced driver. [. . .] He would like to learn from a much older woman — you don't have to be that careful with her. He would like to learn how to deal with young girls, who won't put up with as much nonsense. Does this have anything to do with civilization? [. . .] He will cautiously teach her everything she needs for love, but then he will turn to more rewarding goals and more difficult tasks in regard to the female enigma. The eternal enigma. Some day he will be her teacher.][14]

As this passage depicting Klemmer's intentions already suggests, what ensues between Klemmer and Erika is a struggle for the dominant subject position in the relationship, whereby Erika, who is in cultural-historical terms attempting to usurp the subject position — as teacher, as subject of the gaze, and as sexual subject — traditionally allocated to the male, is predestined to come off worse. In their first extended sexual encounter in a girls' toilet in a school where they have been attending an orchestra rehearsal, Erika is able to retain the upper hand. At the conclusion of this scene, she promises to write him a letter in which she will lay out the rules of their relationship and what he is permitted to do to her — as indeed she subsequently does, setting down in writing a catalogue of masochistic fantasies of being bound, beaten, and violated by Klemmer, and forcing him to read the letter in her presence. In other words, while accepting the necessity (as she views it) of her inferior position in the sexual relationship, her status as object, Erika nevertheless sees the control and precise direction of the ways in which she is to be treated as object as a way of paradoxically reasserting herself as the subject rather than the object of the relationship. The narrative leaves the reader in some doubt as to whether Erika's masochistic desires are genuine, however:

> Erika zwingt Klemmer zum Lesen eines Briefs und *fleht innerlich dabei, daß er sich über den Inhalt des Briefs, kennt er ihn erst, hinwegsetzen möge bitte. Und sei es nur aus dem einen Grund, daß es wahrhaftig Liebe ist, was er empfindet,* und nicht nur deren lockerer Anschein, der auf den Matten glänzt. (*KS* 266, italics added)

> [Erika forces Klemmer to read the letter; *she mentally begs him to transcend the contents of the letter once he has read it. If only because what he feels is truly love* and not just a flimsy mirage shining on the meadows. (*KS* 213, italics added)]

She wishes to assert herself within the relationship, but also longs for her "Erlösung" ("redemption"; *KS* 257/206) in the form of a love that does not treat her as a mere object. Klemmer responds with ridicule (*KS* 271/217), then abuse, and Erika is abandoned once more to the relationship with her mother. Following what is perhaps the novel's most provocative scene, in which Erika throws herself with "cryptosexual" intent (*KS* 293/234) on her mother, revealing her pubic hair in a quasi-Freudian enactment of the girl-infant's realization that the mother is castrated (*KS* 294/234), the novel moves toward its close in a series of scenes in which Erika is finally and utterly humiliated — first reduced to begging on her knees for Klemmer's affection, subsequently violently beaten and raped by him, on his terms now, not hers, and lastly seeing him among a group of friends of his own age, apparently in a new liaison with a young female fellow-student. The novel ends with Erika leaving the house armed with a knife, intent on exacting revenge, but ultimately turning the knife against herself in an apparent failed attempt at suicide. As Marlies Janz has demonstrated, the close of the novel paraphrases the final scene of Kafka's *Der Proceß* (The Trial), but with the twist that Jelinek's Erika K., unlike Kafka's Josef K., does not even have the distinction of suffering a pointless death (81–82).

This is an outrageous and deliberately shocking narrative, the tale of a spinsterish woman who lives with her elderly mother, which progressively unfolds into scenes of sexual violence and masochistic fantasy. As ever with Jelinek, the shock effect is derived in large part from the distorting play with familiar linguistic registers. Prominent among these is, on the one hand, the language of bourgeois individualism, notably through the text's focus on artistic striving and music-making, and, on the other, allusions to psychoanalytic theory through the representation of family and sexual relations. The character Erika marks the point at which these discourses intersect: what is being displayed in her is the conflict between a woman's aspiration to cultural subjecthood in established bourgeois terms and the objectification and demotion of the female body in the same bourgeois cultural tradition. In other words, what we are dealing with here is another doubled figure: the female as both would-be subject and object. In Jelinek's treatment, the character's resulting internal conflict becomes a textbook pathological case study.

Erika's self-construction as bourgeois individual subject and her belief, characteristic of Enlightenment male subjectivity, in her singularity as an individual are emphatically established in a passage set early on in the narrative:

> Erika sagt heute schon von sich, sie sei eine Individualistin. Sie gibt an, daß sie sich nichts und niemandem unterordnen kann. Sie ordnet sich auch nur schwer ein. Etwas wie Erika gibt es nur ein einziges Mal und dann nicht noch einmal. Wenn etwas besonders unverwechselbar ist, dann nennt man es Erika. [. . .] Erika läßt sich nicht mit anderen zusammenfassen, und seien sie noch so gleichgesinnt mit ihr. Sie würde sofort hervorstechen. Sie ist eben sie. Sie ist so wie sie ist, und daran kann sie nichts ändern. [. . .] Erika ist eine stark ausgeprägte Einzelpersönlichkeit und steht der breiten Masse ihrer Schüler ganz allein gegenüber, eine gegen alle, und sie dreht am Steuerrad des Kunstschiffchens. (*KS* 18–19)

> [Erika says that she, Erika, is an individualist. She claims she cannot submit to anyone or anything. She has a hard time just fitting in. Something like Erika comes along only once, and then never again. If something is especially irreplaceable, it is called Erika. [. . .] Erika will not be lumped with other people, no matter how congenial they may be. She would instantly stick out. She is simply who she is. She is herself, and there's nothing she can do about it. [. . .] Erika is a sharply defined individual, a personality. She stands alone against the broad mass of her students, one against all, and she turns the wheel of the [little] ship of art. (*KS* 12–13, translation modified)]

The manner of narration here exposes her self-delusion. The passage demonstrates in classic form the technique of gradually shifting from reported speech ("Erika sagt [. . .] von sich, sie sei") to free indirect style: the phrases "Sie ist eben sie" ("She is simply who she is") and "Sie ist so wie sie ist, und daran kann sie nichts andern" ("She is herself, and there's nothing she can do about it") read as the transposition into the third-person of statements Erika might make about herself. In other words, the narration is revealing what Erika believes herself to be, not what she actually is. Moreover, the double use of "etwas" ("something"), culminating in the application to Erika of the neuter pronoun — "so nennt man es Erika" ("it is called Erika") — at least desexes her and at most implies her status as an object. The fact that the passage is repetitive, over-emphatic, acts further to undermine the truth content of its surface statements. The paragraph concludes with a direct allusion to the nineteenth-century bourgeois humanist tradition, which functions here to articulate Erika's hypertrophied sense of self as she attempts to place herself alongside one of the tradition's great artists: "Wenn ein Schüler nach ihrem Ziel fragt, so nennt sie die Humanität, in diesem Sinn faßt sie den Inhalt des Heiligenstädter Testaments von Beethoven für die Schüler zusammen, sich neben den Heros der Tonkunst mit aufs Postament zwängend" ("When a student asks her what her goal is, she says, "Humanity," thus summing up Beethoven's *Heiligenstadt Testament* for her pupils — and squeezing in next to the hero of music, on his pedestal"; *KS* 19/13).

The origin of Erika's belief in her own singular identity is shown in the text to be her mother in her function as Erika's main authority figure (*KS* 18/12). Given Frau Kohut senior's economic ambitions, the belief in her singularity that she has inculcated into her daughter reveals itself as a vehicle of the mother's social aspirations: Erika is to set herself apart from the masses, be something special — and thereby also raise her mother's social status. Bourgeois individualism is unmasked by the text as ideological, an aspirational target placed at the pinnacle of a hierarchically ordered class system, as is further suggested by the novel's representation of reluctant children driven to the conservatory to learn music in fulfillment of their parents' middle-class strivings.

Yet if ideology is false consciousness, which is how it is defined in classical Marxist theory, it is nevertheless still a form of consciousness. Erika's overweening sense of her own individuality, though uncovered by the text as an effect of language, translates itself into a characteristically aggressive self-assertion, notably in Erika's deployment of her knowledge of music and in her role as teacher, which she uses to subject her pupils to merciless humiliation. Her conceptualization of herself as a cut above the rest runs up against an obstacle, however, when she is forced to confront her sex and her sexuality. In Erika's recollections of her earlier sexual liaisons, it is the moment of coitus that topples the woman from the pedestal to which she aspires:

> Zuerst zog sie einen gewissen Genuß daraus, sich als Pianistin, wenn auch zur Zeit außer Dienst, aufblasen zu können. Keiner dieser Herren hatte je eine Pianistin daheim auf dem Kanapee sitzen gehabt. Sofort verhält der Mann sich ritterlich, und die Frau genießt die Aussicht im weiten Umkreis, über den Mann hinweg. Doch beim Liebesakt bleibt keine Frau lang grandios. Recht bald nahmen die jungen

Herren sich charmante Freiheiten heraus, die auch noch im Freien andauerten. Keine Autotür wird mehr aufgehalten, Spott wird über Ungeschicklichkeiten ausgegossen. Die Frau wird hernach belogen, betrogen, gequält und nicht oft angerufen. (*KS* 96)

[At first, she enjoyed preening herself: a pianist, albeit temporarily not performing. None of these men had ever had a pianist sitting on his sofa. Each man instantly behaved like a gentleman, and the woman enjoyed a wide view, over and above the man. But when she's having sex, no woman remains grandiose. The young men soon took charming liberties, both indoors and outdoors. Car doors were no longer held open, fun was poked at clumsiness. The woman was then lied to, cheated on, tormented, and often not called. (*KS* 75)][15]

The key to Erika's disturbed attitude to sex has, understandably enough, been sought by a number of commentators on the novel in the representation of her relationship to her domineering mother. As with Erika's conviction of her singularity, it is her mother who appears as the source of her fear of sexual involvement: "Die Mutter ist gegen eine spätere Heirat Erikas, weil sich meine Tochter nirgends ein- und niemals unterordnen könnte" ("Mother is against Erika's marrying later on, because 'my daughter could never fit in or submit anywhere'"; *KS* 19/13). One should hesitate to read too much into the characters' supposed psychology, however. Elizabeth Wright rightly remarks on the peculiar resistance of this text to a psychoanaytical reading, notwithstanding the fact that at first glance it seems to beg for one.[16] Janz goes further, and proposes that the reason why the novel does not leave room for psychoanalytical interpretation is that the relationships between its figures are already expressed in psychoanalytical terms within the text (72). The point is that Jelinek is transposing psychoanalytical theorems into what Janz terms pseudo-realistic narration. Her intention in doing so is to expose psychoanalysis as a regulatory discourse through the grotesque staging of its theoretical assumptions. Thus the mother-daughter relationship reproduces the mother-child dyad of Lacanian psychoanalytic theory, but without the intervention of the father as the "third term" that regulates the entry of the child into the symbolic order in the course of the oedipal phase. The father's transportation into the mental asylum is presented in the text as the family's loss of the "phallus," and in his absence Erika becomes a phallic substitute.[17] Her phallic status is presented in the image of the marital bed shared with her mother, but also, for example, in her occupation of the male position as the master of the gaze in the peepshow sequence:

Sie geht nicht in die Abteilung für Angestellte des Hauses, sondern in die Abteilung für zahlende Gäste. Es ist die wichtigere Abteilung.

Diese Frau will sich etwas anschauen, das sie sich zu Hause viel billiger im Spiegel betrachten könnte. [. . .] Erika schreitet, ganz Herrin, in die Venusgrotte hinein. (*KS* 66–67)

[She does not walk into the employee section, she steps into the section for paying guests — the more important section. This woman wants to look at something that she could see far more cheaply in her mirror at home. [. . .] Erika, thoroughly a professor, strides into the Venus grotto. (*KS* 51, translation modified)][18]

Likewise, in relaying her wishes for their sexual relationship to Klemmer in written form, Erika can be seen as asserting her phallic position. As Janz suggests: "In the bureaucratic administration and communication in written form even of her fantasies of subordination, Erika retains control and power" (79).

In terms of Freud's account of the development of female/feminine sexuality, however, Erika's attempts to occupy the phallic position *as a woman* mean that she is in effect psychosexually arrested within the oedipal conflict, for attaining "normal" femininity involves the girl-child's acceptance of her own castration and the transferral of her desire from the mother as primary love-object to the father as the possessor of the penis. As Freud sets out in his 1933 lecture on "Die Weiblichkeit" (Femininity), failure to make this transition may lead to neurosis:

The discovery that she is castrated is a turning-point in a girl's growth. Three possible lines of development start from it: one leads to sexual inhibition or to neurosis, the second to change of character in the sense of a masculinity complex, the third, finally, to normal femininity.[19]

Freud's description of the masculinity complex in this lecture appears particularly relevant to the representation of Erika, displaying as she does an identification with the "phallic mother," while resisting the necessary "wave of passivity" that, according to Freud, "opens the way to the turn towards femininity."[20] In Jelinek's representation, though, the identification with the phallic mother — shown in the way she reproduces her mother's domineering behavior in the relations with those weaker than herself, such as her pupils at the conservatory[21] — is presented as the product of her mother's construction of her identity. Erika's *underlying* sexual desires are in conflict with her phallic status, and reveal the passive traits that Freud equates with "normal" femininity.

Erika's castration complex vis-à-vis the "boy's far superior equipment," as Freud calls it,[22] is demonstrated in flashback scenes from her childhood and youth in the novel's first part, notably in a scene with her cousin Burschi where she is wrestled to the ground and ends with her lips pressed longingly against his penis (*KS* 55/42–43). Throughout, the novel reproduces established cultural gender binaries. The male, notably in the figures of Burschi and later of Klemmer, appears as both sportsman and as scientist in training (Klemmer is not only Erika's star pupil at the conservatory, but also a student of technology, while Burschi is reading medicine). As master both of knowledge and of his own and others' bodies, the young male is shown to occupy with un-self-conscious confidence the position of cultural subject allocated to him within the symbolic order. The female, by contrast, is represented as corrupt corporeality. Particularly with regard to her sex, Erika is afflicted by her awareness of her body as organic matter: "Zwischen ihren Beinen Fäulnis, gefühllose weiche Masse. Moder, verwesende Klumpen organischen Materials" ("Rot between her legs, an unfeeling soft mass. Decay, putrescent lumps of organic material"; *KS* 246/197); "Im Gehen haßt Erika diese poröse, ranzige Frucht, die das Ende ihres Unterleibs markiert" ("Striding along, Erika hates that porous, rancid fruit that marks the bottom of her abdomen"; *KS* 247/198).[23] Moreover, in her visit to the peepshow, what Erika sees in the female body on display is what the male sees, presented in the language of Lacanian psychoanalysis: "Der Mann schaut auf das Nichts, er schaut auf den reinen Mangel" ("The man looks at nothing, he looks at pure lack"; *KS* 67/52). Erika internalizes this cultural construction of her sex; indeed, in her own self-perception she ultimately becomes nothingness (247/198).

In Erika's abnormal behavior, which reaches its climax in the letter composed for Klemmer with its catalogue of masochistic fantasies, Jelinek represents her figure's attempts to reconcile contrary impulses. On the one hand, Erika has learned to despise her own sex and to fear objectification by the male in the sexual act. In response to her fears and under the influence of her mother, she has constructed a pseudo-phallic identity for herself, based on conceptions of control and mastery, whether this be as teacher, as musician, as subject of the masculine-connoted gaze, or as the masochist who dictates exactly how she is to be mishandled. On the other hand, she attempts to initiate this masochistic contract precisely because she is in actuality caught by her sexual desires that are both passive and romantic in nature: "Erika liebt den jungen Mann und wartet auf Erlösung durch ihn. Sie gibt kein Anzeichen für Liebe von sich, damit sie nicht unterliegt" ("Erika loves the young man and is waiting for him to redeem her. She reveals no sign of love, so she won't have to endure defeat"; *KS* 257/206). In the desire for redemption in the love relationship, Erika appears as a literary successor to Bachmann's female character *Ich*. The result of the conflict within Erika is presented in the form of an extreme contradiction in Erika's wishes:

> Erika wird sich Klemmer vollkommen entziehen, falls er sich weigern sollte, ihr Gewalt zuzumuten. Doch sie wird jederzeit glücklich über

seine Zuneigung sein, die Gewalt ausschließt gegen das Geschöpf seiner Wahl. Nur unter der Bedingung von Gewalt jedoch darf er sich Erika zulegen. [. . .] Erika wartet darauf, daß Klemmer aus Liebe Gewaltverzicht schwört. Erika wird sich aus Liebe verweigern und verlangen, daß mit ihr geschehen soll, was sie in dem Brief bis ins Detail gehend fordert, wobei sie inbrünstig hofft, daß ihr erspart bleibe, was sie im Brief verlangt. (*KS* 266–67)

[Erika will withdraw from Klemmer completely if he refuses to subject her to violence. But she will always be happy about his affection, which excludes violence against the creature of his choice. He can take Erika only under the condition of violence. [. . .] Erika waits for Klemmer to abjure violence for the sake of love. Erika will refuse for the sake of love, and she will demand that he do to her what she has detailed in the letter, whereby she ardently hopes that she will be spared what is required in the letter. (*KS* 213)]

Jelinek's representation here of the mutually exclusive desires of her psychological case-study corresponds closely to Freud's account of the aetiology of neurosis in the "Allgemeine Neurosenlehre" (General Theory of the Neuroses) of 1917. Freud writes of the "contention between wishful impulses" in the neurotic, whereby "[one] part of the personality champions certain wishes while another part opposes them and fends them off." Defining the conflict more closely, Freud arrives at the proposition that the pathological conflict is to be understood as one between the sexual libido and the nonsexual "ego-instincts" (*Ichtriebe*).[24] This is a plausible diagnosis of Erika's case. Moreover, the conflicting wishes that come to the surface in the scene in which Erika presents her letter to Klemmer permit the interpretation of the letter itself as a neurotic symptom in the terms of Freud's analysis: "Thus the symptom emerges as a many-times-distorted derivative of the unconscious libidinal wish-fulfilment, an ingeniously chosen piece of ambiguity with two meanings in complete mutual contradiction."[25] Even Erika's quasi-rape of her mother following her rejection by Klemmer lends itself to being read as a characteristically grotesque representation of Freud's description of "a return to the first incestuous objects of the libido" as "a feature that is found in neurotics with positively fatiguing regularity."[26]

The identification of multiple correspondences between both Freudian and Lacanian psychoanalytic theory and Jelinek's representation of her characters' psychology raises the question of Jelinek's purpose in thus staging psychoanalytical theorems in her text. At one level, it is clear that what is at issue is a subversive and ironic play with psychoanalytical terminology. As a form of scientific discourse that perpetuates the social demotion of women and denies them access to the status of subject, psychoanalysis was a frequent target of feminist attack in the 1970s: witness, for example, Hélène Cixous's essay "Sorties" or Luce Irigaray's *Speculum of the Other Woman,* both of which take the critique of the definitions of woman in psychoanalytic theory as their starting point for their attack on the Western metaphysical tradition. At another level, however, the representation of Erika as a pathological case study frequently works with, rather than against, psychoanalytical accounts of female sexuality and of neurosis, as I have demonstrated. This suggests a slightly different underlying agenda, namely the demonstration, in grotesque, exaggerated, and thus shocking form, of the consequences in terms of human behavior of life in a society for which the psychoanalytical account of psychosexual identity formation, differentiated according to biological sex, represents an *accurate account* of the social symbolic order. Under these conditions, the female, as always already "castrated," is barred from full cultural subjecthood, embedded as she is in a system that defines the female sex as lacking the signifier of social power. The male, by contrast, is perpetually endorsed as subject, even where he is a member of the exploited lower economic classes. It is not insignificant that the men who frequent the peepshow are the inhabitants of one of the city's poorer districts, who are seduced into spending their paltry earnings on an illusory form of sexual mastery,[27] or that the male of the couple Erika observes copulating in the Praterauen is a Turkish guestworker. In both of these instances, the link is made between the capitalist organization of society, its endemic economic exploitation of the male of lower social status, and the occupation by women of a lower position still in a hierarchical system of the exploitation of weaker others, so that at least in relation to this lowest of the low, the male can believe himself the master.[28] In other words, the predetermination of woman as sexual object for the male with his "far superior equipment" is revealed as integral to the capitalist organization of society.

Freud himself acknowledged that the construction of femininity as passive and masochistic, on which his own theoretical account relied, had a social causation:

> The suppression of women's aggressiveness which is prescribed for them constitutionally and *imposed on them socially* favours the development of powerful masochistic impulses, which succeed, as we know, in binding erotically the destructive trends which have been diverted inwards. Thus masochism, as people say, is truly feminine.[29]

Moreover, he writes that: "Pathology has always done us the service of making discernible by isolation and exaggeration conditions which would remain concealed in a normal state" (121). Jelinek takes Freud at his word,[30] presenting through the pathological case of Erika Kohut a condemnation of a social system — and a system of social signification — in which psychosexual identity formation coincides with the organization of socioeconomic interests. It is a bitter analysis, entirely lacking in the utopian dimension found, for example, in Bachmann's not dissimilar assessment of a masochistic structure in feminine desire in *Malina*. As with the relationship of *Ich* to Ivan and the father/murderer, Erika's masochism is predicated upon a masculine subjecthood constructed through mastery of the other, including the subsumption of the female sexual partner into the trajectory of the male's own subject formation.[31] The implication is that, in desiring the male, the female is, under the given cultural circumstances, in effect colluding in her own objectification.[32] But where Bachmann nevertheless generates at least a shimmer of the "utopia of a humanity which, itself no longer distorted, no longer needs distortion" (Horkheimer and Adorno),[33] Jelinek offers no such alternative perspective. The social system represented in her fictional universe is too seamless, too closed — and Jelinek's own assessment of the possibilities for change within society too pessimistic[34] — to allow for the crucial breach in the system that might hold in suspension the anticipation of another way of being.

In chapter 3, I suggested that the "Sprung in der Wand" (crack in the wall), the site in which Bachmann's female character *Ich* is retained as articulate absence at the conclusion of *Malina*, lends itself to being read as just such a breach in the symbolic order that privileges masculine-connoted singularity and self-containment. In Jelinek's novel, this breach is, as it were, transposed into the incisions made by Erika in her own body in response to her entrapment in an intolerably rigid system of social signification. The motif of Erika's self-mutilation is introduced in the flashback scenes in the novel's first part, notably in connection with her confrontations with self-confident masculinity. Thus it is immediately following the encounter with her cousin Burschi that we first see Erika cutting herself:

> SIE sitzt allein in ihrem Zimmer, abgesondert von der Menge, die sie vergessen hat, weil sie ein so leichtes Gewicht ist. Sie drückt auf niemand. Aus einem vielschichtigen Paket wickelt sie sorgfältig eine Rasierklinge heraus. Die trägt sie immer bei sich, wohin sie sich auch wendet. Die Klinge lacht wie der Bräutigam der Braut entgegen. (*KS* 56)

> [SHE sits alone in her room, isolated from the crowd, which has forgotten her because she is such a lightweight. She jostles no one. From an intricate package, she carefully unwraps a razor blade. She always takes it everywhere. The blade smiles like a bridegroom at a bride. (*KS* 43)]

In a further development of the motif, Erika's self-mutilation is represented as a substitute for the sexual encounter that she sees as necessarily condemning her to degradation and humiliation as the object of another's desire. The language of a later cutting scene alerts us to the fact that her self-harm is a means for the girl Erika, who feels herself so disempowered, to retain a modicum of control over her own body:

SIE setzt sich mit gespreizten Beinen vor die Vergrößerungsseite des Rasierspiegels und vollzieht einen Schnitt, der die Öffnung vergrößern soll, die als Tür in ihren Leib hineinführt. [. . .] Wie die Mundhöhle ist auch dieser Körperein- und -ausgang nicht direkt als schön zu bezeichnen, doch er ist nötig. Sie ist sich selbst ganz ausgesetzt, *was immer noch besser ist, als anderen ausgesetzt zu sein. Sie hat es in der Hand, und eine Hand hat auch Gefühle. Sie weiß genau, wie oft und wie tief.* (*KS* 110, italics added)

[SHE sits down in front of the magnifying side of the shaving mirror; spreading her legs, she makes a cut, magnifying the aperture that is the doorway into her body. [. . .] Like the mouth cavity, this opening cannot exactly be called beautiful, but it is necessary. She is entirely at her own mercy, *which is still better than being at someone else's mercy. It's still in her hands, and a hand has feelings too. She knows precisely how often and how deep.* (*KS* 86)][35]

Notable in both of these quoted scenes is the insistent use of the language of fluidity. The blood "rieselt warm und lautlos und nicht unangenehm. Es ist so stark flüssig. Es rinnt ohne Pause. [. . .] Es rinnt und rinnt und rinnt und rinnt" ("oozes, warm, silent, and the sensation is not unpleasant. It's so liquid. It runs incessantly. [. . .] It runs and runs and runs and runs"; *KS* 57/44); "Die Blutstropfen sickern, rinnen, mischen sich mit ihren Kameraden, werden zu einem steten Rinnsal. Dann ein roter, gleichmäßig und beruhigend rinnender Strom, als sich die einzelnen Rinnsale vereinigen" ("The drops ooze, run, blend with their comrades, turning into a red trickle, then a soothingly steady red stream when the individual trickles unite"; *KS* 111/87). Description of this kind provides striking imagery in illustration of Armando R. Favazza's diagnosis of repetitive episodic self-mutilation as "a morbid form of self-help," an attempt to find "temporary relief from a host of painful symptoms such as anxiety, depersonalization, and desperation."[36] The flow of blood figures a momentary dissolution of the rigid boundaries of discipline and self-containment that constrict Erika, but in an environment controlled by herself. There is a shadowy repetition of these scenes of self-harm in the novel's closing passage, where Erika turns the blade intended for Klemmer upon herself, but the releasing fluidity is no longer emphasized: "An Erikas Schulter klafft ein Riß, widerstandslos hat sich zartes Gewebe geteilt. [. . .] Blut sickert aus ihr heraus" ("A gap yawns in Erika's shoulder; tender tissue has divided unresistingly. [. . .] Blood oozes out of her"; *KS* 352/280).

It is the motif of self-mutilation that forms a first link between *Die Klavierspielerin* and Rainald Goetz's *Irre* (also 1983), like Jelinek's novel a work with an acknowledged autobiographical basis.[37] In Goetz's novel, however, it is the male protagonist Raspe who is the self-harmer, appearing at a party ornamented with fresh rivulets of blood and with a razor blade dangling from a leather thong around his neck:

> Hat jemand lachend auf seine Oberschenkel gewiesen und gesagt, perfekt täuschende Imitation super wahrscheinlich Plastik sag mal wo hast du das her, hat er kommentarlos, jedoch freundlich die an seiner Brust baumelnde Rasierklinge zur Hand genommen, sie auf ein unversehrtes Stück Haut seines Unterarms etwa gesetzt und dann langsam, gut sichtbar und tief in die Haut eingeschnitten. Die so hergestellte Spalte ist für einen Augenblick von hell weißen Wundrändern eingefaßt gewesen, dann hat sie sich, vom Wundgrund her, mit Blut zu füllen begonnen [. . .]. Das frische helle Blut hat der Schwerkraft gehorchend seinen Weg nach unten gesucht, hat sich gekreuzt mit den alten eingetrockneten, brüchig schwarzen Rinnsalen und so hat jede Frage nach der Beschaffenheit der Wunden zu neuen Ornamenten auf der Haut geführt.

> [If anyone pointed laughingly at his thighs and said great imitation takes you in completely probably plastic say where did you get it, he would, without saying a word, though in a perfectly friendly manner, take the razor blade dangling at his breast into his hand, place it on an unscathed piece of skin on his lower arm, for example, and then slowly and in the sight of all cut deep into the skin. The cleft thus produced was for a brief moment framed by the bright white edges of the wound, until it began to fill with blood from the bottom [. . .]. The fresh bright blood, in keeping with the law of gravity, sought a pathway downwards, crossing the old, dried-up, flaky black channels, and so it was that every question as to how the wounds were formed led to new ornaments on his skin.][38]

A comparison of the cutting scenes in the two novels reveals a distinct difference that reproduces the public-private dichotomy familiar within gender discourse. Erika's self-mutilation is a strictly private activity, conducted in the isolation of a closeted space. Goetz's Raspe, by contrast, is a "Spinner" (nutcase; *I* 20) who performs the ritual of cutting his body in public. Yet the progression of the scene indicates that Raspe's self-harm is to be seen as a distorted appeal for understanding, even for love, moreover with a suggestion of homosexual desire, which the character finds difficult to acknowledge to himself:

> Einzig W., so Raspe, habe ihn verstanden, ja, sogar sich selbst in ihm wiedererkannt. Monate später habe er, Raspe, nächtelang Diskussionen mit W. geführt, man habe eine großangelegte Theorie der Selbstverletzung projektiert, wobei es ihm, rückblickend betrachtet, so Raspe, keineswegs nur um diese Theorie gegangen sei, sondern mindestens ebensosehr um die Nähe zu W., was er sich seinerzeit

jedoch nicht einzugestehen erlaubt habe. Statt dessen habe er, während W. eloquent seine Theorie entwickelt habe, sich geradezu überfallen gefühlt, so später Raspe, überfallen gefühlt von dem befremdlichen Wunsch, diese Lippen küssen zu wollen, überdeutliches und irritierendes Begehren, W. zu küssen. (*I* 20)

[W. was the only one who had understood him, said Raspe, even recognizing himself in him. Months afterwards he, Raspe, had had night-long discussions with W., together they had devised an ambitious theory of self-mutilation, though looking back, what had been important to him, said Raspe, was not this theory so much as, at least as importantly, being close to W., which at the time he hadn't allowed himself to acknowledge. Instead, while W. eloquently elaborated his theory, Raspe had felt himself really quite overwhelmed, as he said later, overwhelmed by the disturbing wish to kiss those lips, a plainly felt and persistent desire to kiss W.]

What the two characters, Jelinek's Erika and Goetz's Raspe, appear to have in common is that their self-mutilation is an expression of their sense of failing control over their own lives, their sense, then, of failing subjecthood. And what the consideration of Goetz's novel alongside Jelinek's highlights is that such a failure of subjecthood and such a pathological attempt both to assert a form of physical self-control and to achieve release from a constricting symbolic order is not an exclusively female dilemma. A man, too, may find himself overtaxed by culturally predetermined patterns of male subjectivity that he cannot live up to or actively rejects, and in response to which he may adopt self-destructive behavior, as the pathological symptom of that failure.

Goetz's Raspe: The Male Subject in Crisis as Pathological Case

Rainald Goetz's *Irre* is divided into three sections, entitled "Sich Entfernen" (Distancing Oneself/Taking Oneself Away), "Drinnen" (Inside), and "Die Ordnung" (Order). The first two sections are focused largely on the world of a psychiatric clinic, with the opening section structured as a collage of scenes depicting, often from a highly sympathetic, even internal perspective, a series of patients suffering from severe pathological conditions. These are interspersed with further scenes from the clinic, monologues, statements, letters written by the clinic employees whose job it is to look after the patients, dialogues between an apparent authorial first-person narrator and a friend on theoretical approaches to mental illness and its relation to society, and occasional passages of narrative featuring the character Raspe who appears in the scene already quoted. There is no chronological structure in this first section: the reader encounters it as a sequence of frag-ments with no clear or comprehensible relation between them.

The second section, "Drinnen," is a traditionally structured, third-person narrative with a discernible chronology that relates the story of Raspe, a young psychiatrist who arrives at the clinic as his first job after the completion of his studies. Unable to uphold the requisite boundary between himself and his patients, or to support the methods, such as elec-tric shock treatment, used by some of the doctors to suppress the patients' symptoms, and increasingly in doubt as to the meaning of his work, Raspe gradually slides into depression and paranoia. Early in his employment, he begins to seek relief from the unbearable nature of his job with nightly visits to clubs where he drinks heavily. Later he turns to drugs and to the anarchic punk scene, gets involved in violent brawls, until finally he arrives at "die Aktion mit den Schnittwunden, Rasierklingenschnittwun-den am ganzen Körper, von der Kleidung bedeckt, vom Arztkittel, ja, vom Arztkittel immer noch" (the action with the cut-wounds, razor-blade-cut-wounds over his whole body, covered by his clothing, by the doctor's coat, yes, still by the doctor's coat; *I* 225). The section closes with a scene in the clinic's garden, Raspe among the patients, unable to differentiate between them and himself:

> Ich denke schon, ich bin ein Delinquent. Habe ich Schuld auf mich geladen?, welche Schuld? Gefesselt saß Raspe auf der Bank und fühl-lte in sich plötzlich einen Freiheitsrausch.
> Alles war am Ende eins. (*I* 227)

> [I suppose it's true, I'm a delinquent. Have I heaped guilt on myself? What guilt? Transfixed, Raspe sat on the bench and felt within him-self a sudden ecstasy of freedom.
> It was all one in the end.]

In retrospect, the scenes from the first section can be slotted by the reader into the chronology of the second section's narrative, understood as insights into characters seen in the latter from an external perspective, or grasped as fragments of a critique of psychiatry.

The third and final section, "Die Ordnung," reverts to a piecemeal structure, now narrated — or, more accurately, *written,* for the nature of the text as text is emphasized — by a first-person authorial narrator/writer who has Raspe's experiences and a history of breakdown behind him. In other words, the nature of novel as an autobiographical project is implied in retrospect, whereby the name "Raspe" can now be understood as functioning as a fictional device to hold together a coherent narra-tive presenting the writer's experience at a distance from himself and in the third-person perspective. A progression is implied, in that in this final section the narrator has turned his back on the "ÄrzteArschlöcher" (doctor-arseholes) and found a sphere of activity for himself "in der KULTUR" (in CULTURE; *I* 236). There remains, too, some sense of chronological development, in that the narrative moves from a period of recovery from breakdown at the beginning of the section through a sequence of months toward the goal of the text's end-point: "Das *Ende*" (The *end; I* 314). At the same time, however, this third section functions simply as a "*space*" (*I* 299, English in original) for the idiosyncratic collection of fragments of perception, opinion, emotive expression, dialogue, images: "Und der einzige, der dieses irre Projekt zusammenhalten kann, ist logisch ein gescheit irres und zugleich irr gescheites ICH" (And the only one who can hold together this crazy project is, logically, a cleverly crazy and at the same time crazily clever "I"; *I* 279).

Not unlike the conservatory of music in Jelinek's *Die Klavierspielerin*, the psychiatric clinic in Goetz's novel functions as a site in which the illusions of bourgeois Enlightenment subjectivity can be explored and exposed. Just as Erika Kohut defined herself before her own consciousness as an individual subject through recourse to the historical goals of Enlightenment thought — "When a student asks her what her goal is, she says, 'Humanity'" (*KS* 14/13) — so the medical student Raspe has chosen to pursue a career in psychiatry on the basis of an individual identification with the power of science to improve the human condition:

> Und hatte er etwa sechs Jahre Medizin studiert, um dann als Augenarzt zu enden, als Röntgenologe oder Spezialist für kranke Haut? Nein, der Mensch, der ganze Mensch muß mein Patient sein [. . .]. Und hatten nicht die vielen entkräfteten Augen so zu ihm gesprochen: Nicht mein Körper ist krank, krank ist meine Seele. Notwendig war Raspes Entscheidung für die Psychiatrie. Möglich ist einzig die Psychiatrie. (*I* 164–65)

> [And had he studied medicine for six years only to end up as an ophthalmologist, radiologist, or specialist in skin diseases? No, the human being, the whole human being must be my patient [. . .]. And hadn't the many exhausted eyes spoken to him thus: It is not my body that is sick, sick is my soul. Raspe's decision in favour of psychiatry was a necessary one. Psychiatry is the only possibility.]

On his first day in the clinic, Raspe summons into his mind the ambitions that have brought him to this place: they are fantasies of his singularity as an individual, and of the exceptional nature of his gifts. He wants to be a professor, the most extraordinary, most incredible professor, one who will revolutionize German psychiatry (*I* 116).

Yet these dreams of individual achievement, characteristic as much as anything of idealistic youth, soon come up against their limits in the reality of the clinic as a regulatory system. One of Raspe's fellow-doctors on the ward, Bögl, introduces Raspe to the rules that restrict individual agency in the workplace (*I* 122–23). It becomes evident that, beyond the relaxation in the aftermath of the student movement of the stipulation that assistant doctors must wear a tie and keep their hair cut short (*I* 123), the doctors are still bound by the requirements of their place within a strict hierarchy of power, the latter represented in the seating order in the library where the doctors' morning conference is held. At his first morning conference, Raspe in error sits among the professors at the top end of the table (*I* 119–20); on the next occasion, although he has not been reprimanded, he takes his place at the back of the room, as befits his rank as junior (*I* 135). The "house style" (*I* 123), to which all who work in the clinic are subordinate, is ultimately determined by the clinic's director, represented as a caricature of the self-disciplined, physically superb, and humane Enlightenment subject:

> Er hatte weißes ungelichtetes welliges Haar, und in seinem Gesicht war dieses tatenhungrige, entscheidungsfreudige Tiefbraun. War da nicht eine Güte zu erkennen, in den Zügen? Sie waren gestrafft, fast hager, und zeigten doch mehr als Disziplin und Selbstverzicht. (*I* 151)

> [He had a full head of white wavy hair, and in his face was this deep brown that spoke of his hunger for action, his joy in decision-making. Wasn't there a goodness discernible in those features? They were taut, almost gaunt, and yet they displayed more than discipline and self-denial.]

In an early interview with the director, Raspe's notions of treating the whole human being are dismissed as the illusion of youth. The director's research specialty, and so the specialty of the university clinic that operates under his directorship, is biologically oriented psychiatry (*I* 152), which transpires to be a euphemism for the pharmaceutical treatment of psychiatric illness. One of the expectations of Raspe's employment is that he will conduct research on a defined topic in this field. In terms of his daily work with the patients on his ward, Raspe must later ask himself if he is actually anything more than a prescriber of pills (*I* 214).

It is not only the regulatory system within the clinic that deprives the doctors of their agency, but also their helplessness in the face of the intractibility of the patients' psychoses. The drugs administered in the clinic deaden the patients' psychotic symptoms, creating an atmosphere of silent heaviness and of agonizing stasis on the ward (*I* 111). But they do not heal. Patients are routinely discharged from the clinic, only to return again after a few weeks or months (*I* 197). One of the patients, Stelzer, is submitted to the violence of electric shock therapy, which for a time cures him of his obsessive self-harm, but within months he has reverted (*I* 196). Raspe has to ask himself what the sense is of the work he does (*I* 197).

The theme of the doctors' resignation, and their attempts to convince themselves of their ability nevertheless to make a difference, appears in narrative fragments depicting individuals other than Raspe in the novel's first section. Herr Dr. Andreas Hippius, who wears his hair in tousled shoulder-length curls (*I* 40), is shown thinking about the influence of his determined unconventionality on the conformist world of the clinic. His interior monologue betrays that his sense of his own individual agency is in fact limited to the perceived effect of his hair on his environment and his colleagues (*I* 42). Nor is this attempt to retrieve a sense of agency gender-specific. In another interior monologue in this section, a female doctor who has recently achieved success with a research presentation at a conference reflects on her desire to maintain her distance from the system and on her commitment to the patients' interests above all else: "Auch ich spüre in mir die mächtige resignative Tendenz, die alles hier in der Klinik unterjocht. Aber ich bekämpfe sie. Und ich glaube, ich kann etwas erreichen, doch, davon bin ich überzeugt" (I, too, feel within me the powerful resignative tendency that holds everything here in the clinic in its thrall. But I fight against it. And I believe I can achieve something, I do, I'm convinced of it; *I* 87). The rhetorical construction of both scenes betrays the underlying attempt at self-reassurance, which in fact serves to consolidate the novel's diagnosis of the nullity of individual agency in the system represented by the clinic.

The way to succeed under these circumstances, as in the capitalist social order more generally, is not to seek the meaning of one's activities in "changing the world" (*I* 217), but rather pragmatically to accept the limits set by one's surroundings and to pursue success within the given terms: "ebenso hält den tagtäglich praktizierten Leistungsvergleich ein denkendes Subjekt nur aus, wenn es sich den dadurch vorgeschriebenen *Weg zum Erfolg* zu seinem Lebenszweck macht" (likewise the thinking subject can only sustain the daily practice of comparing his attainments with those of others if the *path to success* that is determined in this way becomes for him the purpose of his existence), as Herr Doktor Karl Held states in another of the narrative fragments in the novel's first section (*I* 98–99, italics in the original). If Raspe is at first overwhelmed by his experiences of the clinic, to the point of a dangerous near-dissolution of his identity (*I* 153), as he becomes accustomed to the environment, he adapts, even begins to taste the pleasures of power:

> Es war recht schön, im Kittel so einher zu gehen, wie die anderen, und ernst zu sitzen. Plötzlich war da auch die Macht, ja, die hat gelockt. [. . .] Zu herrschen war eine merkwürdige Lust, und Raspe hatte, ohne recht zu wissen, wie, schon davon geschmeckt. (*I* 172)

> [It felt good to walk about in the doctor's coat as the others did and to sit so seriously. Suddenly one felt the sense of one's own power,

> yes, that was enticing. [. . .] There was a strange pleasure to be had
> in ruling, and Raspe had, without really knowing how it had hap-
> pened, already tasted that pleasure.]

Fantasies of success entice him, expressed as the emphatic assertion of the
individual will: "Größenwahn, wilde Ambitionen auf eine wissenschaftli-
che Blitzkarriere: ich muß ich will ich werde ich will will will" (Delusions
of grandeur, wild ambitions to rise swiftly up the career ladder: I must I
will I'm going to I will will will; *I* 179).

Success in these terms is bought at the price of not *seeing*, however.
Raspe's adaptation to his employment is described in terms of the loss
of the ability to perceive his environment and a concomitant loss of the
pain (*Schmerz*) that afflicted him when the clinic was new to him and his
perceptions were sharp: "Man kennt, was man kennt, und das Auge wird
so stumpf. Der schmerzende Beobachtungszwang hatte längst nachgelas-
sen" (One knows what one knows, and the eye becomes so dulled. The
painful compulsion to observe had long since slackened; *I* 174). Where
he does not succeed in maintaining his self-protective blindness, doubts
return and helplessness — to be obliterated in the nighttime battle against
consciousness:

> Es gab die Tage in der Klinik und ein Funktionieren darin, jenseits
> von Entschlüssen, dennoch nicht nur blind. Begann er darüber
> nachzudenken, schien Raspe das Leben so kompliziert, schlechthin
> unbewältigbar. Da war der Alkohol. (*I* 179)
>
> [There were the days in the clinic and a functioning in it, beyond any
> decision-making, and yet not only unseeing. If he began to reflect
> on what he was doing, life seemed so complicated to Raspe, quite
> unmanageable. That's where alcohol came in.]

Raspe's ability to see his surroundings is restored in a day of crisis,
initiated by the admission of a new patient, in the third chapter of the
novel's second section, and this marks the turning point in the trajectory
of his narrative. "Aufhören, sagte Raspe bei sich, wochenlang blind, und
heute wie unter Beobachtungszwang, woher?, zu welchem Zweck?, diese
fremdgesteuerte Zwangswahrnehmung, Ruhe da, hinter den Augen, im
Kopf" (Stop, said Raspe to himself. He had been blind for weeks, but
today he was as if under a compulsion to observe, why? for what purpose?, this involuntary compulsive perception, be quiet there, behind my
eyes, in my head; *I* 193). Throughout this study so far, sight has figured
as the sense culturally most closely associated with masculine-connoted
mastery. In chapter 4, I quoted Elizabeth Grosz:

> Of all the senses, vision remains the one which most readily con-
> firms the separation of subject from object. Vision performs a

distancing function, leaving the looker unimplicated in or uncontaminated by its object. [. . .] the look is the domain of domination and mastery; it provides access to its object without necessarily being in contact with it.[39]

In the discussion of Max Frisch's *Mein Name sei Gantenbein,* the Gantenbein figure's feigned blindness was shown to conceal his continuing self-definition as observing, controlling, knowing subject. In Jelinek's *Die Klavierspielerin,* one of the ways in which Erika Kohut appropriates a male-connoted position is through the gaze: in the peepshow, on the Praterauen, or as the observer of Klemmer. Sight does not necessarily imply complete detachment from the object of the gaze, however: "In der Zuschauerin arbeitet es zerstörerisch" ("The effect on the spectator is devastating"), comments Jelinek's narrator in the Praterauen sequence (*KS* 143/144). Here Erika reacts physiologically to the scene of copulation she observes: she is overcome by the need to urinate, and the terms in which this is described — "es wird von einem anfänglichen Prasseln zu einem sanften, stetigen Rinnen" ("the initial patter turns into a gentle, steady running"; *KS* 148/148) — recalls the motif of the flowing blood in the cutting scenes, forming another image of flow and liquidity that disrupts the rigidly upheld boundaries of corporeal self-containment. Likewise for Raspe, sight breaks down the boundary between his own identity as doctor and the suffering humanity of his patients. In Raspe, seeing is identificatory, it initiates sym-pathy, the pain of suffering with the patients' misery and disempowerment: "Plötzlich war Raspe von Mitleid und Schmerz erfaßt. Wie sie da alle sitzen im Kreis, die Verwahrlosten und Gepflegten, jeder für sich, alle zusammen, nichts als eine einzige Gestalt des Elends" (Suddenly Raspe was seized by sympathy and pain. How they are just all sitting there, the unkempt and the well-groomed, each alone and all together, nothing but a single figure of wretchedness; *I* 140).

Throughout the novel's first two sections, links in imagery and motif indicate the closeness between Raspe's troubled subjectivity and the psychotic minds of the patients. In particular the fragmentary structure of the opening section, where the reader is as yet unable to distinguish between patient and doctor, serves to erase the boundaries between the different individuals; in the traditional third-person narration of the second section, by contrast, these are situated in their allotted places on either side of the locked doors that divide the ward from the doctors' office in the orderly topography of the clinic. The implication is that the dividing line is in fact thin, upheld by the given order of discourse as much as by real divisions between the sane and the insane. One of the female patients is an alcoholic who drinks against despair (*I* 15–17, 127); the same might be said of Raspe. Tommi Wörmann, a schizophrenic, suffers from megalomania (*I*

127), is a hashish and LSD user, and is forever insisting that he must be discharged immediately as he has urgent business elsewhere: swimming and fishing, meeting his friends, and going out to the pub (*I* 167). His description of his wished-for weekend corresponds closely to the way in which Raspe, not without his own megalomania, spends his free time, and Raspe himself must acknowledge, as he sits over Wörmann's file: "Musik und Drogen, Autoritätskonflikte mit den Eltern, mit seinem Chef, Motorradbegeisterung und Anarchiegelüste — all das war Raspe nicht so fern" (Music and drugs, authority conflicts with his parents and with his boss, an enthusiasm for motorbikes and anarchic desires — it was all far from unfamiliar to Raspe; *I* 148). One of the patients hears voices (*I* 135); Raspe's doubts and self-questionings are likewise described in terms of voices in his head (*I* 149). Stelzer works doggedly at the destruction of his thumbnails, prefiguring Raspe's self-mutilation at the point where he can no longer withstand his internal conflict. For Raspe, as for his patient Fottner, the mind is a prison (*I* 207).

Raspe's nightlife, spent in clubs where he drinks, dances, and brawls, represents an escape from the demands of rational consciousness that define his daytime functioning as doctor and scientist. What he seeks is the dissolution of the coherent narrative of identity, the release into the purely corporeal:

> Das brutalste, ordinärste, grobste Gesicht wollte Raspe haben. Er wollte keine Sprache mehr kennen, außer Brocken von Dialekt. Er wollte eine Faust haben, die umstandslos zuschlägt. Nie wieder wollte er von seinen unerträglich vielen Büchern wissen. (*I* 222–23)

> [Raspe wanted to have the most brutal, vulgar, uncouth face. He wanted to know no language any more, except fragments of dialect. He wanted to have a fist that had no compunction in hitting out. He never wanted to think about his intolerably many books ever again.]

Hubert Winkels reads the nightclub scenes as representing a mimesis of madness.[40] In this sense, Raspe's nightlife is also the enactment of an attempted erasure of the boundaries that separate doctor and patient in the clinic. The difficulty for Raspe is the coexistence of his two incompatible ways of being. Arriving at work the morning after his nights out, he finds himself asking whether he is a changed man or a doubled one: "Gab es ein gespaltenes Gesetz für Nacht und Tag" (Was there a divided law for night and day; *I* 134). The resulting tension is reminiscent of the psychic split into masculine and feminine selves experienced by Bachmann's *Ich* in *Malina*: "Getrennt, meinte Frau Novak, wäre das lebbar, aber so, wie es sei, kaum" ("If they were separated it would be livable, maintained Frau Novak, but scarcely the way it is"; *M* 248/163). However, since traditional "masculine" subjectivity — as coherent self-identity, as rational mastery, and historical agency — is here so radically exposed as an act, an ideology superimposed upon a reality of predetermined functioning within a regulatory social system, the lure of self-dissolution becomes the stronger. Raspe's answer to the question of his identity — "Wer bin ich?" (Who am I?; *I* 221) — is given in terms that correspond to Erika Kohut's self-perception: he is "ein Nichts im All" ("a nothing in the cosmos"; *KS* 221). Self-mutilation, as the end point of his trajectory as an employee of the clinic (*I* 225), becomes, as it did with Erika, a graphic articulation of the psychic crisis. Through the gesture of cutting, the body is transformed into a sign of the internal state: "Von meinem Körper soll nichts heil übrig bleiben. Mein Körper ist die Lüge. In mir, innen, ist alles zerstört. [. . .] Die Lüge ist unerträglich. Ich werde sie beseitigen. Ich werde ihn vernichten und zerstückeln" (Of my body, nothing is to remain unscathed. My body is a lie. Within me, inside, everything is destroyed. [. . .] The lie is unbearable. I'm going to do away with it. I will annihilate my body by cutting it in pieces; *I* 100).⁴¹

The Subjectivity of the Artist:
Symbolic Fragmentation and (Self-) Destruction

During his period of employment within the psychiatric clinic, Raspe seeks release from his daytime existence in the literally antisocial space of the punk rock scene, an early 1980s cultural phenomenon that can be understood as political insofar as it represented a negation of the regulatory discourses of the social establishment through the assertion of aggressive, anarchic, and anti-authoritarian cultural behavior. The nightclub preferred by Raspe and his friends is called Damage. In the final section of the novel *Irre,* the principles of the punk scene are transposed onto the production of the text. It may seem ironic that this section bears the title "Die Ordnung" (Order), as it appears rather to be a *Zerschreiben* — an act of destruction through the writing process — of any kind of order: "Die NEUE ORDNUNG kenne ich noch nicht" (I don't yet know the NEW ORDER; *I* 238). Coherent self-narrative — the basis of what has been described in this study as "masculine" identity — is replaced by "Hackfleisch, Theorie, Sauereien, Hirn und nochmals Hirn, manische Pamphlete, Tratsch und Kalauer und Finden statt Tasten" (Mincemeat, theory, smuttiness, brain, brain and more brain, manic pamphlets, gossip and puns and finding instead of fumbling; *I* 279), held together only by the first-person self-referent "ICH" (*I* 279). "Das ist eine Scheiße, keine Literatur, sagt man mir. Aber das muß wurscht sein, weil es maßlos um die Wahrheit geht und um sonst gar nichts" (This is shit and not literature, they tell me. But I don't care, because this is immoderately about the truth, and nothing else besides; *I* 279). The "truth" of this text is in some senses not dissimilar to the truth of selfhood projected by Bachmann's *Malina,* notably in the third chapter "Von letzten Dingen" (Of Last Things), where fragments of reflection and observation, responses to reading matter, self-representation, and dialogue provide a kind of seismograph of the mind unmediated by traditional literary figuration and narrative structuring, likewise held together as narrative only by the common reference point of the first-person pronoun.[42] Like Bachmann, Goetz draws on the imagery of fire — or more precisely of lava, the burning flow of molten rock — to describe the immediacy of a form of writing focused on the Now, while the future completed text is already anticipated as having cooled into an icy material stored in the archive (*I* 314).

The similarities between Bachmann's *Ich* and Goetz's draw attention to the fact that what is at stake in both texts is a counter-model to a conceptualization of identity that is perceived as underpinning, and as determined by, the contemporary social order. In Bachmann, this is addressed in gendered terms; in Goetz, it is not, just as in Frisch's *Mein Name sei Gantenbein* the fragmentary, inconsistent, spontaneous self underlying the fiction of coherent self-identity was not feminized.[43] The comparison with Frisch's *Gantenbein* in turn draws attention to certain common concerns between the two texts. Notable, for example, is the entrapment of the "living creature" that is the self in the granite of the constricting social role as figured in Frisch's narrator's nightmare of the horse's head, which corresponds to Raspe's entrapment in the "Arbeitsknast" (work-prison; *I* 215) of the clinic, from which his fragmentary, impetuous self-authorship represents the escape. One might also mention the destructive impulse — recall the motif of smashing glass and other objects in Frisch's novel — that accompanies the breakdown of the conventional "masculine" role.

Vis-à-vis the novels from earlier in the period, however, Goetz's text figures a more extreme, more radical, and much angrier dissolution of the coherent self, in keeping with the radicalization of the avant-garde literary text as a site of anti-order in the aftermath of the student movement and the urban terrorism of the 1970s. As Winkels points out, the name "Raspe," along with other names given by Goetz to his fictional protagonists, alludes to the history of the Rote Armee Fraktion, the organization behind the terrorist attacks that disrupted German society in the 1970s.[44] At a public reading in the context of the annual Ingeborg-Bachmann literary competition in Klagenfurt in June 1983, during which he famously slashed himself across the forehead with a razor blade, Goetz created a link between the gesture of self-mutilation and terrorism, as he claimed: "Ohne Blut logisch keinen Sinn. Und weil ich kein Terrorist geworden bin, deshalb kann ich bloß in mein eigenes weißes Fleisch hineinschneiden" (Without blood logically no meaning. And because I didn't become a terrorist, I can only cut into my own white flesh).[45] In Winkels's interpretation: "According to this practice, 'meaning' begins where the sign impacts upon the body, where pain arises, where blood flows [. . .] as the guarantee of a no-longer-phantasmatic, but 'real' violence of the symbolic" (239). With the public gesture of self-mutilation, Goetz erases the boundary between the literary text and the person of the author, while the text he reads to accompany the gesture reveals the act of self-harm as a now-consciously-undertaken transposition of the terrorist act aimed against the fabric of society into the symbolic act of self-destruction.

Such (self-) destruction, as an aspect of Goetz's textual practice in *Irre*, also links to the overall theme of madness in the novel. If cutting is a pathological behavior that provides a symbolic release from the constrictions, anxieties, and stresses imposed upon the self by the social environment, the novel's final section adopts a further pathological manifestation, namely mania, as a textual principle: "Ein MANIKER brüllt in mir. Der brüllt so laut, dauernd möchte der aus mir heraus brüllen" (A MANIAC is bellowing inside me. He's bellowing so loudly, he's constantly trying to bellow his way out from within me; *I* 238). This provides a psychological category by which to define the "perpetual flux of impetuous thoughts" and the "audacity and fury" that characterize the fragmentary text of "Order."[46] Mania is here the principle by which the coherent self/text disintegrates into "Hackfleisch" (mincemeat) as the symbolic representation of a life that has been cut in pieces (*I* 279).

Madness has entertained close relations with the literary text in modernity, as Michel Foucault observes in his conclusion to *Madness and Civilization:* "The frequency in the modern world of works of art that explode out of madness no doubt proves nothing about the reason of that world [. . .] yet this frequency must be taken seriously, as if it were the insistence of a question" (272). Founding his observations on Nietzsche and Artaud as exemplary figures, Foucault concludes: "Madness is the absolute break with the work of art; it forms the constitutive moment of abolition, which dissolves in time the truth of the work of art" (273). In this totality of negation, the (still and despite everything, linguistic, that is, meaning-ful) confrontation with the absence of meaning in the work of art, Foucault nevertheless struggles to find a form of utopian challenge:

> By the madness which interrupts it, a work of art opens a void, a moment of silence, a question without an answer, provokes a breach without reconciliation where the world is forced to question itself. [. . .] Henceforth, and through the mediation of madness, it is the world that becomes culpable (for the first time in the Western world) in relation to the work of art; it is now arraigned by the work of art, [. . .] compelled by it to a task of recognition, of reparation, to the task of restoring reason *from* that unreason and *to* that unreason. (273–74, italics in original.)

As for Goetz himself: at the novel's conclusion, he reverts briefly to the fictional device of the character Raspe, narrated from the third-person perspective and in the conventional narrative preterite, as a means of reflecting in retrospect on the implications of a textual practice modeled on madness as the vital negation of a stultifying social order. Here, we find an acknowledgement that the logical conclusion of such a practice must ultimately be the total annihilation of self and world:

> Wohl ahnte Raspe, daß DIE ZYKLOTHYMIE, derart zum vitalen Prinzip erhoben, mit progressiver Dynamik in immer wüstere Exzesse von Überhebung und Wahrheit und in eine ebenso immer noch maßlosere Verzagtheit, Selbstverlorenheit und Lebenserschöpfung und also einbahnstraßenmäßig in die Welt- und Selbstzerstörung und also final logisch in die Katastrophe führen müsse [. . .]. (*I* 328)

> [Raspe had the certain conviction that CYCLOTHYMIE, raised to a vital principle in this way, would necessarily lead with its progressive dynamic to ever-wilder excesses of arrogance and truth and so to an ever-more immeasurable despair, self-loss, and existential exhaustion and so directly down a one-way street to the destruction of the world and of the self and so logically in the end to catastrophe.]

It is just such a trajectory of dynamic negation interchanging with despair and self-loss and leading ultimately to a symbolic self-annihilation that will be encountered again in the form of an abbreviated history of avant-garde male authorship in modernity in Heiner Müller's Die *Hamletmaschine,* to be examined in the next chapter.

Jelinek and Goetz: Gender and Authorship

The two novels that have been in the focus of discussion here, Jelinek's *Die Klavierspielerin* and Goetz's *Irre,* are undoubtedly very different works: the one a pseudo-realistic narrative that stages psychoanalytical theorems in order to expose the contradictions, experienced by a female character aspiring to cultural subjecthood, between such an aspiration and the positioning of woman as sexual object within the socioeconomically determined symbolic order; the other, an autobiographically motivated representation of the crisis and wilful self-dissolution of a male figure who finds himself unable to sustain a professional identity as doctor and scientist. However, the comparison of the two, based in the first instance on the linking motif of self-mutilation, reveals that what these texts have in common is a central concern with psychological conflict: between, on the one hand, a socially institutionalized conceptualization of subjectivity, based on professional mastery, self-discipline, knowledge (whether of music or of psychiatric medicine), and institutional position as the guarantor of social power, which both texts expose as ideological, and, on the other, an accumulation of counter-desires that might be summarized as a longing for the suspension of such a rigorously contained and containing identity, whether in the self-loss of the sexual relationship or in the obliteration of the pain of singular consciousness through alcohol or drug consumption and in ecstatic dance. Both texts are to be understood as critiques of contemporary society and its construction of the boundaries between self and other (whether male and female, or the medical scientist and the patient). In both, the psychopathology of the central character constitutes a symbolic condemnation of a social order that confines the individual in roles always already discursively predetermined, whereby self-mutilation, and in the case of Erika Kohut, the masochistic letter, become symptomatic of an intolerable contradiction: the desire for release, for the dissolution of containing boundaries crossed with the continuing compulsion to assert (self-) control. Both authors attack language as the means by which social normality is constructed, Goetz through the destructive *Zerschreiben* or de-composition of narrative order, Jelinek through her characteristic jarring — and, it must be said, often very funny — combinations of imagery and linguistic registers, which serve in this instance ruthlessly to expose the link between psychosexual identity formation and socioeconomic interests.

While these parallels are indications of the texts' common cause as aesthetic responses to the contemporary social order, the gender differential nevertheless places them at quite different points on the spectrum of 1980s literature. Jelinek's fictional universe depends on a clear dichotomy between male and female. In using psychoanalysis as a basis for her character configurations, she produces a scenario that confirms sexual difference — *genital* difference — as that which underpins the distribution of social power. The notion of the individual subject as historical agent has, in Jelinek's extremely negative estimation, been destroyed in contemporary market-dominated society, even though it continues to be in the interest of a commercial society to suggest to its members that they are singular and noninterchangeable individuals.[47] Nevertheless, her texts represent the *illusion* of subjectivity as being more readily available to the male within society, upheld as he is by a traditional social bias in favor of the male-subject-as-norm that confirms his sense of himself as an "Einzelpersönlichkeit" (individual personality).[48] Her coruscating social critique thus depends on the representation of the female, always already defined as body and as sexual object, as the social order's most abject victim. For all Jelinek's protestations at the categorization,[49] this situates her among feminist writers whose chief political target is a society perceived as perpetuating the privileges of the male sex.

Goetz is less interested in gender: one notes that he does not portray the male and female doctors as having a distinctively different relationship to their position of social authority. Goetz's is a fictional world in which the historically, in fact, quite recent changes in the social position of women are not at issue, but rather accepted: male and female work alongside each other in the clinic (though the female staff are evidently in the minority). Authority is established, in other words, on the basis of social signifiers other than genital difference: the doctor's coat, the keys that lock and unlock the doors to the wards, the ability to use scientific terminology — all of these indicators of professional position allocated according to education and training, from which in this period women are no longer debarred. Perhaps a different picture would have emerged if Goetz had explicitly addressed male-female sexual relations, which remains the area where the persisting imbalance of power between the sexes is most evident. In *Irre,* however, the representation of sexuality, to the extent that it does feature, is largely confined to a hesitant and oblique indication of the problematics of homosexual desire, which underpins Goetz's absorption in issues of masculine identity.

Such self-absorption is, of course, the privilege of the male-subject-as-norm. Moreover, in fleeing from the model of Enlightenment subjectivity — the scientist who masters the diseases of human nature, or at any rate, masters his subject — Goetz's *Ich* in effect simply moves into another already existing form of male subjectivity. As Hubert Winkels's enthusiastic appraisal of Goetz's impact upon the literary scene illustrates, perhaps against its own intention, the rejection of the socially sanctioned "masculine" role as self-disciplined, career-minded professional in favor of a manic, aggressive, fragmentary self-authorship within the "*space*" of the literary text in the novel's final section in fact has recourse to a model of masculine identity that is as old as modernity itself:

> From time to time the public arena of literature has a need, in order to reassure itself of its own existence, for the ostracized young man whose fury makes one lustful, whose lack of illusion to the point of intoxication makes one sober, and whose torment makes one all-consumingly sympathetic; it has a need for the autobiographical genius of the annihilation of world and self. (250)

In the reading of the text presented here, I have emphasized the nature of Goetz's novel as symptomatic of a continuing crisis in masculine identity in the post-1945 period. But in effect Goetz's authorship marks the return of a figure familiar enough from the German literary tradition of the modern period since its beginnings in the eighteenth century: the wounded genius with a predisposition to insanity and self-destruction.[50] Goetz's particularity is his updating of this figure to the environment of late-twentieth-century pop and media culture.[51]

Jelinek's authorial persona in the public sphere appears, by contrast, as more complex and challenging, a new phenomenon characteristic of the significant shift taking place in the possibilities for women in the aftermath of the new feminism. Unlike her female characters, Jelinek as author does not appear a victim. *Die Klavierspielerin* may contain auto-biographical impulses, but the text itself conveys an intellectual control and an invulnerability that are quite at odds with its representation of the female protagonist's humiliation and self-loss. One might go further and claim that Jelinek's public reputation as indubitably one of the most important German-language writers of the past three decades rests to a considerable degree on her refusal of any kind of stereotypical "feminine" identity, on the fascinating tension between conventional expectations of "women's writing" and the fact of her texts' cynicism, aggression, and signal lack of any kind of utopian dimension. This may mark a departure from the pigeonholing of the woman writer as the guardian spirit of pur-portedly "feminine" values, but it also sheds an interesting light on the extent to which masculine-connoted characteristics — coldness, intellectual assuredness, technical prowess, self-assertion, even aggressiveness — con-tinue to figure in the public estimation of what constitutes success. What emerges, in the final analysis, from the bleak world depicted in the two novels discussed in this chapter is that there is not really a space within this late-modern social order that allows the incorporation of vulnerability, openness, relationality — those aspects of the human psyche that have tra-ditionally been associated with "femininity" and consigned to the private sphere — as viable, even admirable characteristics into the public domain. Jelinek, as author, has recognized this, and intelligently she plays the game. But the motto of the game is: it is always war (*M* 236/155).

Notes

[1] Peter Wagner, *A Sociology of Modernity* (London and New York: Routledge, 1994), 123. See discussion in chapter 2 above.

[2] The work of Michel Foucault in particular explored the influence of "discourse" and discursive systems on the shaping of bodies and selves.

[3] The debate in French feminist circles on the notion of an *écriture féminine* was particularly influential, and fed into discussion among German feminists of a spe-cifically female aesthetic (see below). Toril Moi considers the not-unproblematical claims concerning *l'écriture féminine* in the work of Hélène Cixous in *Sexual/Tex-tual Politics*, 102–26.

[4] Silvia Bovenschen, "Über die Frage: gibt es eine 'weibliche' Ästhetik?," first published in *Ästhetik und Kommunikation* 7.25 (September 1976): 60–76; quoted here from the slightly abridged version in *Die Überwindung der Sprachlo-sigkeit: Texte aus der neuen Frauenbewegung*, ed. Gabriele Dietze (Darmstadt und Neuwied: Luchterhand, 1979), 82–115, here 89. Subsequent references appear in the text as parenthetical page numbers.

[5] Herbert Marcuse, "Marxismus und Feminismus," *Zeitmessungen* (Frankfurt, 1975), 13, quoted from Bovenschen, "Über die Frage: gibt es eine 'weibliche'

Ästhetik?," 94. She criticizes Marcuse for his use of the word "undermine" (*unterminieren*), questioning its relation to the proposed "feminine" quality of nonviolence.

[6] Riki Winter, "Gespräch mit Elfriede Jelinek," in *Dossier 2: Elfriede Jelinek,* ed. Kurt Bartsch and Günther A. Höfler (Graz-Vienna: Droschl, 1991), 9–19, here 12–13.

[7] See Linda C. DeMeritt, "A 'Healthier Marriage': Elfriede Jelinek's Marxist Feminism in *Die Klavierspielerin* and *Lust*," in *Elfriede Jelinek: Framed by Language,* ed. Jorun B. Johns and Katherine Arens (Riverside, CA: Ariadne, 1994), 107–28.

[8] The latter registers are particularly prominent in *Wolken. Heim* (literally, Home. In the Clouds, 1990) and *Totenauberg* (a play on the name of the village where the philosopher Martin Heidegger lived, Todtnauberg, 1991).

[9] Marlies Janz comments usefully on Jelinek's study in the late 1960s of the work of the French theorist Roland Barthes, from which she develops a method combining structuralist semiology with Marxist ideology critique: Janz, *Elfriede Jelinek* (Stuttgart: Metzler, 1995), vii. Subsequent references appear in the text as parenthetical page numbers.

[10] Elfriede Jelinek, "Ich schlage sozusagen mit der Axt drein," *Theaterzeitschrift Berlin* 7 (1984): 14–15, quoted here from Yvonne Spielmann, "Ein unerhörtes Sprachlabor. Feministische Aspekte im Werk von Elfriede Jelinek," in *Dossier 2,* ed. Bartsch and Höfler, 21–40, here 35.

[11] See Jelinek's statements on the autobiographical features in *Die Klavierspielerin* in Winter, "Gespräch mit Elfriede Jelinek," 9–11; and her unusually self-revelatory comments in the 1990 interview "Ich lebe nicht. André Müller spricht mit der Schriftstellerin Elfriede Jelinek," *Die Zeit,* 22 June 1990, 55–56.

[12] See Allyson Fiddler, "Reading Elfriede Jelinek," in *Post-War Women's Writing in German: Feminist Critical Approaches,* ed. Chris Weedon (Providence, RI, Oxford: Berghahn, 1997), 291–304, here 300.

[13] Winter, "Gespräch mit Elfriede Jelinek," 13.

[14] Elfriede Jelinek, *Die Klavierspielerin: Roman* (Reinbek bei Hamburg: Rowohlt, 1983), 82–83 / *The Piano Teacher,* trans. Joachim Neugroschel (London: Serpent's Tail, 1989), 64–65. Subsequent references appear in the text, identified as *KS* (in German to the original edition, in English to the Neugroschel translation).

[15] This passage in Jelinek's novel contains allusions to Bachmann's *Malina,* notably the reference in the next paragraph to Erika scratching with her fingernails the back of whatever man she happens to be with, which recalls an element in *Ich*'s excursus on men in the third chapter of Bachmann's novel; compare Bachmann, *Werke,* vol. 3, 271/*Malina,* trans. Boehm, 179. Jelinek's interest in Bachmann comes across through her frequent mentions of her in the interview with Riki Winter. She was also the author of the screenplay for Werner Schroeter's 1991 film of Bachmann's novel. Subsequent references to *Malina* appear in the text, identified as *M* (in German to the *Werke* edition, in English to the Boehm translation).

[16] Elizabeth Wright, "Eine Ästhetik des Ekels. Elfriede Jelineks Roman 'Die Klavierspielerin,'" in Heinz Ludwig Arnold, ed., *Elfriede Jelinek, Text + Kritik* 117 (January 1993): 51–59, here 51.

[17] See Janz, *Elfriede Jelinek*, 72. See also Hedwig Appelt's Lacanian reading of the novel in *Die leibhaftige Literatur: Das Phantasma und die Präsenz der Frau in der Schrift* (Weinheim, Berlin: Quadriga, 1989), 111–33, including the analysis of the mother-daughter relationship, 113.

[18] The German describes Erika as "Herrin," combining the German word for "Mister," but also "master" or "lord" with a feminine suffix "-in": as it were, "lord and mistress."

[19] Sigmund Freud, "Femininity" [1933], in Freud, *Standard Edition*, vol. XXII: *New Introductory Lectures on Psycho-Analysis and Other Works* (London: Hogarth Press, 1964), 112–35, here 126.

[20] Freud, "Femininity," 130.

[21] See Sigmund Freud, "Female Sexuality" [1931], in Freud, *Standard Edition*, vol. XXI: *The Future of an Illusion, Civilization and its Discontents and Other Works* (London: Hogarth Press, 1961), 236: "It can easily be observed that in every field of mental experience, not merely that of sexuality, when a child receives a passive impression it has a tendency to produce an active reaction. It tries to do itself what has just been done to it."

[22] Freud, "Femininity," 126.

[23] See Spielmann, "Ein unerhörtes Sprachlabor," 31: "Jelinek demonstrates the social antagonism upon which her figures founder through two motivic strands: there is a direct line from the female body, defined as the epitome of nature, to putrefaction and decay, while the male's mastery of his body through the drill of sport leads to the mastery of nature and destruction of the environment."

[24] Sigmund Freud, "Some Thoughts on Development and Regression — Aetiology," from the "General Theory of the Neuroses," in Freud, *Standard Edition*, vol. XVI: *Introductory Lectures on Psycho-Analysis* (London: Hogarth Press, 1963), 349–50.

[25] Freud, "The Paths to the Formation of Symptoms," from the "General Theory of Neuroses," in Freud, *Standard Edition*, vol. XVI, 360.

[26] Freud, "Some Thoughts on Development and Regression — Aetiology," 341.

[27] See Yasmin Hoffmann's analysis of the peepshow scene in *Elfriede Jelinek: Sprach- und Kulturkritik im Erzählwerk* (Opladen, Wiesbaden: Westdeutscher Verlag, 1999), 168–71.

[28] See Jelinek's statement (one of which she is fond, and repeats elsewhere) in an interview with Josef-Hermann Sauter: "As we know, there is no man so poor, exploited or broken that he does not have someone even worse off than he is, namely his wife": Sauter, "Interviews mit Barbara Frischmuth, Elfriede Jelinek, Michael Scharang," *Weimarer Beiträge* 27, no. 6 (1981): 109–17, here 109.

[29] Freud, "Femininity," 116 (italics added).

[30] See Sabine Wilke, "'Ich bin eine Frau mit einer männlichen Anmaßung': Eine Analyse des 'bösen Blicks' in Elfriede Jelineks *Die Klavierspielerin*," *Modern*

Austrian Literature 26, no. 1 (1993): 115–44, here 129: "With the aid of her artful language Jelinek unmasks the inherent violence of the discourse on woman by taking it at its word."

[31] Klemmer draws close to adopting, at least in fantasy, the position of the murderer in Bachmann's scenario, as he considers the erotic attractions of the relationship delineated in Erika's letter: "Er ist stolz auf Proben, die er ablegen wird, er wird sie vielleicht beinahe töten!" ("He is proud of the trials he will undergo. Why, he may very nearly kill her!"; *KS* 296/236).

[32] This is, needless to say, a pessimistic and cynical assessment of male-female relations. Jelinek's text grants that the female potentially commands a form of subjectivity: "Die Frau hat es ganz in der Hand, dem Mann zärtliche Rücksichtsnahme beizubringen" ("The woman has it quite within her power to teach the man tender consideration"; *KS* 249/199, translation modified), but this is still predicated upon the sexual relationship as a form of power struggle.

[33] Max Horkheimer and Theodor W. Adorno, *Dialectic of Enlightenment: Philosophical Fragments*, ed. Gunzelin Schmid Noerr, trans. Edmund Jephcott (Stanford: Stanford UP, 2002), 93.

[34] See Jelinek in the Sauter interview: "I am completely incapable, it is almost like a physical incapacity, of depicting positive utopias. I just cannot do it. The moment I try to do so I become flat and unconvincing. Quite apart from the fact that I am, rather against my own social convictions [she is referring to her membership of the Communist Party at that time], a pessimist as far as changing the current conditions is concerned." On the other hand, Jelinek sees in the spontaneous emotional reaction of her readers *against* the negativity of her fictional world the utopian impulse that is absent within the work itself: "I think that it is legitimate for an author to represent conditions in all their negativity and, through the exaggeration of this negativity, to arouse spontaneous emotions in the sense that one recognizes: this is so dreadful, this has to be changed, for it can't go on like this": Sauter, "Interviews mit Barbara Frischmuth, Elfriede Jelinek, Michael Scharang," 115.

[35] Hubert Winkels offers a psychoanalytic interpretation of this passage, reading the cut, which is executed with Erika's father's razor, as the symbolic substitution of the intervention of the father in the mother-child dyad; see Winkels, "Panoptikum der Schreckensfrau. Elfriede Jelineks Roman 'Die Klavierspielerin,'" in Winkels, *Einschnitte: Zur Literatur der 80er Jahre* (Cologne: Kiepenheuer & Witsch, 1988), 60–77, here 71. The reading is persuasive in some respects, but cannot account for a more literal reading of the scene as addressing the phenomenon of self-harm among adolescent girls. In interview, Jelinek has laid claim to the autobiographical basis of this scene; see "Ich lebe nicht. André Müller spricht mit der Schriftstellerin Elfriede Jelinek," 55. On the self-mutilation scenes, see also Tobe Levin, "*Die Klavierspielerin*: On Mutilation and Somotaphobia," in *'Other' Austrians: Post-1945 Austrian Women's Writing*, ed. Allyson Fiddler (Bern: Peter Lang, 1998), 225–34.

[36] Armando R. Favazza, *Bodies Under Siege: Self-Mutilation in Culture and Psychiatry* (Baltimore: Johns Hopkins UP, 1996), xix; see also his extensive discussion of pathological self-mutilation, 232–60. When Favazza began work on this

book project in the early 1980s (the first edition was published in 1987), there was still very widespread clinical ignorance about cutting as a behavior; i.e., when Jelinek published *Die Klavierspielerin*, there was as yet very little medical understanding of the motivations. In the meantime, cutting, like eating disorders among teenage girls, has become much more widely discussed and understood. See also Marilee Strong, *A Bright Red Scream: Self-Mutilation and the Language of Pain* (London: Virago, 2000) for a more accessible account of the experiences of those who self-harm.

[37] See Hubert Winkels's discussion of the autobiographical basis of the novel in "Krieg den Zeichen. Rainald Goetz und die Wiederkehr des Körpers," in Winkels, *Einschnitte*, 221–59.

[38] Rainald Goetz, *Irre* (Frankfurt am Main: Suhrkamp, 1983), 19. Subsequent references appear in the text, identified as *I*. There is no published English translation of this novel.

[39] Elizabeth Grosz, *Jacques Lacan: A Feminist Introduction* (London and New York: Routledge, 1990), 38.

[40] Hubert Winkels, "Krieg den Zeichen," 246. Subsequent references appear in the text as parenthetical page numbers.

[41] This quotation comes from the final narrative fragment in the novel's opening section, attributed to a female patient as she contemplates suicide. Like many of the fragments in this first section, it bears a relation to Raspe's own mental state as revealed in the continuous narrative of the second section. The motif of the broken body as a sign that articulates inner conflict reminds of another work of the 1980s, Anne Duden's *Übergang* (The Opening of the Mouth, 1982), in which a female narrator experiences the smashing of her face in an attack as a relief, since the discrepancy between external and internal reality is thus erased; see the title story in Anne Duden, *Übergang* (Berlin: Rotbuch, 1982).

[42] Structurally not dissimilar, these final chapters by Bachmann and Goetz nevertheless succeed in articulating very different characters. Bachmann's *Ich* is often self-defensive, but not aggressive, and remains largely oriented toward others; Goetz's *Ich*, by contrast, is self-absorbed, both troubled and arrogant, wounded and furious.

[43] See chapter 4.

[44] See Winkels, "Krieg den Zeichen," 230. The name Raspe alludes to Jan-Karl Raspe, one of the four leading members of the Rote Armee Fraktion, popularly known as the Baader-Meinhof gang, who were imprisoned at the high-security Stammheim prison in the 1970s (the others were Andreas Baader, Ulrike Meinhof, and Gudrun Ensslin). Further protagonists in Goetz's fictions bear the names Klar (alluding to Christian Klar, another RAF member) and Stammheimer (alluding to the prison where the RAF terrorists were held).

[45] These sentences come from the text read by Goetz at the Klagenfurt reading in 1983, entitled "Subito," reproduced in *Rawums: Texte zum Thema,* ed. Peter Glaser (Cologne: Kiepenheuer & Witsch, 1984); quoted here from Winkels, 239. Again, Anne Duden has suggested a link between her textual practice and terrorist activity; see her poetological essay "Zungengewahrsam. Erkundungen einer

Schreibexistenz," in Duden, *Zungengewahrsam: Kleine Schriften zur Poetik und zur Kunst* (Cologne: Kiepenheuer & Witsch, 1999). See also Heiner Müller's comment in his 1977 "Verabschiedung des Lehrstücks": "Humanism only occurs now as terrorism": Müller, *Mauser* (Berlin: Rotbuch, 1978), 85.

[46] The phrases here are taken from the definition of mania quoted in Michel Foucault, *Madness and Civilization: A History of Insanity in the Age of Reason* [1961], trans. Richard Howard (London and New York: Routledge, 1989), 119. Subsequent references appear in the text as parenthetical page numbers.

[47] See Winter, "Gespräch mit Elfriede Jelinek," 14.

[48] See *Die Klavierspielerin*, 64/49.

[49] Asked by Josef-Hermann Sauter about her attitude to the categorization of her work as "women's literature," Jelinek replies: "On the contrary, I'd say that my aesthetic method is very unfeminine. I continue to be surprised that my work is put in the category of 'women's literature,' because I've much more often heard that my language and my methods, those of irony and satire, actually have a great hardness": Sauter, "Interviews," 109–10. One notes that Jelinek here conflates "very unfeminine" with "hardness."

[50] Within Goetz's novel itself, the phrase "Hat die Welt eventuell einen Riß?" (Does the world perhaps have a tear in it?; *I* 322) suggests, via the allusion to Georg Büchner's *Novelle*, an authorial identification with J. M. R. Lenz, whose work was notably also very challenging to its time in terms of its fragmentation of traditional form. Meanwhile, the hero Raspe's flight from the world of the clinic to the countryside on his free afternoon (*I* 125) and the importance of weather and the seasons to the mood of the protagonist throughout the novel is reminiscent of Goethe's *Die Leiden des jungen Werther*, which of course likewise addresses the entrapment of the individual in a social world which affords his particular selfhood no space.

[51] There is perhaps little essential difference between the drink and drugs scene in which Raspe/Goetz finds release and the porn cinemas and peepshows of Jelinek's novel; drink and drugs are as integrated into the capitalist economy — the "universal black market" as Bachmann terms it — as is the sex industry. The Ecstasy they offer is a wicked illusion.

7: End Visions: Heiner Müller's *Die Hamletmaschine* and Christa Wolf's *Kassandra*

T HE FINAL TWO CHAPTERS OF THIS STUDY form a single thematic sequence, the focus of which is the relation of the gendered author to the inherited literary and cultural tradition. This chapter looks at two works that revisit and revise mythical figures from the Western cultural tradition from a contemporary perspective: Heiner Müller's 1977 performance text[1] *Die Hamletmaschine* (The Hamletmachine) and Christa Wolf's 1983 prose narrative *Kassandra* (Cassandra). Müller's treatment of Hamlet, as the type of the introspective male intellectual subject, represents in extreme form the crisis in masculine subjectivity and authorship in the post-1945 period that has been one of the central focuses of this book, and the text concludes in a vision of apocalyptic destruction. Wolf's fictional occupation of the role of Kassandra, a figure derived from the Homeric account of the Trojan war, is, by contrast, the attempt to project a model of female subjectivity and authorship with which to counter the violence and destructiveness perceived as inherent in the Western cultural tradition. Yet Wolf's text likewise ends in death. Both texts take, in their respective ways, a fundamentally pessimistic view of the individual subject's possibilities for historical agency, an issue central to the readings presented here. The study concludes in chapter 8 with a reading of a work by Barbara Köhler, a writer from a younger generation: a poem cycle that was written in part as a response to Müller's *Hamletmaschine* and that, I shall argue, succeeds in generating a movement beyond the aporias of both Müller's and Wolf's texts to open up a new perspective on the conceptualization of gendered subjectivity within the modern Western tradition.

All three of these authors lived and worked in the German Democratic Republic, and the works concerned are all products of what the literary histories generally define as the last phase of GDR literature, after the watershed of the expatriation of the singer-songwriter Wolf Biermann in 1976. The expulsion of Biermann from the country and the withdrawal of his GDR citizenship marked for many intellectuals the end of any hope they may have had that the communist regime was open to constructively intentioned criticism, and a state incapable of tolerating criticism appeared necessarily moribund. Many notable writers and artists chose or were forced to leave the GDR between 1976 and the fall of the Berlin wall in 1989, and those critical spirits who stayed did so with a palpable sense of embattlement. In terms of this book's larger narrative of the crisis of Enlightenment in the latter half of the twentieth century in Europe, the crisis among the GDR's intellectuals sparked off by the expatriation of Biermann appears as a pivotal moment in which the hope fostered by many that communism might offer a viable alternative order to the perceived dehumanizing and technocratic developments in Western capitalism was finally lost. From then on, the work of the GDR's most prestigious intellectual figureheads — those writers and artists with the greatest international reputations, of whom Heiner Müller was arguably the most prominent man and Christa Wolf the most prominent woman — was marked by a profound pessimism vis-à-vis communism's potential for reform and also, importantly, by a perception of structural similarities between the social orders of East and West.[2] In this sense, much GDR literature of the late 1970s and the 1980s can be seen as rejoining the mainstream of cultural critique within Western modernity that, as I have been arguing, pervades German-language literature in the post-1945 era.

Heiner Müller's *Die Hamletmaschine*: Exploding the Shakespearean Tradition

The text of Müller's *Die Hamletmaschine* (1977)[3] is just a few pages long, yet the density of the writing and the multitude of quotations and allusions that constitute the text make it an exceptionally difficult work to pin down to any unequivocal, let alone unified meaning. It is this complexity, of course, that gives the text life — especially as a form of provocation to thought for any group attempting to stage it.[4] Müller wrote it after working on a production of Shakespeare's *Hamlet,* directed by Benno Besson at the Volksbühne in East Berlin, which premiered in early 1977. The extremely abbreviated form was achieved by radically reducing an original manuscript of hundreds of pages, and, as Müller stated, marked his attempt to rid himself of a thirty-year obsession with Hamlet.[5] The significance of what he does with the Hamlet material goes beyond a merely personal motivation, however.

For Müller, as is indicated by an address delivered at the Weimar Shakespeare Festival in 1988, Shakespeare's *Hamlet* was an anticipatory "Endspiel" or "endgame" written in the dawn of a time as yet unknown to it.[6] For his generation, Müller claims, reading Shakespeare involves confronting the most recent past, a century of violence perpetrated in the name of Enlightenment:

> der Lange Marsch durch die Höllen der Aufklärung, durch den Blutsumpf der Ideologien. Hitlers geographischer Lapsus: Genocid in Europa statt, wie gewohnt und Praxis heute wie gestern, in

Afrika Asien Amerika. Der Veitstanz der Dialektik in den Moskauer Prozessen. Der lidlose Blick auf die Wirklichkeit der Arbeits- und Vernichtungslager. Die Dorf-gegen-Stadt-Utopie des Hegellesers und Verlaineliebhabers Pol Pot. Die verspätete jüdische Rache am falschen Objekt, klassischer Fall von verspätetem Gehorsam. Der Starrkrampf einer zum Sieger geschlagenen Partei beim Umgang mit der geschenkten oder aufgezwungenen Macht in der Mangel-wirtschaft des realen Sozialismus. (*SD* 105)

[the long march through the hells of Enlightenment, through the bloody swamps of the ideologies. Hitler's geographical lapsus: geno-cide in Europe instead [of] — as usual and today's practice as it was yesterday's — in Africa Asia America. The St. Vitus's dance of dia-lectics during the Moscow trials. The lidless view at the reality of the labor and extermination camps. The village-against-city utopia of the Hegel-reader and Verlaine-lover Pol Pot. The belated Jewish vengeance upon the wrong object, a classical case of belated obedi-ence. The lockjaw of a party, burdened with the victor's role, when it is exercizing the power bestowed or forced upon it in the short-age-ridden economy of real-existing Socialism. (*SD* 119, translation modified)]

Striking in Müller's list of political catastrophes in this passage are the many supposed representatives of the oppressed of history who became destroyers in their turn. This is the impact of the references to the ven-geance of the Jews "upon the wrong object," i.e., the Palestinians, and to Communist and revolutionary leaders (the Moscow trials allude to Stalin, and Pol Pot of Cambodia is mentioned explicitly) who have gone down in history for the bloodiness and terror of their regimes. The avengers of injustice and tyranny, it is implied, once they have attained power, become the next tyrants. This view of history informs Müller's understanding of Hamlet's dilemma. Like Orestes, a classical model, Hamlet cannot avenge murder without himself being drawn into the cycle of murder and blood-shed. Moreover, in his acute self-awareness, he realizes this, hence his inability to act. And yet again, in his inaction, he becomes an accomplice to the tyrant's retention of power. Hamlet as the type of the intellectual becomes Müller's identificatory figure in the political scenario of the pres-ent. Reading *Hamlet,* and seeing it as a model of the processes of history to which he has himself been witness in the twentieth century, Müller recognizes the historical choice between a form of revolutionary action that perpetuates the historical cycle of murder and injustice or, for the intellectual who does not act but merely reflects upon the consequences of action, the fate of becoming the accomplice of power. As he wrote in a 1977 fragment on Antonin Artaud, an important influence on Müller's conceptualization of theater in his later works: "Artaud, die Sprache der

Qual. Schreiben aus der Erfahrung, daß *die Meisterwerke die Komplicen der Macht sind*. Denken am Ende der Aufklärung [. . .]" ("Artaud, the language of anguish. *Writing out of the experience that the masterpieces are the accomplices of power*. Thinking at the end of Enlightenment [. . .]").[7]

The only genuinely revolutionary way forward is to attain a new historical position that the drama of Shakespeare is no longer capable of mirroring: "Shakespeare ist ein Spiegel durch die Zeiten, unsre Hoffnung eine Welt, die er nicht mehr reflektiert. Wir sind bei uns nicht angekommen, solange Shakespeare unsre Stücke schreibt" ("Shakespeare is a mirror through the ages, our hope a world he doesn't reflect anymore. We haven't arrived at ourselves as long as Shakespeare is writing our plays"; *SD* 106/119). If Shakespeare's drama still has a mythological force for us, and if, as Müller also claims in his 1988 Shakespeare speech, myth is conceived of as a machine to which other machines can be connected, then Müller's purpose in his own "endgame" is to *overload* this machine, to push it to its limits until the mythical machinery jams — for only then can something new beyond the limits of the text become imaginable: "Der Mythos ist ein Aggregat, eine Maschine, an die immer neue und andre Maschinen angeschlossen werden können. Er transportiert die Energie, *bis die wachsende Beschleunigung den Kulturkreis sprengt*" ("Myth is an aggregate, a machine to which always new and different machines can be connected. It transports the energy *until the growing velocity will explode the cultural field*"; *SD* 106/120, italics added). In this perspective, Müller's *Die Hamletmaschine* symbolically increases the velocity of the mythical "machinery" of Shakespeare's drama, with the aim of imaginatively exploding the cultural structures mirrored within it.

The text has a residual structure from traditional European drama, with the five scenes or *Bilder* corresponding to the traditional five acts. However, in Müller's treatment the form has become extremely compressed, and the conventional textual form of the drama, above all the allocation of speeches to clearly demarcated characters, is suspended. There is a discernible continuity of development, in that scenes 1 and 4 deal with Hamlet, and scenes 2 and 5 with Ophelia, and these characters undergo a progression across their respective two scenes. They do not interact with one another, however, except in the central "Scherzo," the one point at which they meet and exchange dialogue.

Scenes 1 and 4, the Hamlet scenes, are the most notable for their cultural overload, the accumulation of both historical references and (often distorted) quotations that summon other authors and other texts into the drama. Richard Weber and Theo Girshausen, in their commentary on *Die Hamletmaschine*, see the "Stechschritt" ("goose-stepping"; *HM* 545/53) in scene 1 as an allusion to the GDR army, which establishes the relation of the scene to contemporary East German politics. They also register a web of references to twentieth-century Communist history in scene 4: the Russian revolution via a quotation from Pasternak's *Doctor Zhivago* and a self-quotation from Müller's own earlier play *Zement* (Cement), the Stalinist era, and the Hungarian uprising of 1956.[8] The line "Hier kommt das Gespenst das mich gemacht hat" ("Here comes the ghost who made me"; *HM* 545/53) in scene 1 summons up not only the ghost of Hamlet's father, but also the "specter of Communism" from the famous opening sentence of the *Communist Manifesto*. These historical references point to Müller's specific concern with Communism, and in particular his loss of hope in the Communist state in the face of the injustices wrought in its name: the "Denkmal"(monument) that features in scene 4 may suggest Stalin, but the name is "interchangeable," and what it actually stands for is the "Versteinerung einer Hoffnung" ("petrification of a hope"; *HM* 549/56). Morever, the (distorted) quotations from and allusions to literary and other sources cumulatively amount to a kind of compressed compendium of an entire cultural tradition. There are further references to Shakespearean characters, apart from the Hamlet figure: "RICHARD THE THIRD I THE PRINCEKILLING KING" in scene 1 (*HM* 545/53) and "MACBETH" in scene 4 (*HM* 552/57), both figures in whom the struggle for power is represented and both murderers of kings. "OH MY PEOPLE WHAT HAVE I DONE UNTO THEE" (*HM* 545/53) quotes the Good Friday Reproaches from the Christian tradition,[9] while "Unsern täglichen Mord gib uns heute / Denn Dein ist das Nichts" ("Give us this day our daily murder / Since thine is the nothingness"; *HM* 551/57) distorts the familiar words of the Lord's prayer. "A BAD COLD HE HAD OF IT JUST THE WORST TIME / JUST THE WORST TIME OF THE YEAR FOR A REVOLUTION" misquotes T. S. Eliot's poem "Journey of the Magi."[10] Weber and Girshausen further note allusions to Lautréamont and Bonaventura in scene 1, and references to Nietzsche, to Sartre (whose play *La Nausée* is cited verbatim at points), and to Dostoevsky in scene 4.[11] Walter Benjamin's "Angel of history" from the theses *On the Concept of History* is alluded to in the "Scherzo" in the stage direction: "*Ein Engel, das Gesicht im Nacken: Horatio*" ("*An angel, his face at the back of his head: Horatio*"; *HM* 548/55). There are also a number of quotations from Müller's own earlier plays.

The effect of this accretion of associations around the figure of Hamlet may be summed up as twofold. The postmodernist technique of constructing the text by combining fragments from other, pre-existing texts appears as a symptom of historical and cultural exhaustion. As Helen Fehervary puts it: "The author — like his protagonist — has nothing more to say and must content himself with citing literary history and his own works."[12] Fehervary's commentary does not give sufficient emphasis, though, to the degree to which this is a consciously willed exhaustion of a cultural tradition, a demonstrative "endgame." Weber and Girshausen's observations concerning the first scene can usefully be applied to the treatment of the Hamlet figure in the entire piece: "Müller's deployment of the Hamlet plot simultaneously dismantles it. The first scene overloads it with so many problems of an entirely different nature, albeit ones that can potentially be associated with it, that the whole edifice, as it were, collapses under the weight of them" (10). Müller's practice in relation to the Hamlet figure, in other words, is deliberately deconstructive. The aim is to push the imaginary constellation "Hamlet" to the limit of its signification in order to attain — at least in the imagination — a new cultural terrain beyond.

The figure of Hamlet himself in Müller's treatment is a highly complex one. In scene 1 he appears as the residue of the character familiar from Shakespeare's drama: "Ich war Hamlet" ("I was Hamlet"; *HM* 545/53).[13] In the course of the scene, the Shakespearean plot is replayed in terms of Müller's political and aesthetic agenda. Hamlet's uncle and mother, the ghost of his father, Horatio, Polonius, and Ophelia all make their appearance in a compressed, distorted version of the "Hamlet" action, in which the Hamlet figure's desire for self-annihilation provides the central motivation. Thus the insight into the supposedly revolutionary state's perpetration of violence and power-struggle and into the corruption of its figureheads translates into Hamlet's self-disgust, and this in turn into a violent repudiation of his family ties, culminating in the rape of his mother (*HM* 546–47/53–54). Early in scene 4, the Hamlet figure disinvests himself of make-up and costume and is transformed into the "HAMLETDARSTELLER" ("ACTOR PLAYING HAMLET"): "Ich bin nicht Hamlet. Ich spiele keine Rolle mehr. [. . .] Mein Drama findet nicht mehr statt" ("I'm not Hamlet. I don't take part any more. [. . .] My drama doesn't happen anymore"; *HM* 549/56). In this scene, the "Ich" who speaks (i.e., Hamlet, or the actor playing Hamlet) becomes the focus for the representation of the problematics of authorship. Here the traditional signification of Hamlet as the melancholy introvert, hindered in his ability to act by an excess of thought, comes fully into play. In this context, Hamlet takes on meaning as the type of the male intellectual subject of modernity.

A lengthy section of scene 4 is taken up with a representation of a popular revolt, reminiscent not only of the Hungarian uprising of 1956, but also that of 17 June 1953 in the GDR, pivotal moments in the cultural imaginary of the Communist states of Eastern Europe. Here Müller's text imagines a drama in the conditional tense — "Mein Drama, wenn es noch stattfinden würde, fände in der Zeit des Aufstands statt" ("My drama, if it still would happen, would happen in the time of the uprising"; *HM* 550/56) — and the place of the author is projected as being on both sides of the struggle, the chronicler of each, but party to neither. What is expressed here is the vision of a disinterested art form, one, perhaps, that can no longer be accused of being an "accomplice of power." But this requires the suppression of partisan emotion, which is an aspect of humanity itself: as the passage progresses, the author of the projected drama falls back increasingly on mechanistic images to describe his own status: "Ich bin die Schreibmaschine. [. . .] Ich füttere mit meinen Daten die Computer. [. . .] Ich bin die Datenbank" ("I am the typewriter. [. . .] I feed my own data into the computers. [. . .] I am the data bank"; *HM* 551/56). The passage comes to a halt in a recurrence of the Hamlet figure's self-disgust as the author perceives the social irrelevance of this form of literary activity, and once more negates the drama: "Wortschleim absondernd in meiner schalldichten Sprechblase über der Schlacht. Mein Drama hat nicht stattgefunden. Das Textbuch ist verlorengegangen" ("Oozing wordslime in my soundproof blurb over and above the battle. My drama didn't happen. The script has been lost"; *HM* 551/56). He subsequently withdraws from street scene and theater into solipsistic isolation: "Ich gehe nach Hause und schlage die Zeit tot, einig / Mit meinem ungeteilten Selbst" ("I go home and kill the time, at one / with my undivided self"; *HM* 551/56).

The remainder of the scene plays out a series of responses to the moral and cultural dilemma of authorship, a form of experimentation with alternative author positions that is readable as an abbreviated history of the male intellectual avant-garde in modernity. The first section is dominated by the keyword "Ekel" (nausea), reminiscent, as Weber and Girshausen point out, of both Nietzsche and Sartre.[14] Here, the intellectual distances himself from a media-dominated society ("Fernsehn Der tägliche Ekel Ekel" / "Television The daily nausea Nausea"; *HM* 551/56), expressing his disgust "Am präparierten Geschwätz Am verordneten Frohsinn" ("[At] prefabricated babble [At] decreed cheerfulness"; *HM* 551/56) and at the lies peddled in the political sphere. What he sees as he passes through the streets and supermarket halls are, by contrast (and in the contrasting form of verse):

> Gesichter
> Mit den Narben der Konsumschlacht Armut
> Ohne Würde Armut ohne die Würde
> Des Messers des Schlagrings der Faust
> Die erniedrigten Leiber der Frauen
> Hoffnungen der Generationen
> In Blut Feigheit Dummheit erstickt
> Gelächter aus toten Bäuchen
> Heil COCA COLA (*HM* 552)

> [Faces
> Scarred by the consumers battle Poverty
> Without dignity Poverty without the dignity
> Of the knife the knuckleduster the clenched fist

> The humiliated bodies of women
> Hopes of generations
> Stifled in blood cowardice stupidity
> Laughter from dead bellies
> Hail Coca Cola (*HM* 57)]

Here, in acute form, is the negative assessment of mass consumer society familiar from Horkheimer and Adorno's *Dialectic of Enlightenment*, culminating in the reference to the product that most epitomizes the domination of U.S. commercial practices in the postwar global economy. One notes, too, the privileged symbolic value given here to the "humiliated bodies of women." The intellectual's stream of consciousness turns to murderous thoughts to assuage his sense of disgust: "Ein Königreich / Für einen Mörder" ("A kingdom / For a murderer"; *HM* 552/57). But the allusion to Dostoevksy's *Crime and Punishment* summons up an unjust vengeance wreaked upon the wrong individual, a murderous intent visited upon a single victim far from the center of political power: "RASKOLNIKOW AM HERZEN UNTER DER EINZIGEN JACKE DAS BEIL FÜR DEN / EINZIGEN / SCHÄDEL DER PFANDLEIHERIN" ("RASKOLNIKOV CLOSE TO THE / HEART UNDER THE ONLY COAT THE AX FOR THE / ONLY / SKULL OF THE PAWNBROKER"; *HM* 552/57). This section concludes with the insight into the luxury of the intellectual's disgust, distanced as he is from the suffering of the truly underprivileged classes: "Ich bin / Ein Priviligierter Mein Ekel / Ist ein Privileg" ("I am / A privileged person My nausea / Is a privilege"; *HM* 552/57).

As if in response to this insight, the next section enacts as a form of wish-fantasy the annihilation of individual authorship. A speech signaling the desire to withdraw from the daily routines of human life is followed by a stage direction requiring the tearing up of the author's photograph (*HM* 552/57). This initiates the possibility of an unindividuated biological existence after the end of individual subjectivity: "Ich will in meinen Adern wohnen, im Mark meiner Knochen, im Labyrinth meines Schädels. Ich ziehe mich zurück in meine Eingeweide. Ich nehme Platz in meiner Scheiße, meinem Blut" ("I want to dwell in my veins, in the marrow of my bones, in the maze of my skull. I retreat into my entrails. I take my seat in my shit, in my blood"; *HM* 552/57). This move recalls in particular aspects of the work of the German Expressionists, in which the male author seeks to eliminate the pain of a disintegrative social existence in the fantasy of a primordial, formless physicality, as in the following lines by Gottfried Benn:

> O daß wir unsere Ururahnen wären.
> Ein Klümpchen Schleim in einem warmen Moor.
> Leben und Tod, Befruchten und Gebären
> glitte aus unseren stummen Säften vor.[15]

[O that we were our primal primal ancestors.
A little clot of slime in a warm swamp.
Life and death, fecundation and birth,
would slide forth from our mute juices.]

In the progression of Müller's scene, however, this position is negated, in its turn, as the excess of thought associated with the Hamlet figure once again raises the question of the privilege of the male intellectual of Western provenance: "Irgendwo werden Leiber zerbrochen, damit ich wohnen kann in meiner Scheiße. Irgendwo werden Leiber geöffnet, damit ich allein sein kann mit meinem Blut" ("Somewhere bodies are torn apart so I can dwell in my shit. Somewhere bodies are opened so I can be alone with my blood"; *HM* 552–53/57). In a further shift, then, the intellectual desires his transformation into a machine, which brings with it the elimination of the pain of consciousness: "Ich will eine Maschine sein. Arme zu greifen Beine zu gehn kein Schmerz kein Gedanke" ("I want to be a machine. Arms for grabbing Legs to walk on, no pain no thoughts"; *HM* 553/57). The fantasy of the artist as machine has a considerable history in the avant-garde movements of Western modernity, notably in the work of male authors and artists. Müller himself thought of his title *Hamletmaschine* in analogy with the Surrealist Marcel Duchamp's "Machine Célibataire" (Bachelor Machine)[16] while Jonathan Kalb sees the line "I want to be a machine" as alluding to Andy Warhol whose "mechanized art factory" is thus summoned into the text (107). But if this is envisaged as a way of eliminating the conscience that makes cowards of us all that is Hamlet's characteristic affliction,[17] Müller's text exposes the fallacy of the radical gesture. The final section of scene 4 concludes with the Hamlet figure slicing the skulls of the figures of Marx, Lenin, and Mao, as the embodiments on stage of the revolutionary tradition (and represented as naked women). The implication is that the radical, antisocial avant-garde has in fact throughout been complicit in perpetuating the structures of the paternal state — but has done nothing to alleviate the misery of the oppressed, nor to change the social structures that condemn them to such misery. It is this that makes of Hamlet by the end of the scene a figure of counter-revolutionary reaction.[18]

By contrast, the hope of revolutionary *action* — so to speak, the "new" play, the play not written by Shakespeare — is invested in the figure of Ophelia. The trajectories of Hamlet and Ophelia briefly cross in the "Scherzo" scene (scene 3), in which Hamlet expresses his desire to be a woman (*HM* 548/55). This is readable as his wish to be a victim, rather than a perpetrator of history, or, as Kalb puts it: "He [. . .] envies the women their object status, having apparently become overburdened by his intense subjectivity" (116). He changes clothes with Ophelia at this point, and is made up by her as a whore, the privileged allegory of

modernity in much German modernist writing.[19] But it is Ophelia herself
in whom the real energy of the text is realized as, in the much shorter and
less wordy scenes 2 and 5, she emancipates herself from her entrapment
in the role of suffering femininity in a form of counter-trajectory to the
Hamlet plot.

Scene 2 is entitled "DAS EUROPA DER FRAU" ("THE EUROPE
OF WOMEN"; more accurately, of woman) and introduces Ophelia as
the embodiment of those whose only way out of the object status that
confined them was to destroy themselves (one recalls here the female figures of Ingeborg Bachmann's *Todesarten* cycle: Fanny Goldmann, Franza,
Aga Rottwitz): "Ich bin Ophelia. Die der Fluß nicht behalten hat. Die
Frau am Strick Die Frau mit den aufgeschnittenen Pulsadern Die Frau
mit der Überdosis AUF DEN LIPPEN SCHNEE Die Frau mit dem Kopf
im Gasherd" ("I am Ophelia. The one the river didn't keep. The woman
dangling from a rope. The woman with her arteries cut open. The woman
with the overdose. SNOW ON HER LIPS. The woman with her head in
the gas stove"; *HM* 547/54). The scene enacts her rebellion against her
fate thus far and her resurrection as a new revolutionary (the line concerning the river has been read as a reference to Rosa Luxemburg; Kalb
113), destroyer of the bourgeois order and repudiator of the love of men
that has up until now bound her to her victimhood:

> Gestern habe ich aufgehört mich zu töten. Ich bin allein mit mei-
> nen Brüsten meinen Schenkeln meinem Schoß. Ich zertrümmere die
> Werkzeuge meiner Gefangenschaft den Stuhl den Tisch das Bett. Ich
> zerstöre das Schlachtfeld das mein Heim war. Ich reiße die Türen auf,
> damit der Wind herein kann und der Schrei der Welt. (*HM* 547)

> [Yesterday I stopped killing myself. I'm alone with my breasts my
> thighs my womb. I smash the tools of my captivity, the chair the
> table the bed. I destroy the battlefield that was my home. I fling
> open the doors so the wind gets in and the scream of the world.
> (*HM* 54)]

In his 1992 autobiography, Müller makes a link between this scene and
an episode that had caught his interest from the life of Ulrike Meinhof.
Following a failed attack on the offices of the *Spiegel* magazine, a group
around Andreas Baader had, together with Meinhof, wrecked the apartment she shared with her husband, the chief editor of the journal *Konkret,*
and thrown the furniture out of the window. The destruction of the bourgeois environment, the act of leaving behind the bourgeois existence and
embracing illegality: that had interested him, Müller states.[20] The Ophelia figure embodies a purer form of revolutionary anger than Hamlet's
and also an expressly corporeal one (note the references to the breasts,
thighs, and the womb, as well as to the hands and to blood), born out

of the experience of being objectified. Her tearing of the photographs of the men who have (sexually) used her prefigures the tearing of the photograph of the author in scene 4, and signals the female figure's refusal to serve any longer as the Muse and the material base of male authorship. In the text's final scene, her revolutionary anger is raised to fever pitch in an explosive speech that is left to resonate beyond the end of the play, even as she is progressively immobilized by the figures of the two men in doctor's coats who bind her into a wheelchair with gauze in the course of the scene:

> Hier spricht Elektra. Im Herzen der Finsternis. Unter der Sonne der Folter. An die Metropolen der Welt. Im Namen der Opfer. Ich stoße allen Samen aus, den ich empfangen habe. Ich verwandle die Milch meiner Brüste in tödliches Gift. Ich nehme die Welt zurück, die ich geboren habe. Ich ersticke die Welt, die ich geboren habe, zwischen meinen Schenkeln. Ich begrabe sie in meiner Scham. Nieder mit dem Glück der Unterwerfung. Es lebe der Haß, die Verachtung, der Aufstand, der Tod. Wenn sie mit Fleischmessern durch eure Schlafzimmer geht, werdet ihr die Wahrheit wissen. *Männer ab. Ophelia bleibt auf der Bühne, reglos in der weißen Verpackung.* (*HM* 554)

> [This is Electra speaking. In the heart of darkness. Under the sun of torture. To the capitals of the world. In the name of the victims. I eject all the sperm I have received. I turn the milk of my breasts into lethal poison. I take back the world I gave birth to. I choke between my thighs the world I gave birth to. I bury it in my womb. Down with the happiness of submission. Long live hate and contempt, rebellion and death. When she walks through your bedrooms carrying butcher knives you'll know the truth. *The men exit. Ophelia remains on stage, motionless in her white wrappings.* (*HM* 58)]

I will return to the analysis of this highly ambiguous final scene at the end of this chapter in order to read it in parallel with the ending of Wolf's text. For now, let it be stated that there is surely no more succinct and forceful representation than Müller's *Die Hamletmaschine* of the "crisis of Enlightenment," which is at the same time a crisis of male subjectivity as traditionally conceived, the crisis of rationality as offering a means of steering the historical process to the achievement of a perfect society. In this text is encapsulated all the characteristically modern self-disgust of the male subject at his own lack of historical agency and at the self-analytical fragmentation of his consciousness. It is a text of extraordinary self-awareness and also, in the terms of the reading presented here, a blunt critique of the politically ineffectual nature of avant-garde art, while remaining a radically avant-garde text propelled by the aspiration to revolt against the petrifaction of the status quo. Furthermore, the final scene of the play seems to confirm the gesture observed in earlier chapters of this study, that it is precisely in the symbolic position of woman that the potential for cultural change is identified. Helen Fehervary, in an early response to *Die Hamletmaschine*, went so far as to diagnose in Müller's play "the authorial wish for the narrative transferral from male to female authorship."[21] Certainly the time in which Müller was writing, the late 1970s, was a high-point of the new women's movement that, supported by a now vigorously growing feminist literature and literary theory, understood itself as containing the seeds of the overthrowal of the existing cultural order.[22] This provided the historical backdrop for the genesis of Christa Wolf's *Kassandra* project.

Christa Wolf's *Kassandra*: Refusing the Patriarchal Tradition

Wolf's *Kassandra* (1983) was first presented to the public in the form of a series of five lectures, the prestigious Frankfurt poetics lectures that she delivered in May 1982. The first four lectures used non-fictional forms historically associated with female authorship: the travel report (two lectures detailing a journey of Wolf's to Greece in March and April 1980); the diary (covering the period May 1980 to August 1981, and drawing together reflections on reading and aesthetics, as well as contemporary world politics); and the letter (addressed to a friend designated A., and dealing primarily with the concept of a female aesthetics and poetics). A reading from the fictional narrative *Kassandra* (a prepublication draft, different from the final published version of the complete *Erzählung*[23]) formed the fifth and concluding lecture. In its conception, the *Kassandra* project was intended as a web (*Gewebe*) or network (*Netzwerk*) of different narrative forms, containing multiple cross-references and creating tensions of difference that assist the text in avoiding ultimate closure of meaning: a deliberate counter-model to the linear heroic narrative of the male-authored epic against which Wolf was reacting.[24] Furthermore, in its first public form, it actualized other aspects of a conceptual female counter-aesthetics: the work not as transhistorical written text, removed from the body and person of its originator and presented as a coherent, closed and authoritative whole, but as the "living word," "the spoken word" *voiced* by the physically present author in the Now (the time of the *Ich* in Bachmann's *Malina*), a "narrative concept which has the characteristics both of public speech and the offer of conversation and discussion," as Sonja Hilzinger notes in her editorial commentary to the *Werke* edition (420).[25] In short, it was "an extraordinarily complex project which

interrogates aesthetics and politics from the perspective of gender difference, in historical-critical terms and also subjectively" (419).

The first of the Frankfurt lectures begins by addressing the moment
when the figure of Kassandra in Aeschylus's *Oresteia* took possession of
the author Wolf in the form of a voice that tears down the barrier of the
intervening millenia to create pure presence:

> Oh! Oh! Ach!
> Apollon! Ápollon!
> Kassandra. Ich sah sie gleich. Sie, die Gefangene, nahm mich gefan-
> gen, sie, selbst Objekt fremder Zwecke, besetzte mich. [. . .] Drei-
> tausend Jahre — weggeschmolzen.
>
> [*Aiee! Aieeeee!*
> *Apollo! Apollo!*
> Cassandra. I saw her at once. She, the captive, took me captive;
> herself made an object by others, she took possession of me. [. . .]
> Three thousand years — melted away.][26]

Wolf's "occupation"[27] by the mythical figure of Kassandra, the seer who
foretold the fall of Troy but who was fated not to be believed — a marginal
figure in Homer who also appears in the *Oresteia* and in Euripides' *The
Trojan Women* — may have been initiated by her reading of Aeschylus's
dramatic text. However, the fictional monologue of the Trojan Kassandra
that represents the culmination of that imaginative occupation reads as a
counter-narrative to the *Iliad*, the Homeric epic of the siege of Troy told
from the perspective of the Greeks, which revolves above all around the
male figure of Achilles. It is an extraordinarily daring enterprise for a modern author to seek to challenge the hold of one the foundational narratives
of Western culture in this way, but Wolf's intention is no less than this. In
Homer's epic of warring heroes, she sees one of the originary documents
of a form of thinking and a conceptualization of human subjectivity that,
deriving from the patriarchal culture of the ancient Greeks, continues to
inform the Western way of being right up to her own day, the era of the
Cold War between the U.S.-led West and the Soviet-led East. In reenter-
ing the text of Homer's *Iliad* for the purpose of disturbing its inherited
meanings, she, like Müller in *Die Hamletmaschine*, identifies the tradition
of "male" culture as one of violence, bloodshed, and conflict. Within this
cultural tradition, women feature as the objectified Other, excluded from
influence on the course of history and often its passive victims. Her aim is
to bring into view the perspective of this Other as the basis for a new form
of subject constitution.

"Mythologie plus Psychologie" (myth plus psychology), a recipe
taken from her reading of Thomas Mann during the period of her work
on the Kassandra material — in the third lecture she cites his 1941 cor-

respondence with the scholar of ancient Greek mythology, Karl Kerényi (*K* 133/248) — characterizes Wolf's approach to the figures adopted from her classical sources. Her psychological analysis of the Greek heroes familiar from Homeric epic closely follows Horkheimer and Adorno's analysis of the dialectic of the Enlightenment subject.[28] The "identical, purpose-directed, masculine character"[29] of the Greek warriors, intent on the subjection of the more "feminized" Trojans, is represented as having its basis in a catastrophic repression of the emotional and relational impulses of the self. In particular in the repressed homosexual Achill, the apogee of the self-alienated subject in Wolf's rewriting of Homer, these impulses return in distorted form as an excess of violence enacted upon the defeated bodies of those he overcomes in combat: as sadistic perversion, displayed in the scene in which he kills Troilus (*K* 311/74), and necrophilia, in the scene in which he violates the corpse of the defeated Amazon queen, Penthesilea (*K* 365/120). This is highly reminiscent of Horkheimer and Adorno's discussion of the Sadeian libertine whose subjective power is asserted via the mastery of nature and through the objectification and exploitation of all those weaker others who reflect nature back to the self.[30] But the critique extends to others among the Greek heroes. Agamemnon, for example, the commander of the Greek forces, is represented as "ein Schwächling ohne Selbstbewußtsein" ("a weakling who lacked self-esteem"; *K* 286/52) whose "ausgesuchte Grausamkeit im Kampf" ("exquisite cruelty in battle") is the reverse side of the coin to his sexual impotence (*K* 235/10). That the Greeks emerge from the battle for the city as the victors rests on their ability to objectify others, to exploit what the text represents sympathetically as the vulnerable, human aspects of their Trojan opponents. Moreover, since, as the conclusion of the text proclaims, the values of the victors will lay down the law from now on — "Es war ja klar: Allen, die überlebten, würden die neuen Herren ihr Gesetz diktieren" ("It was obvious: The new masters would dictate their law to all the survivors") — the victory of the Greeks over the Trojans is represented as marking the inception of the universal validity of the principle of "self-preservation" that Horkheimer and Adorno identified in the emblematic narrative of individualization in the Odysseus chapter of the *Dialectic*. As Kassandra says to Aineias: "Bald, sehr bald wirst du ein Held sein müssen" ("Soon, very soon you will have to become a hero"; *K* 385/138).

Wolf's project aims to unmask the cost of this version of human subjectivity and to oppose it with a counter-model. The Greek heroes ultimately dominate because of their weddedness to the principle of self-contained individualism, to which the Other can only ever be an object, and their concomitant repression of the relational and combinatory aspects of human psychic activity. The solution to the urgent problem of contemporary history that weighs upon Wolf as a writer in the 1980s, given the contemporary threat of nuclear annihilation, is to be found in a vision that in many respects looks very like the one set out by Herbert Marcuse in *Eros and Civilization* (1955): that of "a non-repressive reality principle involving instinctual liberation [that] would *regress* behind the attained level of civilized rationality."[31] The gradual process of instinctual liberation is exemplified in the biographical development undergone by her central figure Kassandra, from daughter of the royal household, integrated into the hierarchies of patriarchal power and so complicit with its strategies of repression, to outcast living in a temporary community consisting largely of women outside the walls of the citadel: a kind of "Kein Ort. Nirgends" or *ou-topos*. The key to this narrative is that it *also* describes a psychological development, a progress toward self-knowledge. In this, the figure of Kassandra functions as an identificatory figure for Wolf as author in much the same way as Hamlet functions as an identificatory figure for Müller as author in *Die Hamletmaschine*. Kassandra, in Wolf's treatment, becomes the representative of the type of the intellectual, and her role as priestess and seer is hinted at as being parallel to that of the writer.

In the fictional *Erzählung*, Kassandra's public position as priestess and seer, integrated into the palace hierarchy, appears as a masculine-connoted rather than a feminine position. Her choice of the profession of priest and prophet/seer is depicted as a rejection of the usual female biography, as a way of securing her own independence and, importantly, of exercising power, as is suggested in a recollected dialogue with the chief priest of Apollo, Panthoos:

> Zweifellos, sagte er [Panthoos], gebe es Züge in meinem Wesen, die der Priesterschaft entgegenkämen. Welche? Nun — mein Wunsch, auf Menschen Einfluß auszuüben; wie anders sollte eine Frau sonst herrschen können? Ferner: Mein inbrünstiges Verlangen, mich mit der Gottheit auf vertrauten Fuß zu stellen. Und, natürlich, meine Abneigung gegen die Annäherung irdischer Männer. (*K* 255)

> [Beyond doubt, he [Panthous] said, certain of my character traits cut me out for the priesthood. Which traits? Well, my desire to exercise influence over people; how else could a woman hold a position of power? Second: my ardent desire to be on familiar terms with the deity. And of course my aversion to the approaches of mortal men. (*K* 26)]

In occupying this quasi-male subject position, invested with power but bound by the terms on which it is granted, Kassandra, like Müller's Hamlet, becomes an "accomplice of power."[32] This is presented most notably at the moment where Kassandra, realizing that the war is being fought over a phantom, since Helena, the ostensible cause of the conflict, is not in fact in Troy,[33] does not speak out openly, but rather falls into a prophetic "fit," the hallmark of the figure of Kassandra in the classical Greek sources. Wolf's reflecting narrator Kassandra, looking back on her life, acknowledges that her lack of directness was based on her allegiance to the palace:

> Denn warum schrie ich, wenn ich schrie: Wir sind verloren!, warum nicht: Troer, es gibt keine Helena! Ich weiß es, wußte es auch damals schon: Der Eumelos in mir verbot es mir. Ihn, der mich im Palast erwartete, ihn schrie ich an: Es gibt keine Helena!, aber er wußte es ja. Dem Volk hätte ich es sagen müssen. Das hieß: Ich, Seherin, gehörte zum Palast. (*K* 305)

> [For when I shrieked, why did I shriek: "We are lost!"? Why not: "Trojans there is no Helen!"? I know why not, I knew it even then. The Eumelos inside me forbade it me. Eumelos was waiting for me in the palace, it was he at whom I shouted: "There is no Helen!" But of course he already knew it. The people were the ones I should have told. In other words, I the seeress, was owned by the palace. (*K* 69)]

In Wolf's narrative, Kassandra's fits are also subjected to psychological analysis, through which they are diagnosed as affect arising from the tension of the split consciousness — as it were, a "feminine"-inflected version of the return of the repressed, as the cost of the self-discipline that is also self-alienation of the "masculine" subject position. For the nature of her gift as seer is represented as a distinctly *corporeal* and therefore feminine-connoted form of perception, with distinctly physical consequences:

> Ich aber. Ich allein sah. Oder "sah" ich denn? Wie war das doch. Ich fühlte. Erfuhr — ja, das ist das Wort; denn eine Erfahrung war es, ist es, wenn ich "sehe," "sah": Was in dieser Stunde seinen Ausgang nahm, war unser Untergang. Stillstand der Zeit, ich wünsch es niemandem. [. . .] Bis endlich die entsetzliche Qual, als Stimme, sich aus mir, durch mich hindurch und mich zerreißend ihren Weg gebahnt hatte und sich losgemacht. Ein pfeifendes, ein auf dem letzten Loch pfeifendes Stimmchen, das mir das Blut aus den Adern treibt und die Haare zu Berge stehn läßt. Das, wie es anschwillt, stärker, gräßlicher wird, all meine Gliedmaßen ins Zappeln, Rappeln und ins Schleudern bringt. Aber die Stimme schert das nicht. Frei hängt sie über mir und schreit, schreit, schreit. Wehe, schrie sie. Wehe, wehe. (*K* 293–94)

> [But I, I alone saw. Or did I really "see"? What was it, then? I felt. Experienced — yes, that's the word. For it was, it is, an experience when I "see," when I "saw." Saw that the outcome of this hour was

our destruction. Time stood still, I would not wish that on anyone. [. . .] Until finally the dreadful torment took the form of a voice; forced its way out of me, through me, dismembering me as it went; and set itself free. A whistling little voice, whistling at the end of its rope, that makes my blood run cold and my hair stand on end. Which as it swells, grows louder and more hideous, sets all my members to wriggling and rattling and hurling about. But the voice does not care. It floats above me, free, and shrieks, shrieks, shrieks. "Woe," it shrieked. "Woe, woe." (*K* 59)]

The benighted mental state that falls upon Kassandra following this particular scene is described as "Wahn-Sinn als Ende der Verstellungsqual" ("Lunacy: an end to the torture of pretense") and her soul as the site of a battle between two opposing forces (*K* 295/60).[34] A little later, the two principles that oppose each other within Kassandra are identified as the inclination to conform with those in power on the one hand and the craving for knowledge on the other (*K* 298/62–63). The one is linked to public position, honor, and political influence, and is dependent on Kassandra's status as the favorite daughter of her father, Priamos, the king of Troy; the other to an inner vocation and gift, that, when it is granted free reign rather than suppressed, becomes more clearly identifiable as the impulse to a form of perception and wisdom generated from the unbroken, unhindered communication between body and mind. The conflict between the two principles, as long as it lasts, produces corporeal symptoms and illness, as well as mental distress. In other words, like all the representatives of the modern subject encountered in this study, to the extent that she is integrated into a social system that requires of her self-discipline, conformity, and the performance of a publicly accepted and acceptable "ego-narrative,"[35] Kassandra is forced to deny the demands of the repressed parts of her nature, in particular those aspects related to her existence as a corporeal being. As a result, the repressed returns in distorted form: as corporeal symptoms, madness, and also malignant dreams.[36] Once she renounces her loyalty to the palace and to her father, together with the patriarchal principle that he stands for, she no longer suffers from fits and the dreams become more benign, more legible as the promptings of parts of the psyche beyond surface perceptions.

Her passage to the renunciation of the emotional bonds that tie her to the palace and to the king is presented as an inner journey to mental harmony and the realization of her "true" self. By the time Kassandra becomes an accepted member of the community living in the caves by the river Scamander toward the end of the narrative, she is fully committed to "knowledge" and has lost the desire to be integrated into the hierarchies of public power. In terms of the parallels with Müller's Hamlet, Kassandra's path away from complicity with power is, like his, based on a refusal to participate. In her retrospective narrative, this Great Refusal[37] is signaled by her utterance of the word "No."[38] However, the different gendering of the positions of Hamlet and Kassandra produces very different consequences. His is a withdrawal into isolated self-containment, the principle of "masculine" individuation still unquestioned: "I go home and kill the time, at one / with my undivided self." Hers is the relinquishing of one relational construction of the self — the father-daughter relationship — for another, alternative form of relationship, a different collective identity, signaled in the narrative by the use of the pronoun "wir" (we): a community consisting largely of women, but also the elderly, the wounded, and those low in the social hierarchy — in short, a community of the disempowered. That she no longer participates in the war does nothing to stop its course, just as Hamlet's renunciation of action — "My drama doesn't happen anymore" — ultimately leads to an acknowledgement of the complicity even of the one who does not act. However, in the *male* subject, the excess of thought, insofar as it comes between him and action, constitutes a failure of ideal-typical masculinity, the failure to impose his will on the political and historical process, leading to self-hatred. In the *female* figure, by contrast, it offers a platform for a morally critical stance vis-à-vis a social order from which she can construe herself as having been actively excluded. As Anna K. Kuhn points out:

> [Wolf] also assigns to her [Kassandra] advantages peculiar to women: because they are not part of the ruling system, women's underprivileged status as outsiders grants them a greater ability to perceive false consciousness and misconstructions, that is, delusional societal structures.[39]

However, as I hope has become clear, women's non-participation in the ruling system is a fallacy. Women *are* and historically have been accomplices of power, not only through their relationships with their menfolk but, as Kassandra's exemplary biography conveys, also in their own right.[40] It is their sex that creates an interval of difference. "[If] one is a woman one is often surprised by a sudden splitting off of consciousness, say in walking down Whitehall, when from being the natural inheritor of that civilization, she becomes, on the contrary, alien and critical," wrote Virginia Woolf in *A Room of One's Own*.[41] Figuratively speaking, the daughter of the palace is as much the "natural inheritor" of the civilization as the son. Her sex, though, furnishes her with the privilege of the "splitting off of consciousness" that enables her to set herself apart from that same civilization if she so desires it. But to what extent, then, is the narrative's utopian projection bound to a conceptualization of femaleness?

Kassandra's movement away from the patriarchal connection[42] is guided at crucial junctures of the narrative by Arisbe, a woman from the common people and the figure in whom, more than in any other in the narrative, the traces of the memory of an ancient matriarchal culture are preserved. She is constructed in the narrative as a counter-figure to the palace and the parental bonds that tie Kassandra to it. At the point at which Kassanda first goes to seek her out for information about the palace past, Arisbe is described as the inhabitant of a "Neben-, ja Gegenwelt" ("by-world, counterworld": *K* 281/48). Thereafter it is notable how often Arisbe is a presence during Kassandra's "crisis" episodes, steering her growing self-knowledge and interpreting her dreams. The Scamander community into which Kassandra is accepted at the end of her inner development has Arisbe as its most authoritative figure. Because she is a female figure, and because the community of the powerless in which she is such a prominent figure is organized around the worship of a female deity, Arisbe appears as the embodiment of the matriarchal principle, in opposition to the patriarchal principle represented by the king, Priamos. In the light of these observations, Kassandra's progress appears at first sight to be one backward through time, a regression "behind the attained level of civilized rationality" (Marcuse), describing a movement from the patriarchal order, which both represents the principle of individuation but also divides individuals from one another (as self-other, friend-foe, male-female, and so on), back into a matriarchal order, the time of the group, the clan, of the collective, unindividualized community in which the separation of thinking and feeling, of reason and emotion, of mind and body *has not yet taken place*. The cultural "memory" of a state preceding the birth of the rational subject as the individual paradoxically divided against his own nature has, at any rate, been identified by a number of commentators as the goal of Wolf's archaeological quest, among them Sigrid Weigel:

> The figure of Kassandra becomes an image for the desire for originary unity. The concept of the "undivided" in Horkheimer/Adorno — a helpless linguistic attempt to describe, from the perspective of a division that has already taken place, a state which precedes this division — becomes in Wolf a projection of unity.[43]

In the Frankfurt lectures, however, Wolf distances herself decisively from a contemporary feminist thinking that finds in the idea of the matriarchate a form of social model. (It is notable, too, that Wolf makes it a principle to include male figures among the members of the Scamander community, notably Anchises, the father of Aineias.) She identifies in the habitual exclusion of women from the shaping of culture over thousands of years the weak point of culture out of which it becomes self-destructive, described as its "Unfähigkeit zur Reife" ("inability to grow up" or, better, to be mature). However, the rejection of the achievements of rational thought just because they are the products of a male-dominated culture does not assist the attainment of cultural maturity, nor does the imaginary regression to prerational stages of human civilization:

Die Sippe, der Clan, Blut und Boden: Dies sind nicht die Werte, an die Mann und Frau von heute anknüpfen können; daß diese Schlagworte schreckliche Regressionen bieten können, sollten gerade wir wissen. Es gibt keinen Weg vorbei an der Persönlichkeitsbildung, an rationalen Modellen der Konfliktlösung, das heißt auch an der Auseinandersetzung und Zusammenarbeit mit Andersdenkenden und, selbstverständlich, Andersgeschlechtlichen. Autonomie ist eine Aufgabe für jedermann, und Frauen, die sich auf ihre Weiblichkeit als einen Wert zurückziehen, handeln im Grunde, wie es ihnen andressiert wurde: Sie reagieren mit einem großangelegten Ausweichmanöver auf die Herausforderung der Realität an ihre ganze Person. (*K* 148)

[The tribe, the clan, blood-and-soil — these are not values to which men and women of today can adhere. We Germans, of all people, should know that these catchwords can supply pretexts for hideous regressions. There is no way to bypass the need for personality development, for rational models of the resolution of conflict, and thus also for confrontation and cooperation, with people of dissident opinions and, it goes without saying, people of different sex. Autonomy is a task for everyone, and women who treat their femininity as a value they can fall back on act fundamentally as they were trained to act. They react to the challenge which reality poses to them as whole persons with a large-scale evasive maneuver. (*K* 260–61)][44]

What Kassandra represents, then, once she has become part of the Scamander community, is not after all a *regression,* but a projected *next stage* of the cultural development of the subject, as seen from Wolf's own historical perspective. In other words, it is in her capacity as an identificatory figure for the author's own process of *Selbsterkenntnis* or self-knowledge, rather than as a figure from a particular mythological constellation (the historical "seam" between matriarchy and patriarchy), that she has model character.[45] As a double-gendered figure, who seeks to reconcile the masculine-connoted and the feminine-connoted aspects of the psyche — the capacity for rational analysis and insight based on individuation on the one hand, and corporeal perception, intuition, dreaming, bodily presence, sensuality and eroticism on the other — she is the embodiment of Wolf's attempt to imagine a synthesis of the conceptual opposition between the masculine and the feminine inherited from the Western philosophical tradition. In this sense, Wolf's own position is one that is only possible *subsequent to* Horkheimer and Adorno's diagnosis that the malaise of modernity is attributable to the division of the rational, masculinized subject against his own nature. Her Kassandra narrative is to be seen as an attempt to imagine, in Gerhard Neumann's words, "the reconciliation of the opposition of culture and nature" (261) that Horkheimer and Adorno do not pursue in the *Dialectic,* and to provide images through which to actualize what Neumann describes as the "imaginability of a subject that no longer makes others its 'object,' but rather leads the 'I' to a 'you' and finds a 'we,' 'the thing of greatest importance'" (250). That the figure through whom she projects this position is female has to do with the fact that, as found throughout this study, this form of relational subjectivity is more easily conceptualized through the symbolic figure of the double-gendered female than through any symbolic male figure.

Looking at Arisbe more closely in the light of the above, it becomes apparent that she is not, after all, or not only, a representative of the matriarchate, but a figuration of the principle of self-knowledge or *Selbsterkenntnis.* While this seems a very Greek and also very Enlightenment concept — in the fourth lecture, Wolf notes that the phrase "Know thyself" derives from the god Apollo at Delphi[46] — Arisbe's form of *Selbsterkenntnis* is not so much Apollonian as rooted in corporeal experience, and as such representative of a synthesis of rational cognition and corporeal sensibility.[47] In her interrogation of Kassandra's dreams and symptomatic behavior at the mid-point of the narrative, she occupies a role very like that of the rational, analytical Malina in the dream chapter of Bachmann's novel. She serves here as an externalized authority before whom Kassandra undertakes her self-interrogation. By the end of the narrative, though, she is the voice of the text's projection into an imagined future of humanity, the bearer of the work's utopian desire:

> Du meinst, Arisbe, der Mensch kann sich selbst nicht sehen. — So ist es. Er erträgt es nicht. Er braucht das fremde Abbild. — Und daran wird sich nie was ändern? Immer nur die Wiederkehr des Gleichen? Selbstfremdheit, Götzenbilder, Haß? — Ich weiß es nicht. Soviel weiß ich: Es gibt Zeitenlöcher. Dies ist so eines, hier und jetzt. Wir dürfen es nicht ungenutzt vergehen lassen.
> Da, endlich, hatte ich mein "Wir." (*K* 369)

> ["You think that human beings cannot see themselves, Arisbe?" "That's right. They cannot stand it. They need the alien image." "And will that never change? Only ever the repetition of the same? Self-estrangement, idols, hatred?" "I don't know. This much I do know: There are gaps in time. This is one of them, here and now. We cannot let it pass without taking advantage of it."
> There at last I had my "we." (*K* 124, translation modified)]

Something is wrong, though. For Kassandra's narrative does not end on the opening onto the future. Rather, like Bachmann's novel before it, it ends with a murder — the slaughter of Kassandra by Klytemnestra. The "gap in time" that is the site of utopia in Wolf's *Kassandra* is, in the final analysis, uncannily similar to the crack in the wall in which Bachmann's

Ich comes to a halt at the end of *Malina:* it is an imaginary breach in the existing order, but what is projected in it has no place in history. This could be read as a consequence of the fact that a social system is not yet in sight that could sustain and support the reconceptualization of the subject proposed through Wolf's narrative. But there is a more negative interpretation: that Wolf, in the end, however unconsciously, wanted to retain the moral purity of the position *apart* from the course of history, with its concomitant accusatory gesture, the "alien and critical" stance that is her privilege as a woman within the established binary opposition of male and female. I see this as the key to the much-debated issue of the closure of Wolf's narrative, which appears in direct contradiction to her discussion of the fragmentary, multiplicit, and open nature of a conceptual "female" aesthetics in the Frankfurt lectures.[48]

Hamletmaschine and *Kassandra*: Endings / Stasis

Both texts considered in this chapter, Heiner Müller's *Die Hamletmaschine* and Christa Wolf's *Kassandra,* contain representations of the passage of female figures from victimhood to a form of autonomy, from objects of history to would-be subjects. In both, the emergence of the female figures from the background of history appears to offer a potential counter-model to an exhausted or denounced masculine subject construction. Yet both texts end in stasis: Ophelia "motionless in her white wrappings" and Kassandra powerless before the gates of death: "Hier ende ich, ohnmächtig, und nichts, nichts was ich hätte tun oder lassen, wollen oder denken können, hätte mich an ein andres Ziel geführt" ("Here I end my days, helpless, and nothing, nothing I could have done or not done, willed or thought, could have led me to a different goal"; *K* 227/3). Why this immobility, this inability to take *action?*

In the case of Wolf's *Kassandra,* one argument that has been put forward is that it is because Wolf is constrained by her sources. Sigrid Weigel notes that Wolf's commitment to the historicization of myth in her project means that she has no choice but to reproduce the ending as handed down by tradition.[49] She also comments that this is a more general risk when working with mythical material, for while myths are often variable and open to re-interpretation, they are structurally closed to the extent that they provide images for historical experiences and as such become fixed to defined, unequivocal meanings.[50] Sonja Hilzinger proposes that, while Wolf's narrative sought to counter the objectification of Kassandra in the myth as passed down, the latter nevertheless continues to express historical reality: "the 'site' of Kassandra's process of coming to consciousness remains the interior monologue, to which, under the given conditions, there is no corresponding possibility of agency" (421). The challenge of the narrative under these circumstances, argues Hilzinger, lies in the fact that it "problematizes the way in which this fatal necessity has come about" (422).

This means, though, that the murder of Kassandra at the close of Wolf's narrative has distinct parallels with the elimination of *Ich* at the end of Ingeborg Bachmann's *Malina*. In chapter 3, I proposed that Bachmann's novel should be read as a critique of "masculine" subjectivity, as presenting a history of the construction of the male-subject-as-norm in the terms of the Western tradition that makes visible and tangible what has been eradicated from consciousness in that construction of selfhood. The novel's last sentence, "Es war Mord" ("It was murder"), rings out in accusation against the prevailing cultural conditions under which the spontaneous, open, vulnerable, and would-be-relational self that is figured in the female figure *Ich* becomes unviable as a subject position. But I also drew attention to those moments toward the end of the dream chapter where, under the guidance of Malina in the role of quasi-psychoanalyst, *Ich* begins to move away from her status as victim and to discover in herself the capacity for violence that her dreams so far have identified exclusively with the father figure. Following this self-discovery, *Ich* relinquishes her resistance to Malina's view that "war" is all-pervasive and as such is a constituent part even of *Ich* herself:

> MALINA: Es ist Krieg. Und du bist der Krieg. Du selber.
> ICH: Ich nicht.
> MALINA: Wir alle sind es, auch du.
> ICH: Dann will ich nicht mehr sein [. . .].
>
> [MALINA: It's war. And you are the war. You yourself.
> ME: Not me.
> MALINA: We all are, you included.
> ME: Then I don't want to be anymore [. . .].][51]

The logical consequence of the acknowledgement that there is no other order except "eternal war" (*M* 236/155) is that all hope of social transformation must be abandoned. It is just such a lack of any kind of utopia that haunts Elfriede Jelinek's writing. Bachmann's *Ich* does not pursue this course. Rather, *Ich* is eradicated as a character position in order to preserve *as an idea* the utopian potential figured in her. This relies upon her exclusion from the social order as a still explicitly female figure. The breach in the wall in which *Ich* is held in suspension at the end of the novel is in this respect the site of her total self-realization as a figure of the abstract "feminine":

> MALINA: An der richtigen Stelle hast du nichts mehr zu wollen. Du wirst dort so sehr du sein, daß du dein Ich aufgeben kannst. Es wird die erste Stelle sein, auf der die Welt von jemand geheilt ist. (*M* 313)

> [MALINA: In the proper place you will have nothing more to want. There you will be yourself so much that you'll be able to give up your "I." It will be the first place where someone has healed the world. (*M* 208, translation modified)]

Wolf's Kassandra repeats this gesture. Ostensibly, she chooses not to accompany her lover Aineias on his journey to become the founder of Rome (and the hero of Virgil's *Aeneid*) because she does not wish to see him transformed by the conditions that prevail following the fall of Troy:

> Es war ja klar: Allen, die überlebten, würden die neuen Herren ihr Gesetz diktieren. Die Erde war nicht groß genug, ihnen zu entgehen. Du, Aineias, hattest keine Wahl: Ein paar hundert Leute mußtest du dem Tod entreißen. Du warst ihr Anführer. Bald, sehr bald wirst du ein Held sein müssen.
> [. . .] Einen Helden kann ich nicht lieben. Deine Verwandlung in ein Standbild will ich nicht erleben. (*K* 385)

> [It was obvious: The new masters would dictate their law to all the survivors. The earth was not large enough to escape them. You, Aeneas, had no choice: You had to snatch a couple of hundred people from death. You were their leader. "Soon, very soon, you will have to become a hero."
> [. . .] I cannot love a hero. I do not want to see you transformed into a statue. (*K* 138)]

But surely what she is in actuality avoiding is her own transformation into a historical agent under the prevailing historical conditions that, as *Ich* realizes at the end of the dream chapter in *Malina*, will require her to acknowledge and develop her own violent propensities alongside the other, more pacifist aspects of the self. As the mention of loving in the passage just quoted betrays, what Kassandra's renunciation permits is, in contrast, the retention at least of the *idea of love,* the most positive aspect of the "feminine" as male-created culture has defined it, even as it is acknowledged that it will have no place in the historical order of the world after the end of the war. Far from representing a way forward into the future, then, Kassandra in the end collapses back into an already well-established "feminine" cultural position, that of offering a "corrective" within the cultural imagination to the narratives of masculine subjectivity, as described by Adorno:

> Where it claims to be humane, masculine society imperiously breeds in woman its own corrective, and shows itself through this limitation implacably the master. The feminine character is a negative imprint of domination. But therefore equally bad. [. . .] The glorification of the feminine character implies the humiliation of all who bear it.[52]

Müller's Ophelia in the final scene of *Die Hamletmaschine* — or Ophelia/Elektra, since the scene opens with the claim that it is Elektra speaking — looks very different. Her speech in this scene definitively rejects her womanhood and its concomitant humiliation:

> Ich stoße allen Samen aus, den ich empfangen habe. Ich verwandle die Milch meiner Brüste in tödliches Gift. Ich nehme die Welt zurück, die ich geboren habe. Ich ersticke die Welt, die ich geboren habe, zwischen meinen Schenkeln. Ich begrabe sie in meiner Scham. Nieder mit dem Glück der Unterwerfung. (*HM* 554)

> [I eject all the sperm I have received. I turn the milk of my breasts into lethal poison. I take back the world I gave birth to. I choke between my thighs the world I gave birth to. I bury it in my womb. Down with the happiness of submission. (*HM* 58)]

She accepts the conditions of "eternal war" as the price of her entry into history: "Es lebe der Haß, die Verachtung, der Aufstand, der Tod. Wenn sie mit Fleischmessern durch eure Schlafzimmer geht, werdet ihr die Wahrheit wissen" ("Long live hate and contempt, rebellion and death. When she walks through your bedrooms carrying butcher knives you'll know the truth"). The predominant reading among Müller's commentators has been that the Ophelia/Elektra figure in this final scene stands, as the embodiment of "the declassified of history,"[53] for a "violent, revolutionary force"[54] and for the "anguish of the oppressed."[55] In this representative role, she becomes a paradigm of hate-filled uprising,[56] in contrast to the melancholic, infantile, and self-hating Hamlet.[57] The men who bind her into immobility while she rages have, meanwhile, been read by Norbert Otto Eke as "agents of history, presumably psychiatrists" (102), an interpretation more or less supported by a statement of Müller's own: "the revolution, as represented by Ophelia/Elektra, is finally silenced [. . .] by the psychiatrists or whatever we assume these men in their white smocks are."[58]

This reading is problematic, however, in that it fails to engage with the many paradoxes of this scene. It is not just that Ophelia's speech promises both self-destruction and, if her paradigmatic value as maternal woman per se is accepted, the destruction of humanity in general, an aspect that is acknowledged by some, though surprisingly few, of the commentators to date.[59] Nor is it just that, in view of the content of Ophelia/Elektra's speech, the men in doctor's coats cannot unequivocally be regarded as the agents of a reactionary force, nor her release from her bonds at the close as entirely desirable.[60] The greatest paradox is rather that this angry female figure, who *appears* to project the revolution and revenge of the victims of history as they take the limelight from the now-redundant male actor/author/intellectual, is of course still male-authored. This in turn raises the question whether this Ophelia/Elektra is anything other than the product and projection of that same male intellectual tradition that Müller would seem to be intent on deconstructing in this text.

On closer inspection, the scene indeed proves to be full of male authors. Conrad is obviously here ("Im Herz der Finsternis" / "In the heart of darkness"), as are Sartre and Artaud ("Unter der Sonne der Folter" / "Under the sun of torture").[61] Shakespeare's Lady Macbeth is echoed ("Come to my woman's breasts / And take my milk for gall, you murdering ministers"),[62] and Euripides' Medea is present at least as a shadow. The final sentence of Ophelia's speech is attributed by Müller to Susan Atkins, a woman admittedly, but a member of the Charles Manson "family" who turned to violent crime under the influence of a disturbed, vengeful, but evidently charismatic man.[63] Girshausen and Weber suggest that the quotation from Hölderlin, "WILDHARREND / IN DER FURCHTBAREN RÜSTUNG / JAHRTAUSENDE" ("FIERCELY ENDURING / MILLENIUMS / IN THE FEARFUL ARMOR"), that heads the scene is an indication of Hamlet's continuing presence on stage following the conclusion of the previous scene,[64] while Schulz and Lehmann have postulated that this in turn indicates a "continuation of the 'Hamlet'-speech in the revolt of the woman [. . .], who articulates the (self-) hatred and the unfulfilled longings of the man enclosed in the armour of history."[65] This reading is convincing in view of the fact that Ophelia's speech promises the realization of Hamlet's wish for a world without mothers, as expressed in scene 1 (*HM* 546/53). And in Ophelia's self-designation as "Elektra" it is possible to see the transposition of the "Hamlet" plot from male to female character, as may be seen with particular clarity from the following speech by Sophocles' Electra (in Watling's translation):

> Imagine,
> Imagine what it means to see, day after day,
> Aegisthus sitting in my father's chair, wearing
> The clothes he wore, pouring the same libations
> At the altar where he killed him: and, last outrage,
> The murderer going to his bed with *her* —
> Must I still call her mother? — with his mistress.
> For she still lives with the criminal, unashamed,
> Unafraid of retribution.[66]

The conclusion to be drawn from these observations can only be that the Ophelia figure in the final scene of *Die Hamletmaschine* is a further manifestation of the text's troubled male author figure, a transvestite Hamlet perhaps (Hamlet and Opehlia exchanged clothes in scene 3), or, at the very least, an instance of what Helen Fehervary has termed the "narrative colonization of female silence,"[67] whereby the objectified female body becomes the (albeit here constrained) executor of male apocalyptic desire. For wherever the vision of death and apocalypse has been encountered in this study, it has always been as the logical end point of the historical trajectory of Enlightenment modernity's conceptualization of the "masculine" subject — from Bachofen to Horkheimer and Adorno, from the historical fall of Nazism to the fictional fall of Troy, from Hannah Arendt's diagnosis of humanity's flight from the human condition to Günther Anders's and Christa Wolf's fear of nuclear "annihilism." This "masculine" subjectivity is socially endorsed insofar as it transcends human physical and material nature and emotional vulnerability, but, in Horkheimer and Adorno's analysis, it enacts its revenge on objectified nature for the constraints imposed upon it by culture. It appears only able to attain release from those constraints through lascivious (self-) destruction. Seen in this light, the men who bind Müller's Ophelia/Elektra into immobility are not so much the agents of malign reactionary forces or abstract history itself as the agents of a masculine imagination that both conjures up and acts to recontain a "feminine" destructiveness simultaneously fascinating and fearful to it. It might even be admissible to see the dominant principle of aesthetics in the Western tradition in this dual movement — the oscillation between desire and, since desire in masculine culture always conjures up the association with death, the recontainment of desire.[68]

We seem to have arrived at an impasse. Within the framework of the gender dualities that have been the object of investigation in this study, the "masculine" subject of modernity desires his self-dissolution, but can only ever attain the repetition of the same. Meanwhile, the "feminine," though the meanings once ascribed to it within a male-authored culture are now occupied by women writers, continues to figure as a "corrective" to an increasingly historically discredited and exhausted masculine culture. Yet it does so without offering a basis on which to generate anything but what Horkheimer and Adorno called the "the utopia of a humanity which, itself no longer distorted, no longer needs distortion" (H-A 93). The problem, as I see it, is the conflation of the position of the emergent female subject with an inherited symbolic "femininity," which only deceptively offers a platform for cultural renewal, since it is precisely excluded from historical agency. As I argued in chapter 2, the theoretical work of Hélène Cixous and Luce Irigaray, in which woman was conflated with the "unconscious" of the culture, while setting out to liberate revolutionary energies, in fact entrapped women and their writing within a set of significations that had consistently defined the "feminine" within Western modernity. The real promise lies, I believe, in the complex nature of the emergent female subject: her conceptually slippery status as both subject and object, as both self and other, as rational, intellectual agent who carries with her the cultural memory of existence on the shadow side of Enlightenment, and as a living, corporeal presence entering into the inheritance of the Western philosophical tradition. For this symbolic position contains, in a way far less accessible to the symbolic male subject, the potential for rethinking the structure of subjectivity altogether. And is not the lesson of twentieth-century history that this is what is needed: to change the subject?

Notes

[1] The form of this text, as will be discussed, is in revolt against the Western dramatic tradition and as a text for the stage sets considerable challenges to would-be performers. At the same time, it is written with the *idea* of performance in mind — as the residual conventions from the drama, such as stage directions and attribution of speeches to character positions, indicate. Under the circumstances, the term "performance text" appears more appropriate than "drama."

[2] Helen Fehervary, writing in the early 1980s, notes differences between East and West in the structural relationship of art to the public sphere, but lists the key issues within critical artistic practice in the GDR as "the legacy of instrumental rationality, the patriarchy and the dialectical impotence of Enlightenment," seen as the basis for a negatively assessed "technocratic state socialism": Fehervary, "Autorschaft, Geschlechtsbewußtsein und Öffentlichkeit. Versuch über Heiner Müllers 'Die Hamletmaschine' und Christa Wolfs 'Kein Ort Nirgends,'" in *Entwürfe von Frauen in der Literatur des 20. Jahrhunderts*, ed. Irmela von der Lühe (Berlin: Argument, 1982), 132–53, here 132.

[3] Heiner Müller, "Die Hamletmaschine," in Müller, *Werke*, ed. Frank Hörnigk, vol. 4 (Frankfurt am Main: Suhrkamp, 2001), 543–54 / "Hamletmachine," in *Hamletmachine and Other Texts for the Stage*, ed. and trans. Carl Weber (New York: Performing Arts Journal Publications, 1984), 49–58. Subsequent references appear in the text, identified as *HM* (in German to the *Werke* edition, in English to the Weber translation).

[4] "Eventually any theatre artists intent on doing Müller's work will find themselves faced with a heady and alarming freedom, for the key to the staging must, to a far greater degree with Müller's plays than with any other major body of dramatic work, be invented upon the occasion — by the historically informed, politically engaged imaginations of those doing the staging." Tony Kushner, "Foreword," in *A Heiner Müller Reader: Plays, Poetry, Prose*, ed. and trans. Carl Weber (Baltimore and London: Johns Hopkins UP, 2001), xvi.

[5] See Müller, quoted by Jonathan Kalb in *The Theater of Heiner Müller* (Cambridge: Cambridge UP, 1998), 108–9: "I think the main impulse is to strip things to their skeleton, to rid them of their flesh and surface. Then you are finished with them." Subsequent references to Kalb's work appear in the text as parenthetical page numbers.

[6] Heiner Müller, "Shakespeare eine Differenz" [1988], in *Heiner Müller Material: Texte und Kommentare*, ed. Frank Hörnigk (Göttingen: Steidl, 1989), 105 / "Shakespeare a Difference," in *A Heiner Müller Reader*, 118–21, here 119. Subsequent references appear in the text, identified as *SD* (in German to the *Texte und Kommentare* edition, in English to the *Heiner Müller Reader*).

[7] In *Heiner Müller Material*, ed. Hörnigk, 20, italics added.

[8] Richard Weber and Theo Girshausen, "Notate zur HAMLETMASCHINE," in *Die Hamletmaschine: Heiner Müllers Endspiel*, ed. Theo Girshausen (Cologne: Prometh, 1978), 16. Subsequent references appear in the text as parenthetical page numbers.

[9] In Arlene Akiko Teraoka's reading, the allusion is mediated by T. S. Eliot's poem "Ash Wednesday"; see Teraoka, *The Silence of Entropy or Universal Discourse: The Postmodernist Poetics of Heiner Müller* (New York, Bern, Frankfurt am Main: Peter Lang, 1985), 90.

[10] T. S. Eliot, "Journey of the Magi," in Eliot, *Collected Poems 1909–1962* (London: Faber and Faber, 1974), 109–10.

[11] See Weber and Girshausen, "Notate zur HAMLETMASCHINE," 14, 16.

[12] Fehervary, "Autorschaft, Geschlechtsbewußtsein und Öffentlichkeit," 138.

[13] See Müller's own comment: "All that is left of Shakespeare's play went into this first scene": Carl Weber, "Heiner Muller: The Despair and the Hope," *Performing Arts Journal* 12 (1980): 139–40; quoted from Teraoka, *The Silence of Entropy*, 91, and 204–5 n. 8.

[14] See also Kalb's commentary, *The Theater of Heiner Müller*, 111–12.

[15] Gottfried Benn, *Gesammelte Werke*, ed. Dieter Wellershof (Wiesbaden: Limes, 1958–61), vol. 3: *Gedichte*, 25.

[16] See notes to "Hamletmaschine" in Müller, *Werke*, vol. 4, 593. On the "bachelor machine," see Sigrid Weigel's discussion in her essay "Hans Bellmer Unica Zürn: 'Auch der Satz ist wie ein Körper . . .'? Junggesellenmaschinen und die Magie des Imaginären," in Weigel, *Topographien der Geschlechter: Kulturgeschichtliche Studien zur Literatur* (Reinbek bei Hamburg: Rowohlt, 1990), 67–113, especially the section 87–92. The work that was foundational for discourse on the "bachelor machine" was Michel Carrouges, *Les Machines Célibataires* (1954).

[17] William Shakespeare, *Hamlet*, ed. G. R. Hibbard (Oxford: Oxford World Classics, 1998), 241 (act 3, scene 1).

[18] See Teraoka, *The Silence of Entropy*, 109: "The intellectual Hamlet becomes the counter-revolutionary who betrays the revolt of the masses." Norbert Otto Eke also reads the conclusion of the scene as figuring Hamlet's betrayal of the goals of revolution; see Eke, *Heiner Müller: Apokalypse und Utopie* (Paderborn/Munich/Vienna/Zurich: Schöningh, 1989), 101.

[19] For a discussion of Walter Benjamin's conceptualization of the whore as the privileged allegory of modernity, see Weigel, *Body- and Image-Space*, chapter 6: "From Images to Dialectical Images: The Significance of Gender Difference in Benjamin's Writings," 80–94, and here especially 92–94.

[20] Heiner Müller, *Krieg ohne Schlacht: Leben in zwei Diktaturen* (Cologne: Kiepenheuer & Witsch, 1992), 294.

[21] Helen Fehervary, "Die erzählerische Kolonisierung des weiblichen Schweigens," in *Arbeit als Thema in der deutschen Literatur vom Mittelalter bis zur Gegenwart*, ed. R. Grimm and J. Hermand (Königstein/Ts.: Athenäum, 1979), 192.

[22] The contemporary novel by Günter Grass, *Der Butt* (The Flounder, 1977), is similarly symptomatic of the perception by a male author that history as shaped by men had run its course — even though this work can clearly be read as an attempt by the male author to occupy the new cultural space being opened up by feminist thinking.

[23] See the "Fünfte Vorlesung. Kassandra. Arbeitsfassung der Erzählung," reproduced from the typescript held in the Christa Wolf archive in the Stiftung Archiv der Akademie der Künste in Berlin, compared with the televised broadcast of the fifth lecture, in Christa Wolf, *Werke*, ed. Sonja Hilzinger, vol. 7: *Kassandra: Voraussetzungen einer Erzählung* (Munich: Luchterhand Literaturverlag, 2000), 197–223.

[24] See Sonja Hilzinger's commentary in Wolf, *Werke*, vol. 7, 420. Subsequent references appear in the text as parenthetical page numbers.

[25] On voice and physical presence as the marks of a "female" aesthetics counter to the "male" tradition of written text which enables the aspiration to outlive the present, see Gerhard Neumann's thought-provoking and insightful essay "Christa Wolf: *Kassandra*. Die Archäologie der weiblichen Stimme," in *Erinnerte Zukunft. 11 Studien zum Werk Christa Wolfs*, ed. Wolfram Mauser (Würzburg: Königshausen & Neumann, 1985), 233–64. Subsequent references appear in the text as parenthetical page numbers.

[26] Christa Wolf, *Kassandra* [here the first lecture], quoted from *Werke*, vol. 7, 15–16 / *Cassandra: A Novel and Four Essays*, trans. Jan van Heurck (London: Virago, 1984), 144–45. Further references to *Kassandra* appear in the text, identified as *K* (in German to the *Werke* edition, in English to the van Heurck translation).

[27] See discussion in chapter 3 above of Ingeborg Bachmann's notion of the "occupation" of one's own "I" by the "I"s encountered in reading.

[28] For further commentary on the connections evident between Wolf's work and that of Horkheimer and Adorno, see Sigrid Weigel, "Vom Sehen zur Seherin. Christa Wolfs Umdeutung des Mythos und die Spur der Bachmann-Rezeption in ihrer Literatur," in *Christa Wolf. Ein Arbeitsbuch. Studien — Dokumente — Bibliographie*, ed. Angela Drescher (Berlin and Weimar: Aufbau, 1989), 169–203, especially 178–79; and Brigid Haines and Margaret Littler, *Contemporary Women's Writing in German: Changing the Subject* (Oxford: Oxford UP, 2004), 87.

[29] Max Horkheimer and Theodor W. Adorno, *Dialectic of Enlightenment: Philosophical Fragments*, ed. Gunzelin Schmid Noerr, trans. Edmund Jephcott (Stanford: Stanford UP, 2002), 26. Subsequent references appear in the text as parenthetical page numbers, identified as H-A.

[30] See discussion in chapter 2 above.

[31] Herbert Marcuse, *Eros and Civilization*, 143. See discussion in chapter 2 above.

[32] On this point, see Eva Ludwiga Szalay's insightful article "'I, the seeress, was owned by the palace': The Dynamics of Feminine Collusion in Christa Wolf's *Cassandra*," *Women in German Yearbook* 16 (2000): 167–90.

[33] In Homer, the war is fought over Helen, the wife of the Greek king Menelaos, who had been abducted by the Trojan prince, Paris. Wolf uses different sources, which allow the interpretation that Helen was never actually brought to Troy, and psychologizes the effect: Paris and his father Priamos, fearing for the loss of

masculine honor if it is revealed that Paris failed to bring back his "booty," choose to create the illusion that Helen is in Troy.

[34] See Weigel, "Vom Sehen zur Seherin," 178: "In madness the repressed and what was constrained through pretense gets some breathing space. Here, the Other, excluded by the logic of opposites, 'comes to language.'"

[35] See discussion of Max Frisch's *Mein Name sei Gantenbein* in chapter 4 above.

[36] Christa Wolf's work since the 1980s displays a consistent interest in psychosomatic illness. See in particular the essay "Krankheit und Liebesentzug. Fragen an die psychosomatische Medizin," *Neue Deutsche Literatur* 34, no. 10 (1986): 84–102, and her 2002 prose narrative *Leibhaftig*.

[37] The phrase is adopted from Herbert Marcuse's *One-Dimensional Man* (1964), an indictment of the totalitarian character of contemporary industrialized society, which took to a new stage Horkheimer and Adorno's arguments in the *Dialectic*. Marcuse's notion of the Great Refusal, also central to *An Essay on Liberation* (1969), became a key inspiration behind the student movement of 1968 and after in Germany. See commentary in Keith Bullivant and C. Jane Rice, "Reconstruction and Integration: The Culture of West German Stabilization 1945 to 1968," in *German Cultural Studies: An Introduction,* ed. Rob Burns (Oxford: Oxford UP, 1995), 242–43.

[38] This is a leitmotif word in Kassandra's emancipation from the palace; see *Kassandra* 307, 372, 377/70, 127, 131.

[39] Anna K. Kuhn, *Christa Wolf's Utopian Vision: From Marxism to Feminism* (Cambridge: Cambridge UP, 1988), 188.

[40] Eva Ludwiga Szalay's discussion is very helpful in elucidating this point; see Szalay, "The Dynamics of Feminine Collusion in Christa Wolf's *Cassandra*" (details in note 32, above), especially 187 n. 9.

[41] Virginia Woolf, *A Room of One's Own* (London: Granada, 1977), 93. See discussion in chapter 2 above.

[42] See Myra Love, "Christa Wolf and Feminism: Breaking the Patriarchal Connection," *New German Critique* 16 (Winter 1979): 31–53.

[43] Weigel, "Vom Sehen zur Seherin," 187. Ortrud Gutjahr explores Wolf's quest for cultural memories which can provide pointers for the future of humanity in her essay "'Erinnerte Zukunft': Gedächtnisrekonstruktion und Subjektkonstitution im Werk Christa Wolfs," in *Erinnerte Zukunft*, ed. Mauser, 53–80, though the concept of "memory" in the essay remains somewhat undefined. See also Sabine Wilke's critique of Wolf's supposed reading of the matriarchate as a source of cultural memory in "Kreuz- und Wendepunkte unserer Zivilisation nach-denken: Christa Wolfs Stellung im Umfeld der zeitgenossischen Mythos-Diskussion," *The German Quarterly* 61, no. 2 (Spring 1988): 213–28, especially 221.

[44] The metaphor of "maturity" shows how much Wolf's thinking owes to the writings of the German Enlightenment, in which "die Erziehung des Menschengeschlechts" (the education of the human race; Lessing) and "Mündigkeit" (maturity; Kant) indicate the transferral of the categories of individual development onto humanity in its entirety.

[45] Weigel notes the conflicts arising from Wolf's dual purpose in the narrative. On the one hand, the project is aimed at reconstructing "the (imagined) social and historical coordinates" of the myth; on the other, Kassandra becomes for her an identificatory figure in the path to "autonomy." See "Vom Sehen zur Seherin," 174–77.

[46] Wolf, "Vierte Vorlesung," *Werke*, vol. 7, 184.

[47] Haines and Littler's reading of *Kassandra* through the work of Adriana Cavarero and Christine Battersby brings out the relevance of recent philosophies of embodied subjectivity to Wolf's project; see *Changing the Subject*, 91–97.

[48] The key critics to discuss the problem of the narrative closure of the *Erzählung* are Sigrid Weigel, in "Vom Sehen zur Seherin," and Sibylle Kramer, "Eine unendliche Geschichte des Widerstands. Zu Christa Wolfs Erzählungen 'Kein Ort. Nirgends' und 'Kassandra,'" in *Christa Wolf Materialienbuch*, ed. Klaus Sauer (Darmstadt and Neuwied: Luchterhand, 2nd, extended edition 1983), 121–42. See also Ricarda Schmidt, "Über gesellschaftliche Ohnmacht und Utopie in Christa Wolfs *Kassandra*," *Oxford German Studies* 16 (1985): 109–21.

[49] Sigrid Weigel, *Die Stimme der Medusa: Schreibweisen in der Gegenwartsliteratur von Frauen* (Reinbek bei Hamburg: Rowohlt, 1989), 306.

[50] Weigel, *Die Stimme der Medusa*, 279.

[51] Bachmann, *Werke*, vol. 3, 185 / *Malina*, trans. Boehm, 121. Subsequent references to *Malina* appear in the text identified as *M* (in German to the *Werke* edition, in English to the Boehm translation).

[52] Theodor W. Adorno, *Minima Moralia: Reflections from a Damaged Life*, trans. E.F.N. Jephcott (London: New Left Books, 1974 (Berlin and Frankfurt am Main: Suhrkamp, 2001), 95–96, translation modified. See discussion in chapter 2 above.

[53] Eke, *Apokalypse und Utopie*, 103.

[54] Teraoka, *The Silence of Entropy*, 119.

[55] Genia Schulz, "Abschied von Morgen. Zu den Frauengestalten im Werk Heiner Müllers," *Text + Kritik* 73 (January 1982), 65.

[56] Klaus Teichmann, *Der verwundete Körper: Zu Texten Heiner Müllers* (Freiburg: Burg, 1986), 180.

[57] See Schulz, "Abschied von Morgen," 64. For further commentary in a similar vein to the above on the Ophelia/Elektra figure in this scene, see Schulz, *Heiner Müller* (Stuttgart: Metzler, 1980), 151, 154–56; Georg Wieghaus, *Heiner Müller* (Munich: Beck, 1981), 111–12; Katherine Vanovitch, *Female Roles in East German Drama 1949–1977* (Frankfurt Main: Peter Lang, 1982), 124–25; Horst Domdey, *Produktivkraft Tod: Das Drama Heiner Müllers* (Cologne: Böhlau, 1998), 55–56.

[58] See Carl Weber, "Heiner Müller: The Despair and the Hope," *Performing Arts Journal* 12 (1980): 135–40, here 140, quoted from Teraoka, *The Silence of Entropy*, 209, note 33.

[59] Schulz grants, for example, that the scene offers "no positive utopia of liberation" ("Abschied von Morgen," 62). Carlotta von Maltzan, by contrast, while acknowledging that Ophelia/Elektra's revenge on the masculine order entails self-destruction as well as destruction, is nevertheless oddly intent on rescuing a notion of the utopian character of the scene; see von Maltzan, "'Der Tod ist eine

Frau.' Die Darstellung der Rolle der Frau bei Heiner Müller," *Acta Germanica* 16 (1983): 255. A similar attempt is undertaken by Eke, *Apokalypse und Utopie*, 104, and Domdey, *Produktivkraft Tod*, 56.

[60] Eke recounts an episode from the production history in which, at the close of the West German première in Essen in 1979, members of the audience began to liberate Ophelia from her wheelchair; see Eke, *Apokalypse und Utopie*, 104–5, note 77. Eke himself reads Ophelia/Elektra's final immobilization as "a silent appeal to a praxis beyond the limits of the text" (104).

[61] The quotation comes from Sartre's preface to Frantz Fanon's *Les damnés de la terre* [first published 1961] (Paris: Gallimard, 1991), 60, and is used by Müller in his 1977 piece about Antonin Artaud, cited earlier: Müller, "Artaud, die Sprache der Qual," 20.

[62] William Shakespeare, *Macbeth*, act 1, scene 5 (Harmondsworth: New Penguin Shakespeare, 1967).

[63] See Müller, *Krieg ohne Schlacht*, 294, where Müller refers to an article in *Life* magazine as his source for the quotation from Atkins. The implicit connection made in this passage of his memoirs with Ulrike Meinhof and the history of the RAF in Germany is more explicit in a statement of Müller's quoted in *Hamletmachine and Other Texts for the Stage*, 51: "I found it interesting that the Manson family was the pragmatic, unideological, puritan, Christian variant of European terrorism in the U.S.A." Weber in his commentary wrongly attributes the sentence to "Squeaky" (i.e. Lynette) Fromme, another member of the Manson "family," who was convicted of attempting to assassinate U.S. President Gerald Ford in 1975. Girshausen and Weber, meanwhile, give the source of the quotation as Susan Atkins's testimony during her trial for the Tate-LaBianca murders in 1969, for which she, together with the "leader" Charles Manson and two other women, was convicted: "Notate zur HAMLETMASCHINE," 22. A reading of the Manson phenomenon as symptomatic of a social and political malaise in the U.S. society of the Vietnam war period, which, in the language used, suggests parallels to the rather later Baader-Meinhof phenomenon in Germany, and which also emphasizes Manson's instrumentalization of the girls in his entourage, can be found in Steven V. Roberts, "Charlie Manson: One Man's Family," *The New York Times Magazine*, 4 January 1970, 10–11 and 29–35.

[64] Girshausen and Weber, "Notate zur HAMLETMASCHINE," 22.

[65] Genia Schulz and Hans-Thies Lehmann, "Protoplasma des Gesamtkunstwerks. Heiner Müller und die Tradition der Moderne," in *Unsere Wagner: Joseph Beuys, Heiner Müller, Karlheinz Stockhausen, Hansjürgen Syberberg*, ed. Gabriele Förg (Frankfurt am Main: 1984), 57–58, as paraphrased by Eke, *Apokalypse und Utopie*, 104.

[66] Sophocles, *Electra and Other Plays*, trans. E. F. Watling (Harmondsworth: Penguin, 1953), 76.

[67] See Fehervary, "Die erzählerische Kolonisierung des weiblichen Schweigens," and especially the commentary on the Ophelia figure in *Die Hamletmaschine*, 190–92.

[68] Fredric Jameson's *The Political Unconscious: Narrative as a Socially Symbolic Act* (1981) is illuminating in its consideration of the way in which narrative forms, in particular, are characterized by "strategies of containment" that organize the energies unleashed within the text into structures that are ideologically acceptable.

8: Beyond the Impasse?: Barbara Köhler's "Elektra. Spiegelungen"

QUESTIONED ABOUT HER POEM-CYCLE "Elektra. Spiegelungen" (Electra. Mirrorings) in an interview recorded in 1993, Barbara Köhler said: "Perhaps the whole cycle was a commentary on, a mirroring of *Die Hamletmaschine*." In the same interview, she describes the work as an attempt "to escape the murder-machinery," and as having more to do with the work of mourning (*Trauerarbeit*) than with (by implication Müller's) vendetta.[1]

The texts that make up the cycle "Elektra. Spiegelungen," written between 1984 and early 1985, are among the earliest in Köhler's first collection, *Deutsches Roulette* (1991),[2] and so stand at the very inception of her oeuvre. It was a period in which she was a participant in the so-called "unofficial scene" in the GDR, a term used to designate the loosely connected groups of writers, visual artists, photographers, printmakers, songwriters, and musicians who in large part avoided state-controlled institutions for the publication and dissemination of their work, instead circulating hand-printed *samizdat* editions among friends and co-artists and performing in cafés and galleries or in private apartments.[3] Artistic creativity within the confines of this "scene" was often dialogic, collaborative. Thus the "Elektra" cycle was not only conceived as a counter-work to Müller's "Hamlet," but also arose out of a creative exchange between Köhler and the graphic artist Gudrun Höritzsch, in which each responded to the other's work in their own medium.[4] The very first publication of the joint work was in an edition of fifteen copies, with Köhler's poems and Höritzsch's woodcuts interleaved in a folder.[5] The principle of the "dialogue in difference" with visual and installation artists has continued to be an element of Köhler's work since German unification.[6]

The trace of the dialogue with Gudrun Höritzsch disappeared from the post-unification publication of the "Elektra" texts in the conventional Suhrkamp single-authored collection of 1991.[7] But Köhler's response to Heiner Müller remains legible in the form and the images of the poem-cycle as published in the *Deutsches Roulette* edition. The poems enact an elaborate refusal of Müller's vision that nevertheless works extensively with his material, demonstrating the extent to which his *Hamletmaschine*, in its deconstruction of male authorship and its redirection of the textual focus toward the female figure, effectively opened up a conceptual space in which the female author could begin to speak on her own account.

Following in the trail of Wolf's attempt to counter the Homeric tradition in *Kassandra,* Köhler's poetic oeuvre thus begins with the attempt to wrest myth from the hold male authorship has over it.

The first three texts of the eight-poem cycle[8] can be seen as separate and distinct approaches to entering the hall of mirrors that is the Western mythical/literary tradition — distinct and yet together forming a step-by-step sequence. The first poem (*ES* 23/224–25) itself has a threefold opening — "aus irgendeinem vergessenen anfang aus der brandmauer / an der die bühne endet aus dem hintergrund des spiegels / tritt eine gestalt" ("from some forgotten beginning or other from the firewall at which the / stage ends from the background of the mirror a figure appears") — that establishes the preconditions: an imaginary retrieval, reminiscent of Wolf's project in *Kassandra,* of a female figure "kaum sichtbar durch schichten von bil- / dern ablagerungen von geschichte und erinnern" ("barely / visible through the layers of images the sedimentations of history and / memory") and the projection of her into a reconfigured scene. Unlike Wolf's Kassandra, who, as argued in the previous chapter, chooses death in order to preserve in herself the *idea* of an ideal-typical feminine "corrective" to masculine culture rather than engage in history on the given terms, Köhler's as yet unnamed female figure's first utterance is "ICH WILL SCHULD SEIN" ("I WISH TO BEAR THE GUILT"). This reads as a commitment to history and to agency: a promising beginning. Moreover, again in contrast to Wolf's work, the concept of singular identity is at once questioned. In anticipation of the textual method to come, the figure is presented as "verdoppelt verviel- / facht" ("duplicated multiplied"), by implication in the mediating surfaces that reflect her back to herself and to the reader. These multiple figures are unified by the female figure's inclination toward/affection for herself — "eins in allen bildern neigt sie sich zu" ("one in all / images she inclines towards herself") — as the premise, or symptom, of her entry as an autonomous being into history. (The ambiguity of the verb *zuneigen,* which means "to bend toward" but carries connotations of "bearing affection for," is exploited by Köhler here in a manner characteristic of her work with words more generally.) The poem concludes with the vision of a possible alternative to the roles and plots held out for women by a still prevalent tradition. "das spiel von held und / happy end das drama in dem alle rollen opfer sind" ("the game of hero and happy end the drama / in which all the roles are victims")[9] are countered by a new, perhaps female-inflected poetics oriented not toward death and mortality, as Adriana Cavarero has argued the Western metaphysical tradition to be,[10] but toward the time (i.e., life) that precedes death:

> aber es gibt den tod und
> es gibt eine zeit davor

[but there is death and
there is the time before it][11]

The second poem, with its dedication "*Hommage à Heiner Müller*" (*ES* 24–25/225), presents in the Müller idiom a recasting of the Electra myth in implicit response not only to Müller's *Hamletmaschine* but also to his "Elektratext" of 1969.[12] In contrast to the motif of vengeance at the heart of the male-authored versions of the myth, Köhler's focus is on the relationship between the siblings Orestes and Electra that, in Elektra's vision (stanza 1), might have formed the basis of a historical alternative to the family tradition of blood-guilt, murder, and war:

> dem töten ein ende machen wir werden leben in licht und
> klarheit [. . .]

> [let there be an end to the killing in light we'll live in
> clarity [. . .]]

This is an important difference. The notion of the brother-sister pairing, as seen at points throughout this study, represents in the cultural imagination an often productive alternative to the patriarchal and paternalistic tradition that demotes and devalues the "feminine" aspects of the self. Elektra's image of herself that would underpin this vision of the future and that she looks for in Orestes' eyes is, however, not confirmed by his returning gaze:

> ich will mich sehen in deinen augen was schaust
> du mich so an bin ich nicht elektra die schönste unter den
> weibern [. . .]

> [in your eyes I'll see myself but why
> do you look at me thus am I not electra most beautiful of
> women [. . .]]

Rather, she finds herself constructed by his gaze as a barbarian, alien in comparison with the sexualized and objectified women of Phokis, "die wohlerzogenen sanf-/ ten fest im fleisch" ("well-raised and gentle and firm-fleshed"), among whom he grew up in exile. Orestes, unable to contemplate the equality of relationship between male and female that Elektra's sibling love holds out, "flieht vor ihr in die blutspur seiner väter" ("flees from her into the bloody trail of his ancestors"). In other words, the poem reconstructs the historical/mythical genesis of the exclusivity of the patriarchy. The second stanza, which bears Orestes' name, returns to the familiar coordinates of the mythical material, the slaughter of Clytemnestra, and the confirmation of the patriarchal order that will condemn the female principle to silence:

                                            ein neues stück
beginnt und keine rolle vorgesehen für elektra und keine
sprache außer der orests

[a new play's
beginning with no role for electra and no language
but that of orestes]

The poem's final line, however, suspends the drama, simultaneously revealing the artifice of the cultural text and posing the question of the relation between the mirror image of mythical projection and the "real" woman beneath the mask in a gesture reminiscent of Hamlet's transformation into the actor playing Hamlet in scene 4 of *Die Hamletmaschine:* "am schminktisch sitzt elektra legt die maske ab" ("at the dressing-table sits electra removes her mask").[13] In contrast to Wolf's identificatory merging with her central figure in the *Kassandra* narrative, Köhler builds into her poem cycle an overtly self-reflexive level that thematizes the relation of the female would-be subject to the inherited images that circumscribe her.[14]

This issue is explored in the third, and most theoretically complex text of the opening sequence (*ES* 26/225–26). The use of personal pronouns in this poem — above all the blurring of "ich" (I) and "du" (you), as the referents for the lyric subject and the image of herself that she contemplates in the mirror — enacts the impossibility of distinguishing between "authentic" person and culturally generated persona. As a consequence, iconoclasm, the smashing of mythical images of Woman, for example, cannot return the female figure to an a priori authentic self:

es ist nichts hinterm bild es ist
ein spiegel und schlag ich dann treff ich
dein gesicht und mein gesicht

zerfällt [. . .]

[there's nothing behind it the image is
a mirror and if I hit out what I hit is
your face and my face

shattered [. . .]]

This could mean a return to the impossibility of generating significantly new meanings from the tradition that weighs upon us, a version, therefore, of the immobility of Müller's Ophelia/Elektra figure at the conclusion *Die Hamletmaschine*. The crucial breach in the system, however, is found in the critical, analytical perspective of the "andre" or "other" of stanza 2 who "legt die hand an das bild" ("lays a hand on the image").

Her gaze diverges from the masculine construction of the female "you" as love-object in stanza 1: "sein mund spricht liebes er meint dich" ("his mouth speaks of love and it's you that he means").[15] The "sie meint mich" ("it's me that she means") of stanza 2, by contrast, recalls the self-regard or self-inclination evoked in the first poem of the cycle, that *difference* in the relation between a woman and the reflected cultural images of woman that is the mark of feminism.

The following three poems project three different and discrete personae, three different refractions that act to subvert traditional cultural images of Woman. They could be the reflections cast by the "scherben deines blicks" ("fragments of your gaze"; *ES* 26/226) of the end of the third text in the cycle, but the construction of the sequence also recalls the three-part mirrors, so fascinating to children, that used to grace our mothers' dressing tables.[16] The fourth and sixth poems, as the outer wings of the mirror (reflecting in profile), work with figures derived from Müller's *Hamletmaschine:* Ulrike Meinhof, an episode from whose biography inspired Müller's second scene,[17] and Ophelia. Both are substantially recast by Köhler. Where Müller's Meinhof was, in keeping with the tenor of his text, a destroyer of bourgeois social order, Köhler's is the altogether more complex and ambiguous Meinhof of the last days in Stammheim prison,[18] perpetrator and victim in one and thus occupying a space beyond the "märchen von GUTundBÖSE" ("fairytale / of GOODandEVIL") evoked by the poem's allusions to the fairytale of Snow White (*ES* 27/226). And where Müller resurrected Shakespeare's drowned Ophelia to turn her into the raging voice of vengeance, Köhler projects an "ALTGEWORDENE OPHELIA" ("OPHELIA [. . .] GROWN OLD"; *ES* 29/227) who has outlived the deceptions of desire and learned a bitter, although not unhumorous, skepticism with regard to the male plot of history:

> dieses von den jahrhunderten vergessene
> orakel trinkt malzkaffee und wermut vom rest der rente
> weigert sich zu sterben nimmt immer wieder ein leeres
> blatt einen bleistift und macht kreuzchen einen ganzen
> heldenfriedhof für
> > hamlet & konsorten

> [this oracle forgotten
> down the centuries drinks malt-coffee and bitter from whats left of her
> pension money refuses to die and taking her pen again and again on the
> empty page makes crosses a whole heroes cemetery for
> > hamlet & consorts][19]

Between these two texts, as it were, in the central panel of the mirror where gaze meets reflected gaze straight on, the "other" confronts herself and begins to generate a language that expresses her own needs and desires, as opposed to those imagined for her within the male-authored text (*ES* 28/226–27). The key to liberation from male-imposed images of Woman is found in the capitalized "unthinkable sentence": "ICH HABE AUFGEHÖRT / GELIEBT ZU WERDEN" ("I HAVE CEASED / TO BE LOVED"). This parallels and contrasts with the sentence in Müller's second scene marking Ophelia's break with the role she has played hitherto: "Gestern habe ich aufgehört mich zu töten" ("Yesterday I stopped killing myself"; *HM* 547/54). The implication in Köhler's text is that the precondition for the female figure's historical movement is her refusal of her status as love object for the male, which has condemned her to immobility as an object of the male imagination:

> als ich ihm heute nacht sagte
> ich kann mich nicht bewegen ich bin
> tot tot tot hörte das sterben auf
>
> [when I said to him last night
> I cannot move I am dead dead dead
> then the dying stopped]

This is the most aggressive of all the texts of the cycle in its attitude toward the male figure, and contemplates, at any rate in *one* of the possible readings of the ambiguous final lines, the bleakest consequence of the passage to female autonomy:

> ich
> gehe ab von der bühne
> in ein mögliches
> Nichts außerhalb der liebe
>
> [I am
> leaving the stage
> into a possible future of
> Nothing apart from love]

The penultimate poem in the cycle (*ES* 30/227) seems to speak from this bleak space, permeated on the one hand by the wish for an alternative conceptualization of male-female relationship — "nicht länger will ich sein / die abbildung seines nichtseins" ("I no longer want to be / the representation of his non-being") — and on the other by hopelessness that this can be achieved within the space of a mortal existence — "trost bleibt aus" ("comfort remains wanting"). But it also expresses the wish for an ending that can serve as a starting point (a theme that runs throughout the *Deutsches Roulette* collection), and states a commitment to mortal life (the existence as a being that is "endlich") as a span that allows movement and becoming:

> ein ende will
> ich finden und von dort beginnen / denn endlich sind wir
> daß wir endlich werden
>
> [an end I want to find and from there begin
> for that we do not last means we may become at last]

The final poem in the cycle (*ES* 31/228) represents just such an ending. It is a visionary text that projects into a completely other space: "traum hinter dem irrgarten" ("dream beyond the labyrinth"). This final poem, too, resonates with allusions to Müller. Karen Leeder has seen it as a response to the "lift" monologue in Müller's *Der Auftrag* (The Task, 1979),[20] and as a landscape of the imagination it may also recall his "Bildbeschreibung" (Description of a Picture, 1984). Müller describes the scene of "Bildbeschreibung" as a landscape beyond death,[21] but Köhler's in this poem is as much a landscape pre- as post-*histoire*, a world innocent of preconceived images, in which the figures have not yet learned to reproach each other with words like man and woman, to paraphrase another poem in the collection.[22] For at the poem's culmination is an encounter with a figure both undetermined by gender and in other ways held in suspension between different possible — and opposing — meanings:

> irgendwann nehme ich
> eine gestalt wahr. es ist nicht auszumachen ob frau
> oder mann, sich nähernd oder entfernend. die gestalt
> eines menschen breitet die arme eine nicht festlegbare
> gebärde zwischen kreuzigung und flug ich weiß dies ist
> der ort
>   zu gewinnen ohne siegen zu müssen
>
> [at some point my eyes
> discern a figure. I cannot make out if it is a woman
> or a man, approaching or moving away. the figure
> of a person spreads out its arms a gesture not to
> be fixed between crucifixion and flight I know this
> is the place
>   to win without the necessity of victory]

The space the poem constructs is entirely unlocatable except within the mind, or the imagination, as a utopian projection. And yet, in its sensual solidity, the poem holds out the hope of the power of language to occupy the imagination and ultimately to transform physical reality.

The cycle in its entirety articulates the complexity of its own undertaking: to stake a claim to female authorship late in a cultural history shaped by men. Completed two years after Wolf's *Kassandra*, it avoids the pitfall of Wolf's more famous text, with its collapse back into a form of heroic narrative that can only end in death: "Mit der Erzählung geh ich in den Tod" ("Keeping step with the story, I make my way into death").[23] Köhler's appropriation of mythical and mythologizing texts, by contrast, resists closure in its fragmentary and polyperspectival construction of alternative, transitory, and incommensurable identities and in its self-consciousness with regard to the cultural function of images as the mediators of identity. In doing this, it has implications that go beyond the project of realizing a liveable *female* subjectivity.

Reading Köhler's work alongside (but also after) the other works considered in this study illuminates the relation between forms of self-articulation and self-narration and liveable selfhood. Throughout this study, narrative form has appeared as a correlative of the conceptualization of subjectivity. Max Frisch's *Mein Name sei Gantenbein* (chapter 4) has as one of its themes the burdensome constrictions of the *Ich-Geschichte*, or coherent narrative of the self, which is required in order to function as a publicly accepted and acceptable subject under the given conditions of modernity. Frisch opposed this with a counter-model. For him, the *living* self was to be apprehended only in terms of the gaps between words that ostensibly speak of something else or in terms of the tension (*Spannung*) between different statements — a model that avoids fixity:

> Unser Anliegen, das eigentliche, läßt sich bestenfalls umschreiben, und das heißt ganz wörtlich: man schreibt darum herum. Man umstellt es. Man gibt Aussagen, die nie unser eigentliches Erlebnis enthalten, das unsagbar bleibt; sie können es nur umgrenzen, möglichst nahe und genau, und das Eigentliche, das Unsagbare, erscheint bestenfalls als Spannung zwischen diesen Aussagen.

> [What we are really concerned with can only, at best, be written about, and that means, quite literally, we write around it. We encompass it. We make statements which never contain the whole true experience: that cannot be described. All the statements can do is encircle it, as tightly and closely as possible: the true, the inexpressible experience emerges at best as the tension between these statements.][24]

This notion of the relation between language and truth is close to that of Ingeborg Bachmann's character *Ich* in *Malina* (chapter 3). As her analytical alter ego Malina says to her at one point: "Ich glaube dir kein einziges Wort, ich glaub dir nur alle Worte zusammen" ("I don't believe a single word you're saying, just all your words at once").[25] This allows that the conceptualization of *Ich* as a self is irreducible to any single or summarizing statement or *Ich-Geschichte:* she can only be deduced from the sum of all her sometimes mutually contradictory articulations. Indeed, not only Frisch and Bachmann, but all the authors analyzed in the course of this study are demonstrably engaged in the exploration of the complex, fragmentary, and often self-contradictory reality concealed behind the regulated facade of the socially endorsed *Ich-Geschichte*.

In her analysis of Bachmann's *Malina*, Eva Lindemann writes of the "Sprung in der Wand" or crack in the wall into which *Ich* disappears as "the hope of the shattering of the idea of closure" that is also "a hope for the truthfulness of that which is fragmentary."[26] Bachmann's novel affirms the openness and fragmentation figured throughout via its complex compositional technique, and what I have called its symbolic "femininity" as opposed to a "masculinity" based on self-containment and coherent unity. By contrast, the coherent, unified *Ich-Geschichte*, which is both a narrative of the self and an identity that signals conformity to social regulation, transpires in terms of the constraints it imposes to be ultimately death-like, a "mimesis: of death" (Horkheimer and Adorno).[27] Nevertheless, as the texts by male authors analyzed in this study reveal, simple rebellion against the socially imposed restrictions and regulations equally brings death and (self-) destruction, to the extent that it is enacted via a return of the repressed that explodes in violence and rage or expresses itself in the victimization of the weaker Other. This is a central insight of Horkheimer and Adorno's *Dialectic of Enlightenment* — a finding supported by the conclusions of Frisch's *Gantenbein*, Goetz's *Irre* (chapter 6), and Müller's *Hamletmaschine* (chapter 7).

Müller's text, the only dramatic text to be considered in this study, aims for a "truthfulness of that which is fragmentary," and in the puzzles it presents for would-be performers, creates the basis for dynamic transformation in the collective corporeal here-and-now of theater when staged. The text ends in stasis, however, thus demonstrating its entrapment in the tragic heroic form of the Shakespearian tradition that it is simultaneously attempting to explode. Christa Wolf's *Kassandra* project, meanwhile, is explicitly committed to the "truthfulness of the fragmentary" as a counter-model to conventional narrative aesthetics, the latter identified in her introduction to the Frankfurt lectures as the correlation of the self-alienation she is aiming to combat in the political public sphere:

> ich empfinde selbst scharf die Spannung zwischen den Formen, in denen wir uns verabredungsgemäß bewegen, und dem lebendigen Material, das meine Sinne, mein psychischer Apparat, mein Denken mir zuleiteten und das sich diesen Formen nicht fügen wollte. [. . .] Sind also diese Kunst-Objekte ("Werke") auch Produkte der Entfremdung innerhalb dieser Kultur, deren andere perfekte Produkte zum Zweck der Selbstvernichtung produziert werden? (*K* 12)

[I feel keenly the tension between the artistic forms within which we agree to abide and the living material, borne to me by my senses, my psychic apparatus, and my thought, which has resisted these forms. [. . .] So, does this mean that art objects ("works") are products of the alienation of our culture, whose other finished products are produced for self-annihilation? (*K* 142)]

And yet when she came to write the *Erzählung* she found herself reverting to an inherited aesthetic model — in essence, too, that of tragedy. That this was not so much intentionally as against her will is revealed by an entry from her work diary in the third lecture:

> Meteln, 21. Juli 1981
> Erzähltechniken, die ja in ihrer jeweiligen Geschlossenheit oder Offenheit auch Denk-Muster transportieren. Empfinde die geschlossene Form der Kassandra-Erzählung als Widerspruch zu der fragmentarischen Struktur, aus der sie sich für mich eigentlich zusammensetzt. Der Widerspruch kann nicht gelöst, nur benannt werden. (*K* 154)

> [*Meteln, July 21, 1981* Narrative techniques, which in their closedness or openness also transmit thought patterns. I experience the closed form of the Cassandra narrative as a contradiction to the fragmentary structure from which (for me) it is actually composed. The contradiction cannot be resolved, only named. (*K* 266)]

Barbara Köhler takes up the possibilities of "the truthfulness of the fragmentary" where Bachmann left off.[28] Doing so at the beginning of her oeuvre rather than at its end (and without the burden of feeling herself to have been ground down by the "murder-machinery," as Bachmann did at the end of her career), she is intent on eliciting dynamic movement from the aesthetic models with which she works. It is helpful to her that her medium is poetry, for that releases her from the commitment to narrative linearity and closure. In her poem-cycles, not only "Elektra. Spiegelungen," but also, for example, the three-poem "Papierboot" cycle and the nine-poem "ELB / ALB" cycle in *Deutsches Roulette,* the five-poem "Jemand geht" cycle in *Wittgensteins Nichte* (1999) and above all her highly complex *Odyssey* cycle, *Niemands Frau* (2007), she exploits the possibilities of development and progression, while retaining the tension of difference between elements in the cycle in a way that resists any univocal meaning. She is also committed to eliciting semantic plurality in her sequencing of words, to attaining a "simultaneity of several possibilities" in the reading of lines or phrases.[29]

Because multiplicity, fragmentation, and polyvalence appear as feminine-connoted in a culture for which unity, self-identity, and coherence is gendered masculine, Köhler's project is readable in terms of its relevance to the conceptualization of an emergent female subjectivity.[30] However, Köhler's vision of a place and the possibility of an encounter *beyond* gender in the final poem of the "Elektra" cycle suggests also, and simultaneously, her willingness to engage in a venture that could end up undoing the structures of binary, self-other thinking. Indeed, her work of the last two decades since the publication of *Deutsches Roulette* has been a progressive engagement with notions of the subject as mediated through the representational possibilities of both the written and the voiced text, becoming very explicitly interested in the effects of dialogue, communication, and encounters in different media between different and differently embodied selves.[31] Köhler's practice, as a practice that moves beyond the feminist concern with the subjectivity of women within a male-dominated culture, looks to the potential of the manifold nature of emergent female subjectivities — able to participate mentally and corporeally in both the inherited intellectual tradition *and* in its shadow side — to steer a way into a new conceptualization of what it means to be a self in the pluralized, globalizing, medial and so often virtual, and yet still emphatically material, and necessarily relational social collective of the present. The unlocatable and abstract vision on which the "Elektra" cycle ends is classically utopian: the landscape is a no-place and the encounter it describes — in its gender neutrality — apparently impossible under present historical conditions. But it does set an imaginary goal, taking out a wager, as it were, on the fact that the pursuit of truth in terms that are *not* unified, coherent, and categorically unambiguous will take us to a place beyond "eternal war":

> ich weiß dies ist
> der ort
> zu gewinnen ohne siegen zu müssen
>
> [I know this
> is the place
> to win without the necessity of victory]

Notes

1 "'Wie ist überhaupt eine Gleichwertigkeit im Anderssein möglich?' Gespräch mit Barbara Köhler am 11.5.1993," in Birgit Dahlke, *Papierboot: Autorinnen aus der DDR — inoffiziell publiziert* (Würzburg: Königshausen & Neumann, 1997), 297.

2 Information from the author. In the interview with Dahlke, Köhler dates the composition of the texts as before she went to the Literatur-Institut Johannes R. Becher in Leipzig, where she studied from 1985 to 1988: Dahlke, *Papierboot*, 297.

3 See Birgit Dahlke, "'. . . auf einem Papierboot bestehen': Schreiben in der DDR der 80er Jahre," in *Entgegenkommen. Dialogues with Barbara Köhler*, ed. Georgina Paul and Helmut Schmitz (Amsterdam: Rodopi, 2000), 45–61.

[4] See Dahlke, *Papierboot*, 297.

[5] Information from the author.

[6] See, for example, the essays written in conjunction with collaborative installation projects or in response to visual artworks, in Barbara Köhler, *Wittgensteins Nichte: Vermischte Schriften Mixed Media* (Frankfurt am Main: Suhrkamp, 1999).

[7] Babara Köhler, *Deutsches Roulette: Gedichte 1984–1989* (Frankfurt am Main: Suhrkamp, 1991).

[8] Barbara Köhler, "Elektra. Spiegelungen," in Köhler, *Deutsches Roulette*, 23–31 / "Electra. Mirrorings," trans. Georgina Paul, *Comparative Criticism* 21: *Myth and Mythologies* (Cambridge: Cambridge UP, 1999), 224–28. Further references appear in the text, identified as *ES* (in German to *Deutsches Roulette*, in English to the Paul translation).

[9] For a near-contemporary consideration of women as victims in the literary tradition, see Sigrid Weigel, "Die geopferte Heldin und das Opfer als Heldin: Zum Entwurf wieblicher Helden in der Literatur von Männern und Frauen," in Inge Stephan and Sigrid Weigel, *Die verborgene Frau: Sechs Beiträge zu einer feministischen Literaturwissenschaft* (*Argument*-Sonderband 96) (Berlin: Argument, 1983), 138–52.

[10] Adriana Cavarero, *In Spite of Plato: A Feminist Rewriting of Ancient Philosophy*, trans. Serena Anderlini-D'Onofrio and Áine O'Healy (Cambridge: Polity, 1995).

[11] The lines echo Bachmann's in "Lieder auf der Flucht XV" (Songs in flight XV): "Die Liebe hat einen Triumph und der Tod hat einen, / die Zeit und die Zeit danach" (Love has a triumph and death has one, / time and the time thereafter; Ingeborg Bachmann, *Werke*, ed. Christine Koschel, Inge von Weidenbaum, Clemens Münster (Munich/Zurich: Piper, 1978), vol. 1, 147.

[12] See Anthonya Visser, "Bild-Sprache. Barbara Köhlers Texte für öffentliche Räume," in *Entgegenkommen*, ed. Paul and Schmitz, 195–213, here 210.

[13] Compare the stage direction "Legt Maske und Kostüm ab" ("*He takes off make-up and costume*") at the end of Hamlet's first speech in scene 4: Heiner Müller, "Die Hamletmaschine," in Müller, *Werke*, ed. Frank Hörnigk, vol. 4 (Frankfurt am Main: Suhrkamp, 2001), 549 / "Hamletmachine," in *Hamletmachine and Other Texts for the Stage*, ed. and trans. Carl Weber (New York: Performing Arts Journal Publications, 1984), 55; at the end of the scene, the actor is directed to put them on again (553/58). Subsequent references appear as *HM* (in German to the *Werke* edition, in English to the Weber translation).

[14] Sabine Wilke criticized Wolf for falling into the trap of not distinguishing sufficiently between "woman and the image of woman" in *Kassandra*: Wilke, "Kreuz- und Wendepunkte unsere Zivilisation nach-denken: Christa Wolfs Stellung im Umfeld der zeitgenossischen Mythos-Diskussion," *German Quarterly* 61, no. 2 (Spring 1988): 213–28, here 221.

[15] The translations given of this poem here differ slightly from those in the published version.

[16] The fascination of the multiple refractions of the tripartite mirror is the subject of a scene in Christoph Hein's novel *Horns Ende* (Berlin and Weimar: Aufbau, 1985), in which the young boy Thomas plays with his mother's dressing-table

mirror in her absence. The scene functions within the text as a figure for the polyperspectival narration, reflecting the fact "daß es mehrere, zum Teil einander widersprechende Wahrheiten gibt" (that there are several, in part mutually contradictory truths; *Horns Ende*, 26).

[17] See discussion in chapter 7.

[18] Certain parallels suggest the possible influence of Reinhard Hauff's *Stammheim* (1985), a piece of filmed documentary theater based on the transcripts of the Baader-Meinhof trial, in which Meinhof emerges as the most complex and differentiated of the terrorist figures, among other things because of the inclusion by Stephan Aust in his screenplay of passages from her prison diary.

[19] "Wermut" translates literally as "vermouth," but also has the figurative meaning of "bitterness." The translation "bitter" emerged in conversation with the author, as an English substitute that is both a drink and carries the emotional connotation.

[20] Karen Leeder, "Two-Way Mirrors. Construing the Possibilities of the First Person Singular in Barbara Köhler's Poetry," in *Entgegenkommen*, ed. Paul and Schmitz, 63–89, here 76.

[21] See the author's note to "Bildbeschreibung," in Heiner Müller, *Shakespeare Factory I* (Berlin: Rotbuch, 1985), 14.

[22] "Anrede zwo: Diotima an Bellarmin," in Köhler, *Deutsches Roulette*, 12 / "Alloquy Number Two: Diotima to Bellarmin," *Comparative Criticism* 21, 224.

[23] Christa Wolf, *Kassandra*, quoted from *Werke*, vol. 7, 197 / *Cassandra: A Novel and Four Essays*, trans. Jan van Heurck (London: Virago, 1984), 3. Further references to *Kassandra* appear in the text, identified as *K* (in German to the *Werke* edition, in English to the van Heurck translation).

[24] Max Frisch, *Tagebuch 1946–1949*, quoted from Frisch, *Gesammelte Werke in zeitlicher Folge*, vol. 2, 378–79 / *Sketchbook 1946–1949*, 25.

[25] Bachmann, *Werke*, vol. 3, 332 / *Malina*, trans. Philip Boehm (New York, London: Holmes & Meier, 1990), 221. Subsequent references to *Malina* appear in the text, identified as *M* (in German to the *Werke* edition, in English to the Boehm translation).

[26] Eva Lindemann, *Über die Grenze: Zur späten Prosa Ingeborg Bachmanns* (Würzburg: Königshausen & Neumann, 2000), 31. See discussion in chapter 3 above.

[27] Max Horkheimer and Theodor W. Adorno, *Dialectic of Enlightenment: Philosophical Fragments*, ed. Gunzelin Schmid Noerr, trans. Edmund Jephcott (Stanford: Stanford UP, 2002), 44.

[28] On the issue of the poetic influence of Bachmann on Köhler, see Georgina Paul, "Ismene at the Crossroads: Gender and Poetic Influence," *German Life and Letters* 60, no. 3 (2007): 430–46.

[29] See Barbara Köhler and Georgina Paul, "'Ich wäre mir so gerne selbst / verständlich': Ein Gespräch," in *Entgegenkommen*, ed. Paul and Schmitz, 25–44, especially 29.

[30] I emphasized the relevance of Köhler's "Elektra" cycle for the conceptualization of the position of the female writer in the dialectic of Enlightenment in an

earlier publication, using some of the material on Müller and Köhler which also appears here; see Georgina Paul, "Multiple Refractions, or Winning Movement Out of Myth: Barbara Köhler's Poem Cycle 'Elektra. Spiegelungen,'" *German Life and Letters* 57, no. 1 (2004): 21–32.

[31] Apart from the essays in *Entgegenkommen,* ed. Paul and Schmitz, the following offer useful approaches to Köhler's intellectual project: Helmut Schmitz, "Grammatik der Differenz — Barbara Köhlers Suche nach einer nichtidentischen Subjektivität," in *Weiblichkeit als politisches Programm: Sexualität, Macht und Mythos,* ed. Bettina Gruber and Heinz-Peter Preußer (Würzburg: Königshausen & Neumann, 2005), 167–82; Elizabeth Boa, "Revoicing Silenced Sirens: A Changing Motif in Works by Franz Kafka, Frank Wedekind and Barbara Köhler," *German Life and Letters* 57, no. 1 (January 2004): 8–20; Mirjam Bitter, *Sprache. Macht. Geschlecht: Lyrik und Essayistik von Barbara Köhler* (Berlin: trafo, 2007). The *Niemands Frau* cycle has not yet been the subject of scholarly analysis in its completed form.

Bibliography

Primary Texts

Bachmann, Ingeborg. *The Book of Franza & Requiem for Fanny Goldmann.* Trans. Peter Filkins. Evanston, IL: Northwestern UP, 1999.

———. *Ich weiss keine bessere Welt: unveröffentlichte Gedichte.* Ed. Isolde Moser, Heinz Bachmann, and Christian Moser. Munich: Piper, 2000.

———. *Kritische Schriften.* Ed. Dirk Göttsche and Monika Albrecht. Munich: Piper, 2005.

———. *Letzte, unveröffentlichte Gedichte, Entwürfe und Fassungen.* Ed. Hans Höller. Frankfurt am Main: Suhrkamp, 1998.

———. *Malina.* Trans. Philip Boehm. New York and London: Holmes & Meier, 1990.

———. *"Todesarten"-Projekt: Kritische Ausgabe.* Ed. Monika Albrecht and Dirk Göttsche, 4 vols. Munich and Zurich: Piper, 1995.

———. *Werke.* Ed. Christine Koschel, Inge von Weidenbaum, and Clemens Münster, 4 vols. Munich and Zurich: Piper, 1978.

Benn, Gottfried. *Gedichte.* Vol. 3 of *Gesammelte Werke.* Ed. Dieter Wellershof. Wiesbaden: Limes, 1958–61.

Duden, Anne. *Übergang.* Berlin: Rotbuch, 1982.

———. *Zungengewahrsam: Kleine Schriften zur Poetik und zur Kunst.* Cologne: Kiepenheuer & Witsch, 1999.

Eliot, T. S. *Collected Poems 1909–1962.* London: Faber and Faber, 1974.

Fanon, Frantz. *Les damnés de la terre.* Paris: Gallimard, 1991.

Frisch, Max. *Gantenbein.* Trans. Michael Bullock. London: Methuen, 1982.

———. *Gesammelte Werke in zeitlicher Folge.* Ed. Hans Mayer with the cooperation of Walter Schmitz. Frankfurt am Main: Suhrkamp, 1976.

———. *Homo faber: A Report.* Trans. Michael Bullock. Harmondsworth: Penguin, 1974.

———. *Sketchbook 1946–1949.* Trans. Geoffrey Skelton. New York and London: Harcourt Brace Jovanovich, 1977.

Goetz, Rainald. *Irre.* Frankfurt am Main: Suhrkamp, 1983.

Hein, Christoph. *Horns Ende.* Berlin and Weimar: Aufbau, 1985.

Jelinek, Elfriede. *Die Klavierspielerin.* Reinbek bei Hamburg: Rowohlt, 1983.

———. *The Piano Teacher.* Trans. Joachim Neugroschel. London: Serpent's Tail, 1989.

Köhler, Barbara. *Deutsches Roulette: Gedichte 1984–1989.* Frankfurt am Main: Suhrkamp, 1991.

———. "Electra. Mirrorings." Trans. Georgina Paul. *Comparative Criticism* 21: *Myth and Mythologies* (1999): 224–28.

———. *Wittgensteins Nichte: Vermischte Schriften Mixed Media.* Frankfurt am Main: Suhrkamp, 1999.

Müller, Heiner. "Artaud, die Sprache der Qual." In *Heiner Müller Material: Texte und Kommentare,* ed. Frank Hörnigk, 20. Göttingen: Steidl, 1989.

———. "Bildbeschreibung." In *Shakespeare Factory I,* 7–14. Berlin: Rotbuch, 1985.

———. "Die Hamletmaschine." In *Werke,* ed. Frank Hörnigk, vol. 4, 543–54. Frankfurt am Main: Suhrkamp, 2001.

———. "Hamletmachine." In *Hamletmachine and Other Texts for the Stage,* ed. and trans. Carl Weber, 49–58. New York: Performing Arts Journal Publications, 1984.

———. *Mauser.* Berlin: Rotbuch, 1978.

———. "Shakespeare a Difference." In *A Heiner Müller Reader: Plays, Poetry, Prose,* ed. and trans. Carl Weber, 118–21. Baltimore and London: Johns Hopkins UP, 2001.

———. "Shakespeare eine Differenz." In *Heiner Müller Material: Texte und Kommentare,* ed. Frank Hörnigk, 105–8. Göttingen: Steidl, 1989.

Shakespeare, William. *Hamlet.* Ed. G. R. Hibbard. Oxford: Oxford World Classics, 1998.

———. *Macbeth.* Harmondsworth: New Penguin Shakespeare, 1967.

Sophocles. *Electra and Other Plays.* Trans. E. F. Watling. Harmondsworth: Penguin, 1953.

Stampa, Gaspara. *Selected Poems.* Trans. Laura Anna Stortoni and Mary Prentice Lillie. New York: Italica Press, 1994.

Wolf, Christa. *Accident: A Day's News.* Trans. Heike Schwarzbauer and Rick Takvorian. London: Virago, 1989.

———. *Cassandra: A Novel and Four Essays.* Trans. Jan van Heurck. London: Virago, 1984.

———. "Krankheit und Liebesentzug. Fragen an die psychosomatische Medizin." *Neue Deutsche Literatur* 34, no. 10 (1986): 84–102.

———. *No Place on Earth.* Trans. Jan van Heurck. London: Virago, 1995.

———. *Werke.* Ed. Sonja Hilzinger. 12 vols. Munich: Luchterhand, 2000.

Secondary Sources

Ingeborg Bachmann

Albrecht, Monika. *Die andere Seite: Untersuchungen zur Bedeutung von Werk und Person Max Frischs in Ingeborg Bachmanns "Todesarten."* Würzburg: Königshausen & Neumann, 1989.

———. "Mein Name sei Gantenbein — mein Name? Malina: Zum intertextuellen Verfahren der 'imaginären Autobiographie' *Malina.*" In *Ingeborg*

Bachmanns "Malina," ed Andrea Stoll, 265–87. Frankfurt am Main: Suhrkamp, 1992.

Arnold, Heinz Ludwig, ed. *Ingeborg Bachmann: Text + Kritik Sonderband.* Munich: edition text + kritik, 1984.

Bachmann, Ingeborg. *Wir müssen wahre Sätze finden: Gespräche und Interviews.* Ed. Christine Koschel and Inge von Weidenbaum. Munich and Zurich: Piper, 1983.

Behre, Maria, "'Das Ich, weiblich': 'Malina' im Chor der Stimmen zur 'Erfindung' des Weiblichen im Menschen." In *Ingeborg Bachmanns "Malina,"* ed. Andrea Stoll, 210–32. Frankfurt am Main: Suhrkamp, 1992.

Bird, Stephanie. *Women Writers and National Identity: Bachmann, Duden, Özdamar.* Cambridge: Cambridge UP, 2003.

Boschenstein, Bernhard, and Sigrid Weigel, eds. *Ingeborg Bachmann und Paul Celan: Poetische Korrespondenzen. Vierzehn Beiträge.* Frankfurt am Main: Suhrkamp, 1997.

Göttsche, Dirk, and Monika Albrecht, eds. *Bachmann-Handbuch: Leben, Werk, Wirkung.* Stuttgart: Metzler, 2002.

Haas, Franz. "Fechten vor verhängten Spiegeln. Ingeborg Bachmann, Max Frisch und die diskrete Germanistik." *Neue Zürcher Zeitung,* 8 March 2003.

———. "Die Schnäppchenjäger." *Neue Zürcher Zeitung (Internationale Ausgabe),* 16 November 2000.

Hamm, Peter, and Reinhard Baumgart. "Ingeborg Bachmann, *Ich weiß keine bessere Welt:* Eine ZEIT-Kontroverse." *Die Zeit,* 5 October 2000.

Höller, Hans. *Ingeborg Bachmann: Das Werk. Von den frühesten Gedichten bis zum "Todesarten"-Zyklus.* Frankfurt am Main: Anton Hain (Athenäums Programm), 1987.

Jabłkowska, Joanna. "Ingeborg Bachmanns *Malina* und Max Frischs *Mein Name sei Gantenbein* — Varianten derselben Geschichte." *Acta Universitatis Lodziensis: Folia Litteraria* 11 (1984): 69–84.

Jurgensen, Manfred. *Ingeborg Bachmann: Die neue Sprache.* Bern: Peter Lang, 1981.

Lindemann, Eva. *Über die Grenze: Zur späten Prosa Ingeborg Bachmanns.* Würzburg: Königshausen & Neumann, 2000.

Lühe, Irmela von der. "Erinnerung und Identität in Ingeborg Bachmanns Roman 'Malina.'" In *Ingeborg Bachmann. Text + Kritik Sonderband,* ed. Heinz Ludwig Arnold, 132–49. Munich: edition text + kritik, 1984.

Probst, Gerhard F. "Mein Name sei Malina: Nachdenken über Ingeborg Bachmann." *Modern Austrian Literature* 11, no. 1 (1978): 103–19.

Stoll, Andrea, ed. *Ingeborg Bachmanns "Malina."* Frankfurt am Main: Suhrkamp, 1992.

Toman, Lore. "Bachmanns *Malina* und Frischs *Mein Name sei Gantenbein:* Zwei Seiten des gleichen Lebens." *Literatur und Kritik* 12 (1977): 274–78.

Weigel, Sigrid. "'Ein Ende mit der Schrift. Ein andrer Anfang.' Zur Entwicklung von Ingeborg Bachmanns Schreibweise." In *Ingeborg Bachmann.*

Text + Kritik Sonderband, ed. Heinz Ludwig Arnold, 58–92. Munich: edition text + kritik, 1984.

———. *Ingeborg Bachmann: Hinterlassenschaften unter Wahrung des Briefgeheimnisses.* Vienna: Paul Zsolnay, 1999.

Max Frisch

Beckermann, Thomas, ed. *Über Max Frisch I.* Frankfurt am Main: Suhrkamp, 1971.

Bohler, Liette. *Der Mythos der Weiblichkeit im Werke Max Frischs.* New York: Peter Lang, 1998.

Butler, Michael. *The Novels of Max Frisch.* London: Oswald Wolff, 1976.

Geulen, Hans. "Max Frischs *Homo faber.*" In *Frischs "Homo Faber,"* ed. Walter Schmitz, 101–32. Frankfurt am Main: Suhrkamp, 1983.

Haupt, Ursula. *Weiblichkeit in Romanen Max Frischs.* Frankfurt am Main: Peter Lang, 1996.

Heissenbüttel, Helmut. "Max Frisch oder Die Kunst des Schreibens in dieser Zeit." In *Über Max Frisch I,* ed. Thomas Beckermann, 54–68. Frankfurt am Main: Suhrkamp, 1971.

Kaiser, Gerhard. "Max Frischs 'Homo faber.'" In *Max Frisch: Beiträge zur Wirkungsgeschichte,* ed. Albrecht Schau, 80–89. Breisgau: Universitätsverlag Becksmann, 1971.

Knapp, Mona. "'Eine Frau, aber mehr als das, eine Persönlichkeit, aber mehr als das: eine Frau': The Structural Function of the Female Characters in the Novels of Max Frisch." In *Beyond the Eternal Feminine: Critical Essays on Women and German Literature,* ed. Susan L. Cocalis and Kay Goodman, 261–89. Stuttgart: Akademischer Verlag Hans-Dieter Heinz, 1982.

Latta, Alan D. "Die Verwandlung des Lebens in eine Allegorie: Eine Lektüre von Max Frischs Roman *Homo faber.*" In *Frischs "Homo faber,"* ed. Walter Schmitz, 79–100. Frankfurt am Main: Suhrkamp, 1983.

Merrifield, Doris Fulda. *Das Bild der Frau bei Max Frisch.* Freiburg im Breisgau: Universitätsverlag Becksmann, 1971.

Paver, Chloe E. M. *Narrative and Fantasy in the Post-War German Novel: A Study of Novels by Johnson, Frisch, Wolf, Becker, and Grass.* Oxford: Clarendon Press, 1999.

Schau, Albrecht, ed. *Max Frisch: Beiträge zur Wirkungsgeschichte.* Freiburg im Breisgau: Universitätsverlag Becksmann, 1971.

Schmitz, Walter, ed. *Frischs "Homo faber."* Frankfurt am Main: Suhrkamp, 1983.

———. *Max Frisch. Homo faber. Materialien, Kommentar.* Munich, Vienna: Carl Hanser, 1977.

———. *Max Frisch: Das Spätwerk (1962–1982). Eine Einführung.* Tübingen: Francke, 1985.

Rainald Goetz

Goetz, Rainald. "Subito." In *Rawums: Texte zum Thema,* ed. Peter Glaser. Cologne: Kiepenheuer & Witsch, 1984.

Winkels, Hubert. "Krieg den Zeichen: Rainald Goetz und die Wiederkehr des Körpers." In *Einschnitte: Zur Literatur der 80er Jahre,* 221–59. Cologne: Kiepenheuer & Witsch, 1988.

Elfriede Jelinek

Appelt, Hedwig. *Die leibhaftige Literatur: Das Phantasma und die Präsenz der Frau in der Schrift.* Weinheim and Berlin: Quadriga, 1989.

Arnold, Heinz Ludwig, ed. *Elfriede Jelinek, Text + Kritik* 117 (January 1993).

Bartsch, Kurt, and Günther A. Höfler, eds. *Dossier 2: Elfriede Jelinek.* Graz-Vienna: Droschl, 1991.

DeMeritt, Linda C. "A 'Healthier Marriage': Elfriede Jelinek's Marxist Feminism in *Die Klavierspielerin* and *Lust.*" In *Elfriede Jelinek: Framed by Language,* ed. Jorun B. Johns and Katherine Arens, 107–28. Riverside, CA: Ariadne, 1994.

Fiddler, Allyson. "Reading Elfriede Jelinek." In *Post-War Women's Writing in German: Feminist Critical Approaches,* ed. Chris Weedon, 291–304. Providence, RI, and Oxford: Berghahn, 1997.

———. *Rewriting Reality: An Introduction to Elfriede Jelinek.* Oxford and Providence, RI: Berg, 1994.

Hoffmann, Yasmin. *Elfriede Jelinek: Sprach- und Kulturkritik im Erzählwerk.* Opladen and Wiesbaden: Westdeutscher Verlag, 1999.

Janz, Marlies. *Elfriede Jelinek.* Stuttgart: Metzler, 1995.

Jelinek, Elfriede. "Ich schlage sozusagen mit der Axt drein." *Theaterzeitschrift Berlin* 7 (1984): 14–15.

Levin, Tobe. "*Die Klavierspielerin:* On Mutilation and Somotaphobia." In *"Other" Austrians: Post-1945 Austrian Women's Writing,* ed. Allyson Fiddler, 225–34. Bern: Peter Lang, 1998.

Sauter, Josef-Hermann. "Interviews mit Barbara Frischmuth, Elfriede Jelinek, Michael Scharang." *Weimarer Beiträge* 27, no. 6 (1981): 109–17.

Spielmann, Yvonne. "Ein unerhörtes Sprachlabor. Feministische Aspekte im Werk von Elfriede Jelinek." In *Dossier 2: Elfriede Jelinek,* ed. Kurt Bartsch and Günther A. Höfler, 21–40. Graz-Vienna: Droschl, 1991.

Müller, André. "Ich lebe nicht. André Müller spricht mit der Schriftstellerin Elfriede Jelinek." *Die Zeit,* 22 June 1990.

Wilke, Sabine. "'Ich bin eine Frau mit einer männlichen Anmaßung': Eine Analyse des 'bösen Blicks' in Elfriede Jelineks *Die Klavierspielerin.*" *Modern Austrian Literature* 26, no. 1 (1993): 115–44.

Winkels, Hubert. "Panoptikum der Schreckensfrau. Elfriede Jelineks Roman 'Die Klavierspielerin.'" In *Einschnitte: Zur Literatur der 80er Jahre,* 60–77. Cologne: Kiepenheuer & Witsch, 1988.

Winter, Riki. "Gespräch mit Elfriede Jelinek." In *Dossier 2: Elfriede Jelinek,* ed. Kurt Bartsch and Günther A. Höfler, 9–19. Graz-Vienna: Droschl, 1991.

Wright, Elizabeth. "Eine Ästhetik des Ekels. Elfriede Jelineks Roman 'Die Klavierspielerin.'" In *Elfriede Jelinek, Text + Kritik* 117, ed. Heinz Ludwig Arnold (January 1993): 51–59.

Barbara Köhler

Bitter, Mirjam. *Sprache. Macht. Geschlecht: Lyrik und Essayistik von Barbara Köhler.* Berlin: trafo, 2007.

Boa, Elizabeth. "Revoicing Silenced Sirens: A Changing Motif in Works by Franz Kafka, Frank Wedekind and Barbara Köhler." *German Life and Letters* 57, no. 1 (January 2004): 8–20.

Dahlke, Birgit. "'. . . auf einem Papierboot bestehen': Schreiben in der DDR der 80er Jahre." In *Entgegenkommen. Dialogues with Barbara Köhler,* ed. Georgina Paul and Helmut Schmitz, 45–61. Amsterdam: Rodopi, 2000.

———. *Papierboot: Autorinnen aus der DDR — inoffiziell publiziert.* Würzburg: Königshausen & Neumann, 1997.

Leeder, Karen. "Two-Way Mirrors: Construing the Possibilities of the First Person Singular in Barbara Köhler's Poetry." In *Entgegenkommen: Dialogues with Barbara Köhler,* ed. Georgina Paul and Helmut Schmitz, 63–89. Amsterdam: Rodopi, 2000.

Paul, Georgina. "Ismene at the Crossroads: Gender and Poetic Influence." *German Life and Letters* 60, no. 3 (2007): 430–46.

———. "Multiple Refractions, or Winning Movement out of Myth: Barbara Köhler's Poem Cycle 'Elektra. Spiegelungen.'" *German Life and Letters* 57, no. 1 (2004): 21–32.

Paul, Georgina, and Helmut Schmitz, eds. *Entgegenkommen: Dialogues with Barbara Köhler.* Amsterdam: Rodopi, 2000.

Schmitz, Helmut. "Grammatik der Differenz — Barbara Köhlers Suche nach einer nichtidentischen Subjektivität." In *Weiblichkeit als politisches Programm: Sexualität, Macht und Mythos,* ed. Bettina Gruber and Heinz-Peter Preußer, 167–82. Würzburg: Königshausen & Neumann, 2005.

Visser, Anthonya. "Bild-Sprache: Barbara Köhlers Texte für öffentliche Räume." In *Entgegenkommen: Dialogues with Barbara Köhler,* ed. Georgina Paul and Helmut Schmitz, 195–213.

Heiner Müller

Domdey, Horst. *Produktivkraft Tod: Das Drama Heiner Müllers.* Cologne: Böhlau, 1998.

Eke, Norbert Otto. *Heiner Müller: Apokalypse und Utopie.* Paderborn, Munich, Vienna, and Zurich: Schöningh, 1989.

Fehervary, Helen. "Autorschaft, Geschlechtsbewußtsein und Öffentlichkeit. Versuch über Heiner Müllers 'Die Hamletmaschine' und Christa Wolfs

'Kein Ort Nirgends.'" In *Entwürfe von Frauen in der Literatur des 20. Jahrhunderts*, ed. Irmela von der Lühe, 64–85. Berlin: Argument, 1982.

———. "Die erzählerische Kolonisierung des weiblichen Schweigens." In *Arbeit als Thema in der deutschen Literatur vom Mittelalter bis zur Gegenwart*, ed. R. Grimm and J. Hermand, 171–95. Königstein/Ts.: Athenäum, 1979.

Hörnigk, Frank, ed. *Heiner Müller Material: Texte und Kommentare*. Göttingen: Steidl, 1989.

Kalb, Jonathan. *The Theater of Heiner Müller*. Cambridge: Cambridge UP, 1998.

Maltzan, Carlotta von. "'Der Tod ist eine Frau': Die Darstellung der Rolle der Frau bei Heiner Müller." *Acta Germanica* 16 (1983): 247–59.

Müller, Heiner. *Krieg ohne Schlacht: Leben in zwei Diktaturen*. Cologne: Kiepenheuer & Witsch, 1992.

Schulz, Genia. "Abschied von Morgen. Zu den Frauengestalten im Werk Heiner Müllers." *Text + Kritik* 73 (January 1982): 58–70.

———. *Heiner Müller*. Stuttgart: Metzler, 1980.

Schulz, Genia, and Hans-Thies Lehmann. "Protoplasma des Gesamtkunstwerks: Heiner Müller und die Tradition der Moderne." In *Unsere Wagner: Joseph Beuys, Heiner Müller, Karlheinz Stockhausen, Hansjürgen Syberberg*, ed. Gabriele Förg, 50–84. Frankfurt am Main: Fischer, 1984.

Teichmann, Klaus. *Der verwundete Körper: Zu Texten Heiner Müllers*. Freiburg: Burg, 1986.

Teraoka, Arlene Akiko. *The Silence of Entropy or Universal Discourse: The Postmodernist Poetics of Heiner Müller*. New York, Bern and Frankfurt am Main: Peter Lang, 1985.

Vanovitch, Katherine. *Female Roles in East German Drama 1949–1977*. Frankfurt am Main: Peter Lang, 1982.

Weber, Carl. "Heiner Müller: The Despair and the Hope." *Performing Arts Journal* 12 (1980): 135–40.

Weber, Carl, ed. and trans. *A Heiner Müller Reader: Plays, Poetry, Prose*. Baltimore and London: Johns Hopkins UP, 2001.

Weber, Richard, and Theo Girshausen. "Notate zur HAMLETMASCHINE." In *Die Hamletmaschine: Heiner Müllers Endspiel*, ed. Theo Girshausen. Cologne: Prometh, 1978.

Wieghaus, Georg. *Heiner Müller*. Munich: Beck, 1981.

Christa Wolf

Gutjahr, Ortrud. "'Erinnerte Zukunft': Gedächtnisrekonstruktion und Subjektkonstitution im Werk Christa Wolfs." In *Erinnerte Zukunft: 11 Studien zum Werk Christa Wolfs*, ed. Wolfram Mauser, 53–80. Würzburg: Königshausen & Neumann, 1985.

Haines, Brigid. "The Reader, the Writer, Her Narrator and Their Text(s): Intertextuality in Christa Wolf's *Störfall*." In *Christa Wolf in Perspective*, ed. Ian Wallace, 157–72. Amsterdam and Atlanta, GA: Rodopi, 1994.

Kaiser, Herbert, and Gerhard Köpf, eds. *Erzählen, Erinnern: Deutsche Prosa der Gegenwart: Interpretationen.* Frankfurt am Main: Diesterweg, 1992.

Kramer, Sibylle. "Eine unendliche Geschichte des Widerstands: Zu Christa Wolfs Erzählungen 'Kein Ort. Nirgends' und 'Kassandra.'" In *Christa Wolf Materialienbuch,* ed. Klaus Sauer, 121–42. Darmstadt and Neuwied: Luchterhand, 2nd, extended edition, 1983.

Kuhn, Anna K. *Christa Wolf's Utopian Vision: From Marxism to Feminism.* Cambridge: Cambridge UP, 1988.

Love, Myra. "Christa Wolf and Feminism: Breaking the Patriarchal Connection." *New German Critique* 16 (Winter 1979): 31–53.

Mauser, Wolfram, ed. *Erinnerte Zukunft: 11 Studien zum Werk Christa Wolfs.* Würzburg: Königshausen & Neumann, 1985.

Neumann, Gerhard. "Christa Wolf: *Kassandra:* Die Archäologie der weiblichen Stimme." In *Erinnerte Zukunft: 11 Studien zum Werk Christa Wolfs,* ed. Wolfram Mauser, 233–64. Würzburg: Königshausen & Neumann, 1985.

Rey, William H. "Blitze im Herzen der Finsternis: Die neue Anthropologie in Christa Wolfs *Störfall.*" *German Quarterly* 62, no. 3 (1989): 373–83.

Saalmann, Dieter. "Christa Wolf's *Störfall* and Joseph Conrad's *Heart of Darkness:* The Curse of the 'Blind Spot.'" *Neophilologus* 76, no. 1 (January 1992): 19–28.

———. "Elective Affinities: Christa Wolf's *Störfall* and Joseph Conrad's *Heart of Darkness.*" *Comparative Literary Studies* 29, no. 3 (1992): 238–58.

Schmidt, Ricarda. "Über gesellschaftliche Ohnmacht und Utopie in Christa Wolfs *Kassandra.*" *Oxford German Studies* 16 (1985): 109–21.

Szalay, Eva Ludwiga. "'I, the seeress, was owned by the palace': The Dynamics of Feminine Collusion in Christa Wolf's *Cassandra.*" *Women in German Yearbook* 16 (2000): 167–90.

Weigel, Sigrid. "Vom Sehen zur Seherin: Christa Wolfs Umdeutung des Mythos und die Spur der Bachmann-Rezeption in ihrer Literatur." In *Christa Wolf: Ein Arbeitsbuch. Studien — Dokumente — Bibliographie,* ed. Angela Drescher, 169–203. Berlin and Weimar: Aufbau, 1989.

West, Russell. "Christa Wolf reads Joseph Conrad: *Störfall* and *Heart of Darkness.*" *German Life and Letters* 50, no. 2 (April 1997): 254–65.

Wilke, Sabine. "Kreuz- und Wendepunkte unserer Zivilisation nach-denken: Christa Wolfs Stellung im Umfeld der zeitgenossischen Mythos-Diskussion." *The German Quarterly* 61, no. 2 (Spring 1988): 213–28.

Ziller, Ursula. "Christa Wolf: *Störfall: Nachrichten eines Tages.*" In *Erzählen, Erinnern: Deutsche Prosa der Gegenwart: Interpretationen,* ed. Herbert Kaiser and Gerhard Köpf, 354–71. Frankfurt am Main: Diesterweg, 1992.

General

Abrams, Lynn. *The Making of Modern Woman: Europe 1789–1918*. London: Longman, 2002.

Adorno, Theodor W. *Minima Moralia: Reflections from a Damaged Life*. Trans. E. F. N. Jephcott. London: New Left Books, 1974.

———. *Minima Moralia: Reflexionen aus dem beschädigten Leben*. Berlin and Frankfurt am Main: Suhrkamp, 2001.

alternative 108/109 (1976): *Das Lächeln der Medusa*.

Anders, Günther. *Die Antiquiertheit des Menschen*, vol. 1: *Über die Seele im Zeitalter der zweiten industriellen Revolution*. Munich: C. H. Beck, 2nd edition 2002.

Arendt, Hannah. *The Human Condition*. Chicago and London: U of Chicago P, 2nd edition, 1998.

Bachofen, J. J. "Mother Right." In *Myth, Religion, and Mother Right: Selected Writings of J. J. Bachofen*. Intro. Joseph Campbell, trans. Ralph Manheim. Princeton: Princeton UP, 1992.

Battersby, Christine. *Gender and Genius: Towards a Feminist Aesthetics*. London: The Women's Press, 1989.

Bauman, Zygmunt. *Modernity and the Holocaust*. Cambridge: Polity Press, 1991.

Beauvoir, Simone de. *The Second Sex*. Trans. H. M. Parshley. Harmondsworth: Penguin, 1983.

Berman, Marshall. *All That Is Solid Melts Into Air: The Experience of Modernity*. London and New York: Verso, 1983.

Blackmore, John T. *Ernst Mach: His Work, Life and Influence*. Berkeley: U of California P, 1972.

Bovenschen, Silvia. *Die imaginierte Weiblichkeit: Exemplarische Untersuchungen zu kulturgeschichtlichen und literarischen Präsentationsformen des Weiblichen*. Frankfurt am Main: Suhrkamp, 1979.

———. "Über die Frage: gibt es eine 'weibliche' Ästhetik?" In *Die Überwindung der Sprachlosigkeit: Texte aus der neuen Frauenbewegung*, ed. Gabriele Dietze, 82–115. Darmstadt and Neuwied: Luchterhand, 1979.

Bullivant, Keith, and C. Jane Rice. "Reconstruction and Integration: The Culture of West German Stabilization 1945 to 1968." In *German Cultural Studies: An Introduction*, ed. Rob Burns, 209–56. Oxford: Oxford UP, 1995.

Burgard, Peter J., ed. *Nietzsche and the Feminine*. Charlottesville and London: UP of Virginia, 1994.

Burns, Rob, and Wilfried van der Will. *Protest and Democracy in West Germany: Extra-parliamentary Opposition and the Democratic Agenda*. Basingstoke: Macmillan, 1988.

Carter, Erica. *How German Is She?: Postwar West German Reconstruction and the Consuming Woman*. Ann Arbor, MI: U of Michigan P, 1997.

Cavarero, Adriana. *In Spite of Plato: A Feminist Rewriting of Ancient Philosophy.* Trans. Serena Anderlini-D'Onofrio and Áine O'Healy. Cambridge: Polity Press, 1995.

Cixous, Hélène, and Catherine Clément. *The Newly Born Woman.* Intro. Sandra M. Gilbert, trans. Betsy Wing. Theory and History of Literature, vol. 24. Manchester: Manchester UP, 1986.

Clay, Catrine, and Michael Leapman. *Master Race: The Lebensborn Experiment in Nazi Germany.* London: Hodder & Stoughton, 1995.

Conley, Verena Andermatt. *Hélène Cixous: Writing the Feminine.* Lincoln and London: U of Nebraska P, expanded edition 1991.

Deleuze, Gilles, and Félix Guattari. *Anti-Oedipus: Capitalism and Schizophrenia.* Trans. Robert Hurley, Mark Seem, and Helen R. Lane, preface by Michel Foucault. London and New York: Continuum, 2003.

Evans, Richard J. *The Feminist Movement in Germany 1894–1933.* London and Beverly Hills: Sage, 1976.

Favazza, Armando R. *Bodies Under Siege: Self-Mutilation in Culture and Psychiatry.* Baltimore: Johns Hopkins UP, 1996.

Felski, Rita. *The Gender of Modernity.* Cambridge, MA, and London: Harvard UP, 1995.

Foucault, Michel. *Madness and Civilization: A History of Insanity in the Age of Reason.* Trans. Richard Howard. London and New York: Routledge, 1989.

Freud, Sigmund. "Female Sexuality." In *The Standard Edition of the Complete Psychological Works,* vol. 21: *The Future of an Illusion, Civilization and its Discontents and Other Works,* 223–43. London: Hogarth Press, 1961.

———. "Femininity." In *The Standard Edition of the Complete Psychological Works,* vol. 22: *New Introductory Lectures on Psycho-Analysis and Other Works,* 112–35. London: Hogarth Press, 1964.

———. "The Paths to the Formation of Symptoms." From the "General Theory of Neuroses," in *The Standard Edition of the Complete Psychological Works,* vol. 26: *Introductory Lectures on Psycho-Analysis,* 358–77. London: Hogarth Press, 1963.

———. "Some Thoughts on Development and Regression — Aetiology." From the "General Theory of the Neuroses," in *The Standard Edition of the Complete Psychological Works,* vol. 26: *Introductory Lectures on Psycho-Analysis,* 339–57. London: Hogarth Press, 1963.

———. *The Standard Edition of the Complete Psychological Works.* Ed. James Strachey et al., vol. 5: *The Interpretation of Dreams.* London: Hogarth Press, 1953.

———. "The 'Uncanny'" In *The Standard Edition of the Complete Psychological Works,* ed. James Strachey et al., vol. 27: *An Infantile Neurosis and Other Works,* 217–52. London: Hogarth Press, 1955.

Frevert, Ute. *"Mann und Weib, und Weib und Mann": Geschlechter-Differenzen in der Moderne.* Munich: C. H. Beck, 1995.

Freyer, Hans. *Theorie des gegenwärtigen Zeitalters.* Stuttgart: Deutsche Verlags-Anstalt, 1958.

Fromm, Erich, Max Horkheimer, Herbert Marcuse, Hans Mayer, Karl A. Wittfogel, and Paul Honigsheim. *Studien über Autorität und Familie* (English abstracts). Paris: Felix Alcan, 1936.

Fuss, Diana J. "'Essentially Speaking': Luce Irigaray's Language of Essence." In *Revaluing French Feminisms: Critical Essays on Difference, Agency and Culture,* ed. Nancy Fraser and Sandra Lee Bartky, 94–112. Bloomington: Indiana UP, 1992.

———. "The Risk of Essence." In *Essentially Speaking: Feminism, Nature and Difference,* 1–21. London: Routledge, 1990.

Giddens, Anthony. *Modernity and Self-Identity: Self and Society in the Late Modern Age.* Cambridge: Polity Press, 1991.

Gouges, Olympe de. "Declaration of the Rights of Woman." In *Women in Revolutionary Paris, 1789–1795,* ed. Darline Gay Levy, Harriet Branson Applewhite, and Mary Durham Johnson, 87–96. Urbana: U of Illinois P, 1980.

Griffin, Roger, ed. *Fascism.* Oxford: Oxford UP, 1995.

———. *The Nature of Fascism.* London: Routledge, 1993.

Grosz, Elizabeth. *Jacques Lacan: A Feminist Introduction.* London and New York: Routledge, 1990.

———. *Sexual Subversions: Three French Feminists.* St. Leonards: Allen & Unwin, 1989.

Haines, Brigid, and Margaret Littler. *Contemporary Women's Writing in German: Changing the Subject.* Oxford: Oxford UP, 2004.

Herzog, Dagmar, ed. *Sexuality and German Fascism.* New York and Oxford: Berghahn, 2005.

Horkheimer, Max. "Authoritarianism and the Family Today." In *The Family: Its Function and Destiny,* ed. Ruth Anshen, 359–74. New York: Harper & Brothers, 1949.

———. "Authority and the Family." In *Critical Theory: Selected Essays.* Trans. Matthew J. O'Connell et al., 47–128. New York: Continuum, 1992.

———. "The Concept of Man." In *Critique of Instrumental Reason.* Trans. Matthew O'Connell et al., 1–33. New York: Seabury Press, 1974.

Horkheimer, Max, and Theodor W. Adorno. *Dialectic of Enlightenment: Philosophical Fragments.* Ed. Gunzelin Schmid Noerr, trans. Edmund Jephcott. Stanford, California: Stanford UP, 2002.

———. *Dialektik der Aufklärung.* Frankfurt am Main: Fischer Taschenbuch Verlag, 1988.

Huyssen, Andreas. *After the Great Divide: Modernism, Mass Culture, Postmodernism.* Basingstoke and London: Macmillan, 1988.

Irigaray, Luce. *Speculum of the Other Woman.* Trans. Gillian C. Gill. Ithaca, NY: Cornell UP, 1985.

———. *This Sex Which Is Not One.* Trans. Catherine Porter with Carolyn Burke. Ithaca, NY: Cornell UP, 1985.

Izenberg, Gerald N. *Modernism and Masculinity: Mann, Wedekind, Kandinsky through World War I.* Chicago and London: Chicago UP, 2000.

Jameson, Fredric. *The Political Unconscious: Narrative as a Socially Symbolic Act*. Ithaca, NY: Cornell UP, 1981.

Jaspers, Karl. *Man in the Modern Age*. Trans. Eden and Cedar Paul. London: Routledge & Kegan Paul, 1951.

Jerome, Roy, ed. *Conceptions of Postwar German Masculinity*. Albany: State U of New York P, 2001.

Jünger, Friedrich Georg. *Die Perfektion der Technik*. Frankfurt am Main: V. Klostermann, 1946.

———. *Maschine und Eigentum*. Frankfurt am Main: V. Klostermann, 1949.

Klages, Ludwig. *Der Geist als Widersacher der Seele*. 2 vols. Munich: J. A. Barth, 3rd edition 1954.

Kristeva, Julia. *Revolution in Poetic Language*. Trans. Margaret Waller. New York: Columbia UP, 1984.

Lacan, Jacques. "The mirror stage as formative of the function of the I as revealed in psychoanalytic experience." In *Écrits: A Selection*, trans. Alan Sheridan, 1–6. London: Routledge, 2001.

Laqueur, Thomas. *Making Sex: Body and Gender from the Greeks to Freud*. Cambridge, MA, and London: Harvard UP, 1990.

Lasch, Christopher. *The Culture of Narcissism*. London: Abacus, 1980.

Le Rider, Jacques. *Modernity and Crises of Identity: Culture and Society in Fin-de-Siècle Vienna*. Trans. Rosemary Morris. New York: Continuum, 1993.

Lilienthal, Georg. *Der Lebensborn e. V. Ein Instrument nationalsozialistischer Rassenpolitik*. Stuttgart and New York: Gustav Fischer Verlag, 1985.

Mach, Ernst. *Analyse der Empfindungen und das Verhältniss des Physischen zum Psychischen*. Jena: Fischer, 4th edition. 1903.

———. *The Analysis of the Sensations and the Relation of the Physical to the Psychical*. Trans. C. M. Williams and Sydney Waterlow. New York: Dover, 1959.

Marcuse, Herbert. *Counterrevolution and Revolt*. Boston: Beacon Press, 1972.

———. *Eros and Civilization: A Philosophical Inquiry into Freud*. London: Abacus, 1972.

———. "Marxism and Feminism." *Women's Studies* 2, no. 3 (1974): 279–88.

Marx, Karl. *Capital*. New York: International Publishers, 1977.

Mills, Patricia Jagentowicz. *Woman, Nature, and Psyche*. New Haven and London: Yale UP, 1987.

Moi, Toril. *Sexual/Textual Politics: Feminist Literary Theory*. London and New York: Routledge, 1988.

Mosse, George L. *The Image of Man: The Creation of Modern Masculinity*. New York and Oxford: Oxford UP, 1996.

———. *Nationalism and Sexuality: Respectability and Abnormal Sexuality in Modern Europe*. New York: H. Fertig, 1985.

Pauen, Michael. *Pessimismus: Geschichtsphilosophie, Metaphysik und Moderne von Nietzsche bis Spengler*. Berlin: Akademie Verlag, 1997.

Pietzker, Carl. "The Motif of the Man, Who, Although He Loves, Goes to War: On the History of the Construction of Masculinity in the European Tradition." In *Conceptions of Postwar German Masculinity*, ed. Roy Jerome, 133–70. Albany: State U of New York P, 2001.

Roberts, Steven V. "Charlie Manson: One Man's Family." *The New York Times Magazine*, 4 January 1970, 10–11 and 29–35.

Schönfeld, Christiane, ed. *Commodities of Desire: The Prostitute in Modern German Literature*. Rochester, NY: Camden House, 2000.

Sengoopta, Chandak. *Otto Weininger: Sex, Science, and Self in Imperial Vienna*. Chicago and London: U of Chicago P, 2000.

Simmel, Georg. "Female Culture." In *On Women, Sexuality, and Love*, ed. and trans. Guy Oakes, 65–101. New Haven and London: Yale UP, 1984.

———. "Philosophie der Geschlechter. Fragmente." In *Aufsätze und Abhandlungen 1901–1908*, vol. 2 (*Gesamtausgabe*, vol. 8), ed. Alessandro Cavalli and Volkhard Krech, 74–82. Frankfurt am Main: Suhrkamp, 1993.

———. "Weibliche Kultur." In *Aufsätze und Abhandlungen 1909–1918*, vol. 1 (*Gesamtausgabe*, vol. 12), ed. Rüdiger Kramme and Angela Rammstedt, 251–89. Frankfurt am Main: Suhrkamp, 2001.

Spengler, Oswald. *The Decline of the West*. Trans. Charles Francis Atkinson, 2 vols. London: G. Allen & Unwin, 1926–28.

Strong, Marilee. *A Bright Red Scream: Self-Mutilation and the Language of Pain*. London: Virago, 2000.

Thomas, Nick. *Protest Movements in 1960s West Germany: A Social History of Dissent and Democracy*. Oxford: Berg, 2003.

Toews, John E. "Refashioning the Masculine Subject in Early Modernism: Narratives of Self-Dissolution and Self-Construction in Psychoanalysis and Literature, 1900–1914." *Modernism/Modernity* 4, no. 1 (1997): 31–67.

Ulmi, Marianne. *Frauenfragen — Männergedanken: Zu Georg Simmels Philosophie und Soziologie der Geschlechter*. Zurich: eFeF, 1989.

Wagner, Peter. *A Sociology of Modernity: Liberty and Discipline*. London and New York: Routledge, 1994.

Weigel, Sigrid. "From Images to Dialectical Images: The Significance of Gender Difference in Benjamin's Writings." In *Body- and Image-Space: Rereading Walter Benjamin*. Trans. Georgina Paul with Rachel McNicholl and Jeremy Gaines, 80–94. London: Routledge, 1996.

———. "Die geopferte Heldin und das Opfer als Heldin: Zum Entwurf wieblicher Helden in der Literatur von Männern und Frauen." In *Die verborgene Frau: Sechs Beiträge zu einer feministischen Literaturwissenschaft*, ed. Inge Stephan and Sigrid Weigel, 138–52. Berlin: Argument, 1983.

———. "Hans Bellmer Unica Zürn: 'Auch der Satz ist wie ein Körper . . .?' Junggesellenmaschinen und die Magie des Imaginären." In *Topographien der Geschlechter: Kulturgeschichtliche Studien zur Literatur*, 67–113. Reinbek bei Hamburg: Rowohlt, 1990.

———. *Die Stimme der Medusa: Schreibweisen in der Gegenwartsliteratur von Frauen*. Reinbek bei Hamburg: Rowohlt, 1989.

————. "Towards a female dialectic of enlightenment: Julia Kristeva and Walter Benjamin." In *Body- and Image-Space: Re-reading Walter Benjamin*, trans. Georgina Paul with Rachel McNicholl and Jeremy Gaines, 63–79. London: Routledge, 1996.

Weininger, Otto. *Geschlecht und Charakter*. Munich: Matthes & Seitz, 1980.

Whitebrook, Joel. "The *Urgeschichte* of Subjectivity Reconsidered." *New German Critique* 81 (Fall 2000): 125–41.

Wiggershaus, Rolf. *The Frankfurt School: Its History, Theories and Political Significance*. Trans. Michael Robertson. Cambridge: Polity Press, 1984.

Woolf, Virginia. *A Room of One's Own*. London: Granada, 1977.

Index